Marmalade Boy

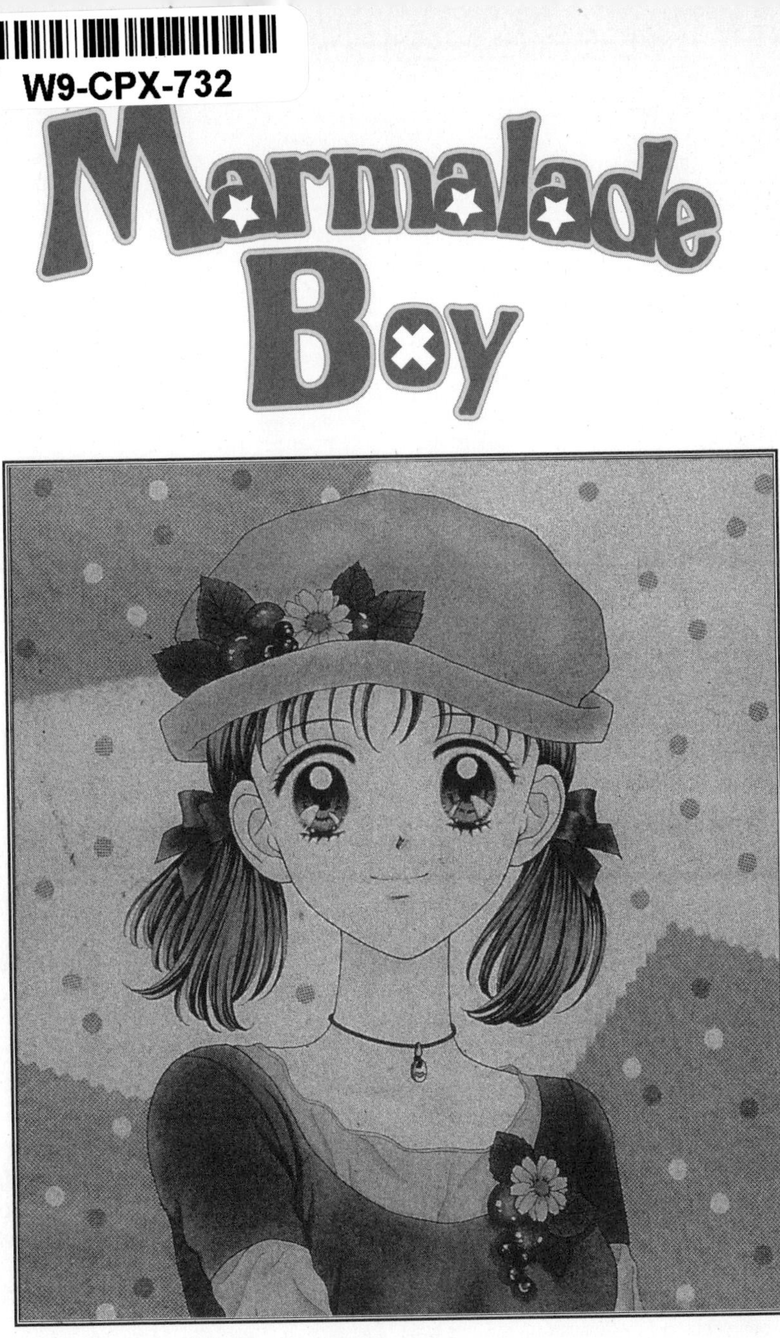

ALSO AVAILABLE FROM 🐾 TOKYOPOP®

MANGA

ANGELIC LAYER*
BABY BIRTH* (September 2003)
BATTLE ROYALE*
BRAIN POWERED* (June 2003)
BRIGADOON* (August 2003)
CARDCAPTOR SAKURA
CARDCAPTOR SAKURA: MASTER OF THE CLOW*
CLAMP SCHOOL DETECTIVES*
CHOBITS*
CHRONICLES OF THE CURSED SWORD (July 2003)
CLOVER
CONFIDENTIAL CONFESSIONS* (July 2003)
CORRECTOR YUI
COWBOY BEBOP*
COWBOY BEBOP: SHOOTING STAR* (June 2003)
DEMON DIARY (May 2003)
DIGIMON
DRAGON HUNTER (June 2003)
DRAGON KNIGHTS*
DUKLYON: CLAMP SCHOOL DEFENDERS* (September 2003)
ERICA SAKURAZAWA* (May 2003)
ESCAFLOWNE* (July 2003)
FAKE*(May 2003)
FLCL* (September 2003)
FORBIDDEN DANCE* (August 2003)
GATE KEEPERS*
G-GUNDAM* (June 2003)
GRAVITATION* (June 2003)
GTO*
GUNDAM WING
GUNDAM WING: ENDLESS WALTZ*
GUNDAM: THE LAST OUTPOST*
HAPPY MANIA*
HARLEM BEAT
INITIAL D*
I.N.V.U.
ISLAND
JING: KING OF BANDITS* (June 2003)
JULINE
KARE KANO*
KINDAICHI CASE FILES* (June 2003)
KING OF HELL (June 2003)

KODOCHA*
LOVE HINA*
LUPIN III*
MAGIC KNIGHT RAYEARTH* (August 2003)
MAN OF MANY FACES* (May 2003)
MARMALADE BOY*
MARS*
MIRACLE GIRLS
MIYUKI-CHAN IN WONDERLAND* (October 2003)
MONSTERS, INC.
NIEA_7* (August 2003)
PARADISE KISS*
PARASYTE
PEACH GIRL
PEACH GIRL: CHANGE OF HEART*
PET SHOP OF HORRORS* (June 2003)
PLANET LADDER
PLANETS* (October 2003)
PRIEST
RAGNAROK
RAVE MASTER*
REAL BOUT HIGH SCHOOL*
REALITY CHECK
REBIRTH
REBOUND*
SABER MARIONETTE J* (July 2003)
SAILOR MOON
SAINT TAIL
SAMURAI DEEPER KYO* (June 2003)
SCRYED*
SHAOLIN SISTERS*
SHIRAHIME-SYO* (December 2003)
THE SKULL MAN*
SORCERER HUNTERS
TOKYO MEW MEW*
UNDER A GLASS MOON (June 2003)
VAMPIRE GAME* (June 2003)
WILD ACT* (July 2003)
WISH*
X-DAY* (August 2003)
ZODIAC P.I.* (July 2003)

CINE-MANGA™

AKIRA*
CARDCAPTORS
JIMMY NEUTRON (COMING SOON)
KIM POSSIBLE
LIZZIE McGUIRE
SPONGEBOB SQUAREPANTS (COMING SOON)
SPY KIDS 2

NOVELS

SAILOR MOON
KARMA CLUB (COMING SOON)

TOKYOPOP KIDS

STRAY SHEEP (September 2003)

ART BOOKS

CARDCAPTOR SAKURA*
MAGIC KNIGHT RAYEARTH*

ANIME GUIDES

GUNDAM TECHNICAL MANUALS
COWBOY BEBOP
SAILOR MOON SCOUT GUIDES

Marmalade Boy

Vol. 6

By

Wataru Yoshizumi

TOKYOPOP®

Los Angeles • Tokyo

Story and Art – Wataru Yoshizumi

Translator - Takae Brewer
English Adaption - Deb Baer
Editor - Amy Court Kaemon
Retouch and Lettering - Rosa Gandara
Cover Layout and Graphic Design - Anna Kernbaum

Senior Editor - Julie Taylor
Managing Editor - Jill Freshney
Production Coordinator - Antonio DePietro
Production Manager - Jennifer Miller
Art Director - Matthew Alford
Director of Editorial - Jeremy Ross
VP of Production & Manufacturing - Ron Klamert
President & C.O.O. - John Parker
Publisher - Stuart Levy

Email: editor@TOKYOPOP.com
Come visit us online at www.TOKYOPOP.com

A  Manga
TOKYOPOP® is an imprint of Mixx Entertainment, Inc.
5900 Wilshire Blvd. Suite 2000, Los Angeles, CA 90036

ISBN:1-59182-190-8

First TOKYOPOP® printing: April 2003

10 9 8 7 6 5 4 3 2 1

Printed in the USA

Main Characters

GINTA SUOU:
MIKI'S CLASSMATE.
IN LOVE WITH ARIMI

ALWAYS HAPPY AND ENERGETIC.

MIKI KOISHIKAWA:
SIMPLISTIC — LOVES YUU

MEIKO AKIZUKI:
MIKI'S BEST FRIEND.
EXTREMELY MATURE!

ARIMI SUZUKI:
YUU'S EX-GIRLFRIEND

LIVES WITH MIKI.

COOL, BUT MEAN!?

YUU MATSUURA:
HOW IS HE GETTING
ALONG WITH MIKI?

KEI TSUCHIYA:
MIKI'S CO-WORKER

THE STORY SO FAR...

DURING BREAKFAST ONE DAY, MIKI'S PARENTS BREAK IT TO HER THAT THEY'RE GETTING DIVORCED! TO MAKE MATTERS WORSE, THEY ALSO ANNOUNCE THAT THEY ARE SWAPPING SPOUSES WITH ANOTHER COUPLE. NOW MIKI HAS FOUR PARENTS AND A NEW STEPBROTHER, YUU, WHO KEEPS TEASING HER. MIKI THINKS YUU'S SWEET ON THE OUTSIDE, BUT HE'S GOT A BITTER STREAK—HE'S A MARMALADE BOY! AS MIKI GETS TO KNOW YUU, SHE DEVELOPS A CRUSH ON HIM.

THINGS GET COMPLICATED WHEN MIKI'S OLD CRUSH, THE TENNIS CHAMP, GINTA, CONFESSES HIS LOVE FOR HER. WITH MAJOR CRUSHES ON BOTH GINTA AND YUU, MIKI FINDS HERSELF WAGING AN INNER BATTLE SHE KNOWS SHE CAN NEVER WIN.

MIKI FINALLY TELLS YUU THAT SHE LOVES HIM. ALTHOUGH THEIR FEELINGS ARE STRONG, THEY DECIDE TO KEEP THEIR FORBIDDEN LOVE SECRET FROM THEIR PARENTS. ONE DAY, YUU IS SELECTED TO BE IN A TV COMMERCIAL. HE CO-STARS WITH SUZU SAKUMA, A POPULAR FEMALE MODEL. SUZU BECOMES FOND OF YUU AND HIRES HIM AS HER TUTOR. MIKI IS FREAKED OUT ABOUT THE SITUATION, SO MIKI AND YUU PLAN TO TAKE A TRIP TOGETHER THIS SUMMER. MIKI IS REALLY LOOKING FORWARD TO IT! SHE NEEDS TO SAVE MONEY FOR THE TRIP, SO SHE GETS A PART-TIME JOB AT AN ICE CREAM PARLOR. AS FATE WOULD HAVE IT, SHE HAS AN UNFORTUNATE FALL IN THE STOREROOM AND SHE LANDS IN THE ARMS OF A MYSTERIOUS BUT UNDENIABLY CUTE CO-WORKER!

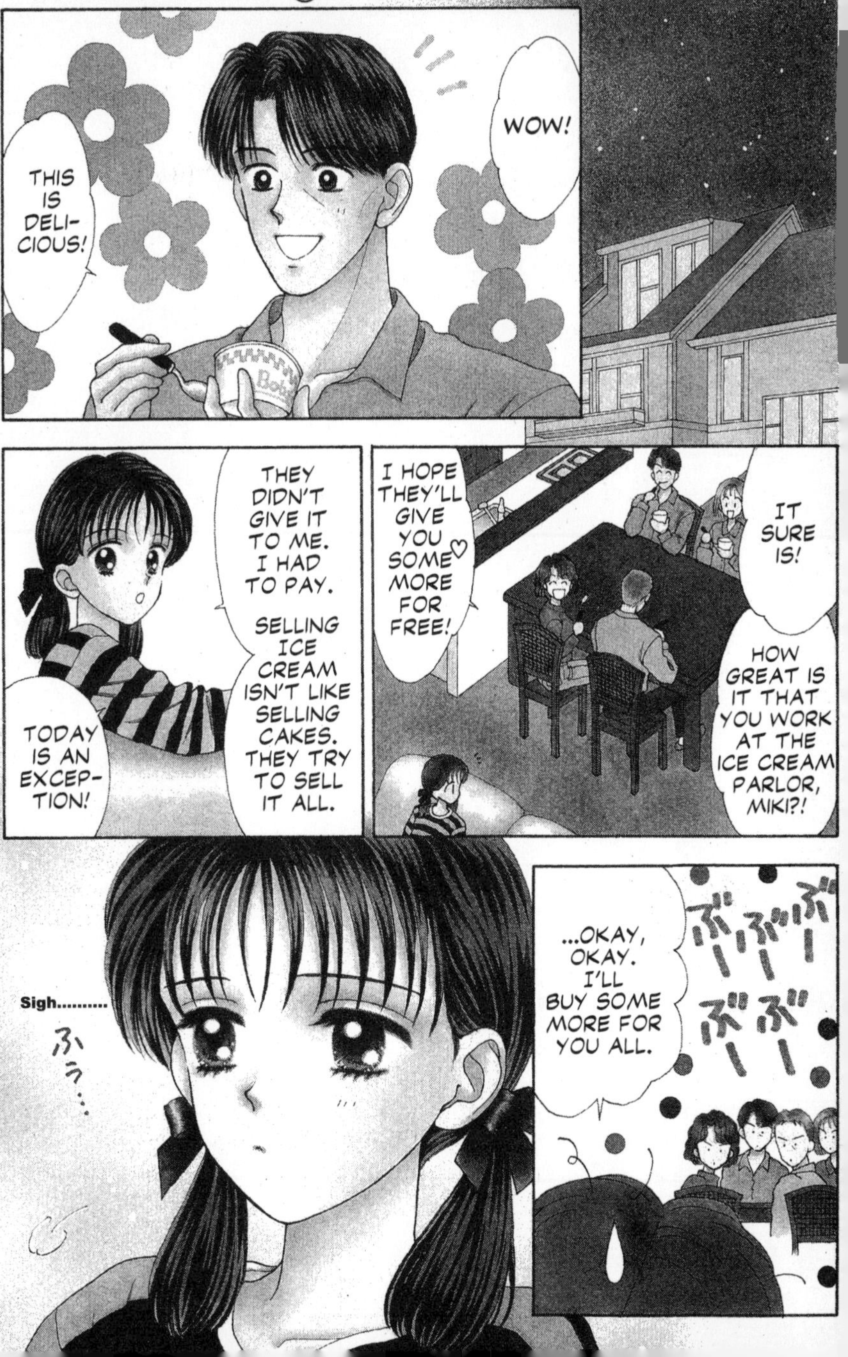
WOW!
THIS IS DELICIOUS!
IT SURE IS!
HOW GREAT IS IT THAT YOU WORK AT THE ICE CREAM PARLOR, MIKI?!
I HOPE THEY'LL GIVE YOU SOME MORE FOR FREE! ♡
THEY DIDN'T GIVE IT TO ME. I HAD TO PAY.
SELLING ICE CREAM ISN'T LIKE SELLING CAKES. THEY TRY TO SELL IT ALL.
TODAY IS AN EXCEPTION!
ぶー ぶー ぶー ぶー ぶー
...OKAY, OKAY. I'LL BUY SOME MORE FOR YOU ALL.
Sigh..........
ふぅ…

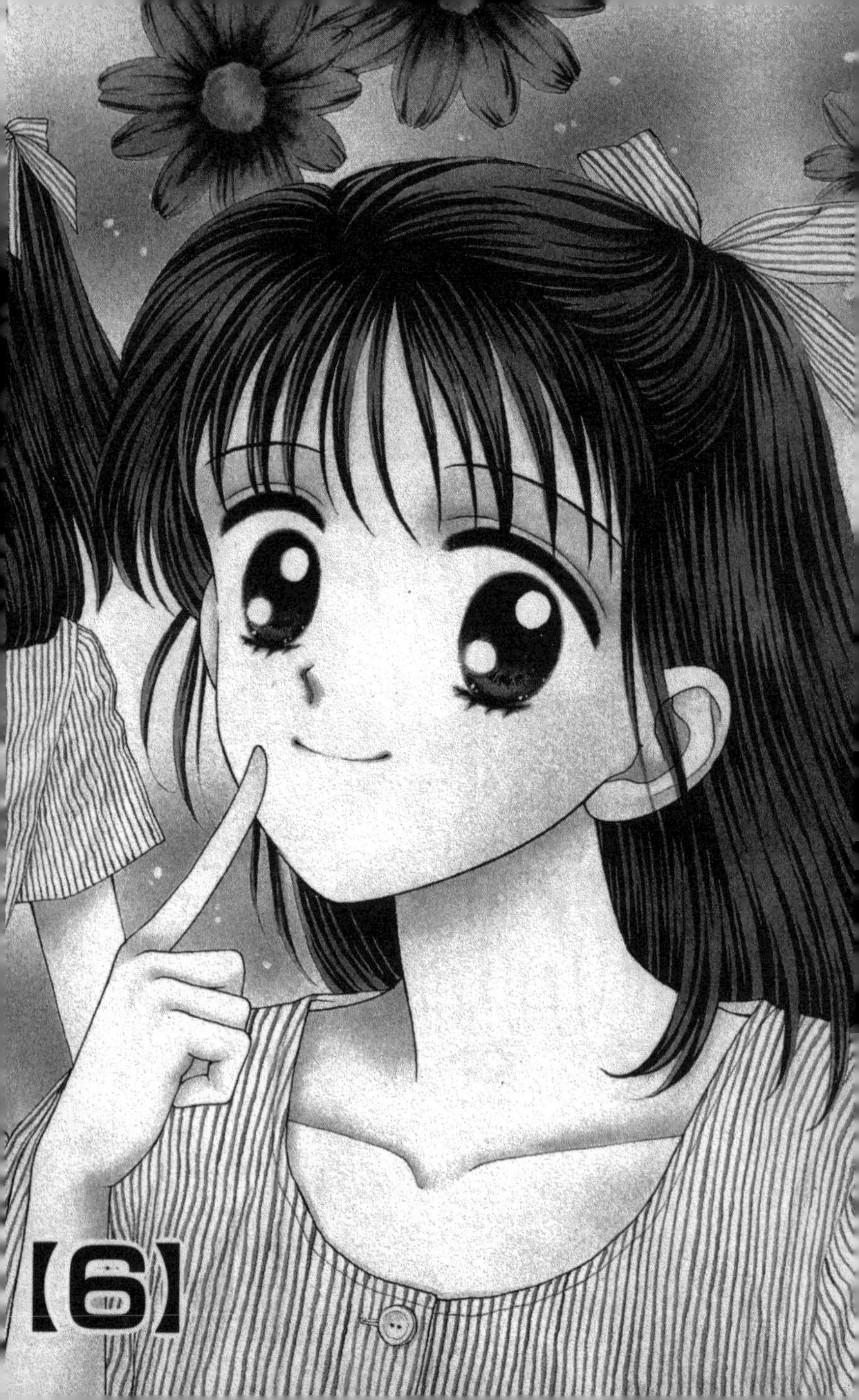
【6】

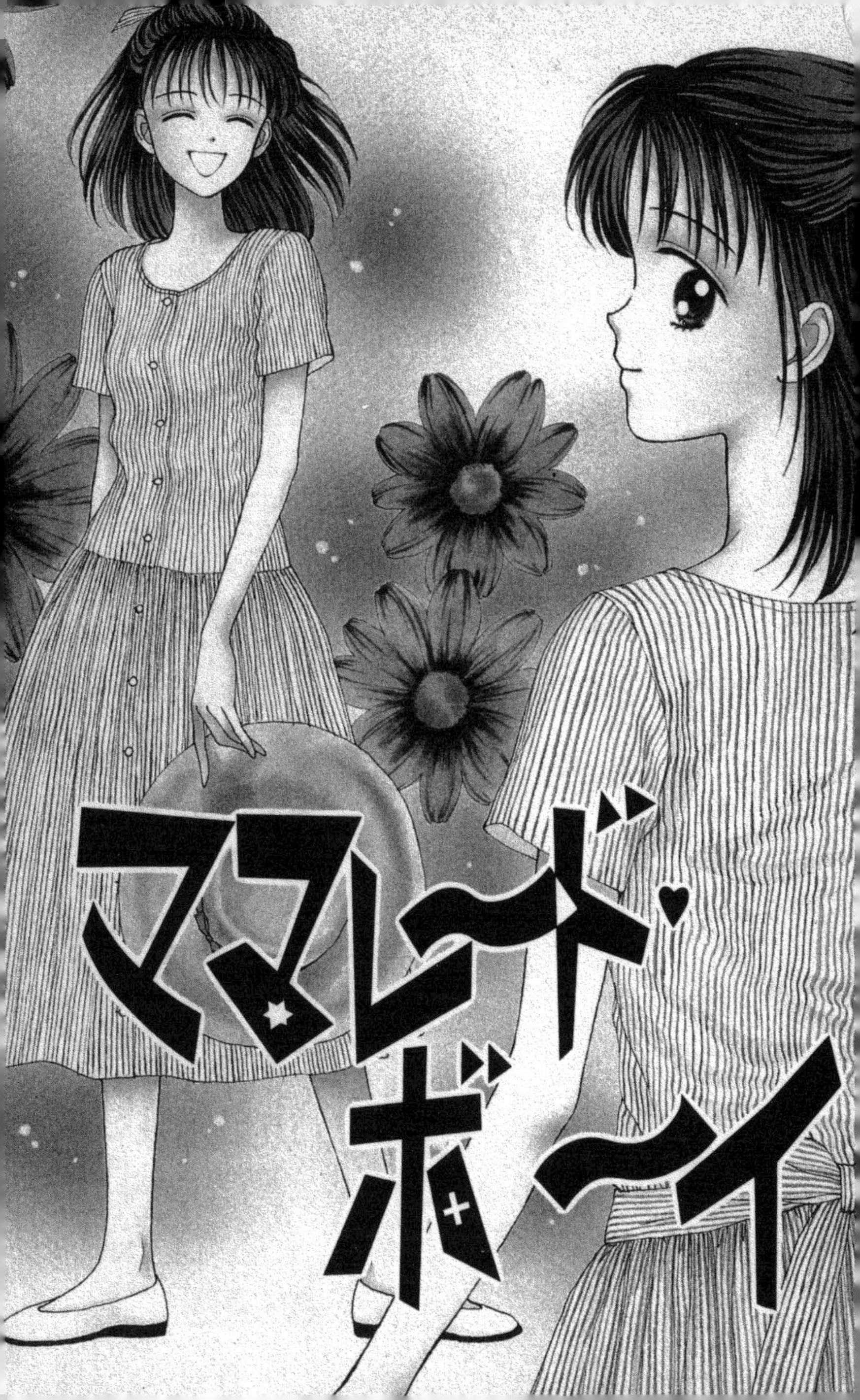
ママレード♥ボーイ

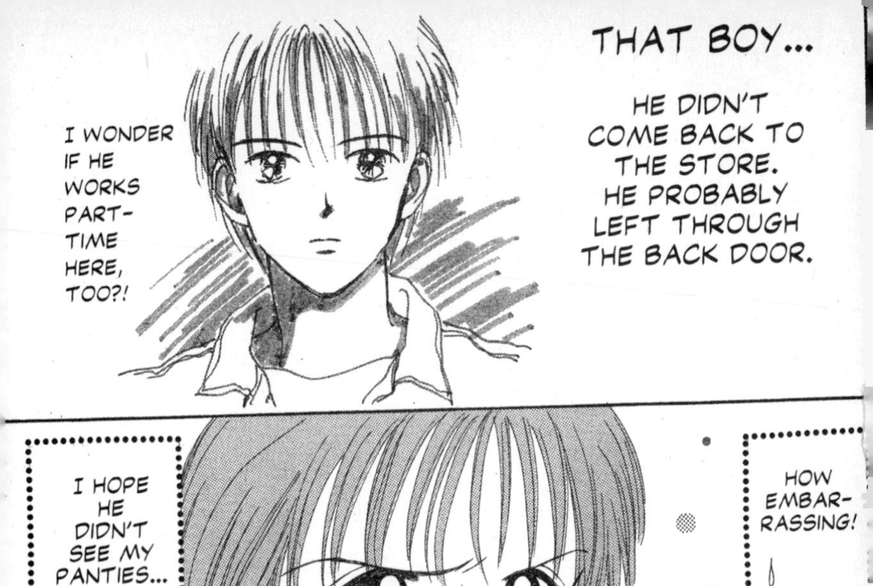
THAT BOY...
HE DIDN'T COME BACK TO THE STORE. HE PROBABLY LEFT THROUGH THE BACK DOOR.
I WONDER IF HE WORKS PART-TIME HERE, TOO?!
HOW EMBARRASSING!
HE WAS IN THE WRONG PLACE AT THE WRONG TIME.
I HOPE HE DIDN'T SEE MY PANTIES...
OH, MY!

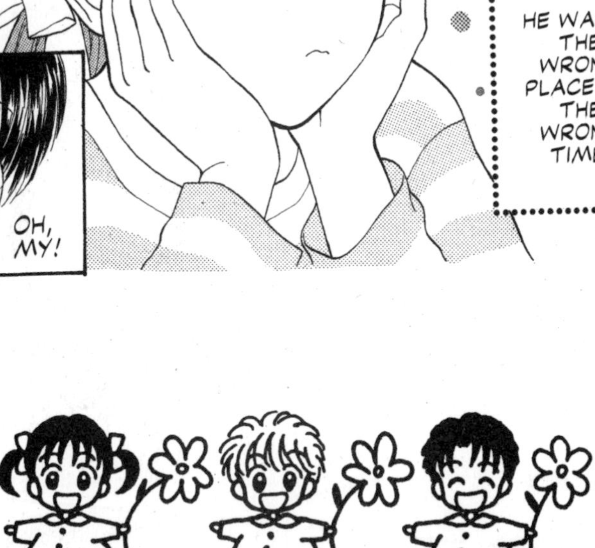

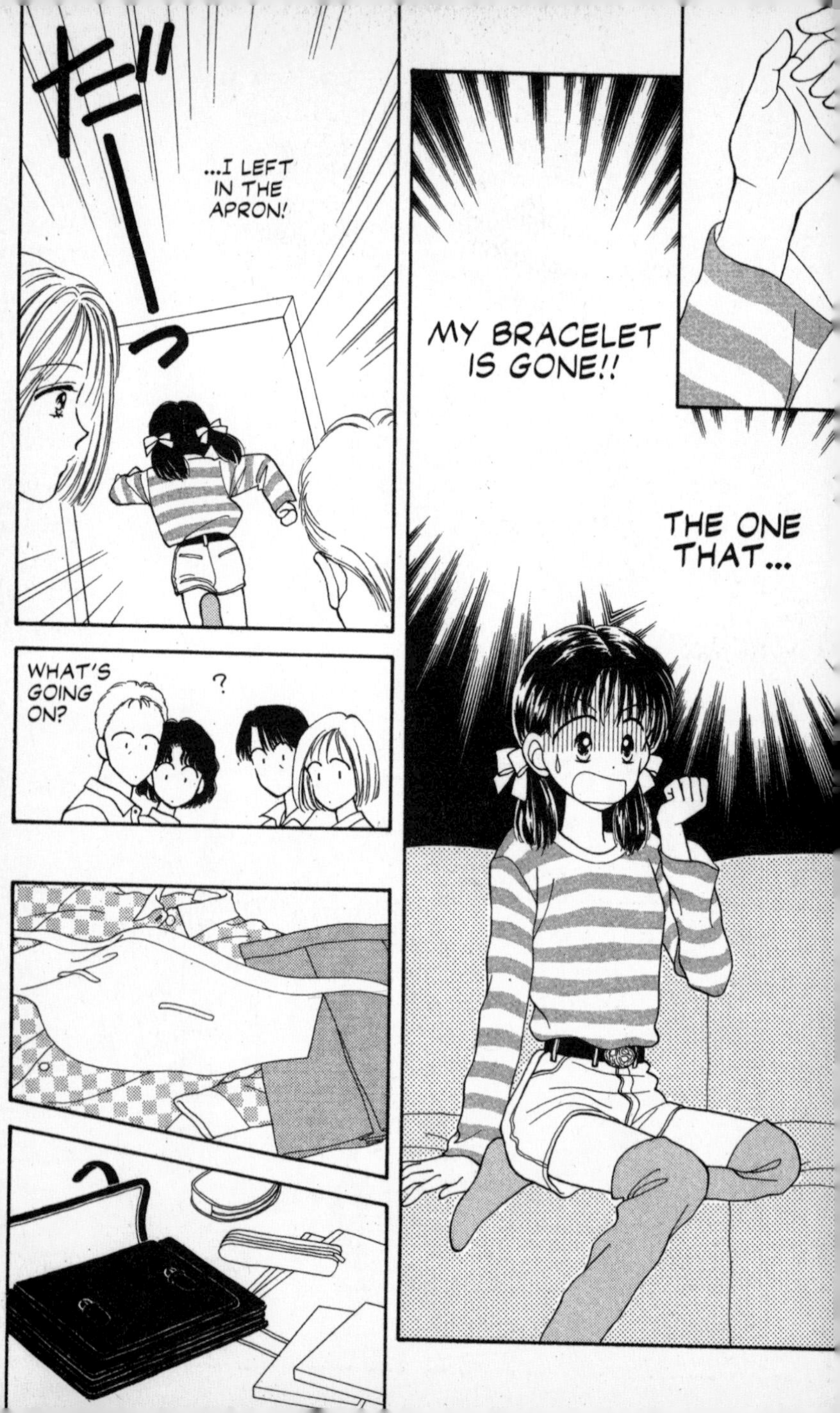
MY BRACELET IS GONE!!
THE ONE THAT...
...I LEFT IN THE APRON!
だーっ
WHAT'S GOING ON?
?

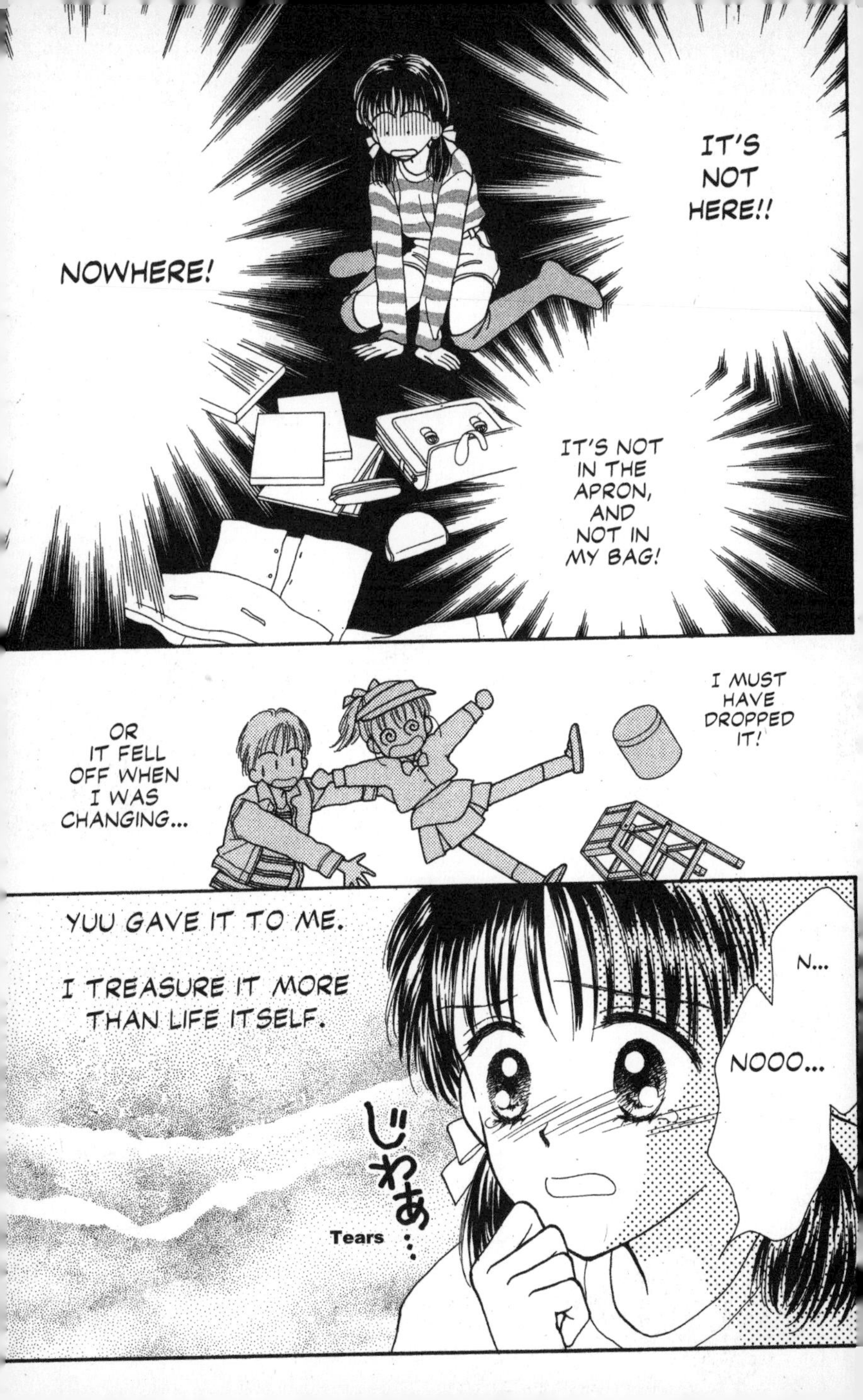
IT'S NOT HERE!!
IT'S NOT IN THE APRON, AND NOT IN MY BAG!
NOWHERE!
I MUST HAVE DROPPED IT!
OR IT FELL OFF WHEN I WAS CHANGING...
N...
NOOO...
YUU GAVE IT TO ME.
I TREASURE IT MORE THAN LIFE ITSELF.
じわぁ…
Tears

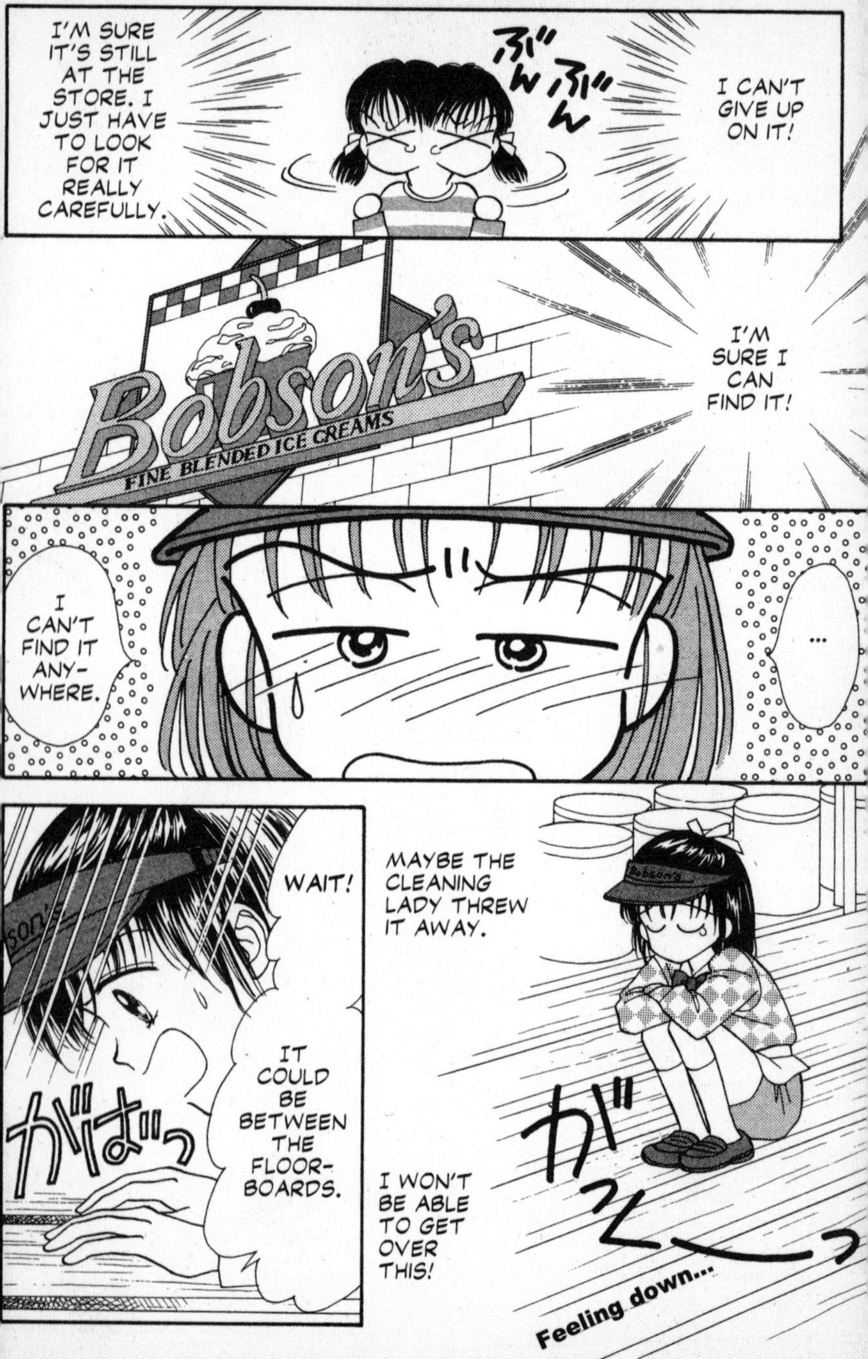
I CAN'T GIVE UP ON IT!
ぶんぶん
I'M SURE IT'S STILL AT THE STORE. I JUST HAVE TO LOOK FOR IT REALLY CAREFULLY.
I'M SURE I CAN FIND IT!
Bobson's
FINE BLENDED ICE CREAMS
...
I CAN'T FIND IT ANYWHERE.
MAYBE THE CLEANING LADY THREW IT AWAY.
I WON'T BE ABLE TO GET OVER THIS!
がくーっ
Feeling down...
WAIT!
IT COULD BE BETWEEN THE FLOORBOARDS.
がばっ

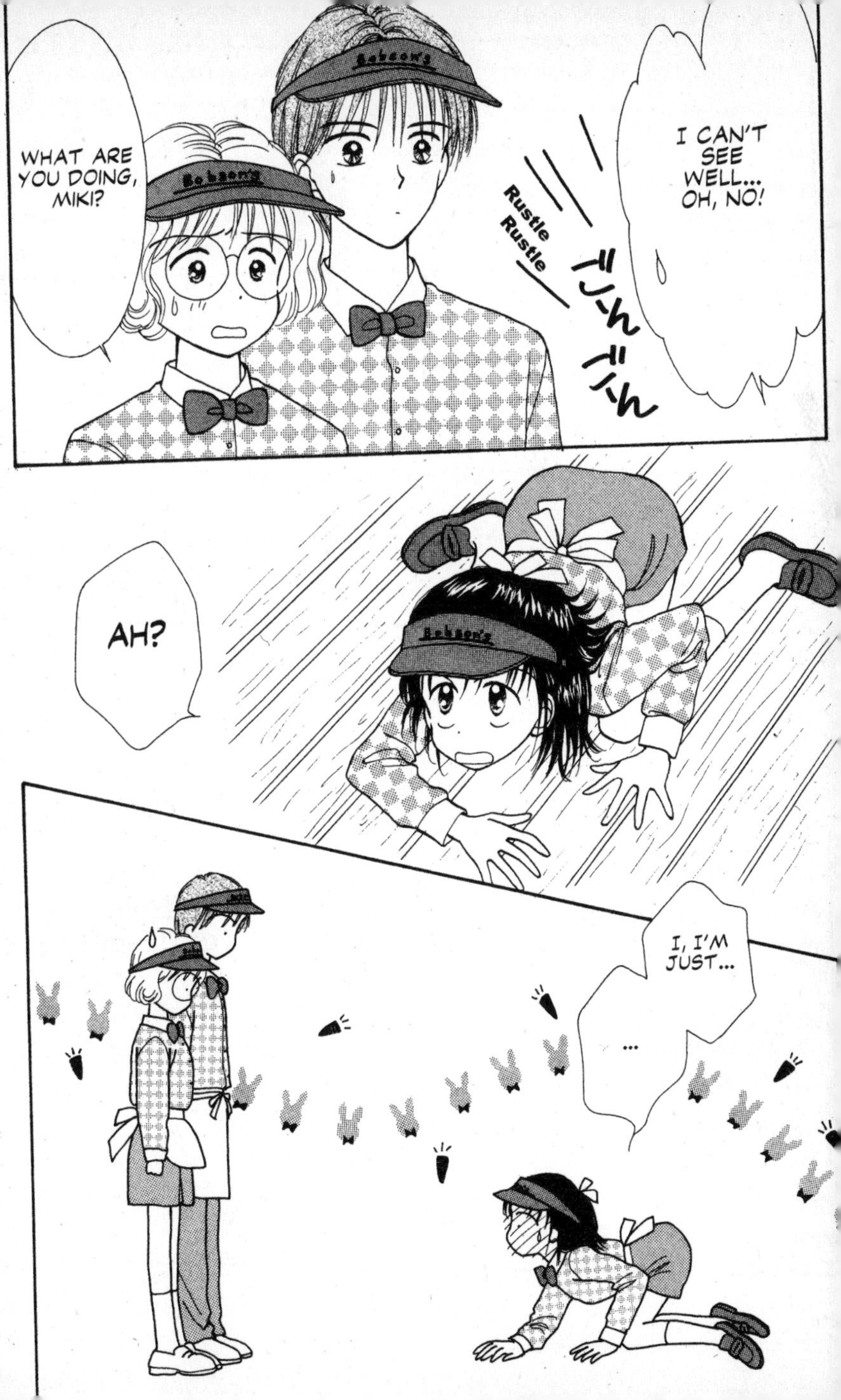
I CAN'T SEE WELL... OH, NO!
Rustle
Rustle
WHAT ARE YOU DOING, MIKI?
AH?
I, I'M JUST...
...

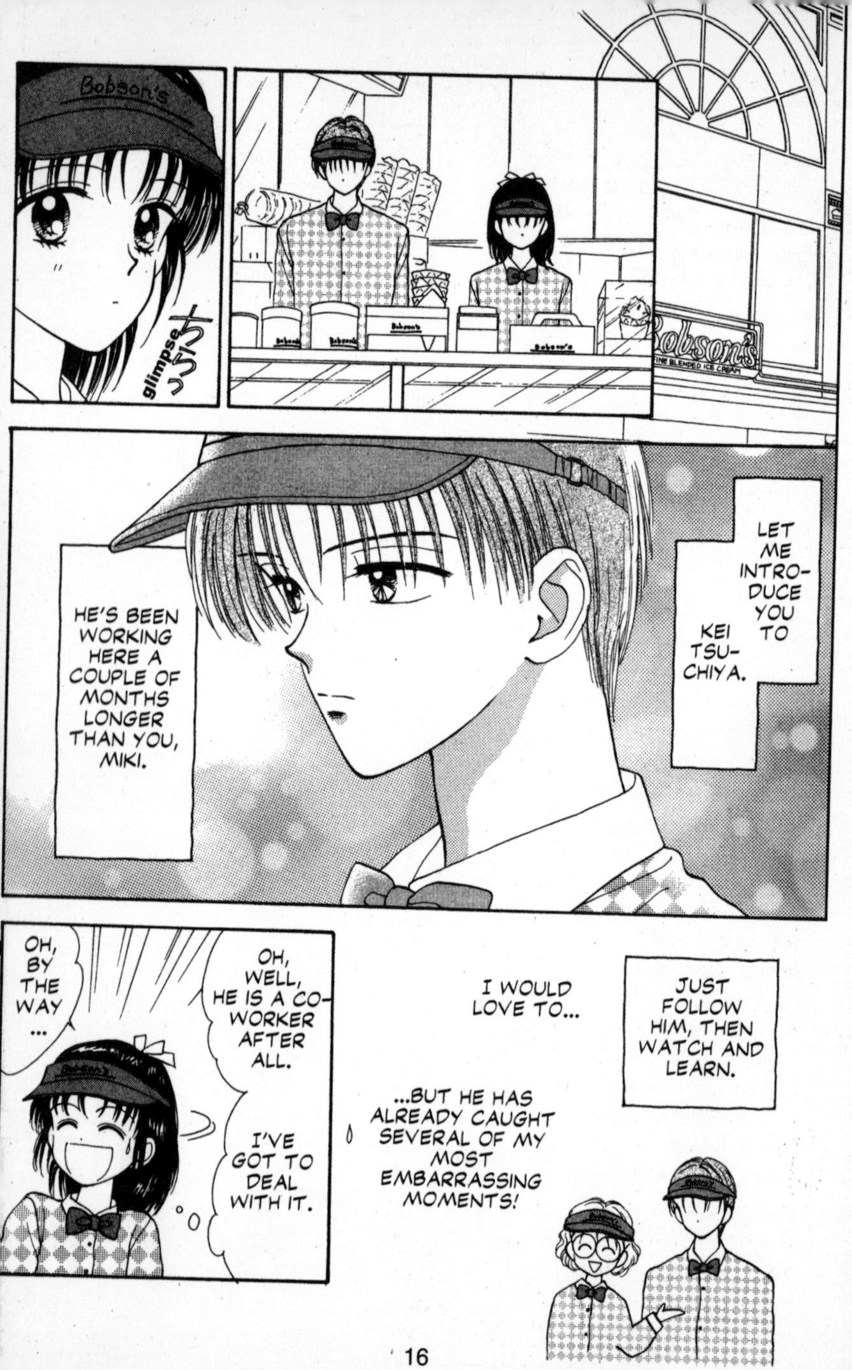
Bobson's
FINE BLENDED ICE CREAM
glimpse
LET ME INTRODUCE YOU TO KEI TSUCHIYA.
HE'S BEEN WORKING HERE A COUPLE OF MONTHS LONGER THAN YOU, MIKI.
JUST FOLLOW HIM, THEN WATCH AND LEARN.
I WOULD LOVE TO...
...BUT HE HAS ALREADY CAUGHT SEVERAL OF MY MOST EMBARRASSING MOMENTS!
OH, WELL, HE IS A CO-WORKER AFTER ALL.
I'VE GOT TO DEAL WITH IT.
OH, BY THE WAY ...

FREE TALK ①

Today is December 21, 1994. We moved our office three days ago, and I am writing this Free Talk at the new office. (I had the deadline extended because of the move.) Time passed so quickly and now Marmalade Boy animation has been on TV for nine months. I couldn't write a Free Talk for the fifth volume so I would like to talk about the animation here. Animation is a great entertainment medium with motion, voices, sounds and music. The actors have been doing a great job portraying the voices of the characters. With the help of music, some scenes are well dramatized and appear even better than in my original work. The TV show has already caught up with the published version but the show takes different turns and twists from the original. Even I sometimes don't know how the story will go, so I'm always excited to watch the TV show!

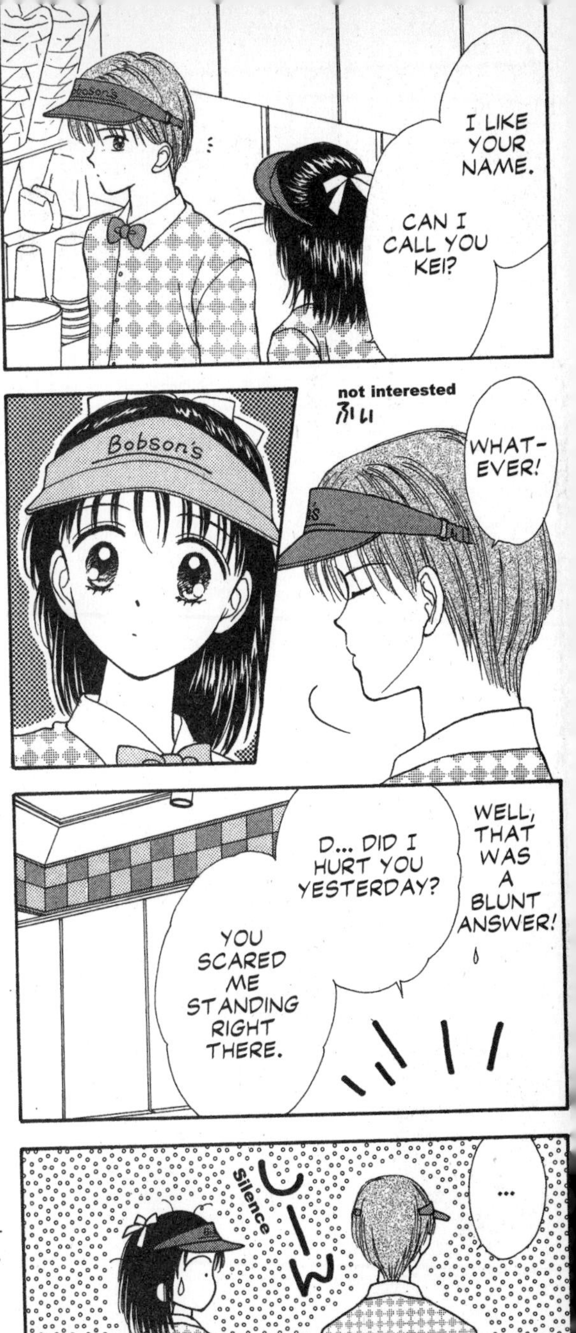
I LIKE YOUR NAME.
CAN I CALL YOU KEI?
not interested
WHATEVER!
WELL, THAT WAS A BLUNT ANSWER!
D... DID I HURT YOU YESTERDAY?
YOU SCARED ME STANDING RIGHT THERE.
...
Silence

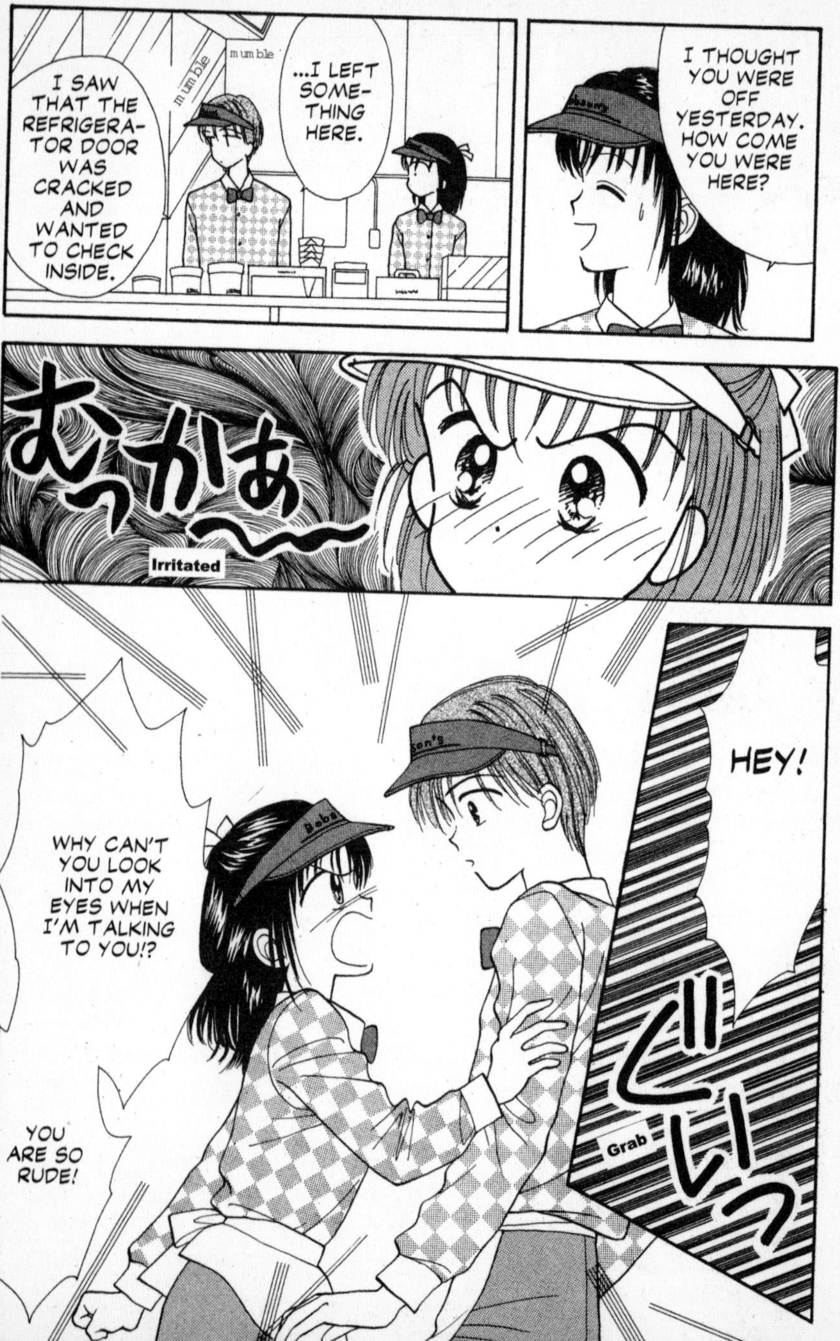
I THOUGHT YOU WERE OFF YESTERDAY. HOW COME YOU WERE HERE?
...I LEFT SOMETHING HERE.
mumble
mumble
I SAW THAT THE REFRIGERATOR DOOR WAS CRACKED AND WANTED TO CHECK INSIDE.
むっかあ〜〜
Irritated
HEY!
ぐいーっ
Grab
WHY CAN'T YOU LOOK INTO MY EYES WHEN I'M TALKING TO YOU!?
YOU ARE SO RUDE!

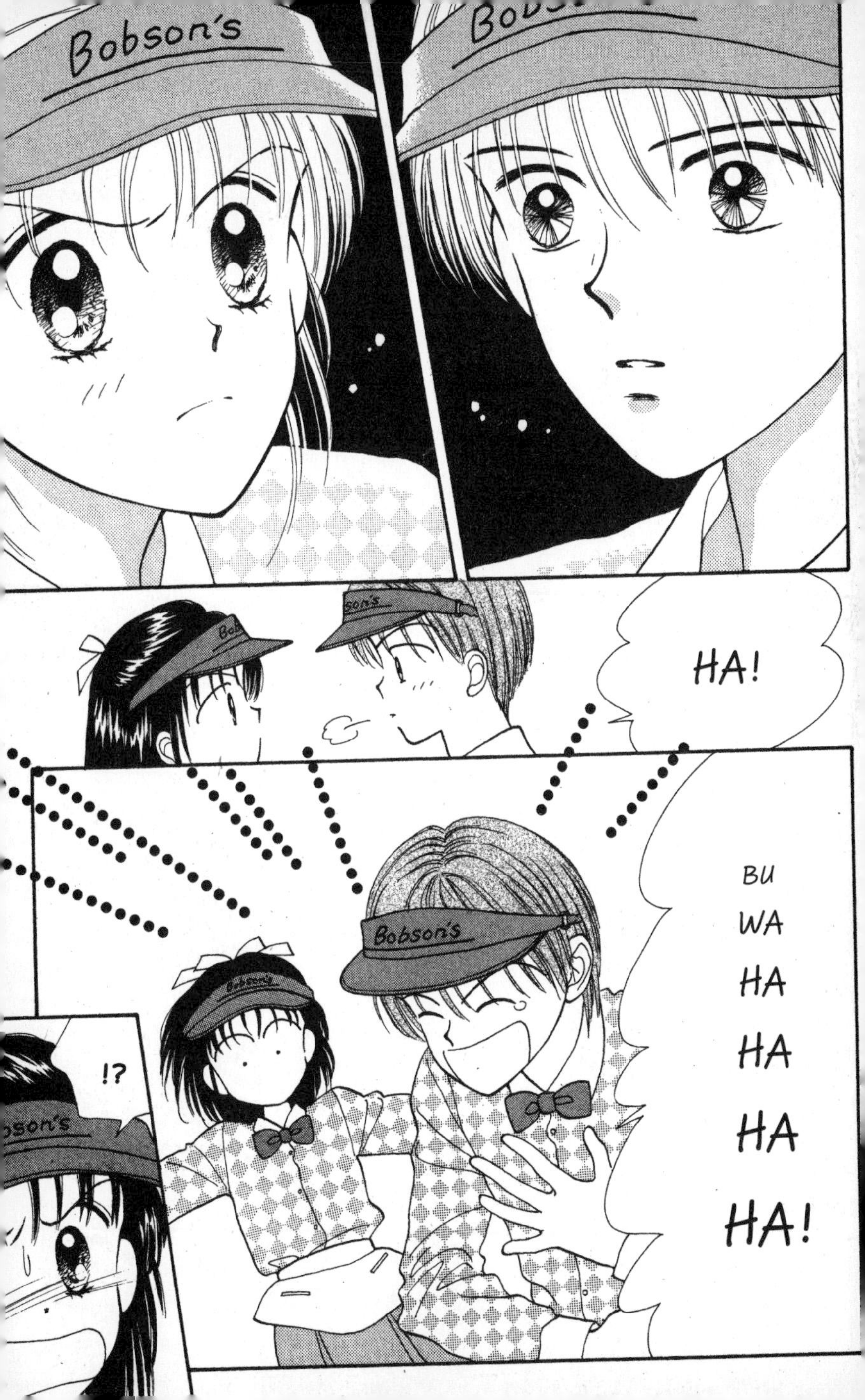
Bobson's
HA!
BU WA HA HA HA HA!
!?

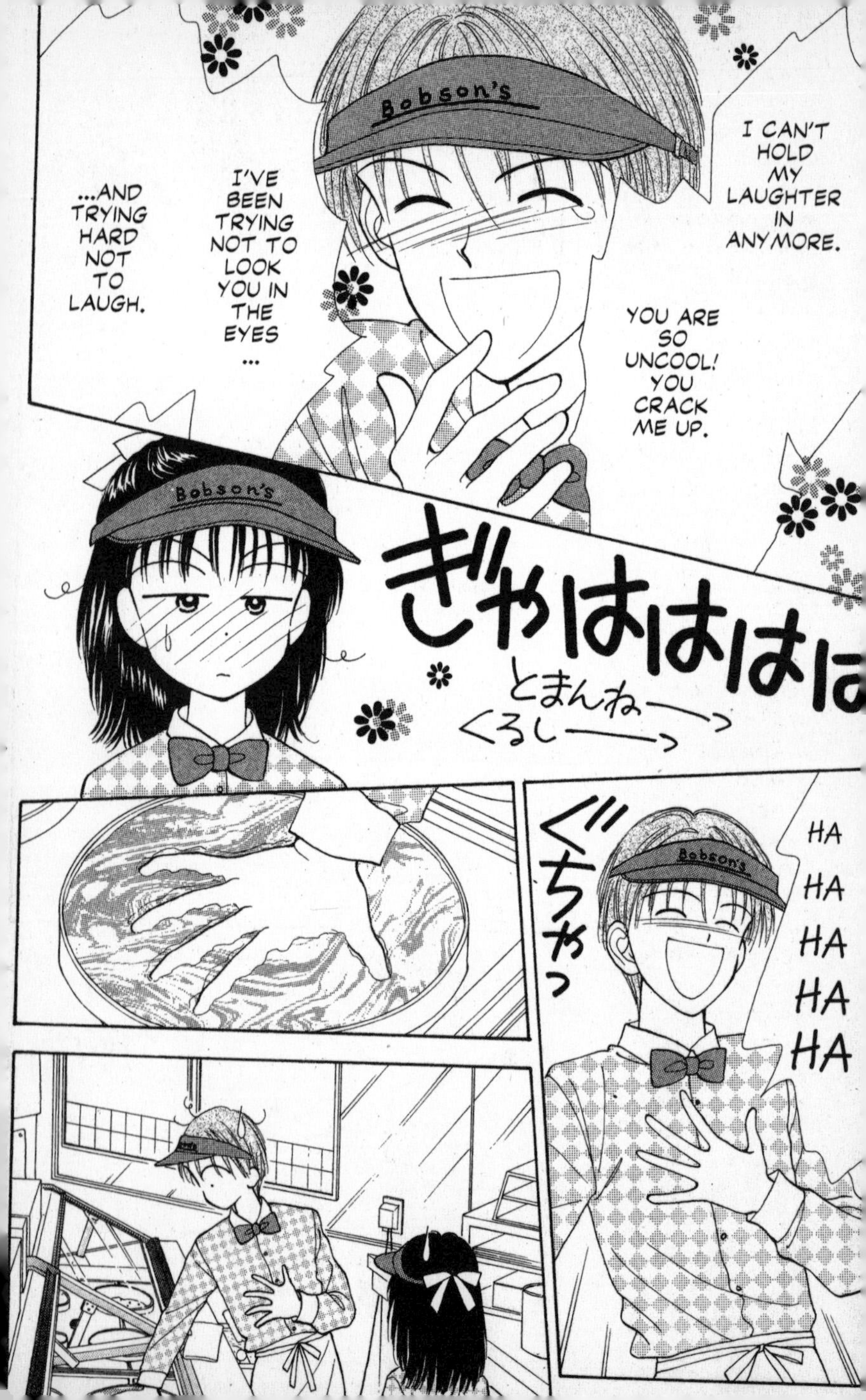

I CAN'T HOLD MY LAUGHTER IN ANYMORE.
YOU ARE SO UNCOOL! YOU CRACK ME UP.
I'VE BEEN TRYING NOT TO LOOK YOU IN THE EYES...
...AND TRYING HARD NOT TO LAUGH.
ぎゃははは
とまんねー
くるしー
HA HA HA HA HA
ぐちゃっ

FREE TALK ②

I sometimes get letters that ask, "why does the anime version of Marmalade Boy have a different story than the original?" or "Can't the anime stick to the original story?" The reality is that the original work can't catch up with the pace of the TV show. Ribon, the magazine, is only monthly, while the TV show is weekly. I hope you enjoy both the original and the animation without worrying too much about slight differences in the characters and their roles. When it comes to the plot for the animation, I leave it up to the production staff. They usually meet me about the story and ask for my advice. Basically, I ask them not to kill anybody and to keep the story happy...

<Two who almost died>

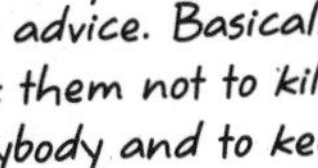

Nachan Anju

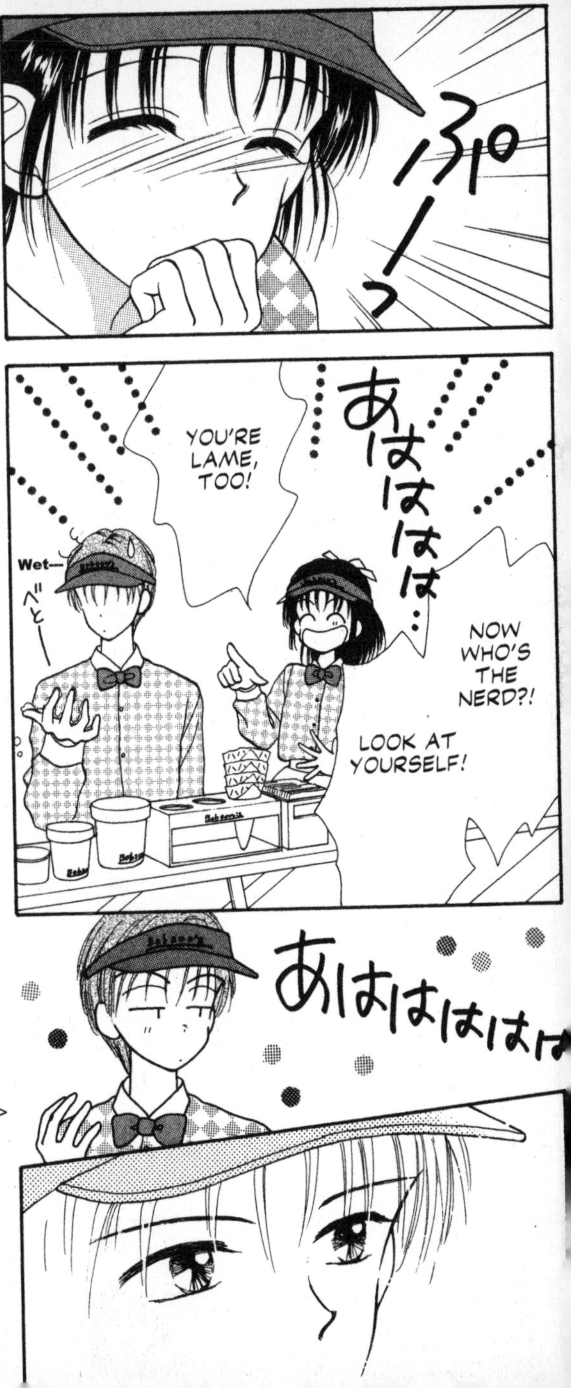

ぷーーっ
あははは…
NOW WHO'S THE NERD?!
LOOK AT YOURSELF!
YOU'RE LAME, TOO!
Wet---
べとー
あはははは

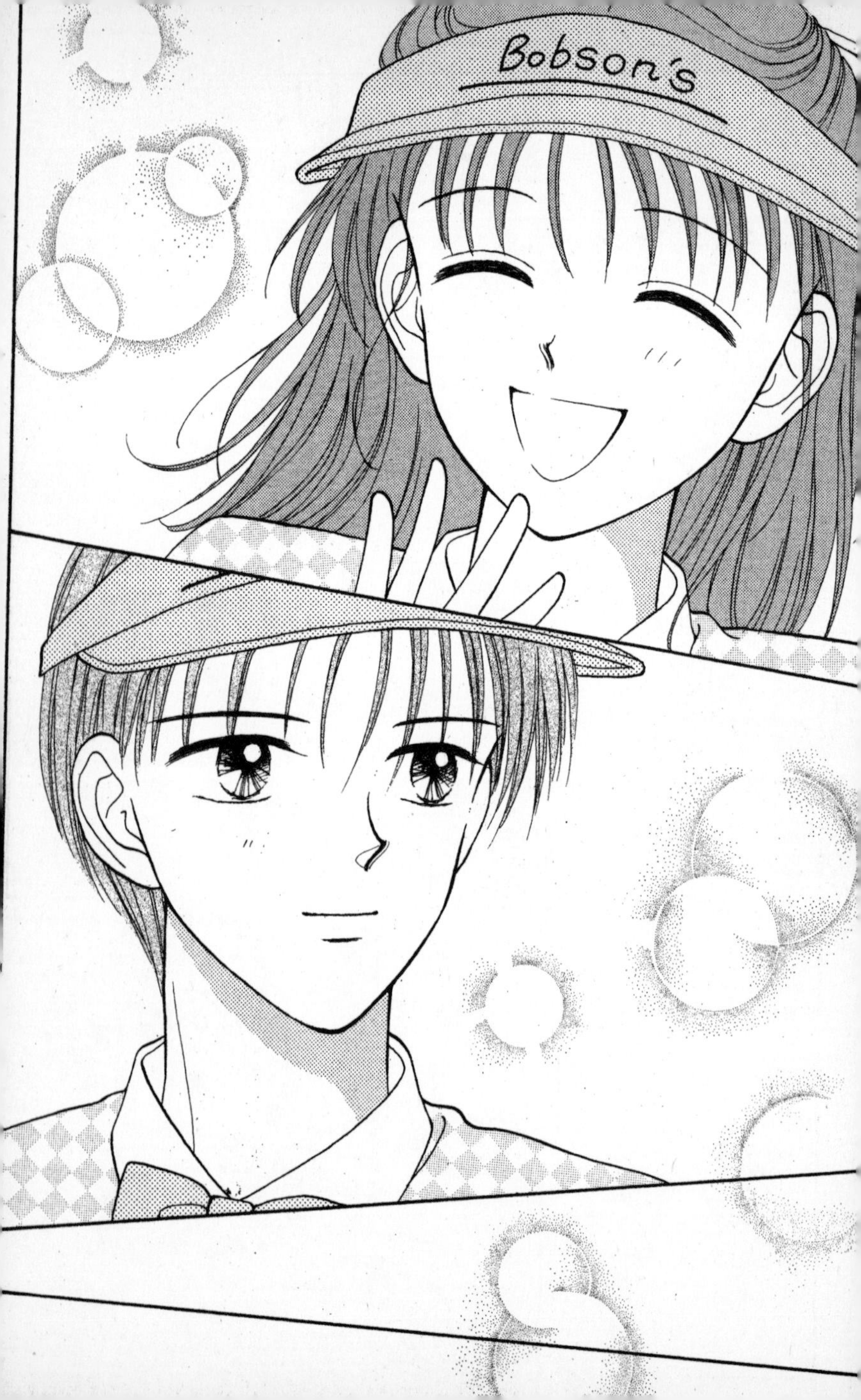
Bobson's

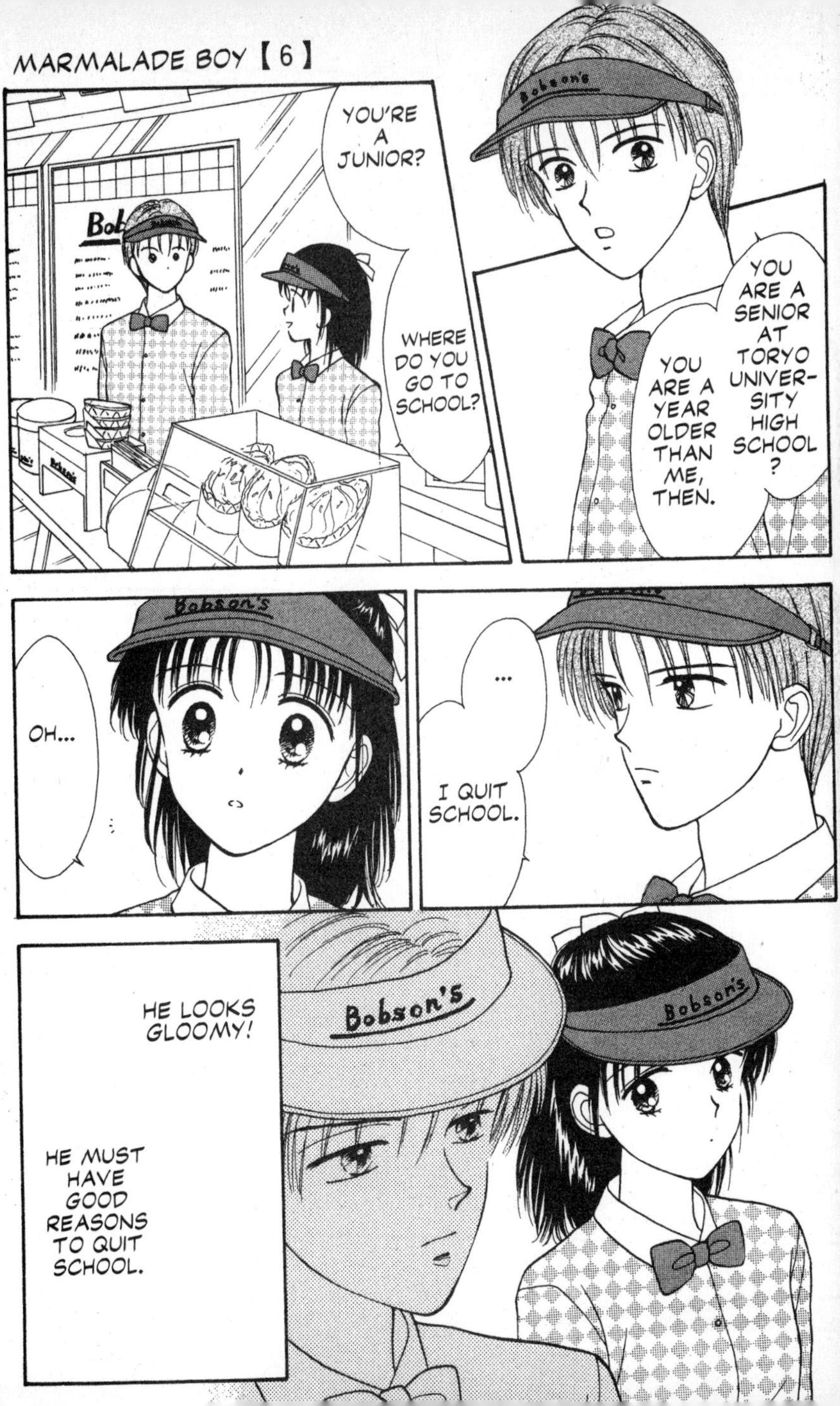
YOU ARE A SENIOR AT TORYO UNIVERSITY HIGH SCHOOL?
YOU ARE A YEAR OLDER THAN ME, THEN.
YOU'RE A JUNIOR?
WHERE DO YOU GO TO SCHOOL?
...
I QUIT SCHOOL.
OH...
HE LOOKS GLOOMY!
HE MUST HAVE GOOD REASONS TO QUIT SCHOOL.

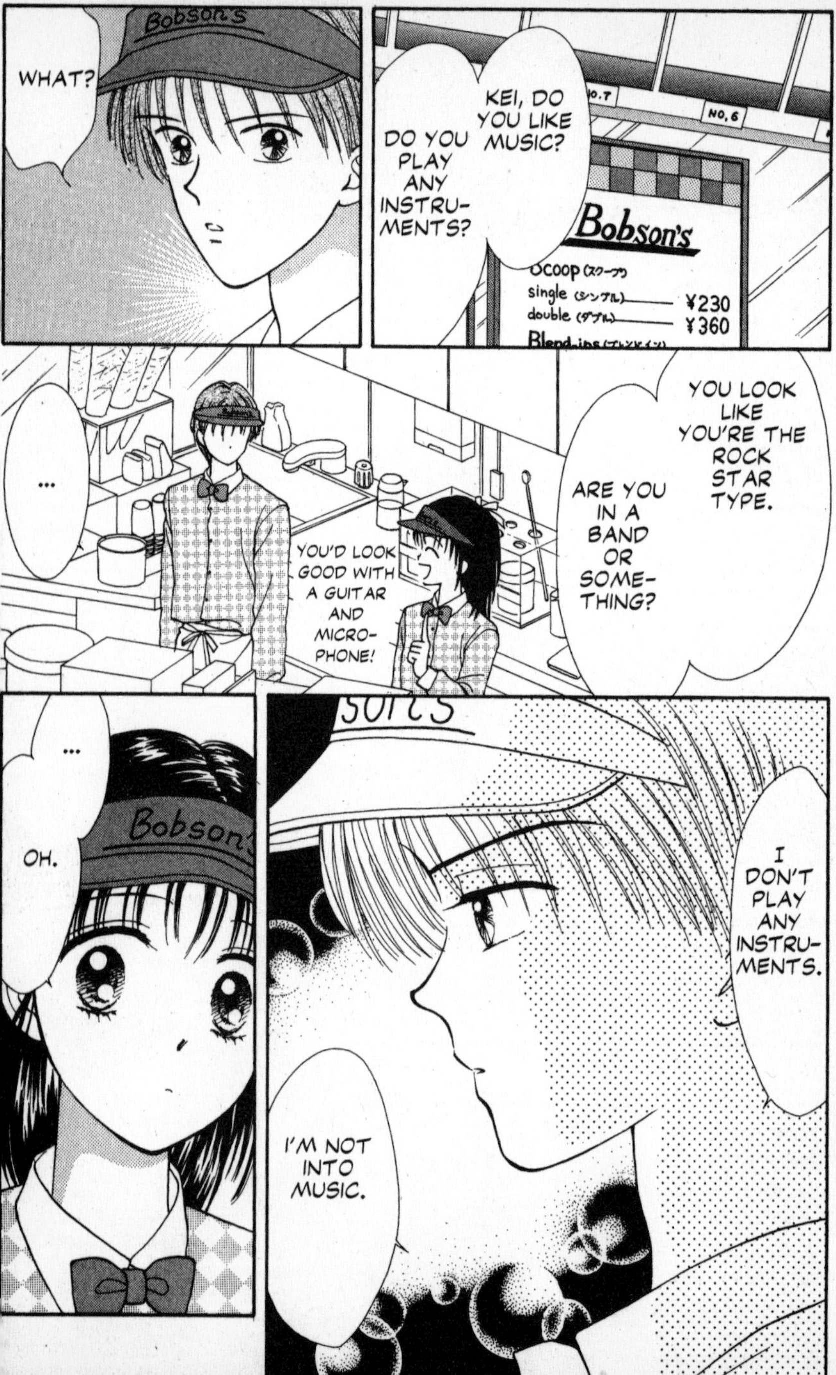
KEI, DO YOU LIKE MUSIC?
DO YOU PLAY ANY INSTRU-MENTS?
NO.7
NO.6
Bobson's
Scoop
single ¥230
double ¥360
WHAT?
YOU LOOK LIKE YOU'RE THE ROCK STAR TYPE.
ARE YOU IN A BAND OR SOME-THING?
YOU'D LOOK GOOD WITH A GUITAR AND MICRO-PHONE!
...
I DON'T PLAY ANY INSTRU-MENTS.
I'M NOT INTO MUSIC.
...
OH.

FREE TALK③

I thought there would be more male fans of the anime version of Marmalade Boy. Surprisingly, I've been receiving a markedly increased number of letters from housewives. Many of them are in their twenties or thirties and have small children. They watch the TV show with their kids, and end up liking it more than their children do! They say it reminds them of their youth. When I write Marmalade Boy, I keep in mind that Ribon, the magazine, is for children and teens in grade school and junior high school. It is my greatest pleasure that people who are much older than the targeted readers enjoy it, too. By the way, Yuu is the most popular character among the adult female readers.

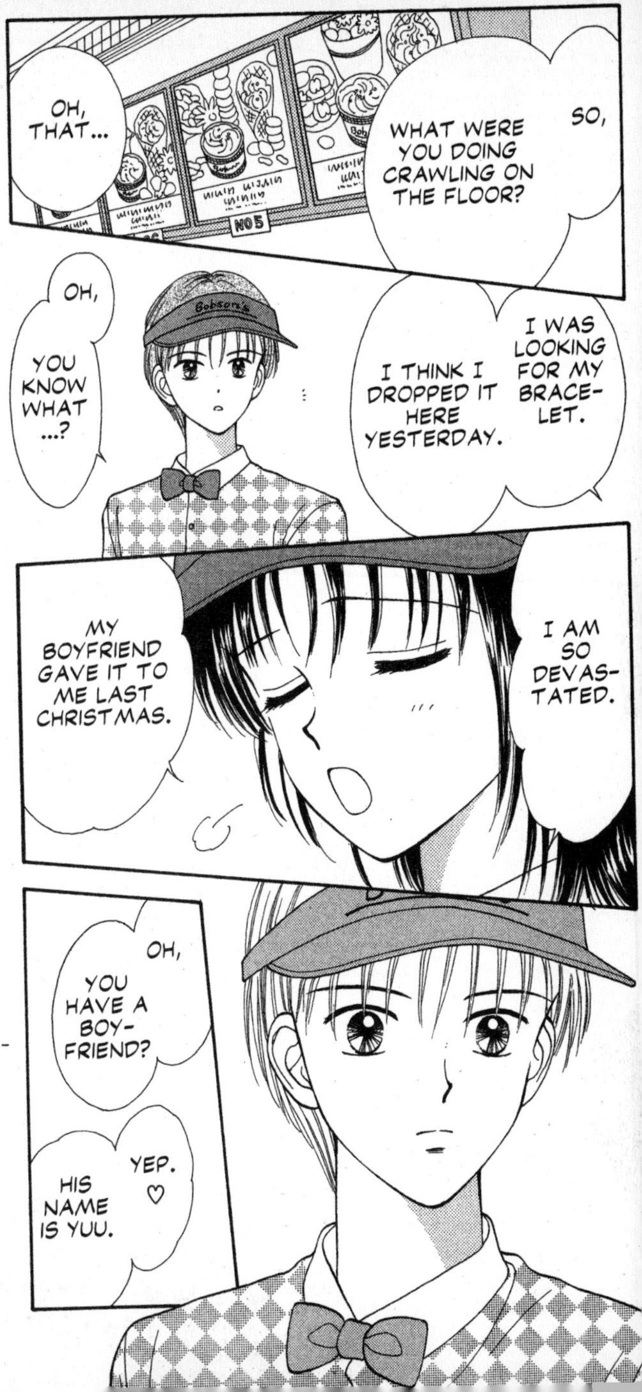
SO, WHAT WERE YOU DOING CRAWLING ON THE FLOOR?
OH, THAT...
NO5
I WAS LOOKING FOR MY BRACELET.
I THINK I DROPPED IT HERE YESTERDAY.
OH, YOU KNOW WHAT...?
I AM SO DEVASTATED.
MY BOYFRIEND GAVE IT TO ME LAST CHRISTMAS.
OH, YOU HAVE A BOY-FRIEND?
YEP. ♡ HIS NAME IS YUU.

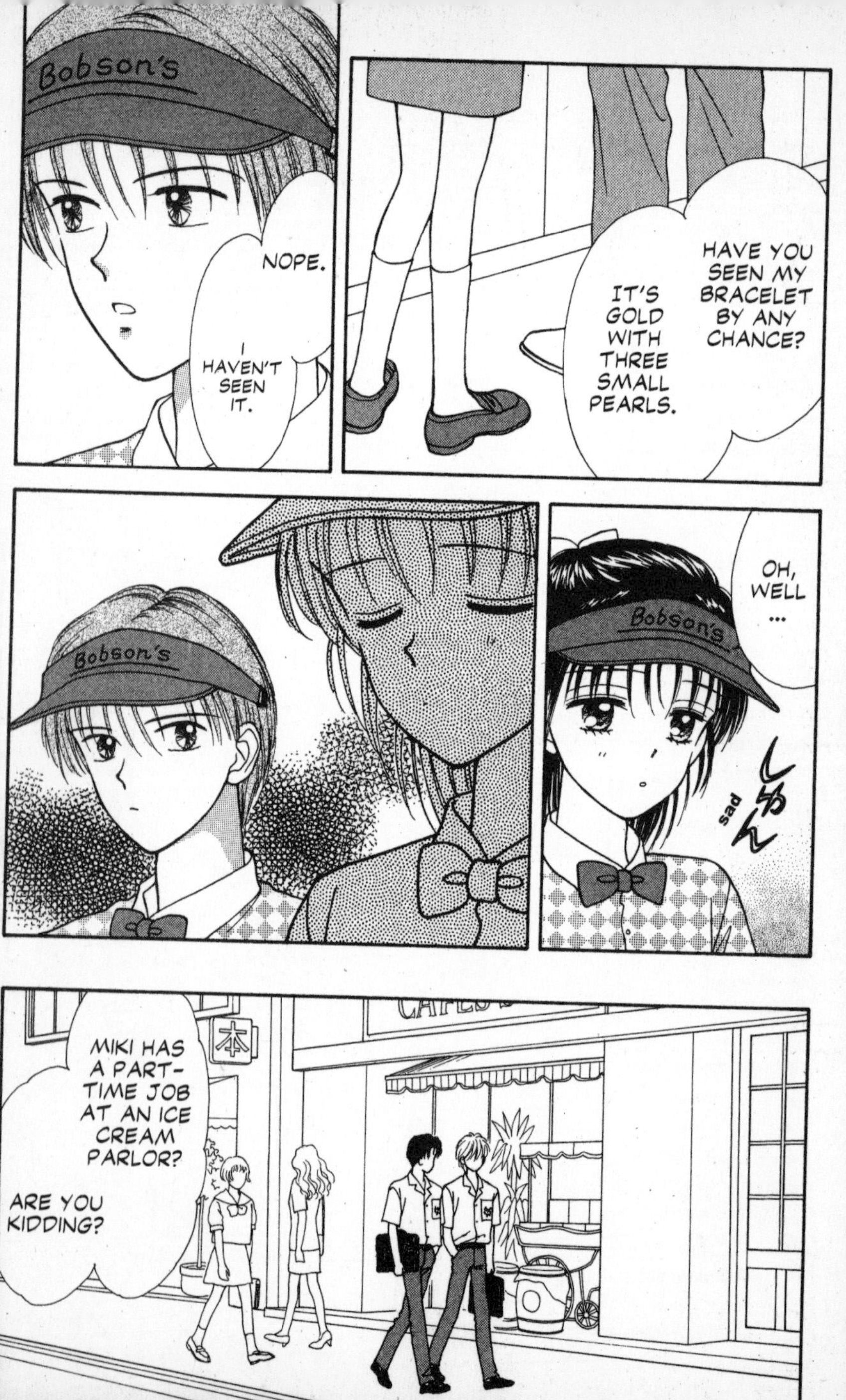
HAVE YOU SEEN MY BRACELET BY ANY CHANCE?
IT'S GOLD WITH THREE SMALL PEARLS.
NOPE.
I HAVEN'T SEEN IT.
OH, WELL ...
しゅん
sad
MIKI HAS A PART-TIME JOB AT AN ICE CREAM PARLOR?
ARE YOU KIDDING?

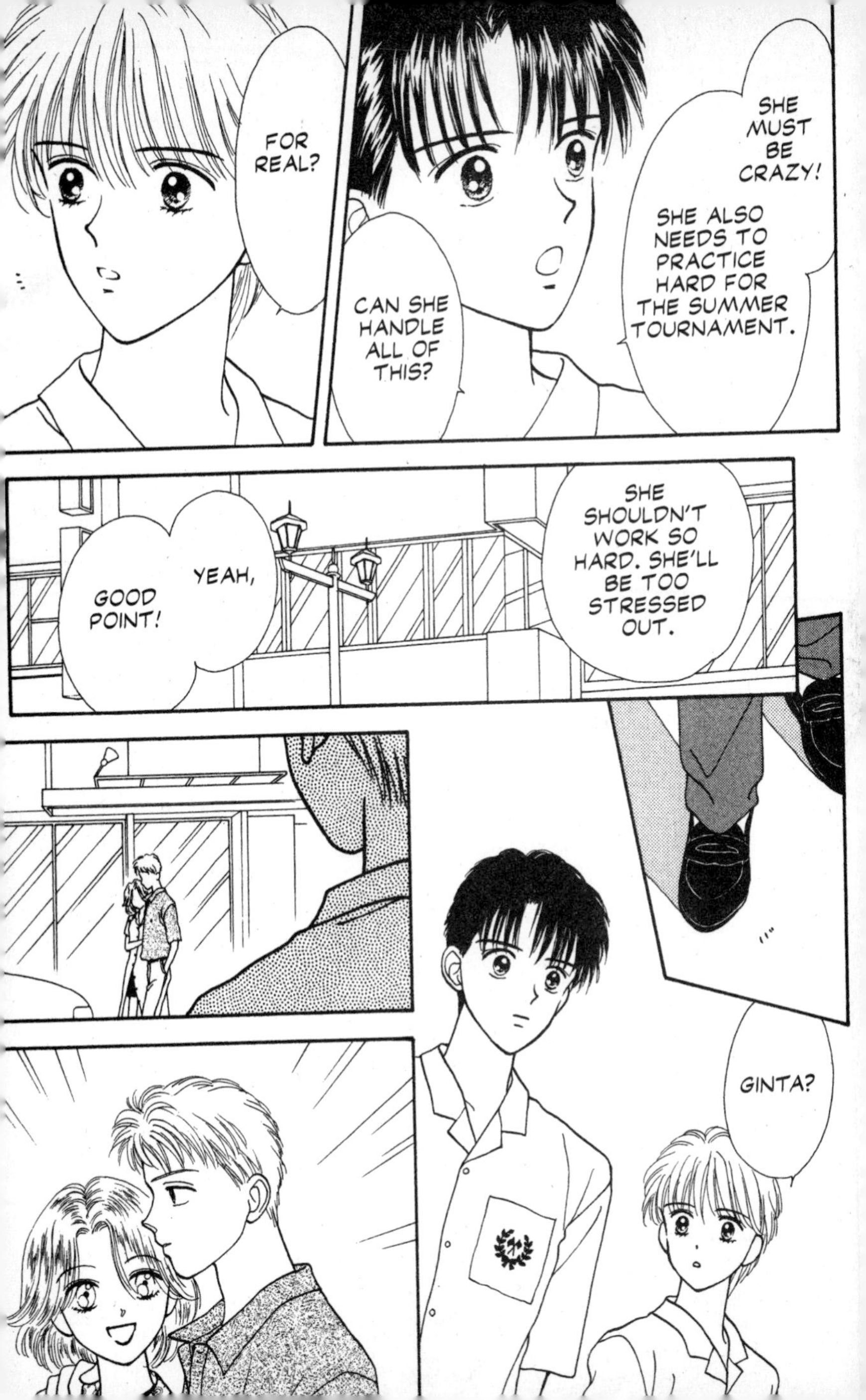
SHE MUST BE CRAZY!
SHE ALSO NEEDS TO PRACTICE HARD FOR THE SUMMER TOURNAMENT.
CAN SHE HANDLE ALL OF THIS?
FOR REAL?
SHE SHOULDN'T WORK SO HARD. SHE'LL BE TOO STRESSED OUT.
YEAH,
GOOD POINT!
GINTA?

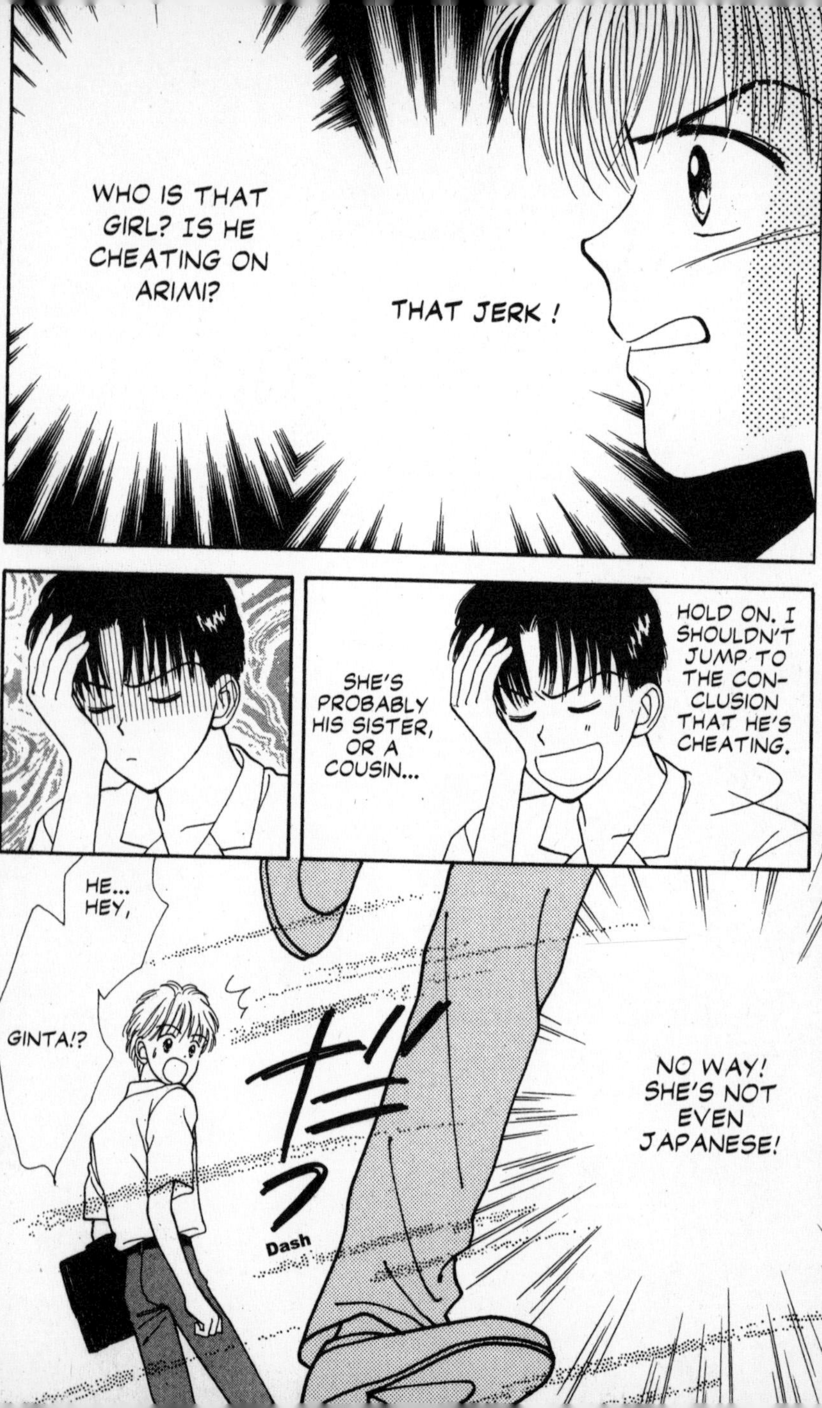
WHO IS THAT GIRL? IS HE CHEATING ON ARIMI?
THAT JERK !
HOLD ON. I SHOULDN'T JUMP TO THE CONCLUSION THAT HE'S CHEATING.
SHE'S PROBABLY HIS SISTER, OR A COUSIN...
NO WAY! SHE'S NOT EVEN JAPANESE!
Dash
HE... HEY,
GINTA!?

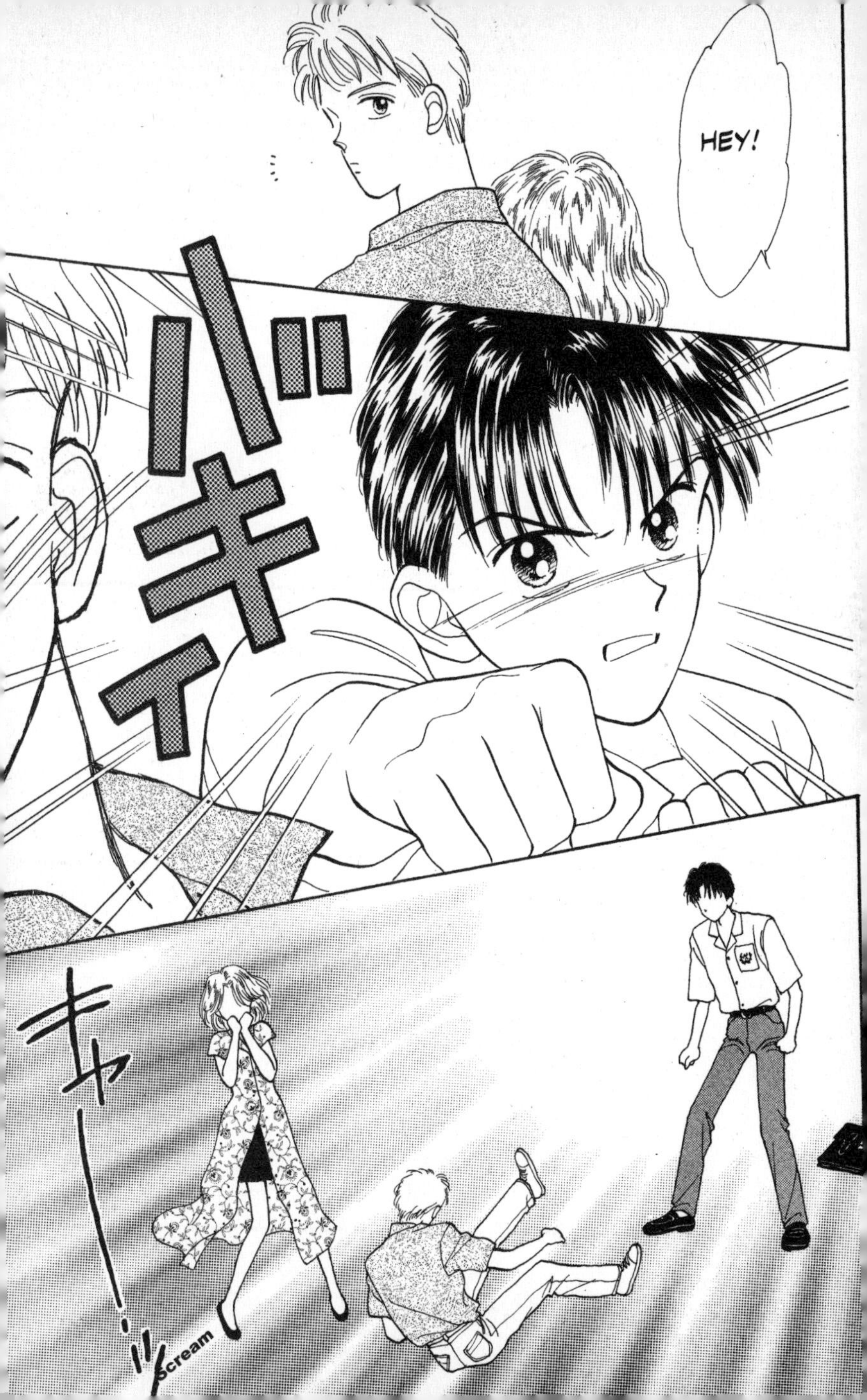
HEY!
バキィ
キャー!!
scream

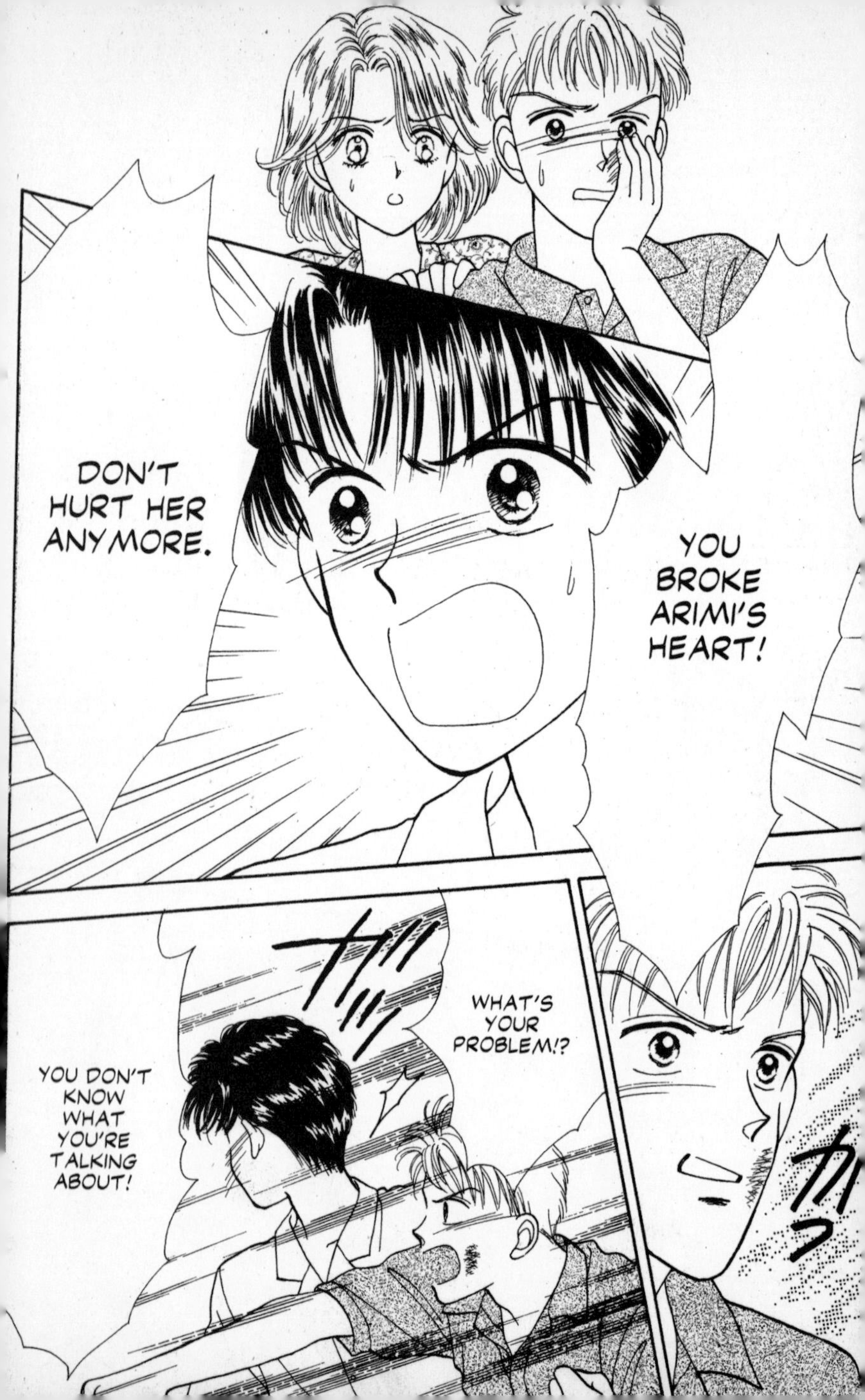
YOU BROKE ARIMI'S HEART!
DON'T HURT HER ANYMORE.
WHAT'S YOUR PROBLEM!?
YOU DON'T KNOW WHAT YOU'RE TALKING ABOUT!

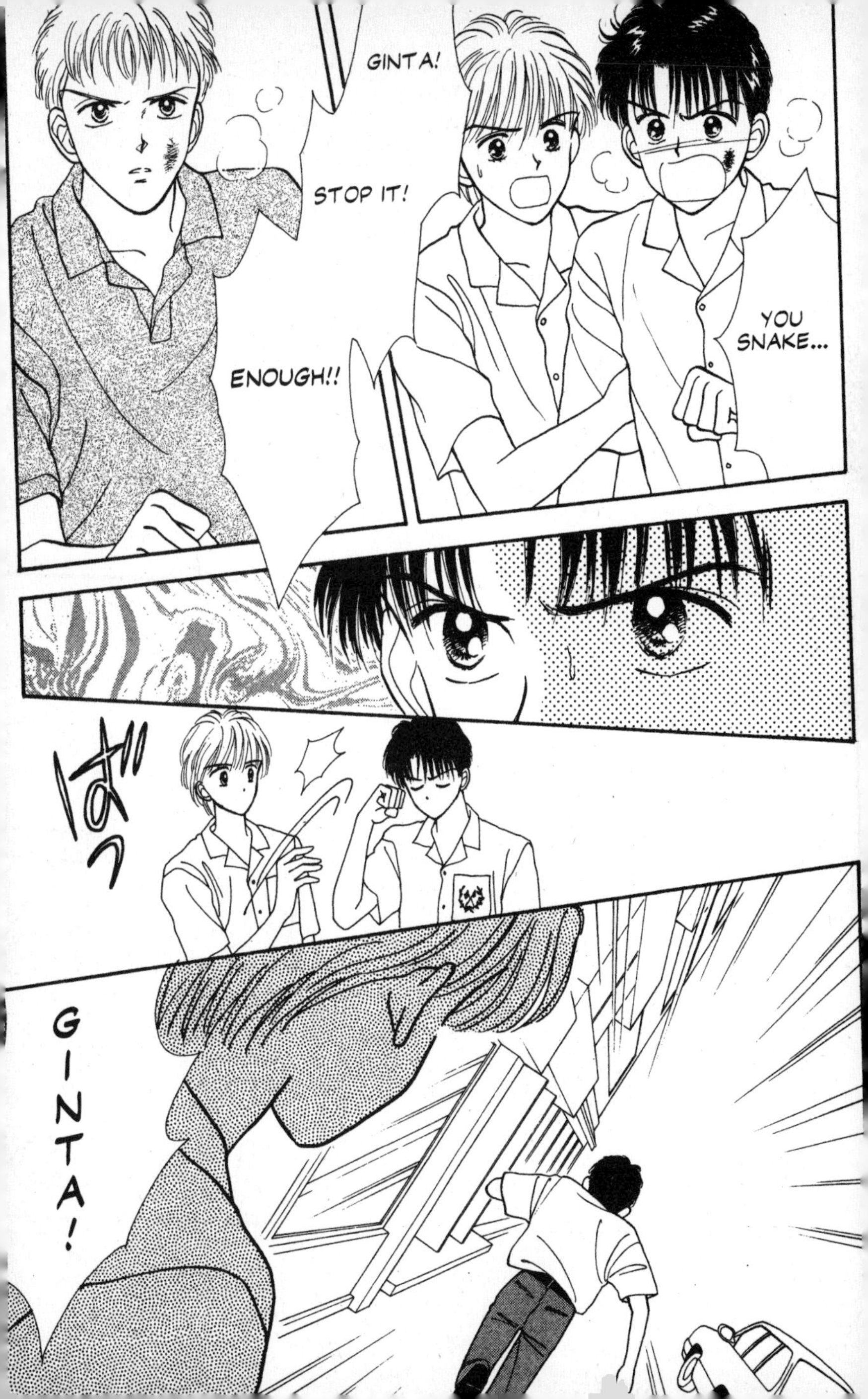
YOU SNAKE...
GINTA! STOP IT! ENOUGH!!
ばっ
GINTA!

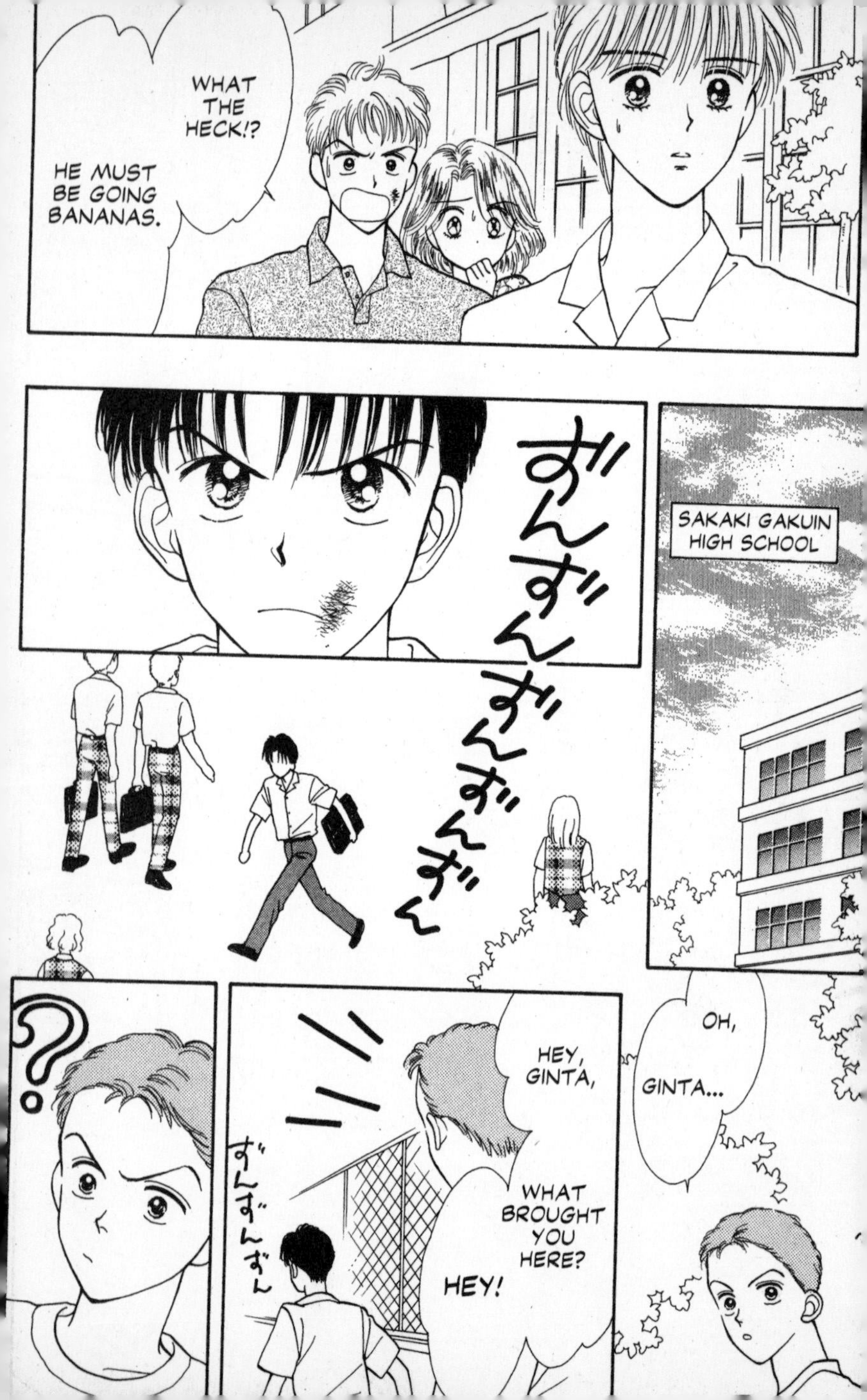
WHAT THE HECK!?
HE MUST BE GOING BANANAS.
SAKAKI GAKUIN HIGH SCHOOL
ずんずんずんずんずんずん
OH,
GINTA...
HEY, GINTA,
WHAT BROUGHT YOU HERE?
HEY!
ずんずん
?

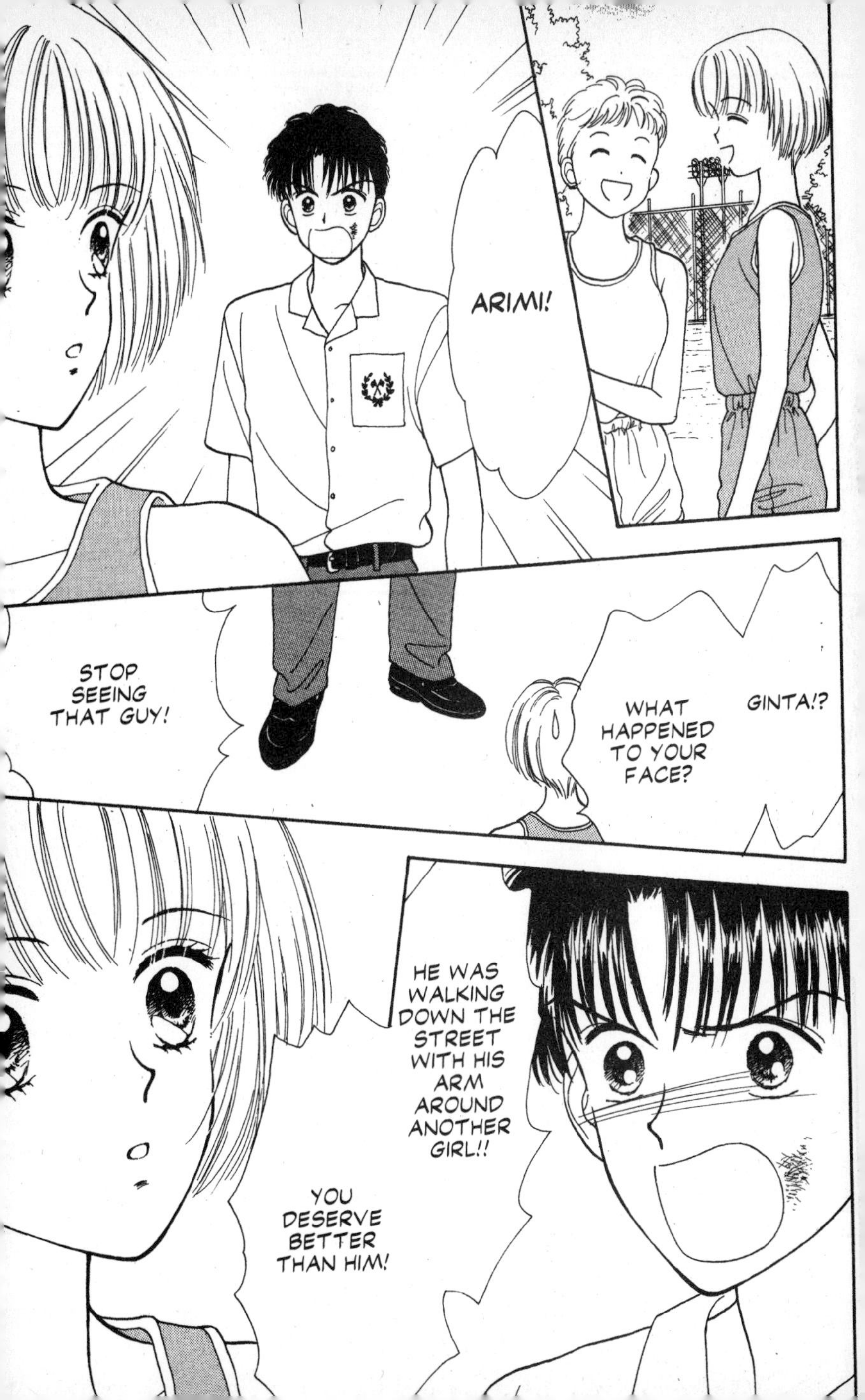
ARIMI!
GINTA!?
WHAT HAPPENED TO YOUR FACE?
STOP SEEING THAT GUY!
HE WAS WALKING DOWN THE STREET WITH HIS ARM AROUND ANOTHER GIRL!!
YOU DESERVE BETTER THAN HIM!

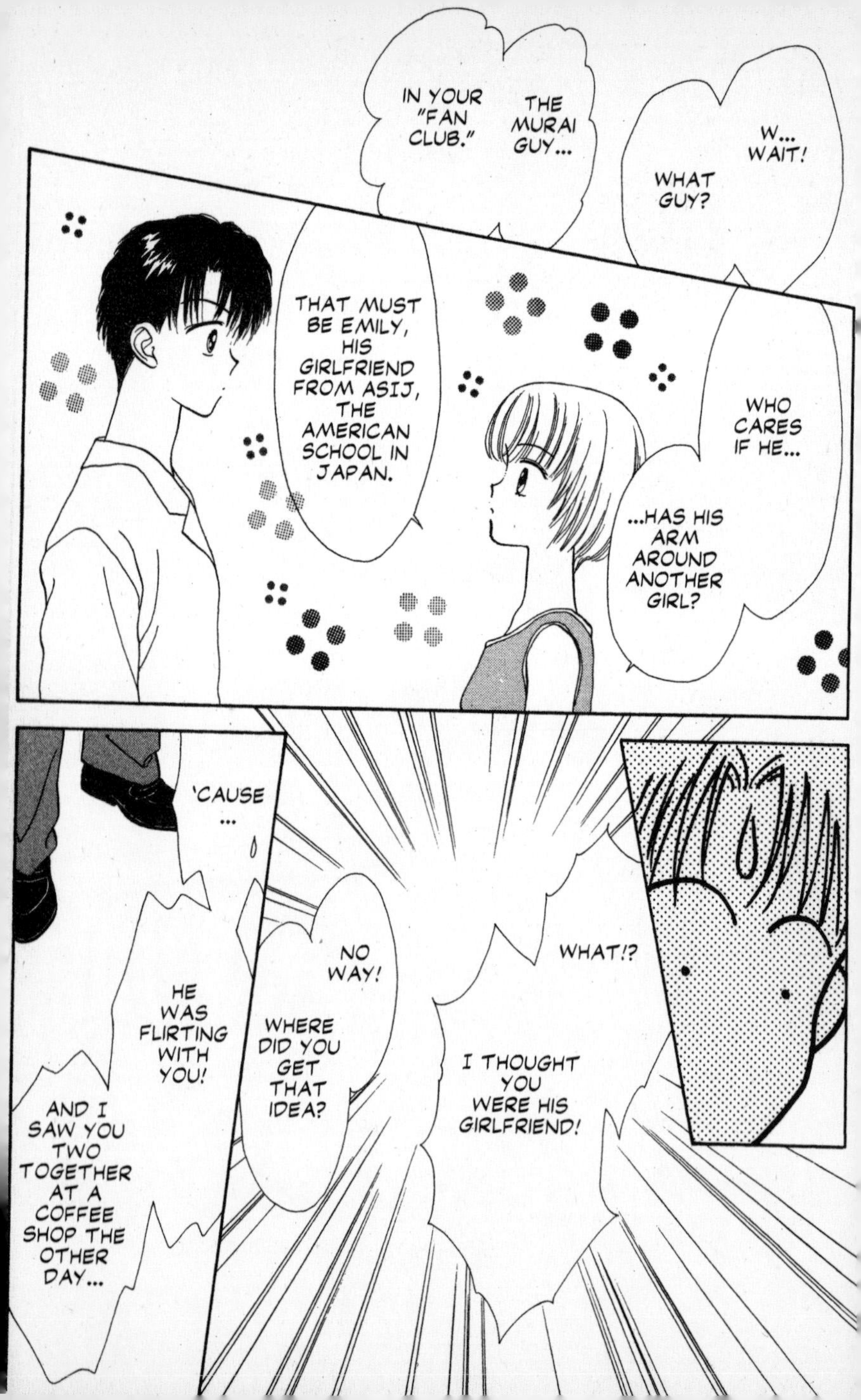
W... WAIT!
WHAT GUY?
THE MURAI GUY...
IN YOUR "FAN CLUB."
WHO CARES IF HE...
...HAS HIS ARM AROUND ANOTHER GIRL?
THAT MUST BE EMILY, HIS GIRLFRIEND FROM ASIJ, THE AMERICAN SCHOOL IN JAPAN.
WHAT!?
I THOUGHT YOU WERE HIS GIRLFRIEND!
NO WAY!
WHERE DID YOU GET THAT IDEA?
'CAUSE...
HE WAS FLIRTING WITH YOU!
AND I SAW YOU TWO TOGETHER AT A COFFEE SHOP THE OTHER DAY...

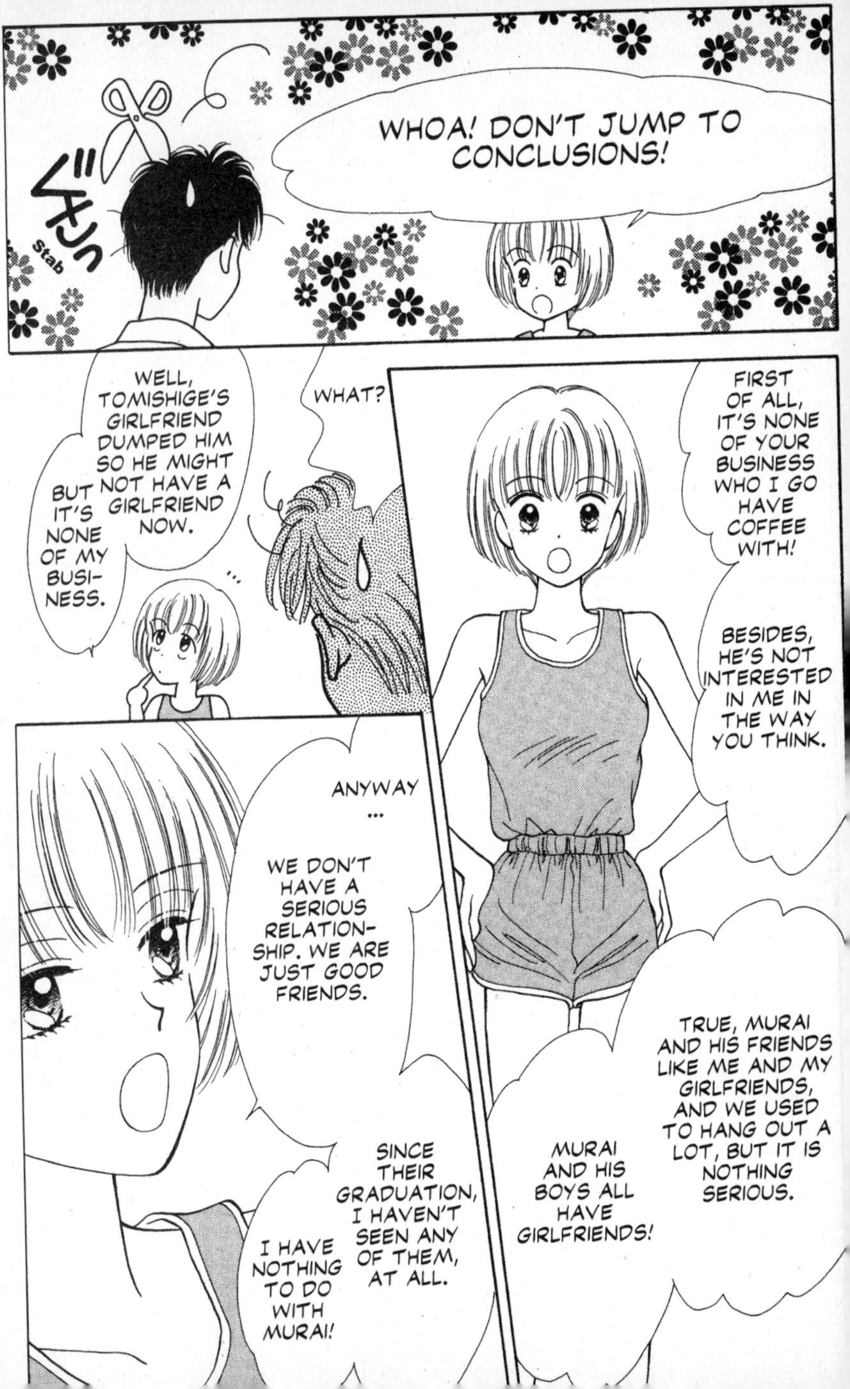
ぐさっ
Stab
WHOA! DON'T JUMP TO CONCLUSIONS!
FIRST OF ALL, IT'S NONE OF YOUR BUSINESS WHO I GO HAVE COFFEE WITH!
BESIDES, HE'S NOT INTERESTED IN ME IN THE WAY YOU THINK.
TRUE, MURAI AND HIS FRIENDS LIKE ME AND MY GIRLFRIENDS, AND WE USED TO HANG OUT A LOT, BUT IT IS NOTHING SERIOUS.
MURAI AND HIS BOYS ALL HAVE GIRLFRIENDS!
WHAT?
WELL, TOMISHIGE'S GIRLFRIEND DUMPED HIM SO HE MIGHT NOT HAVE A GIRLFRIEND NOW.
BUT IT'S NONE OF MY BUSINESS.
...
ANYWAY ...
WE DON'T HAVE A SERIOUS RELATIONSHIP. WE ARE JUST GOOD FRIENDS.
SINCE THEIR GRADUATION, I HAVEN'T SEEN ANY OF THEM, AT ALL.
I HAVE NOTHING TO DO WITH MURAI!

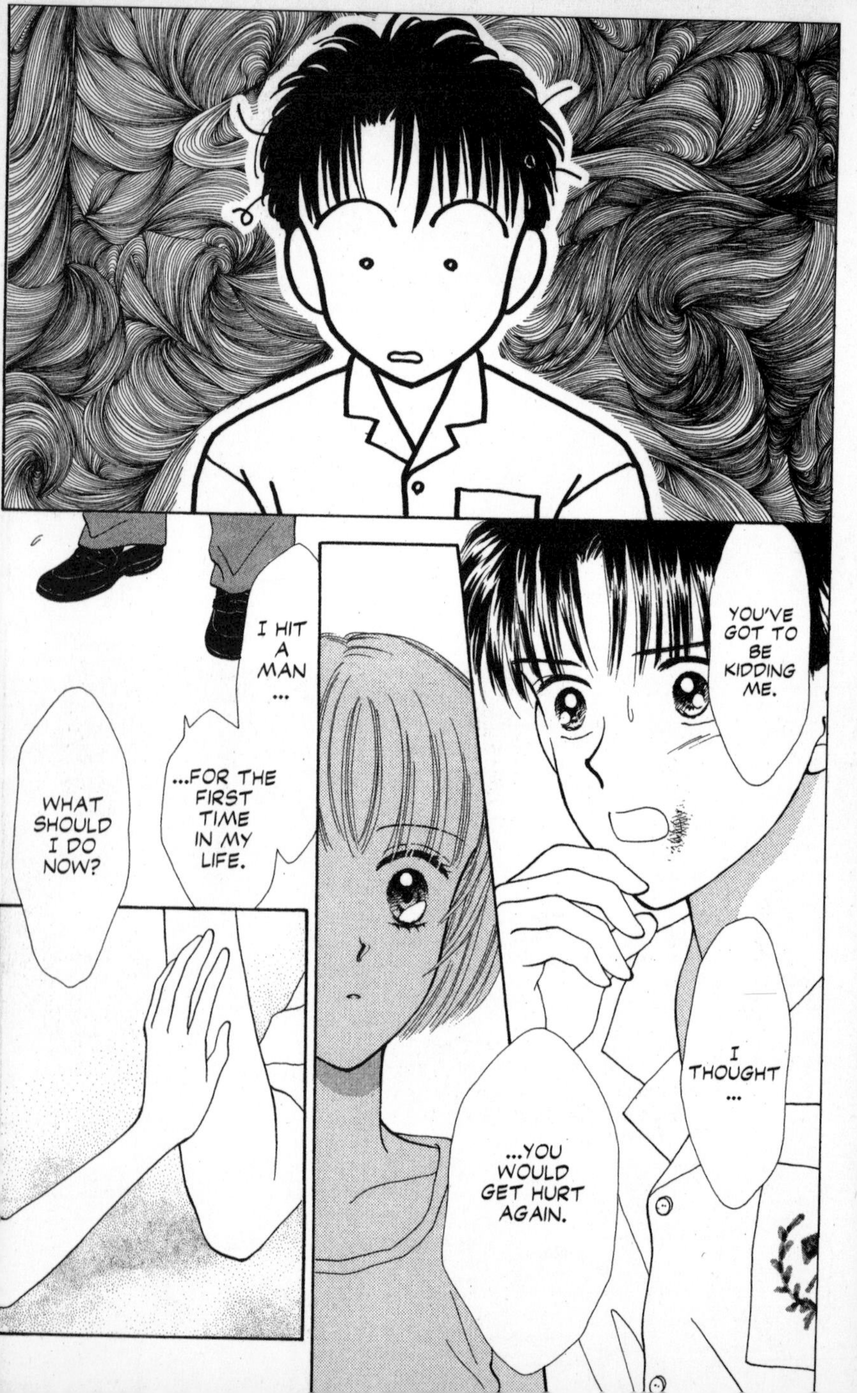
YOU'VE GOT TO BE KIDDING ME.
I THOUGHT...
...YOU WOULD GET HURT AGAIN.
I HIT A MAN...
...FOR THE FIRST TIME IN MY LIFE.
WHAT SHOULD I DO NOW?

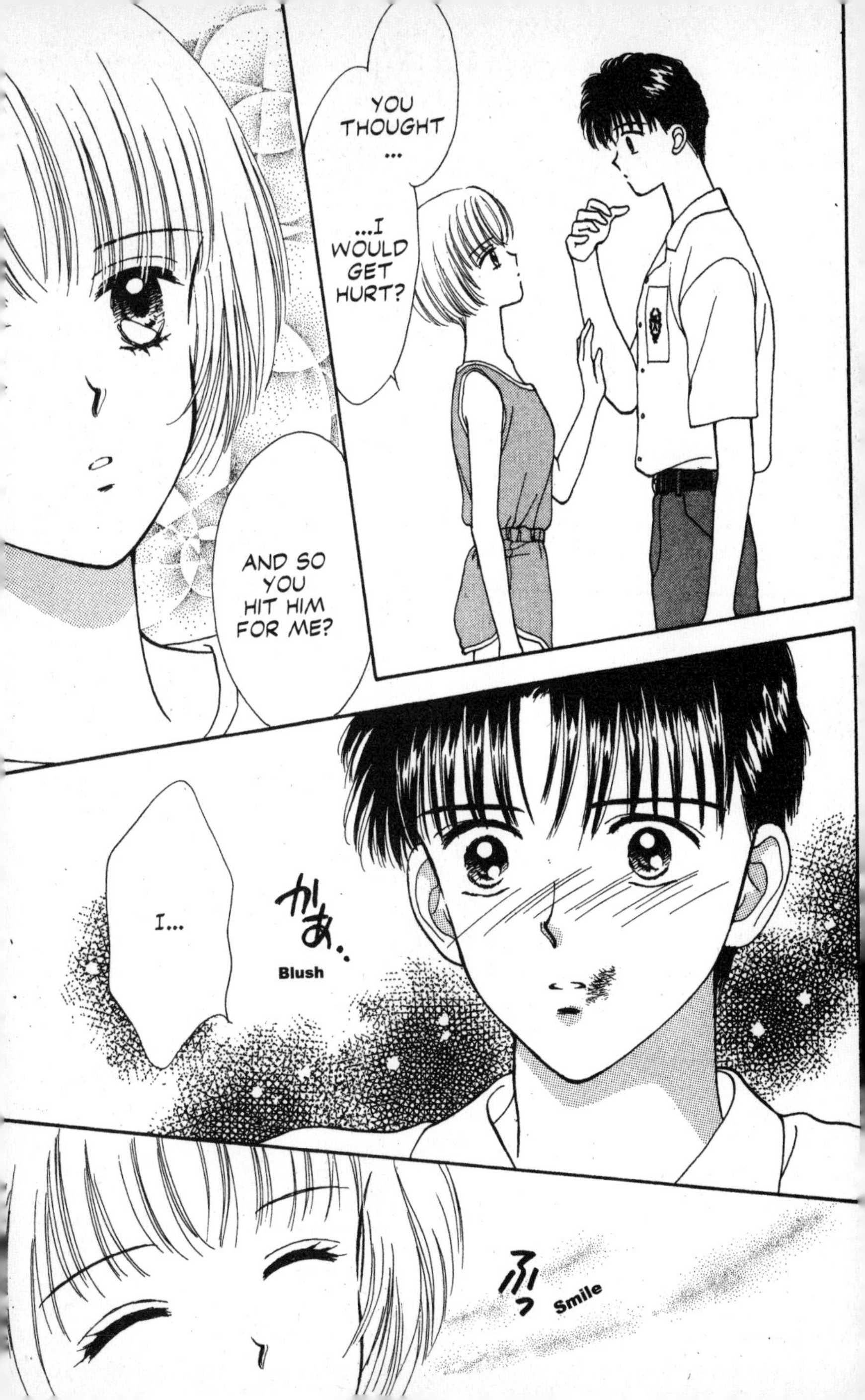
YOU THOUGHT ...
...I WOULD GET HURT?
AND SO YOU HIT HIM FOR ME?
かあ..
Blush
I...
ふっ
Smile

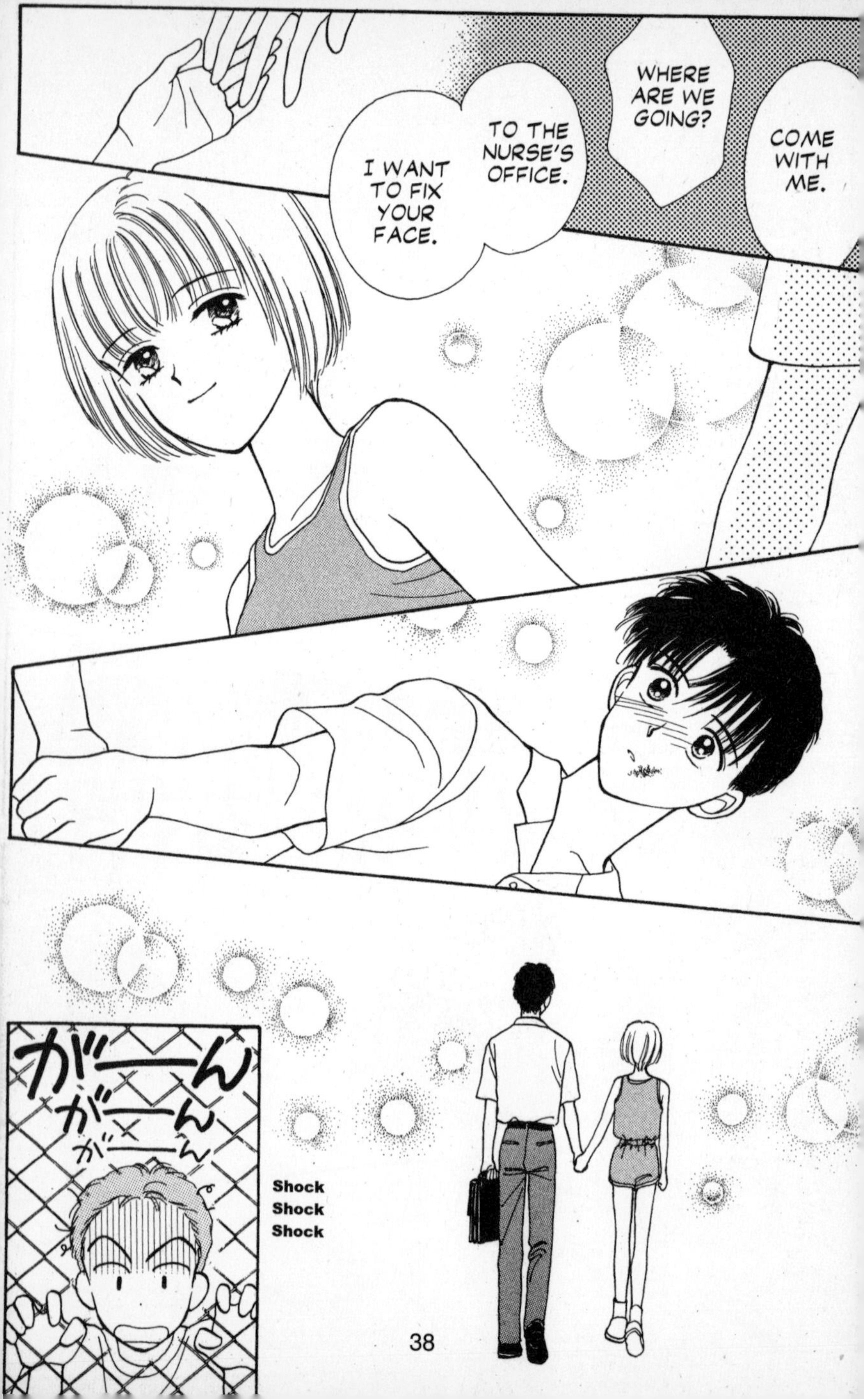
COME WITH ME.
WHERE ARE WE GOING?
TO THE NURSE'S OFFICE.
I WANT TO FIX YOUR FACE.
がーん
がーん
がーん
Shock
Shock
Shock

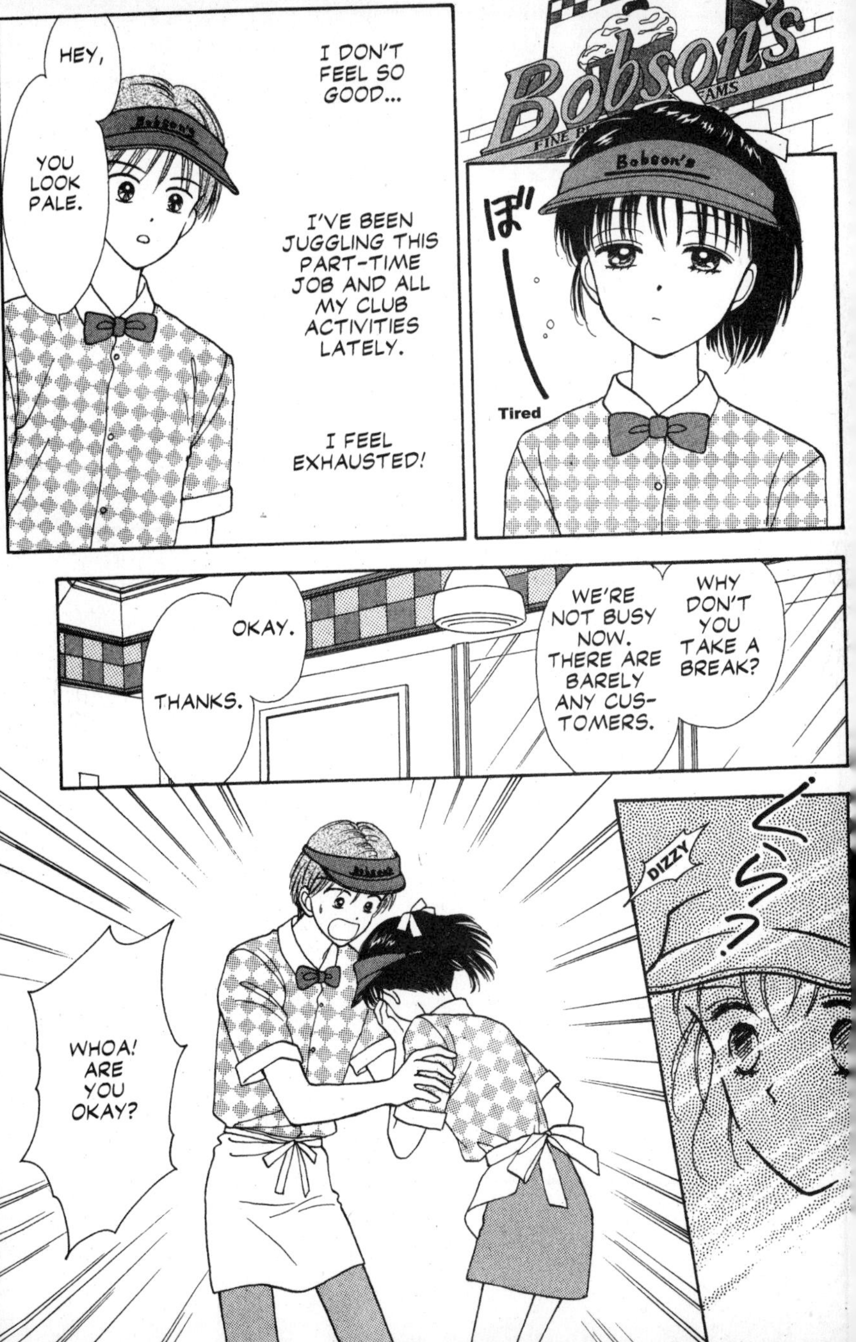
Bobson's
ぼー
Tired
I DON'T FEEL SO GOOD...
I'VE BEEN JUGGLING THIS PART-TIME JOB AND ALL MY CLUB ACTIVITIES LATELY.
I FEEL EXHAUSTED!
HEY,
YOU LOOK PALE.
WHY DON'T YOU TAKE A BREAK?
WE'RE NOT BUSY NOW. THERE ARE BARELY ANY CUS-TOMERS.
OKAY.
THANKS.
ぐらっ
DIZZY
WHOA! ARE YOU OKAY?

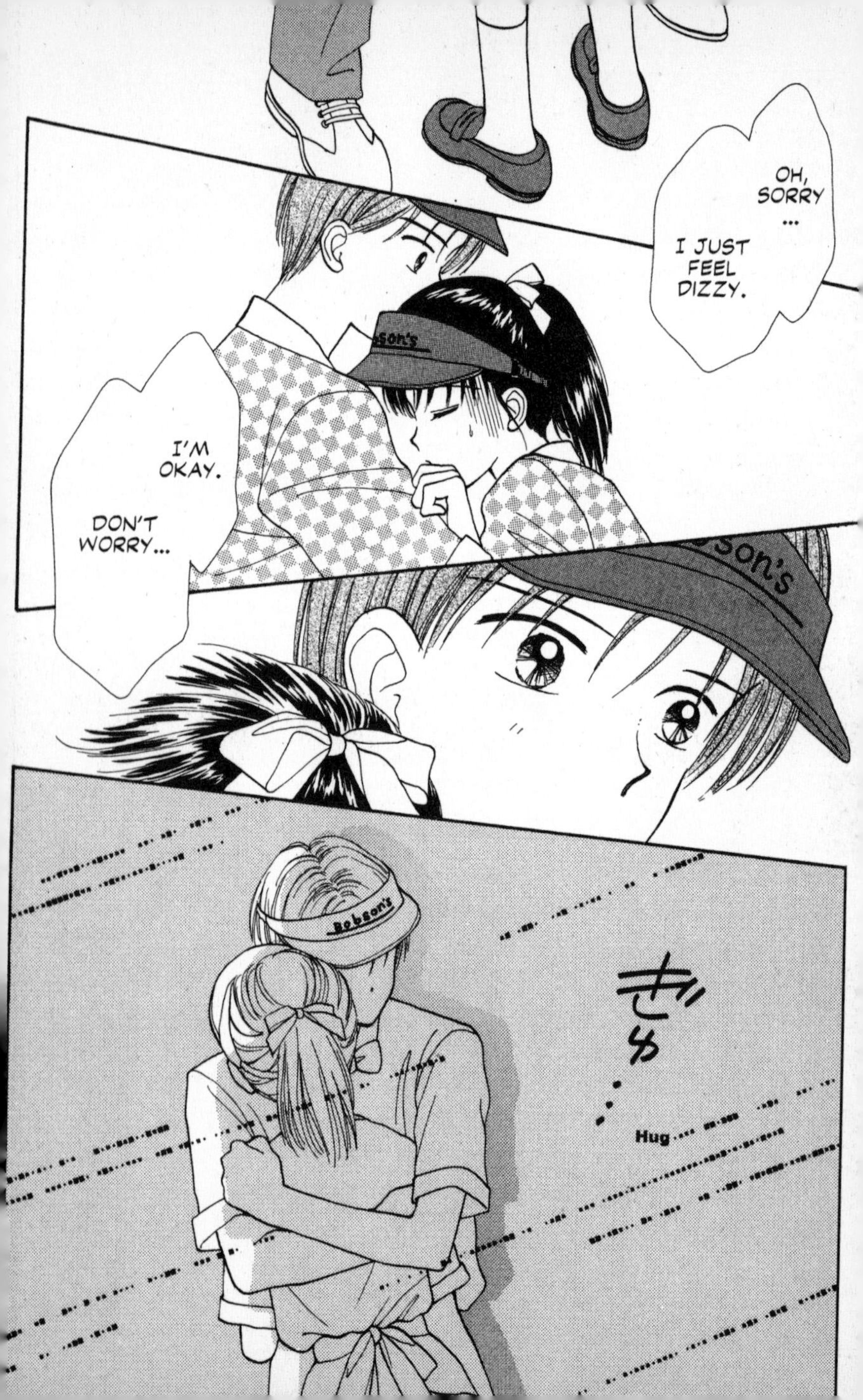
OH, SORRY ... I JUST FEEL DIZZY.
I'M OKAY.
DON'T WORRY...
Bobson's
Hug

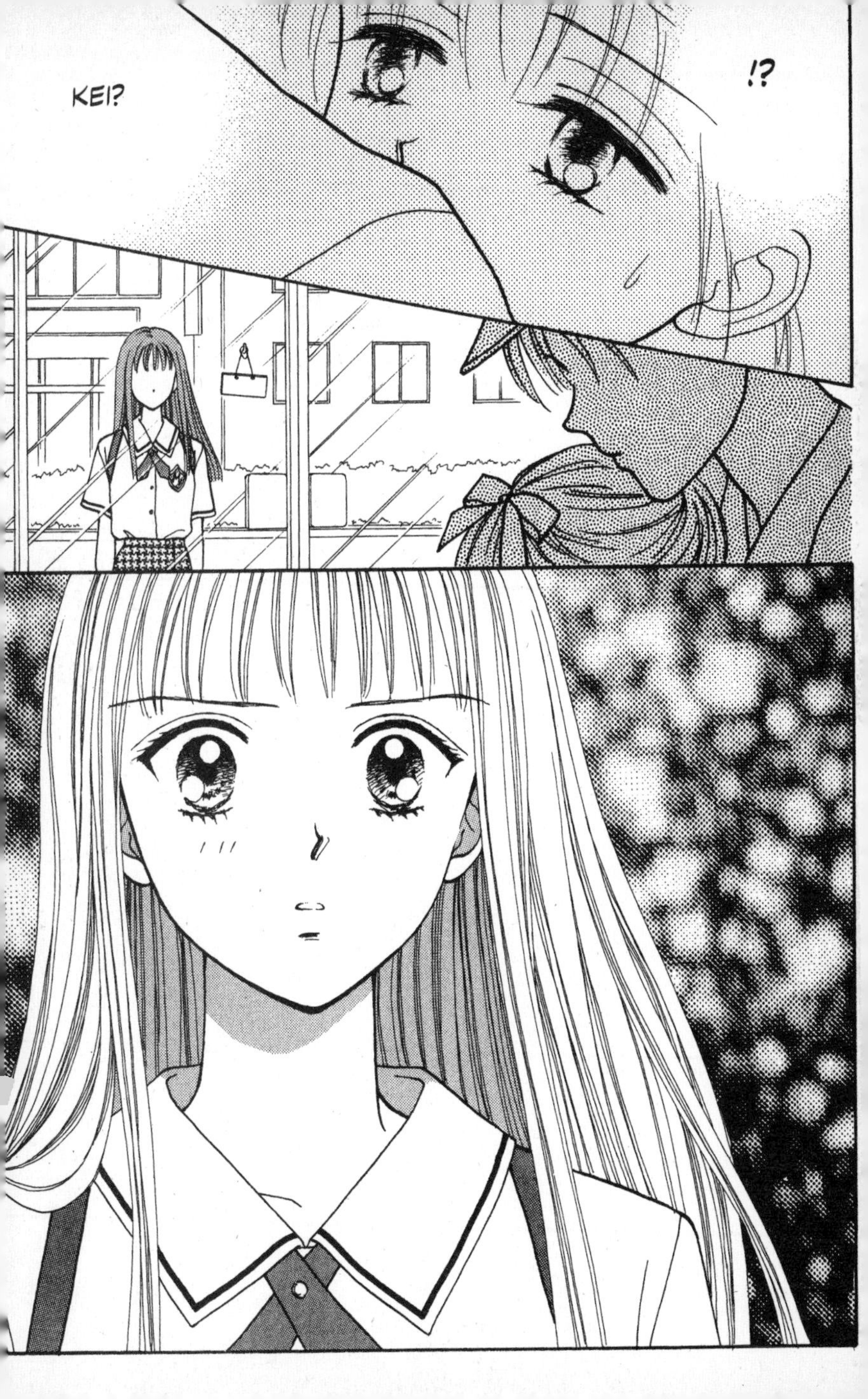
!?
KEI?

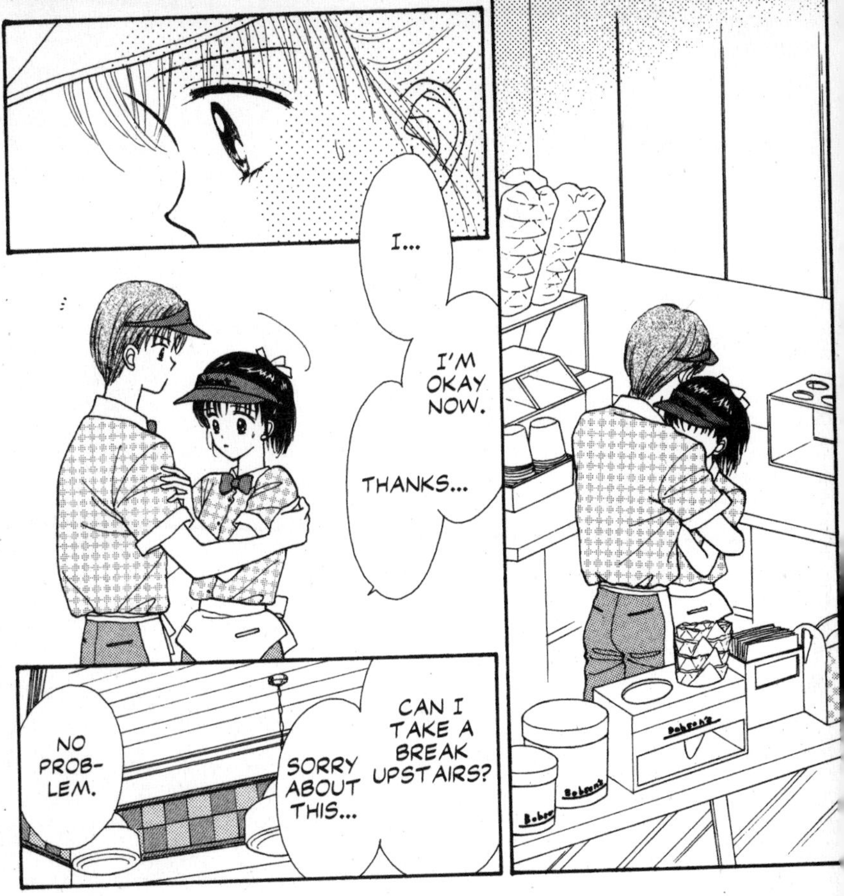
I...
I'M OKAY NOW.
THANKS...
CAN I TAKE A BREAK UPSTAIRS?
SORRY ABOUT THIS...
NO PROB-LEM.

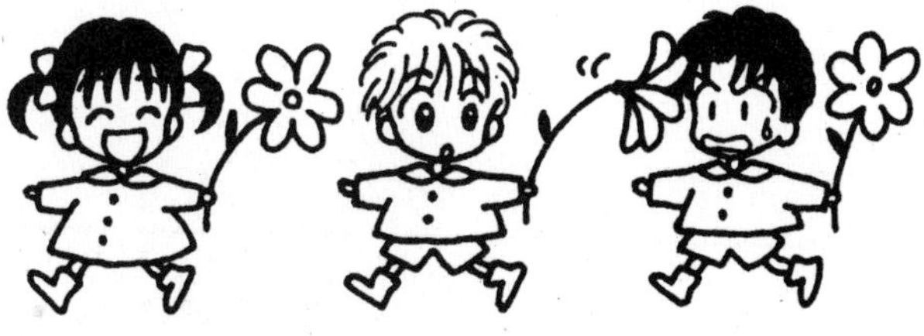

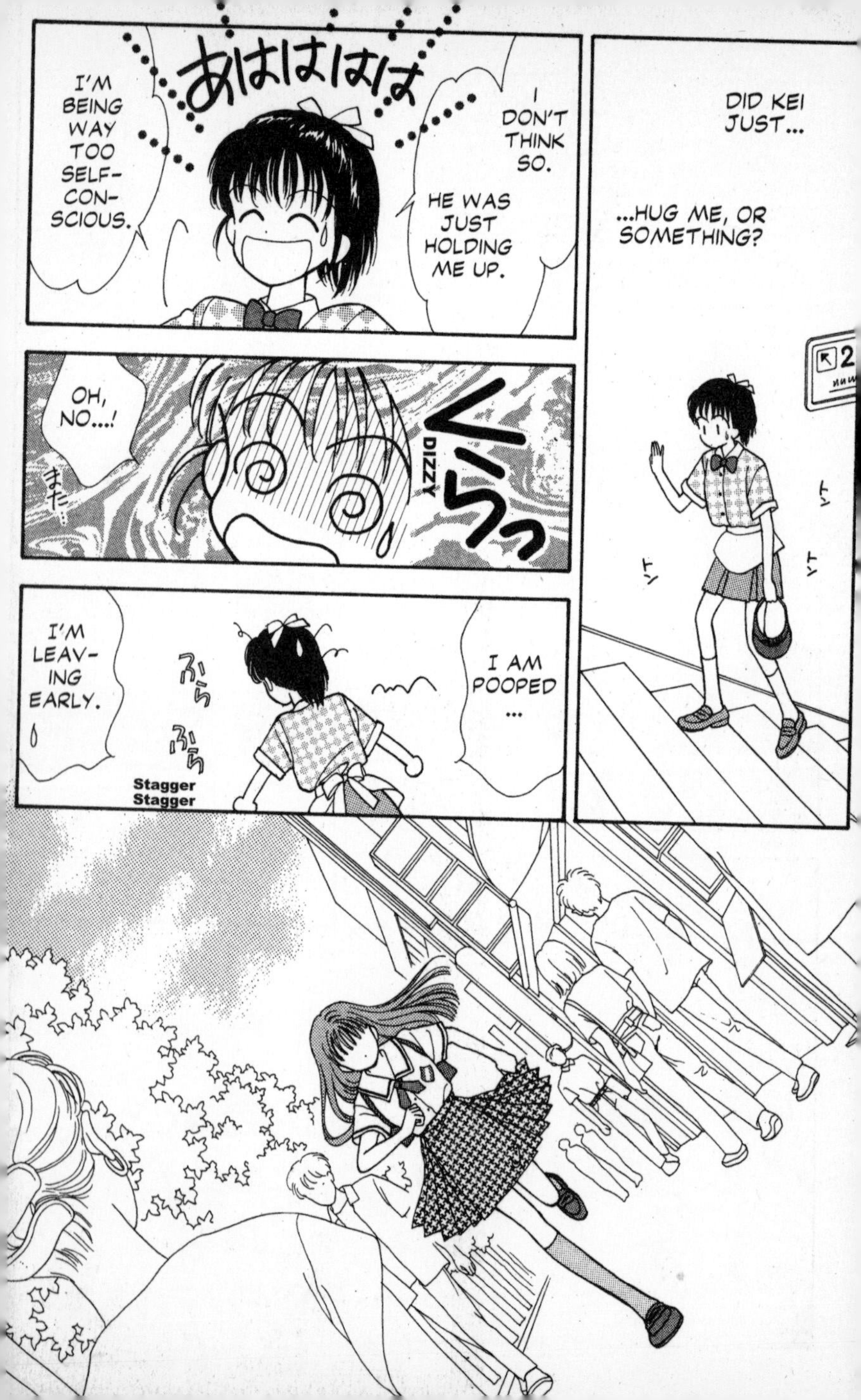
DID KEI JUST...
...HUG ME, OR SOMETHING?
トン
トン
トン
I DON'T THINK SO.
HE WAS JUST HOLDING ME UP.
あははははは
I'M BEING WAY TOO SELF-CONSCIOUS.
くらっ
DIZZY
OH, NO...!
また…
I AM POOPED ...
ふら ふら
Stagger Stagger
I'M LEAVING EARLY.

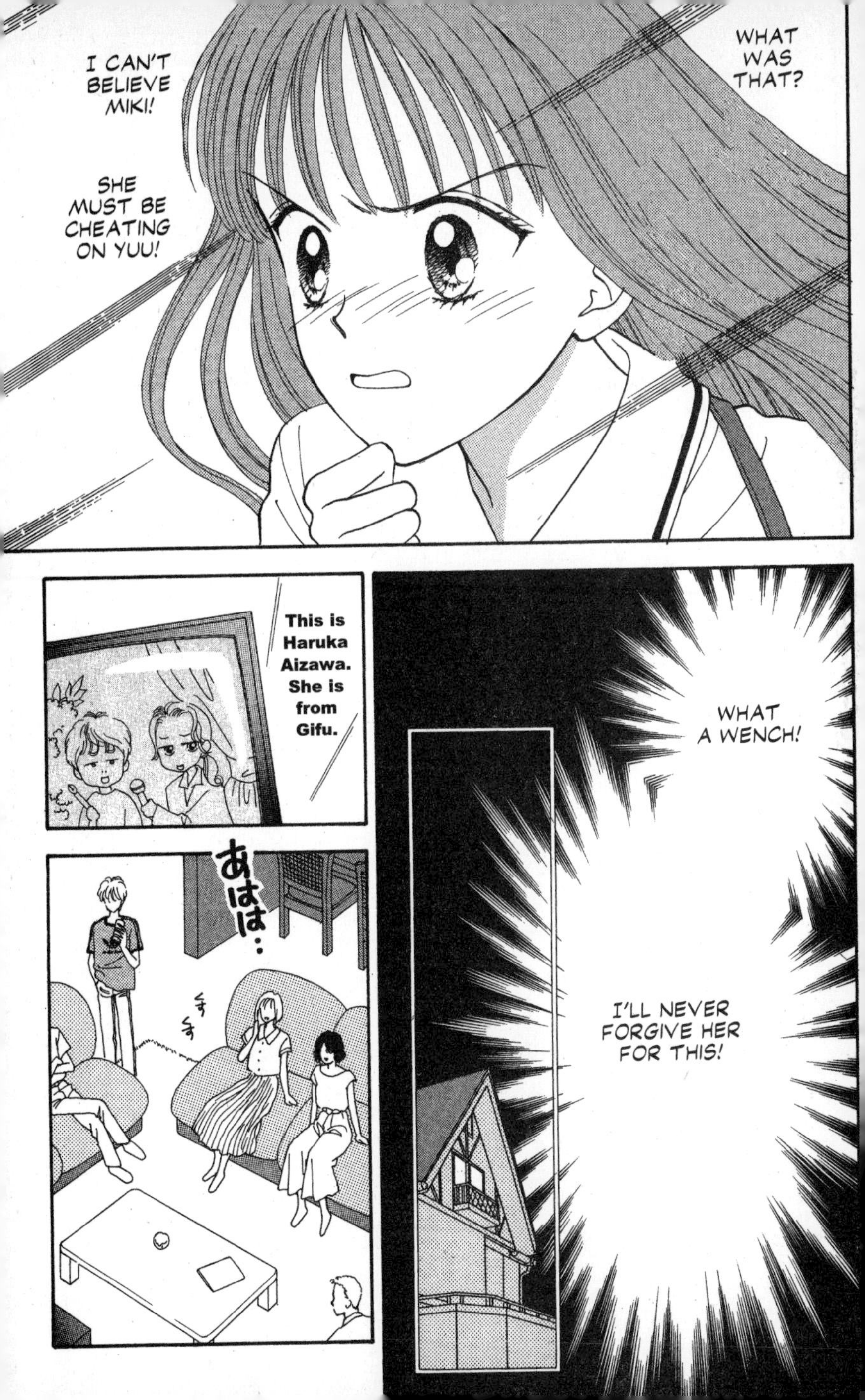
WHAT WAS THAT?
I CAN'T BELIEVE MIKI!
SHE MUST BE CHEATING ON YUU!
WHAT A WENCH!
I'LL NEVER FORGIVE HER FOR THIS!
This is Haruka Aizawa. She is from Gifu.
あはは…
くすくす

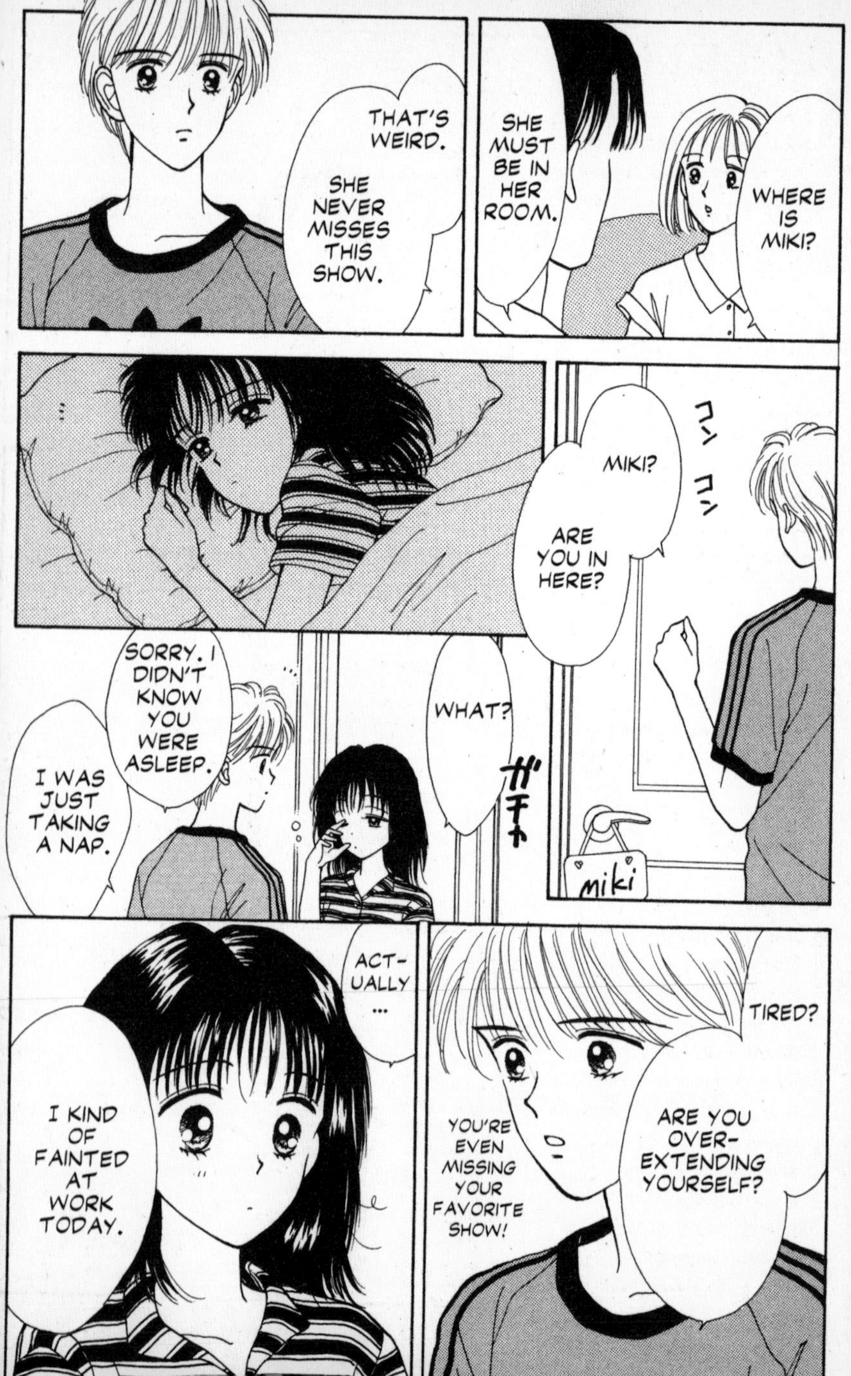
WHERE IS MIKI?
SHE MUST BE IN HER ROOM.
THAT'S WEIRD.
SHE NEVER MISSES THIS SHOW.
コン コン
MIKI?
ARE YOU IN HERE?
...
ガチャ
WHAT?
SORRY. I DIDN'T KNOW YOU WERE ASLEEP.
I WAS JUST TAKING A NAP.
miki
TIRED?
ARE YOU OVER-EXTENDING YOURSELF?
YOU'RE EVEN MISSING YOUR FAVORITE SHOW!
ACT-UALLY...
I KIND OF FAINTED AT WORK TODAY.

FREE TALK ④

I never thought about what kind of voices the characters should have. So when it came to producing the animated version of Marmalade Boy, I was just hoping my favorite actors would play the roles. Mariko Kouda, who does Miki's voice, has such a cute voice, and I am very pleased with her job. Mariko herself is a very attractive lady. She says she's not that photogenic, and she is actually much prettier than how she appears in the picture in Ribon. Ryutaro Okiayu, the voice of Yuu, has a deep, sexy voice—far away from that of a boy. His voice was not something many viewers expected. Ai Yazawa told me with worry in her voice (or was that excitement?): "His too-sexy voice would be too much for love scenes!" (Ha ha!) I first thought his voice was too mature, but I am happy he took the role because he is my favorite male actor among those who auditioned. Most of all, I like Ryutaro's name—it sounds so powerful.

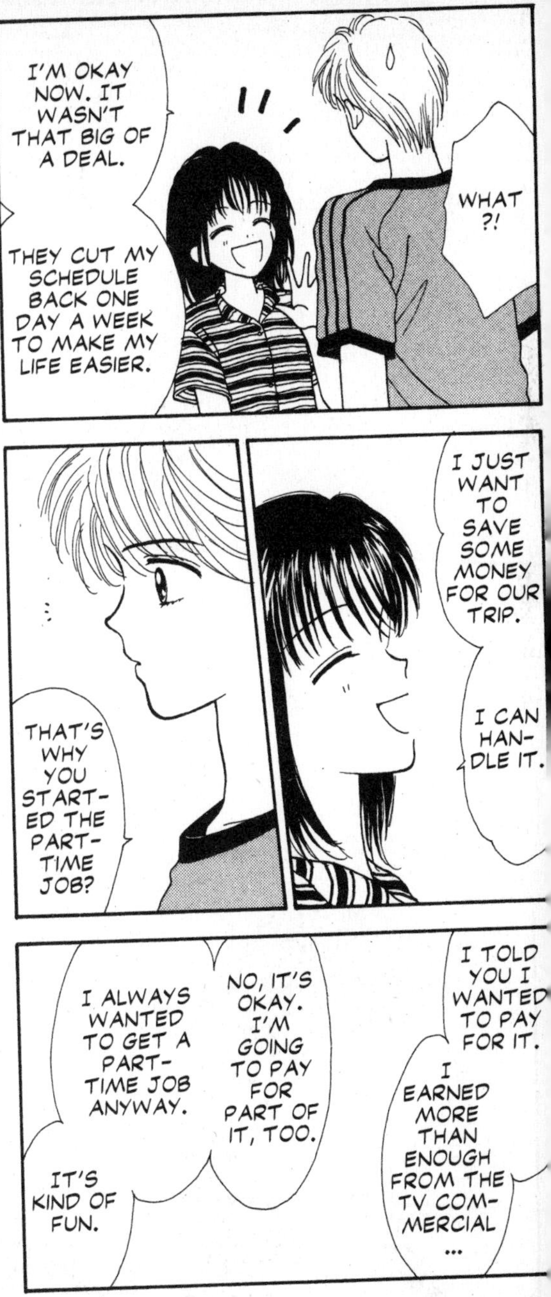
I'M OKAY NOW. IT WASN'T THAT BIG OF A DEAL.
THEY CUT MY SCHEDULE BACK ONE DAY A WEEK TO MAKE MY LIFE EASIER.
WHAT ?!
I JUST WANT TO SAVE SOME MONEY FOR OUR TRIP.
I CAN HANDLE IT.
THAT'S WHY YOU START-ED THE PART-TIME JOB?
I TOLD YOU I WANTED TO PAY FOR IT.
I EARNED MORE THAN ENOUGH FROM THE TV COM-MERCIAL ...
NO, IT'S OKAY. I'M GOING TO PAY FOR PART OF IT, TOO.
I ALWAYS WANTED TO GET A PART-TIME JOB ANYWAY.
IT'S KIND OF FUN.

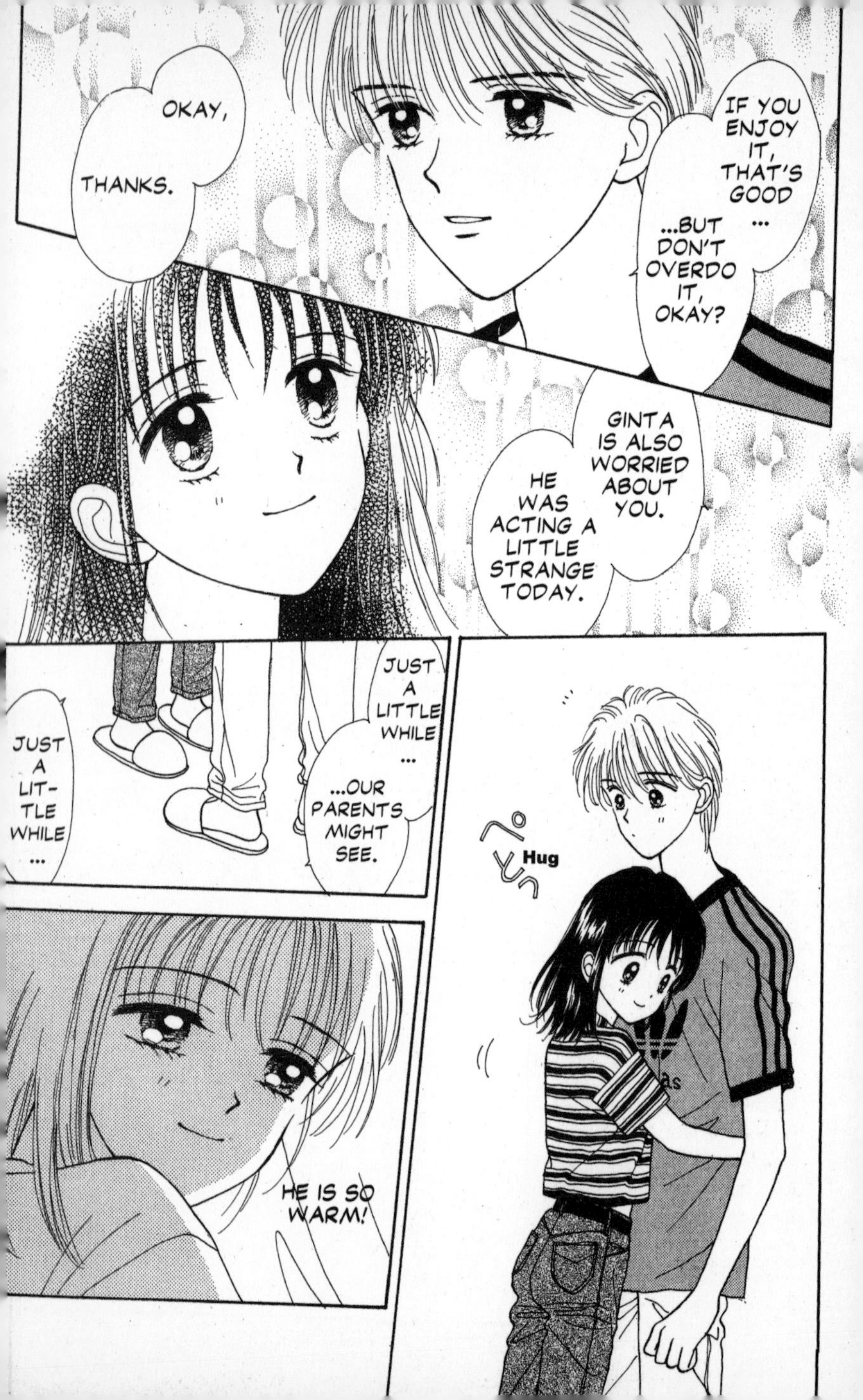
IF YOU ENJOY IT, THAT'S GOOD ...
...BUT DON'T OVERDO IT, OKAY?
OKAY,
THANKS.
GINTA IS ALSO WORRIED ABOUT YOU.
HE WAS ACTING A LITTLE STRANGE TODAY.
Hug
JUST A LITTLE WHILE ...
...OUR PARENTS MIGHT SEE.
JUST A LIT-TLE WHILE ...
HE IS SO WARM!

FREE TALK⑤

Wakana Yamazaki (Meiko's voice) was recommended by Mr. Seki, the producer with Toei Doga Motion Picture, Co., Ltd., so she got the role without auditioning. I had no disagreement about her playing Meiko's role. She has a graceful voice and it's perfect for Meiko's character. I was pleased when Wakana talked to me at the Christmas party held for the Marmalade Boy staff. She told me she read all the episodes of Marmalade Boy. Junichi Kanemaru, as Ginta, is doing a perfect job. He is a great actor with a nice voice. Aya Hisakawa, as Arimi, was also already chosen without an audition. When I first listened to the pilot tape, I was impressed by her performance.

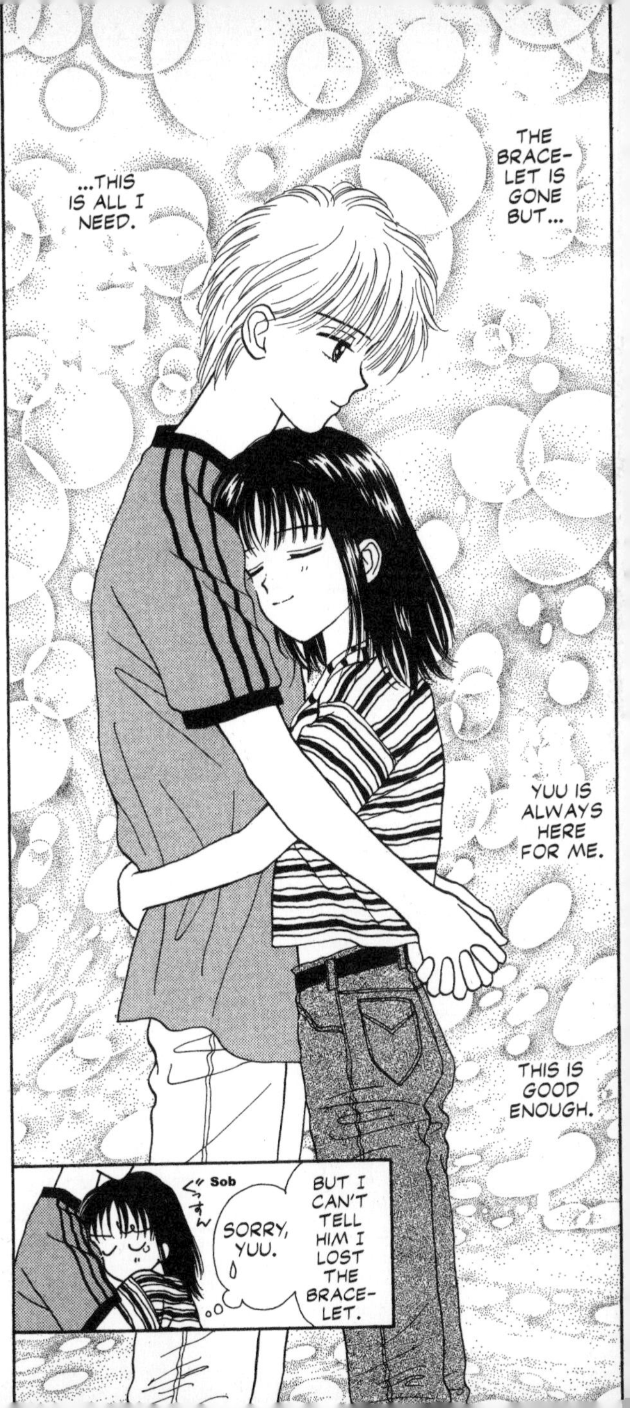
THE BRACELET IS GONE BUT...
...THIS IS ALL I NEED.
YUU IS ALWAYS HERE FOR ME.
THIS IS GOOD ENOUGH.
BUT I CAN'T TELL HIM I LOST THE BRACELET.
SORRY, YUU.
ぐすん Sob

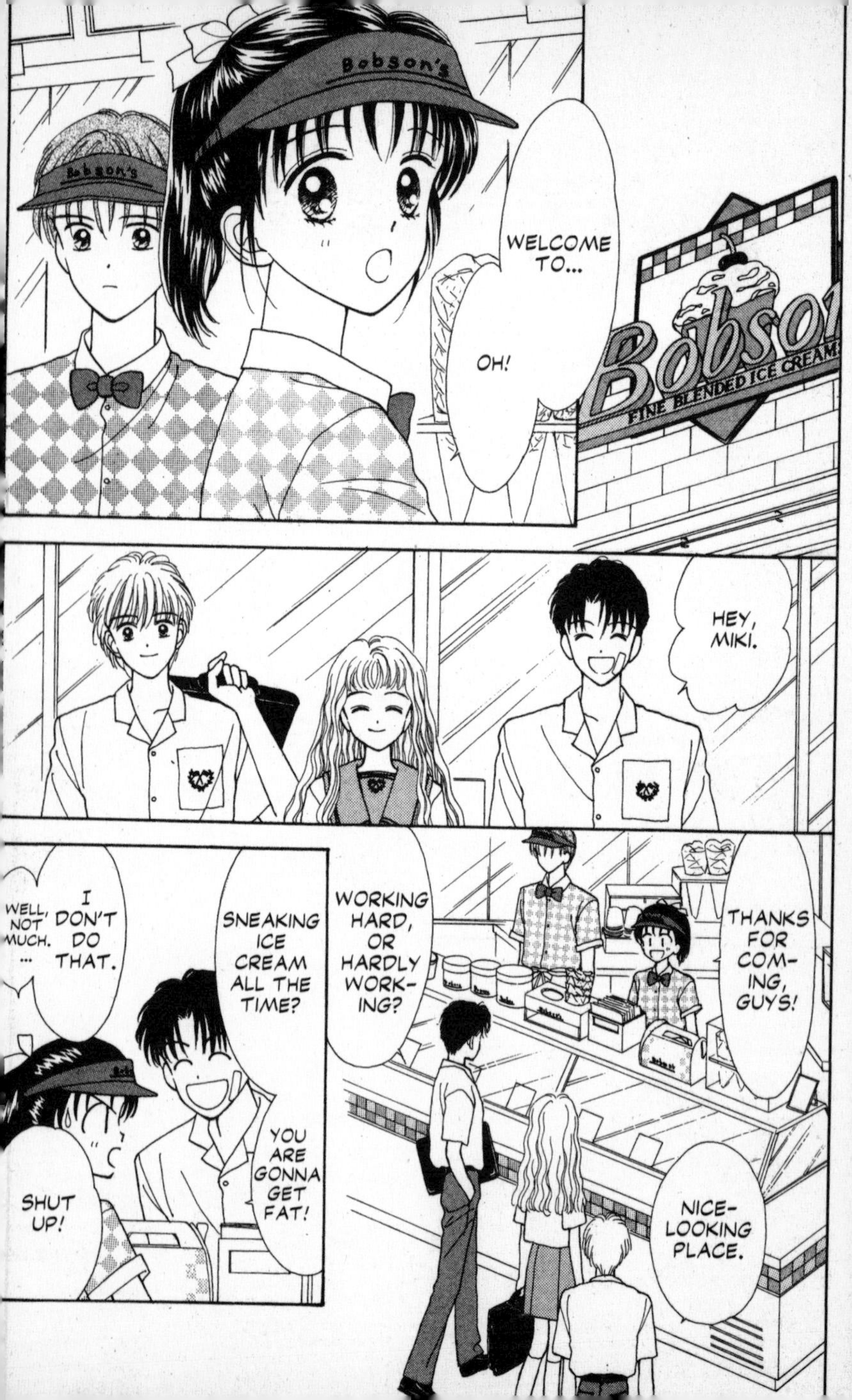
Bobson's
WELCOME TO...
OH!
HEY, MIKI.
THANKS FOR COMING, GUYS!
WORKING HARD, OR HARDLY WORKING?
NICE-LOOKING PLACE.
SNEAKING ICE CREAM ALL THE TIME?
I DON'T DO THAT.
WELL, NOT MUCH. ...
YOU ARE GONNA GET FAT!
SHUT UP!

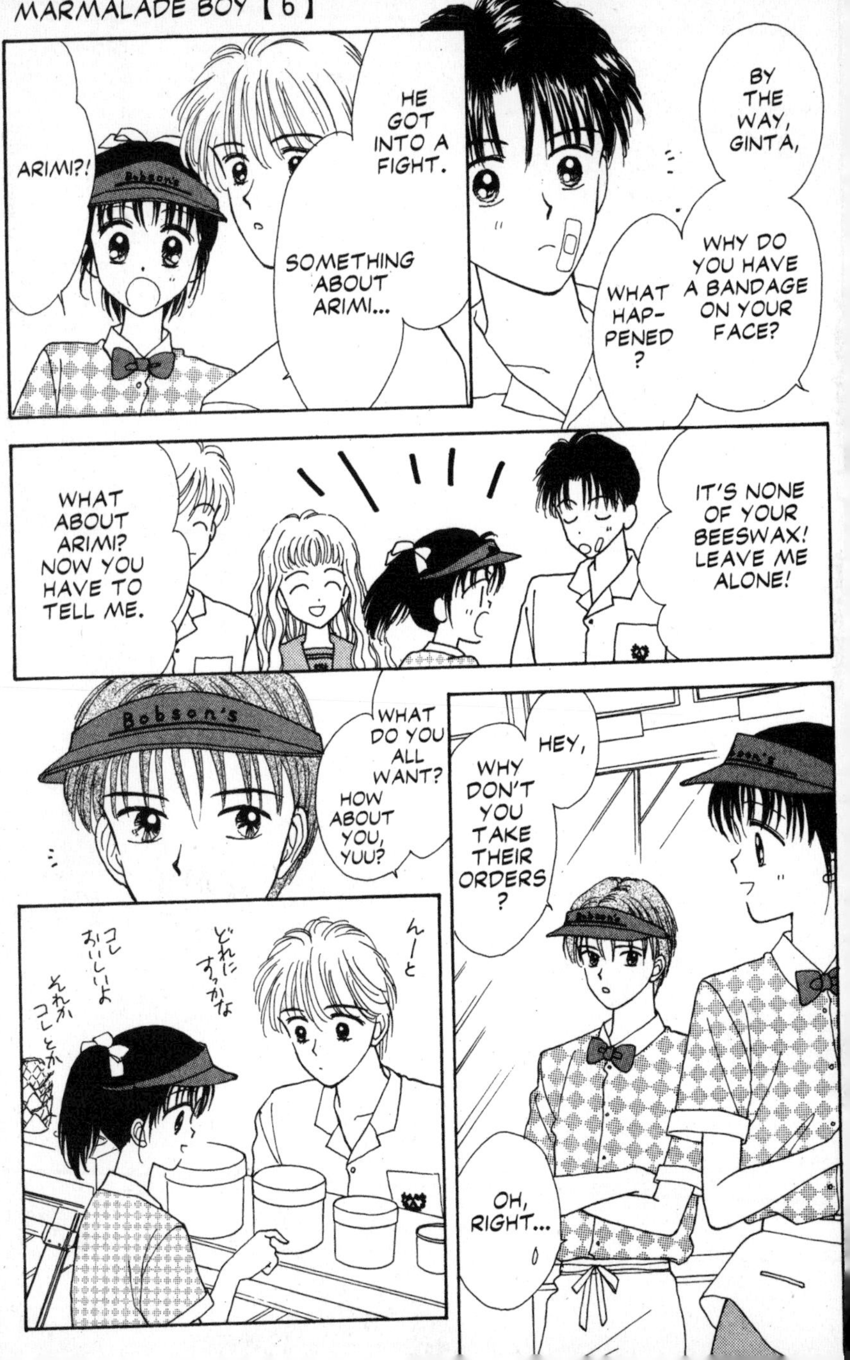
BY THE WAY, GINTA,
WHY DO YOU HAVE A BANDAGE ON YOUR FACE?
WHAT HAPPENED?
HE GOT INTO A FIGHT.
SOMETHING ABOUT ARIMI...
ARIMI?!
IT'S NONE OF YOUR BEESWAX! LEAVE ME ALONE!
WHAT ABOUT ARIMI? NOW YOU HAVE TO TELL ME.
HEY, WHY DON'T YOU TAKE THEIR ORDERS?
OH, RIGHT...
WHAT DO YOU ALL WANT?
HOW ABOUT YOU, YUU?
んーと
どれにすっかな
コレおいしいよ
それかコレとか

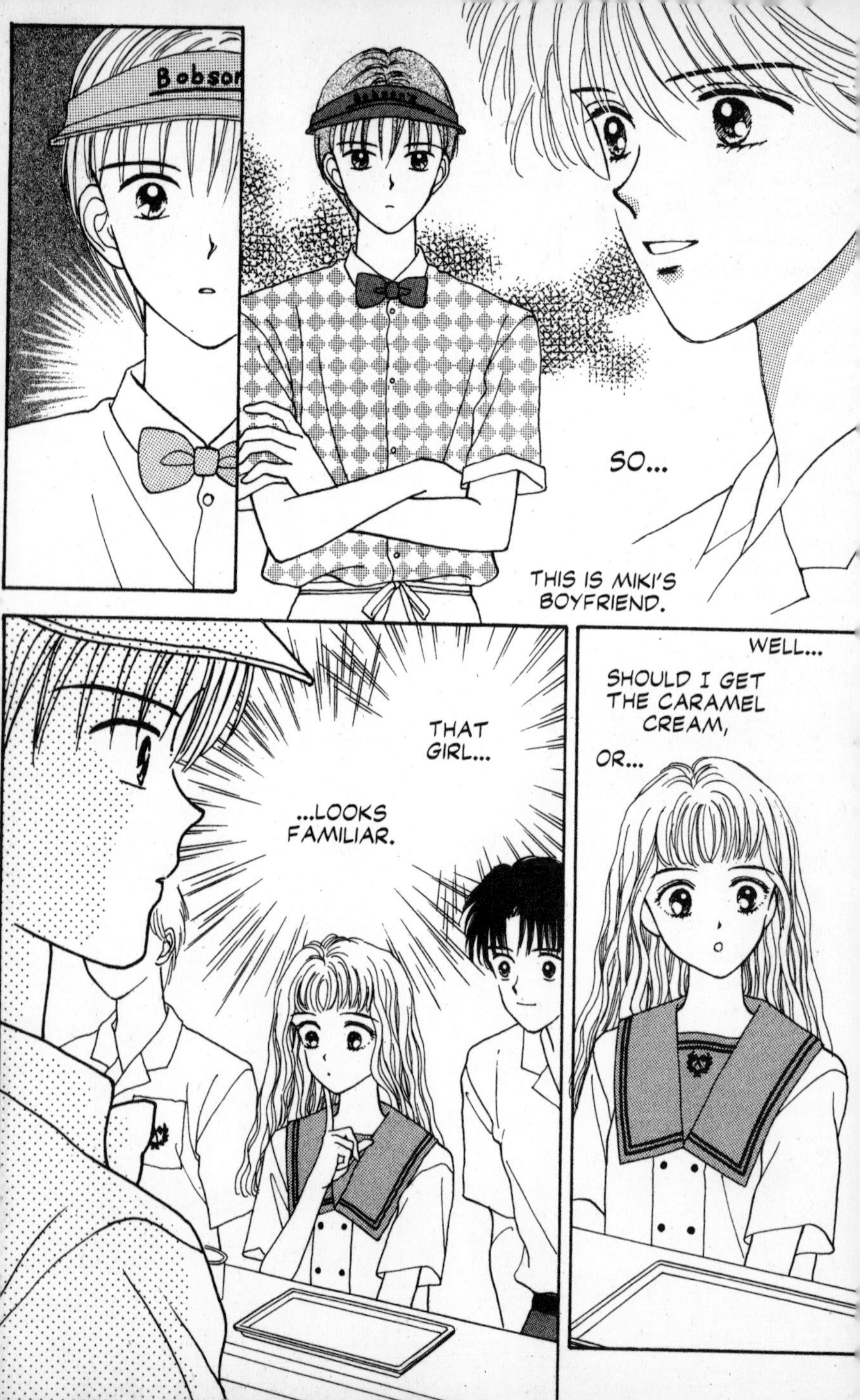
SO...
THIS IS MIKI'S BOYFRIEND.
WELL...
SHOULD I GET THE CARAMEL CREAM,
OR...
THAT GIRL...
...LOOKS FAMILIAR.

FREE TALK ⑥

Of course, all the actors are profession-al and doing excellent jobs, but Hisakawa's job as Arimi is especially impressive. She can convey precise shades of meaning in short lines such as "See you" and "No... it's okay". Although Hisakawa is an excellent actor, her voice is not quite right for Miki. During the audition, Hisakawa tried some of Miki's lines, but she sounded too serious for Miki. I truly think Kouda's voice is perfect for Miki and Hisakawa's for Arimi. I also like the other actors very much, and would like to talk about them all. But if I talk about all the actors, there will be no end to it, so I only talk about the actors for the five main characters.

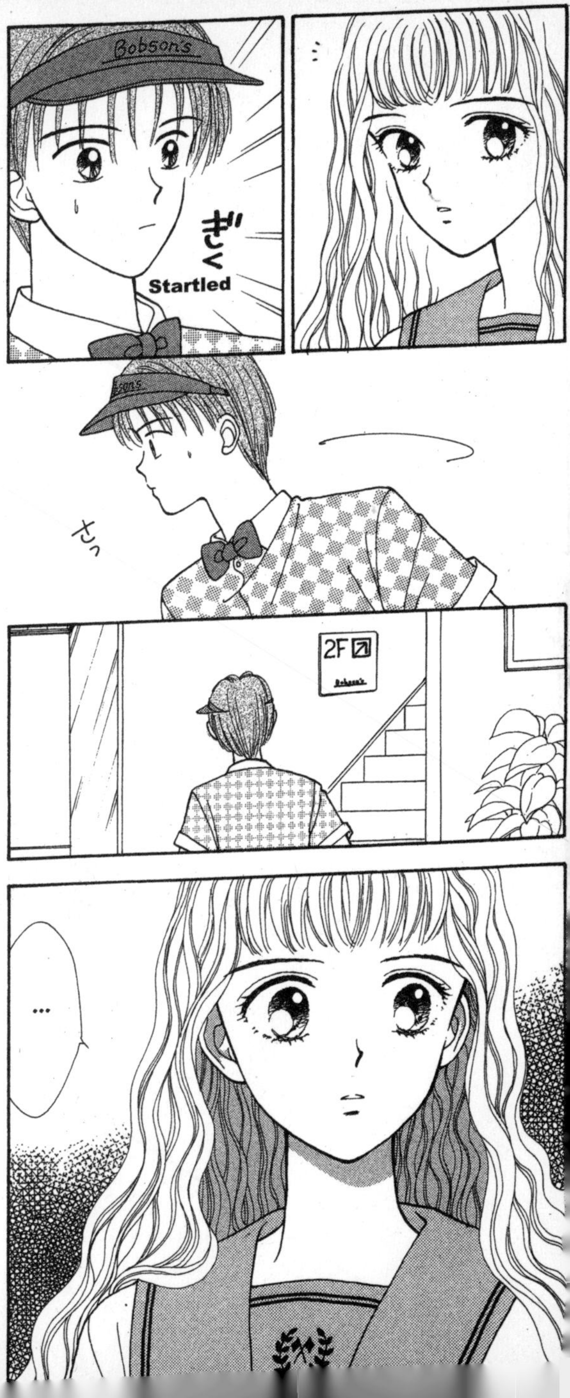
Startled
...

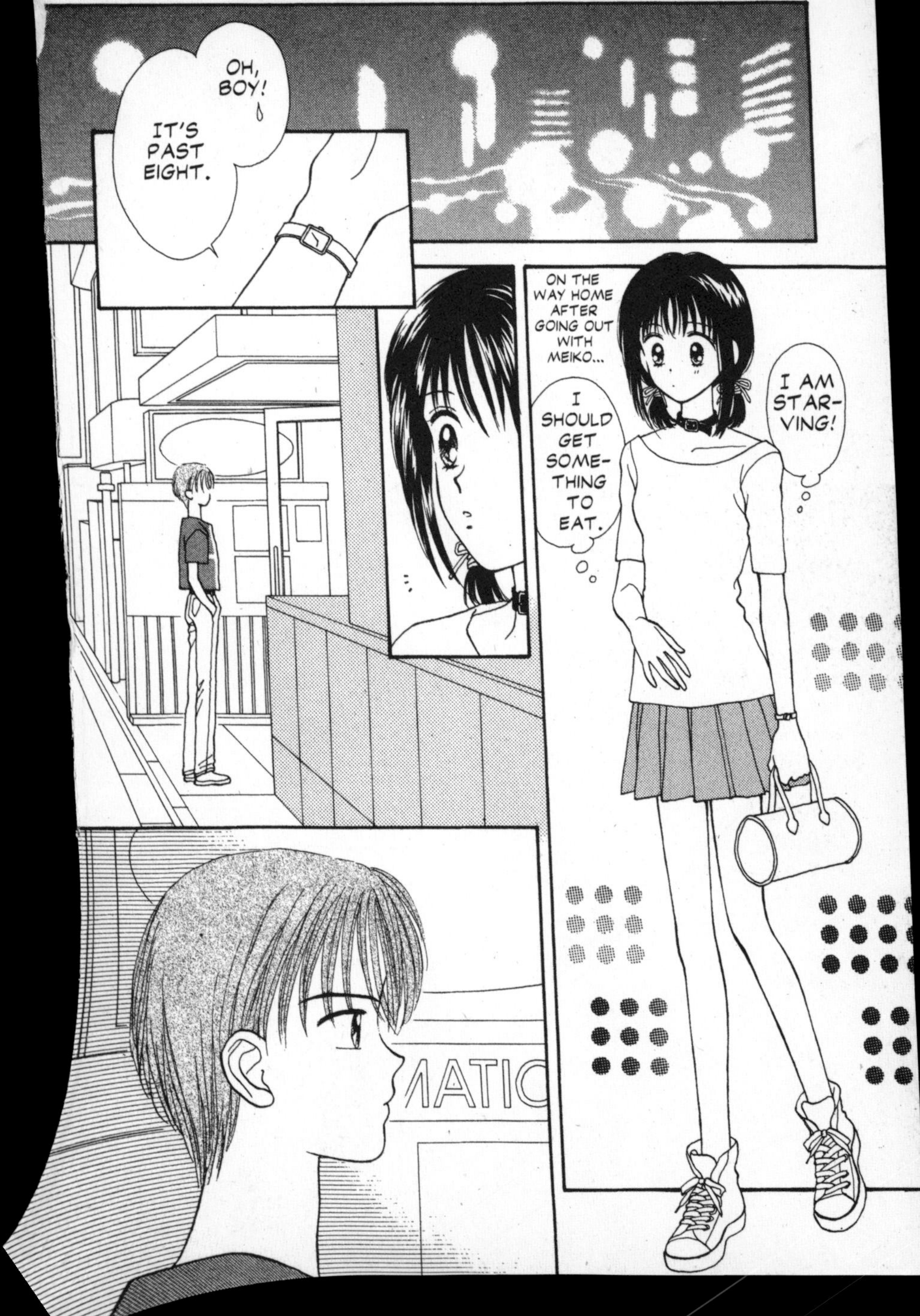
OH, BOY! IT'S PAST EIGHT.
ON THE WAY HOME AFTER GOING OUT WITH MEIKO...
I AM STAR-VING!
I SHOULD GET SOME-THING TO EAT.
MATIC

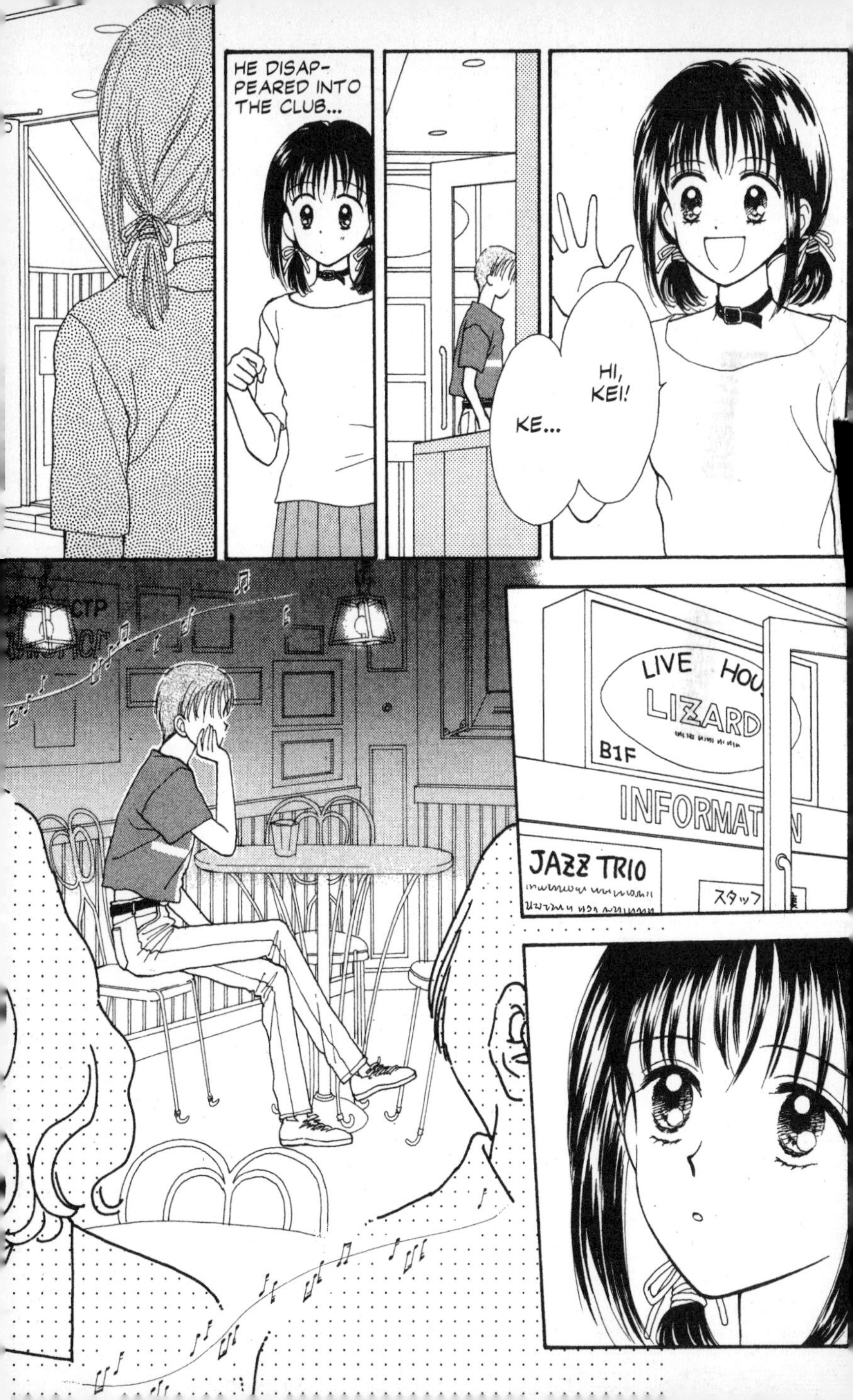
HI, KEI!
KE...
HE DISAPPEARED INTO THE CLUB...
LIVE HOU
LIZARD
B1F
INFORMAT
JAZZ TRIO
スタッフ

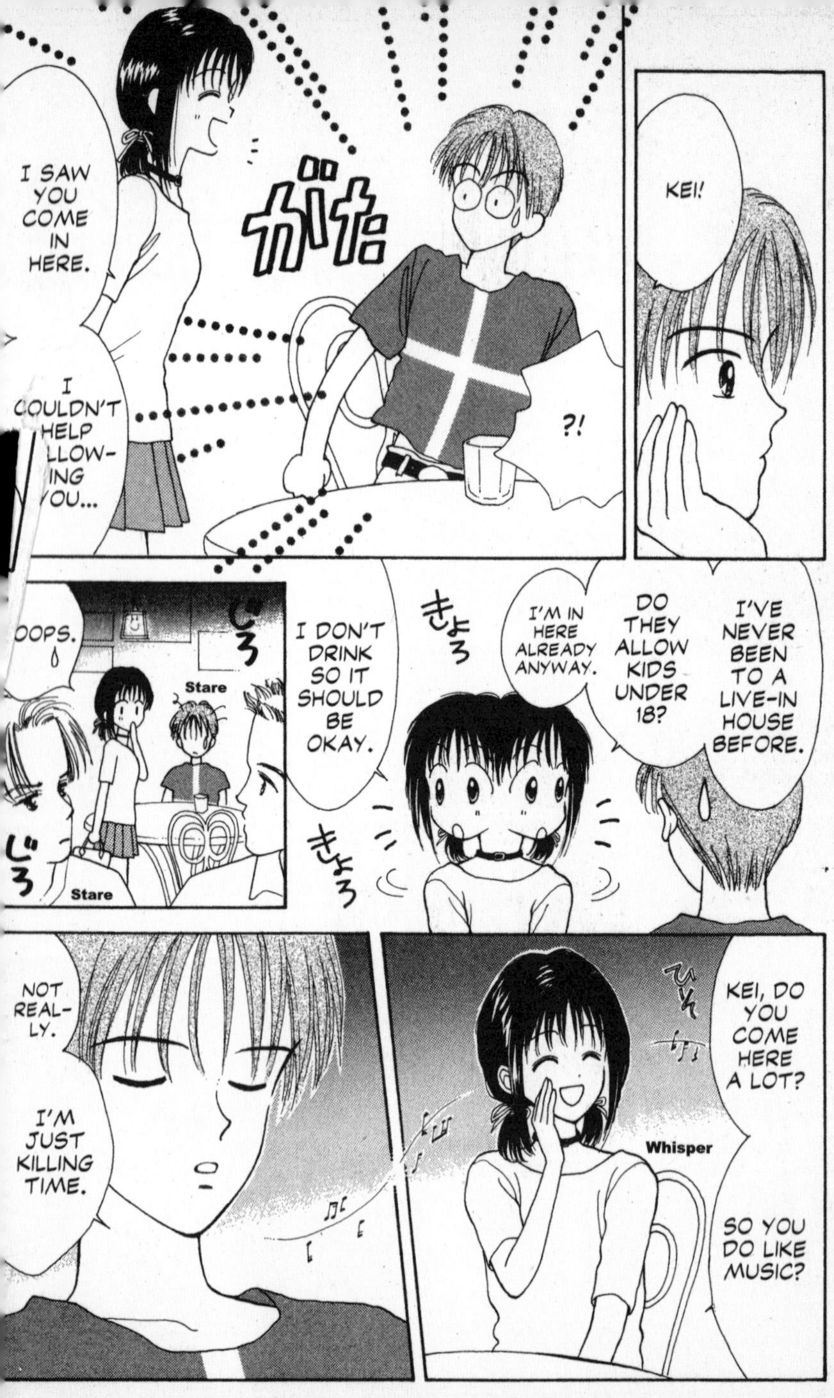
KEI!
?!
がた
I SAW YOU COME IN HERE.
I COULDN'T HELP LLOW-ING OU...
I'VE NEVER BEEN TO A LIVE-IN HOUSE BEFORE.
DO THEY ALLOW KIDS UNDER 18?
I'M IN HERE ALREADY ANYWAY.
きょろ
きょろ
I DON'T DRINK SO IT SHOULD BE OKAY.
じろ
Stare
OOPS.
じろ
Stare
KEI, DO YOU COME HERE A LOT?
ひそ
Whisper
SO YOU DO LIKE MUSIC?
NOT REAL-LY.
I'M JUST KILLING TIME.

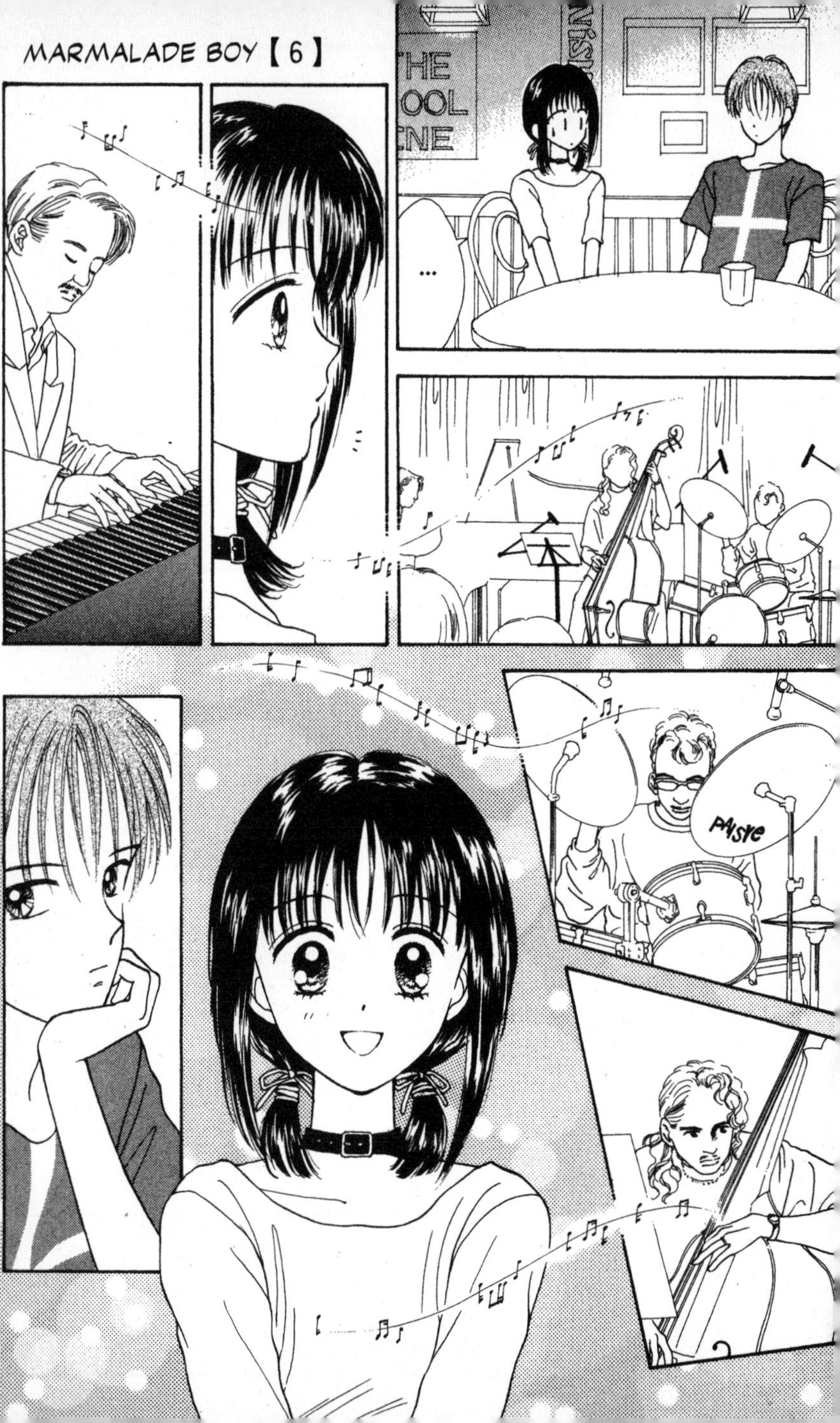
...

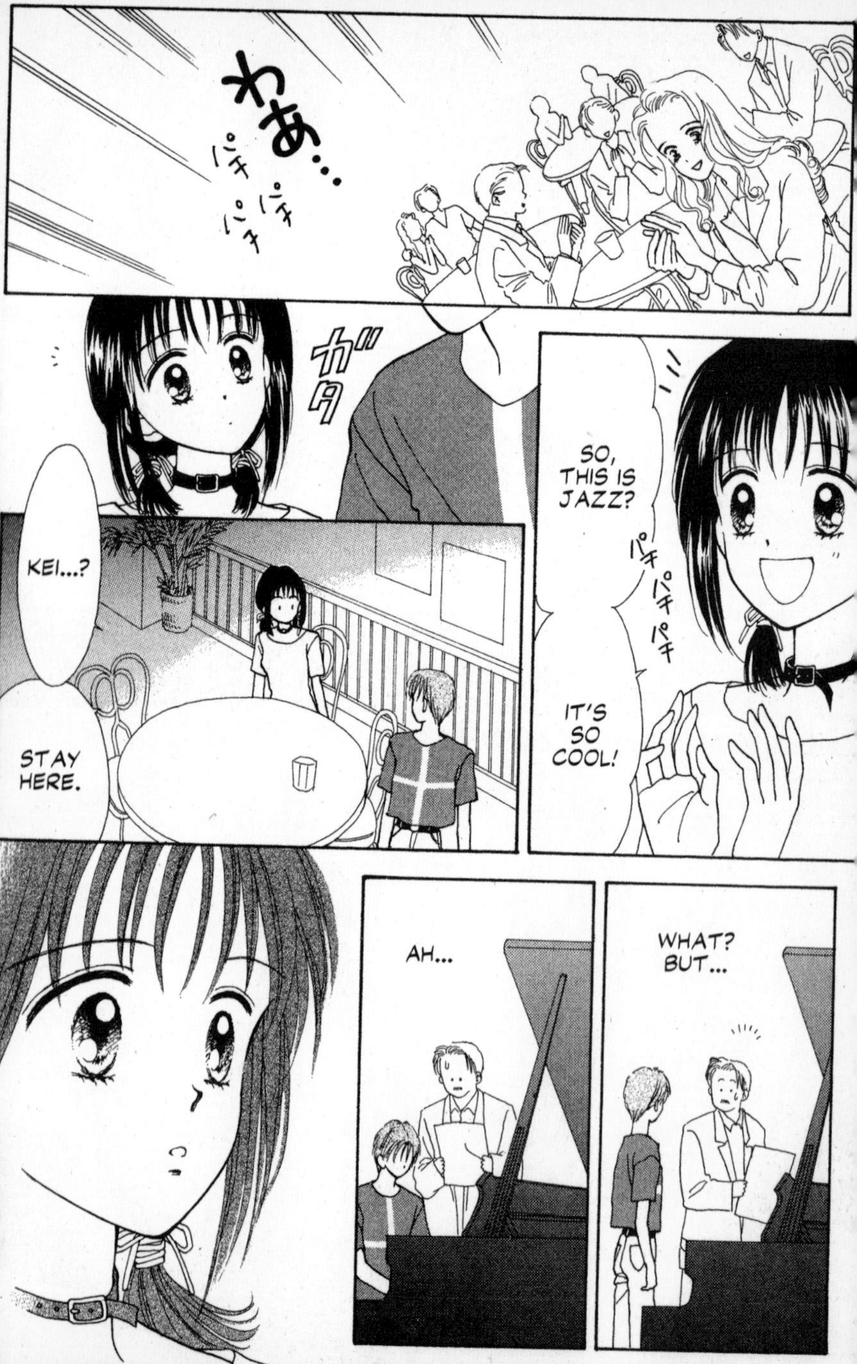
わあ…
パチパチパチ
SO, THIS IS JAZZ?
パチパチパチ
IT'S SO COOL!
ガタ
KEI...?
STAY HERE.
WHAT? BUT...
AH...

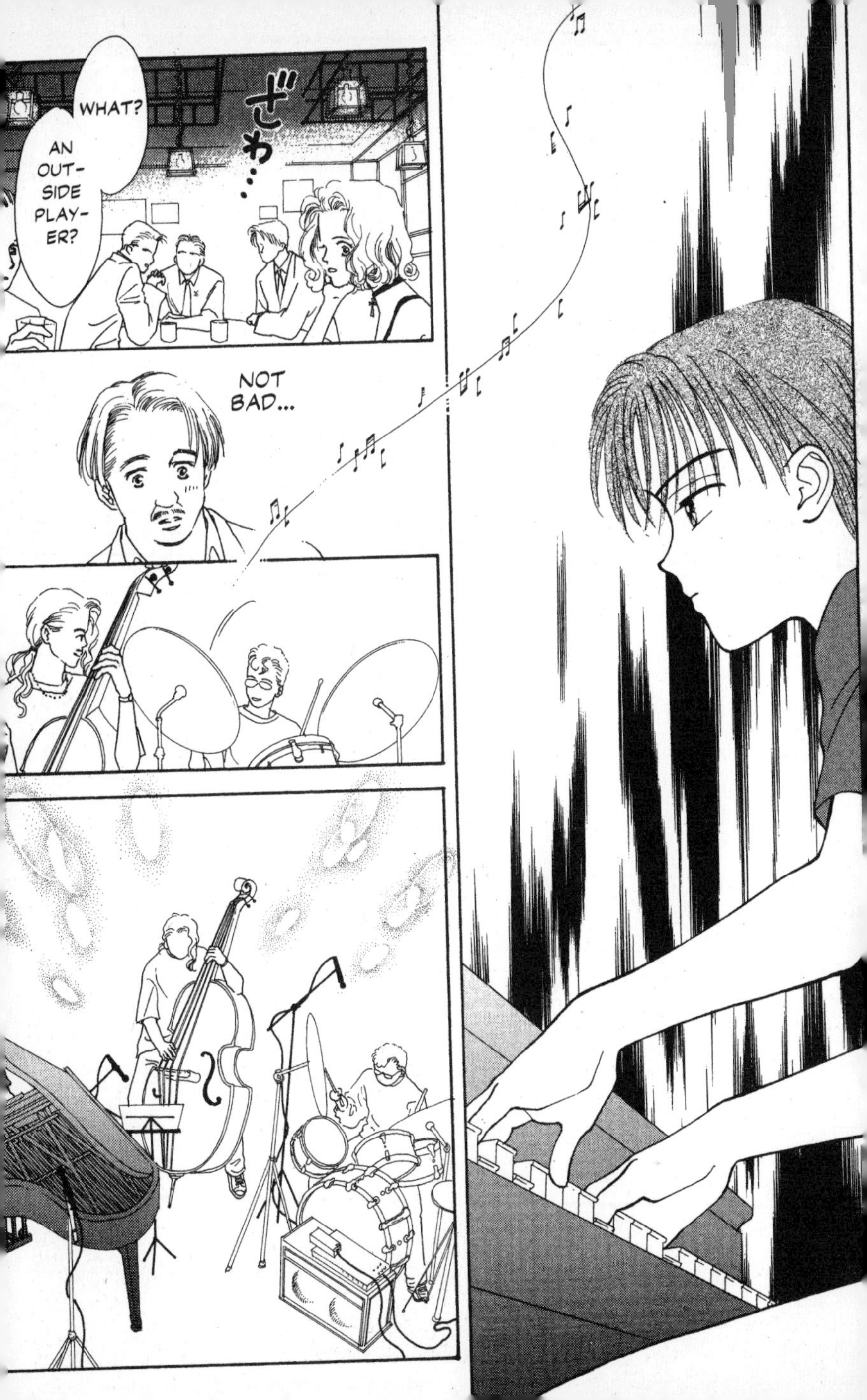
ざわ…
WHAT?
AN OUT-SIDE PLAYER?
NOT BAD...

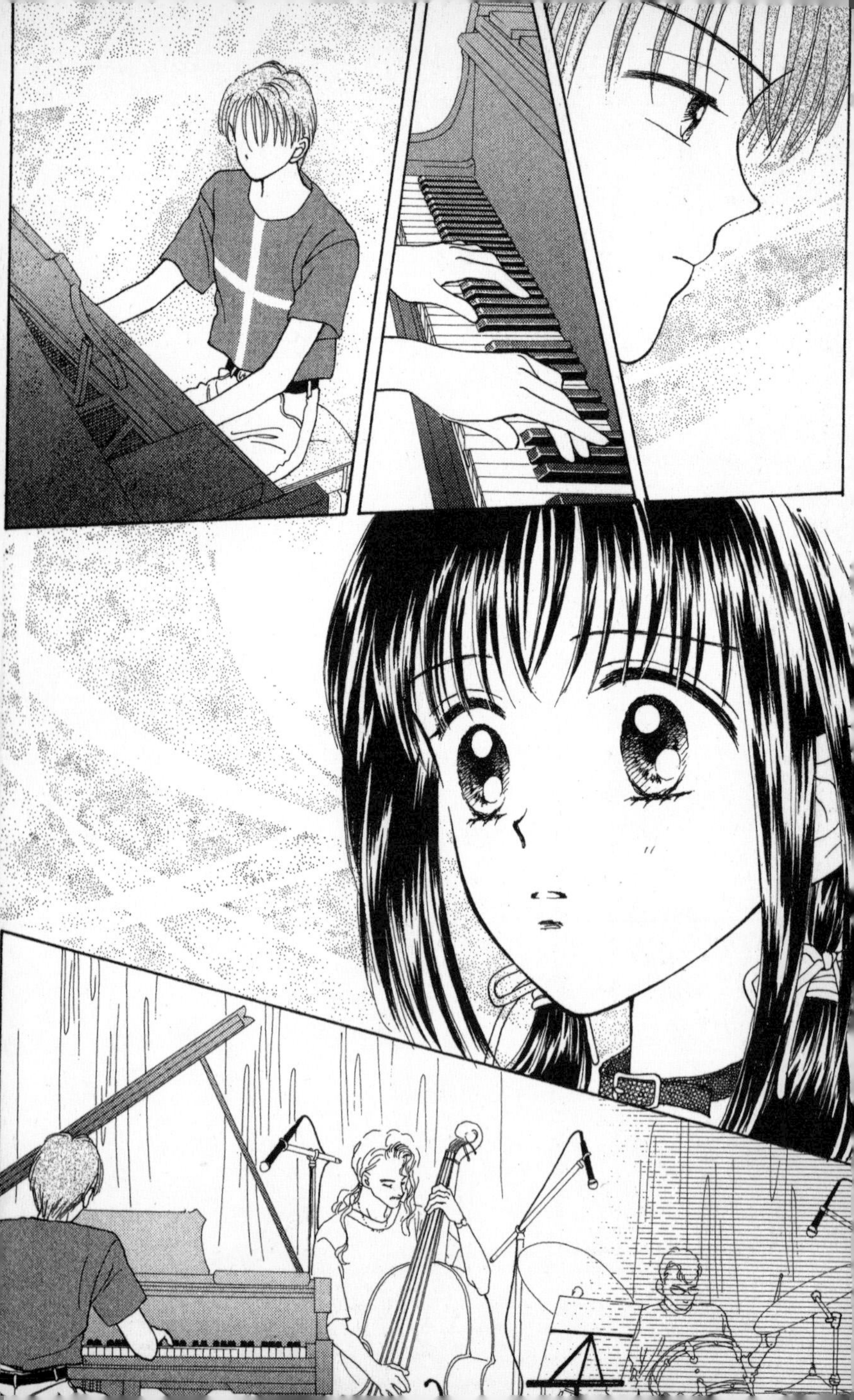

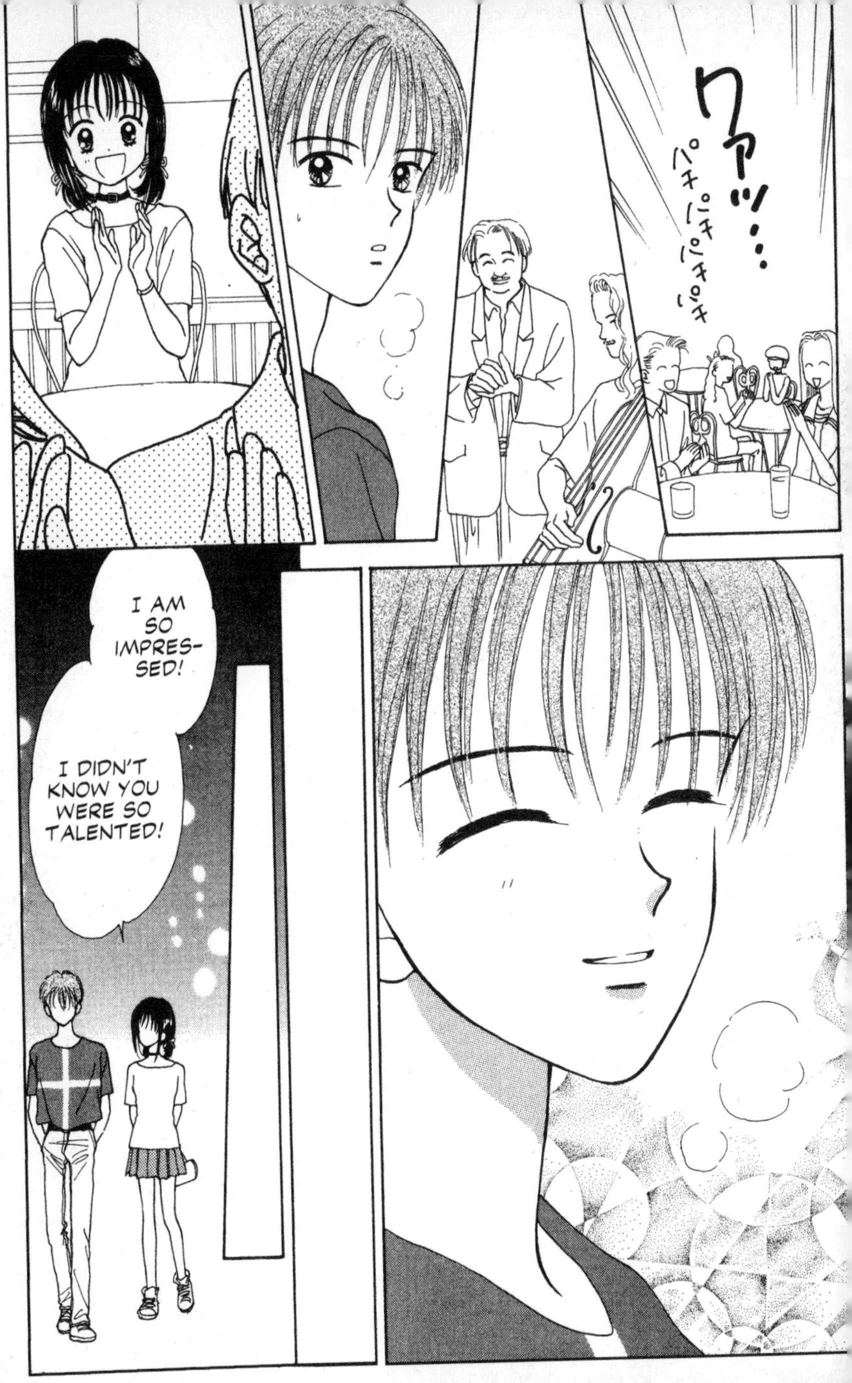
ワァッ・・・
パチパチパチパチ
I AM SO IMPRES- SED!
I DIDN'T KNOW YOU WERE SO TALENTED!

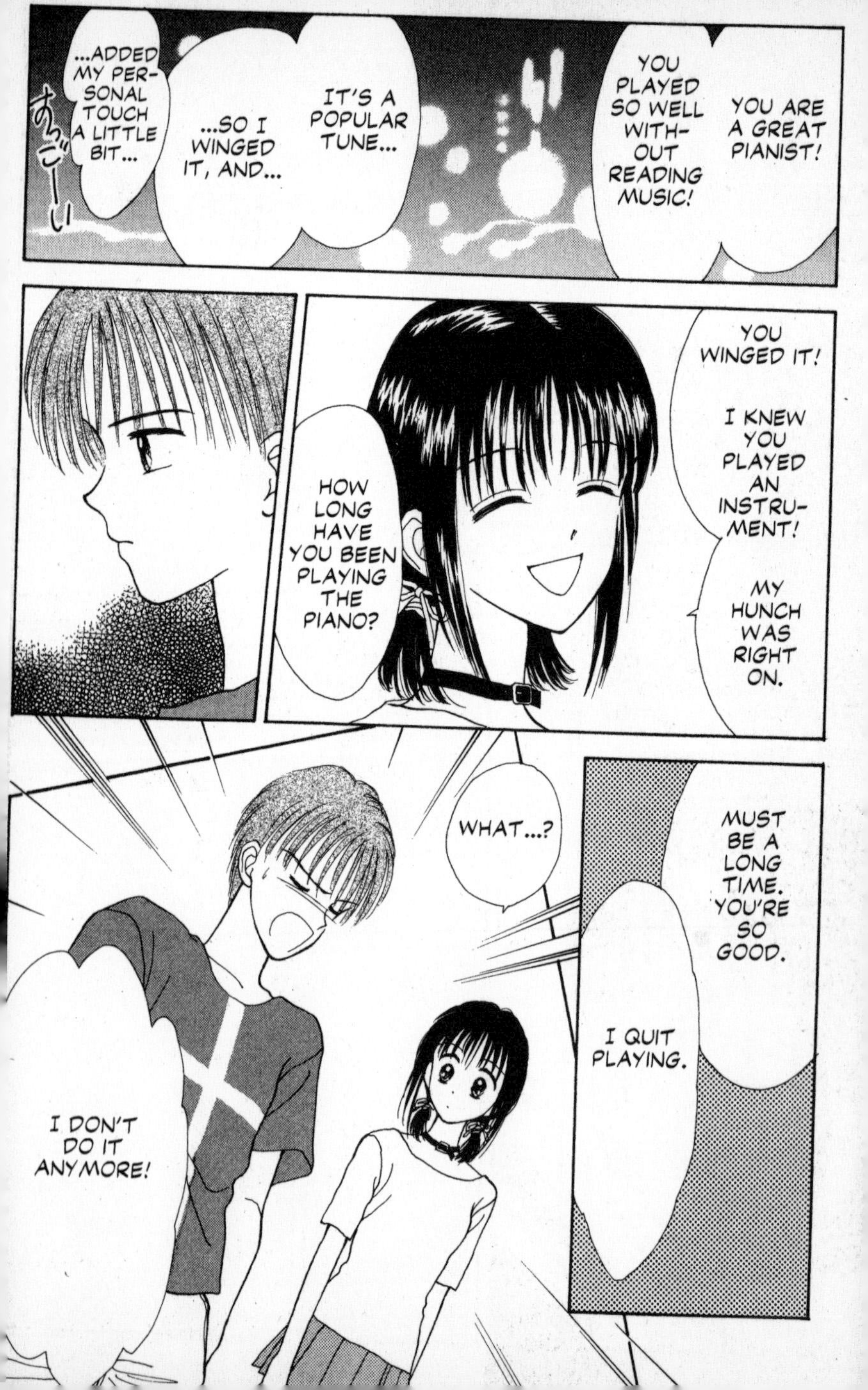
YOU ARE A GREAT PIANIST!
YOU PLAYED SO WELL WITHOUT READING MUSIC!
IT'S A POPULAR TUNE...
...SO I WINGED IT, AND...
...ADDED MY PERSONAL TOUCH A LITTLE BIT...
YOU WINGED IT!
I KNEW YOU PLAYED AN INSTRUMENT!
MY HUNCH WAS RIGHT ON.
HOW LONG HAVE YOU BEEN PLAYING THE PIANO?
MUST BE A LONG TIME. YOU'RE SO GOOD.
I QUIT PLAYING.
WHAT...?
I DON'T DO IT ANYMORE!

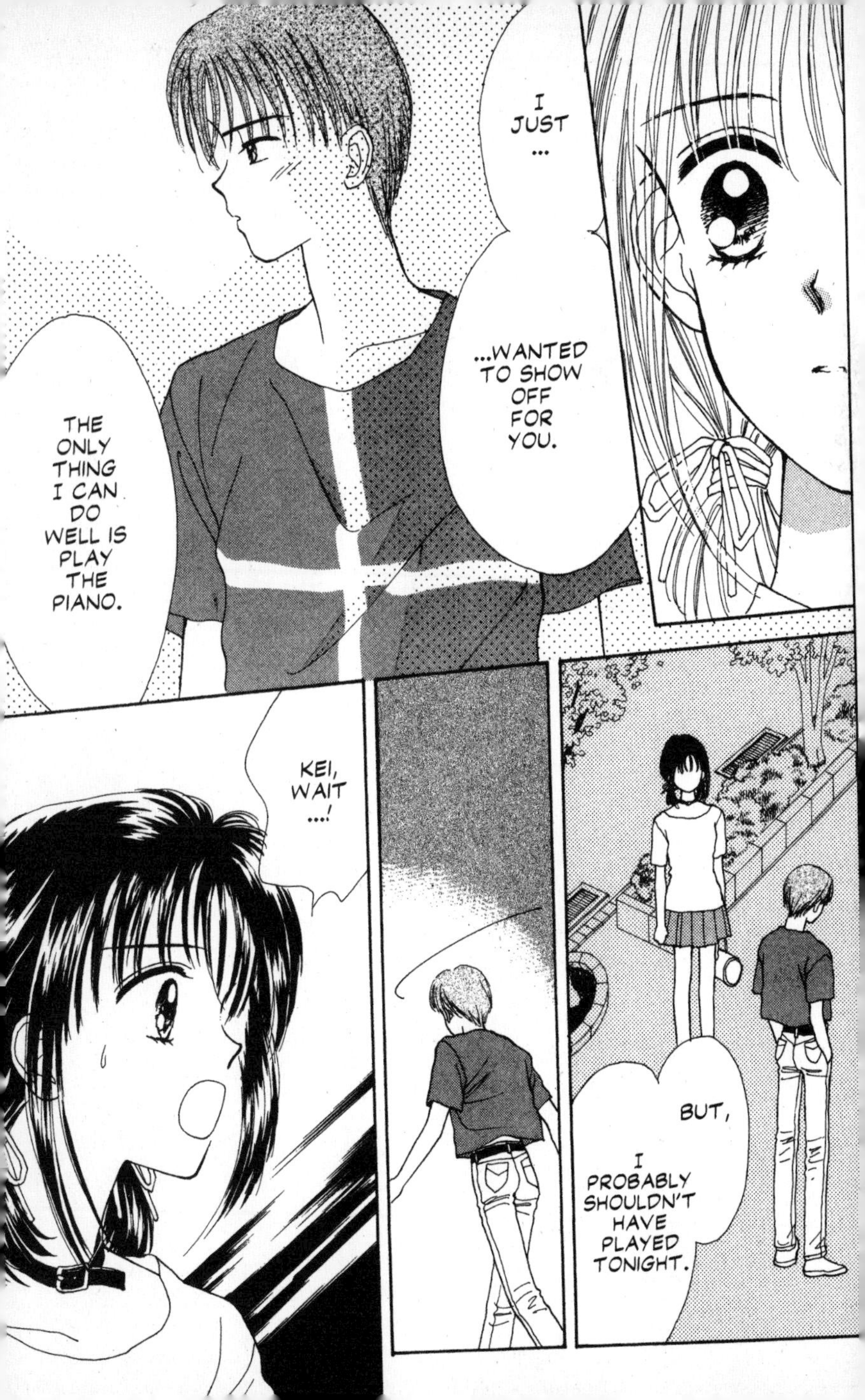
I JUST ...
...WANTED TO SHOW OFF FOR YOU.
THE ONLY THING I CAN DO WELL IS PLAY THE PIANO.
BUT,
I PROBABLY SHOULDN'T HAVE PLAYED TONIGHT.
KEI, WAIT ...!

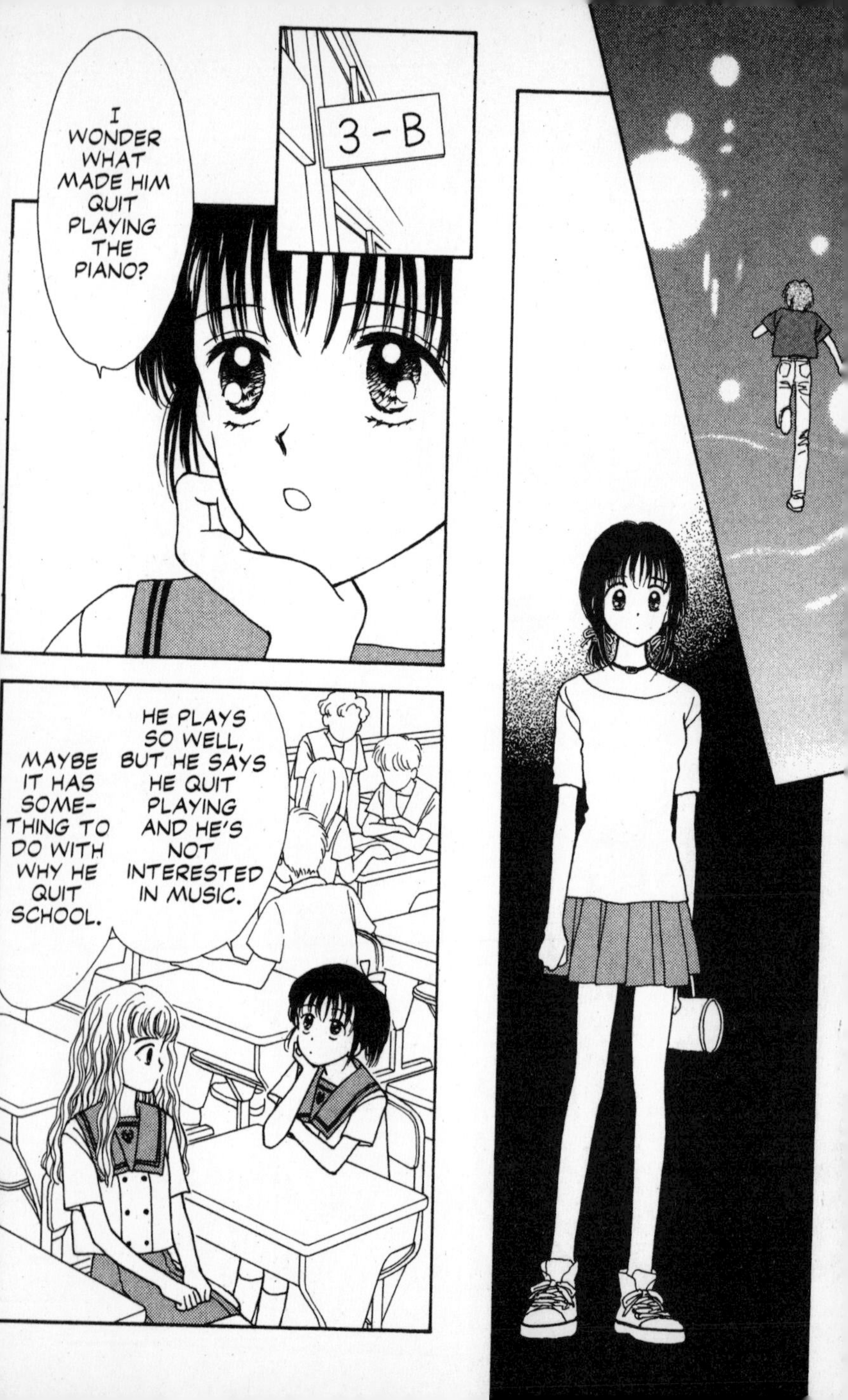
3-B
I WONDER WHAT MADE HIM QUIT PLAYING THE PIANO?
HE PLAYS SO WELL, BUT HE SAYS HE QUIT PLAYING AND HE'S NOT INTERESTED IN MUSIC.
MAYBE IT HAS SOME-THING TO DO WITH WHY HE QUIT SCHOOL.

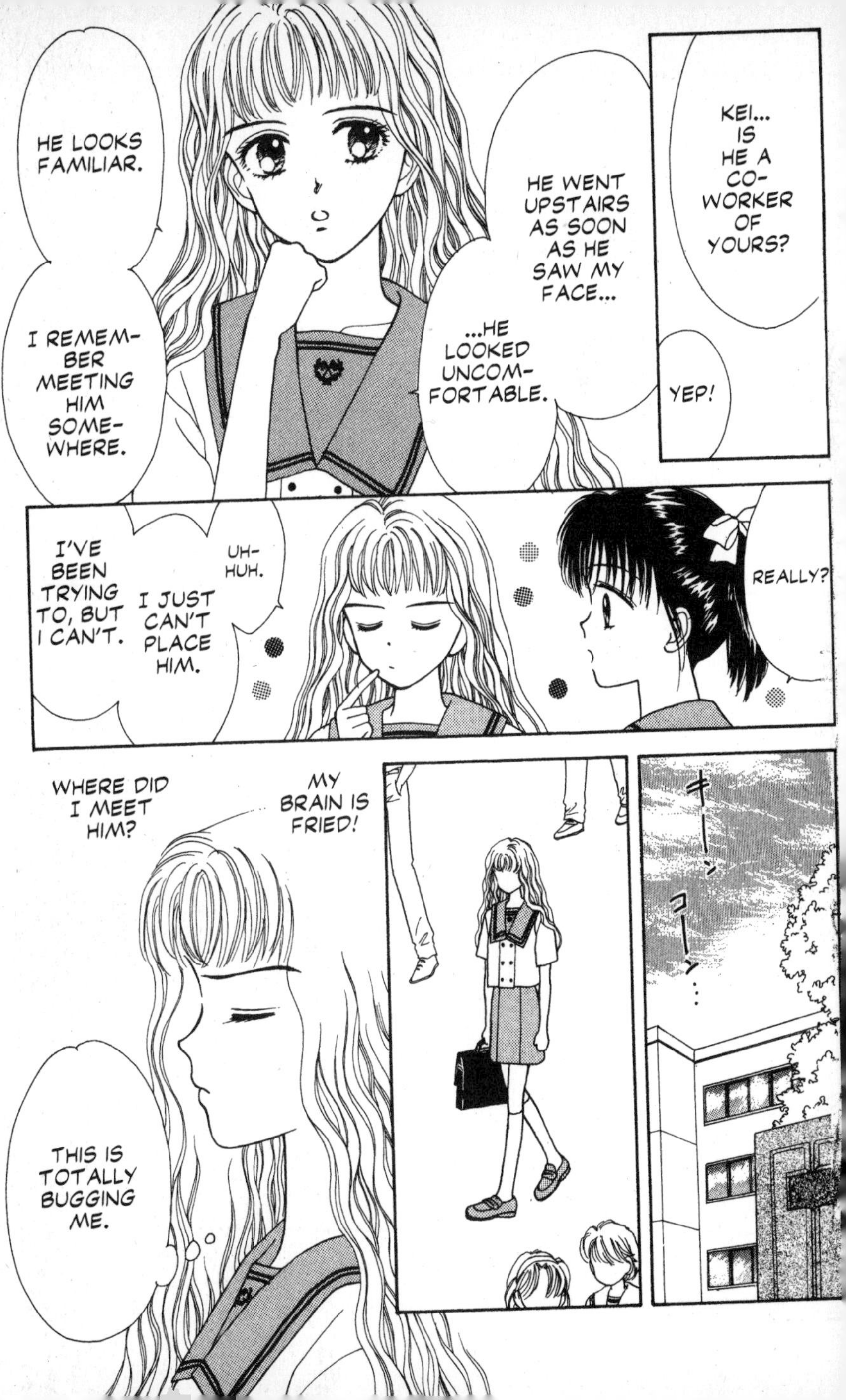
KEI... IS HE A CO-WORKER OF YOURS?
YEP!
HE WENT UPSTAIRS AS SOON AS HE SAW MY FACE...
...HE LOOKED UNCOMFORTABLE.
HE LOOKS FAMILIAR.
I REMEMBER MEETING HIM SOMEWHERE.
REALLY?
UH-HUH.
I JUST CAN'T PLACE HIM.
I'VE BEEN TRYING TO, BUT I CAN'T.
キーン
コーン…
MY BRAIN IS FRIED!
WHERE DID I MEET HIM?
THIS IS TOTALLY BUGGING ME.

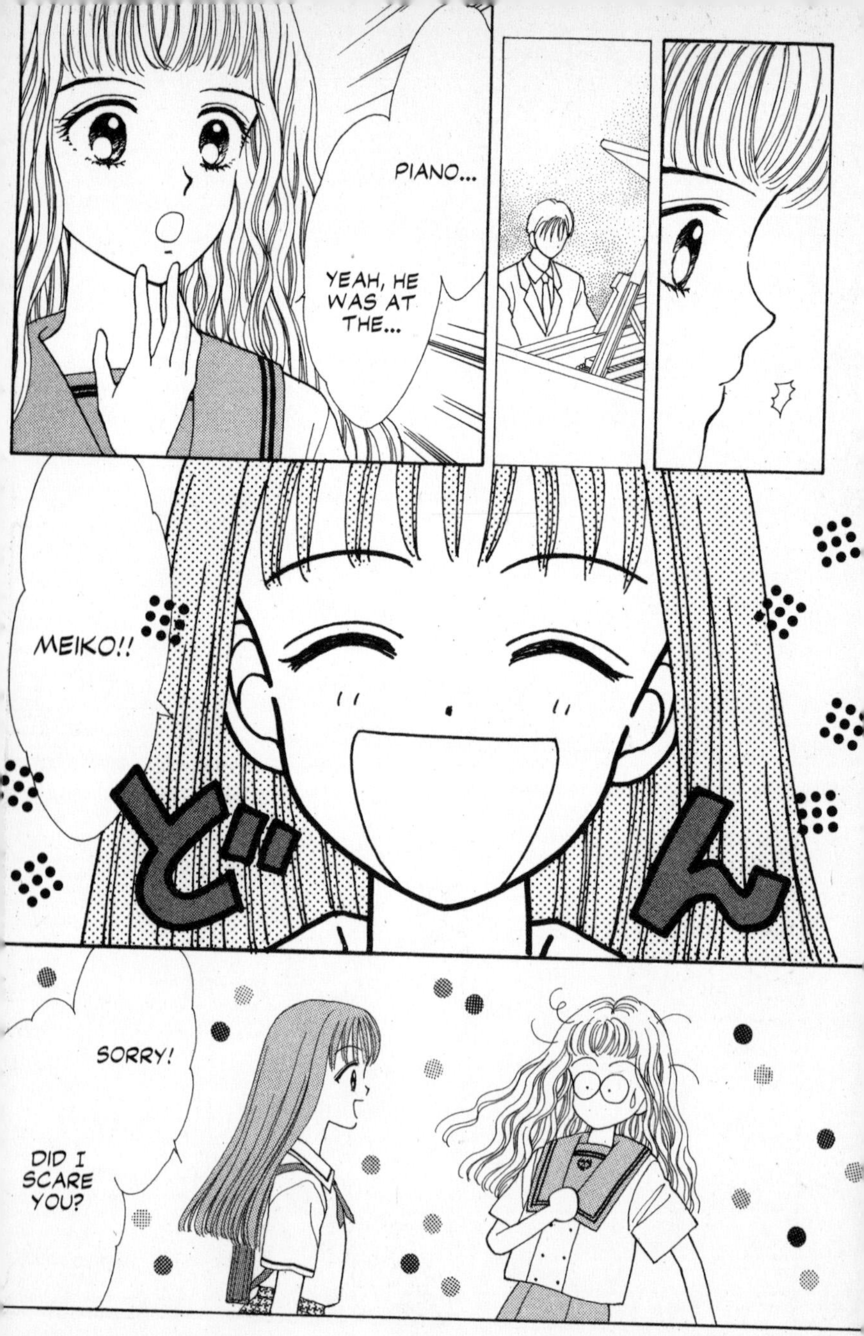
PIANO...
YEAH, HE WAS AT THE...
MEIKO!!
どん
SORRY!
DID I SCARE YOU?

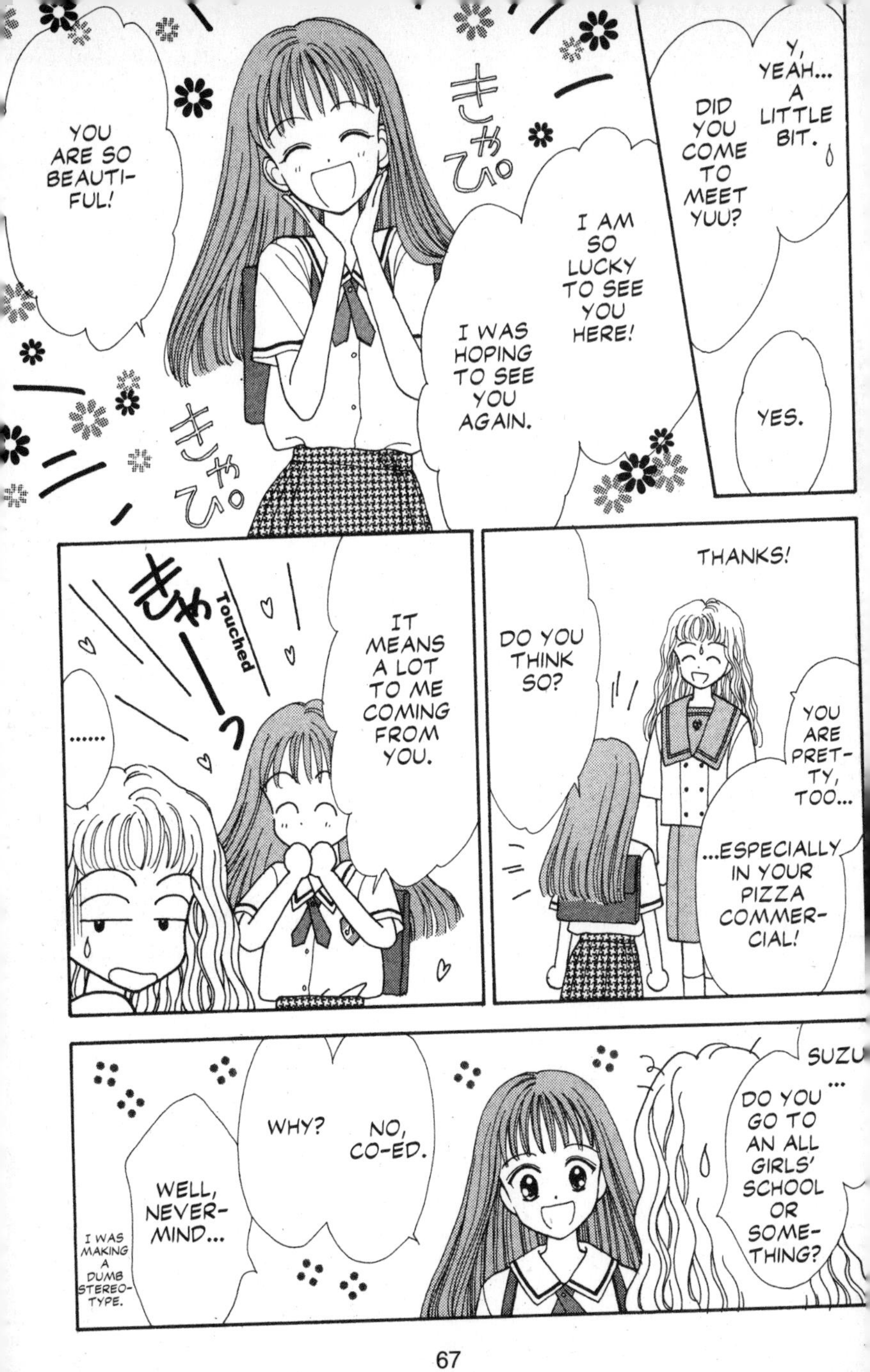
DID YOU COME TO MEET YUU?
Y, YEAH... A LITTLE BIT.
YES.
I AM SO LUCKY TO SEE YOU HERE!
I WAS HOPING TO SEE YOU AGAIN.
きゃぴ
YOU ARE SO BEAUTIFUL!
きゃぴ
YOU ARE PRETTY, TOO...
...ESPECIALLY IN YOUR PIZZA COMMERCIAL!
THANKS!
DO YOU THINK SO?
IT MEANS A LOT TO ME COMING FROM YOU.
きゃーっ
Touched
......
SUZU...
DO YOU GO TO AN ALL GIRLS' SCHOOL OR SOMETHING?
NO, CO-ED.
WHY?
WELL, NEVER-MIND...
I WAS MAKING A DUMB STEREOTYPE.

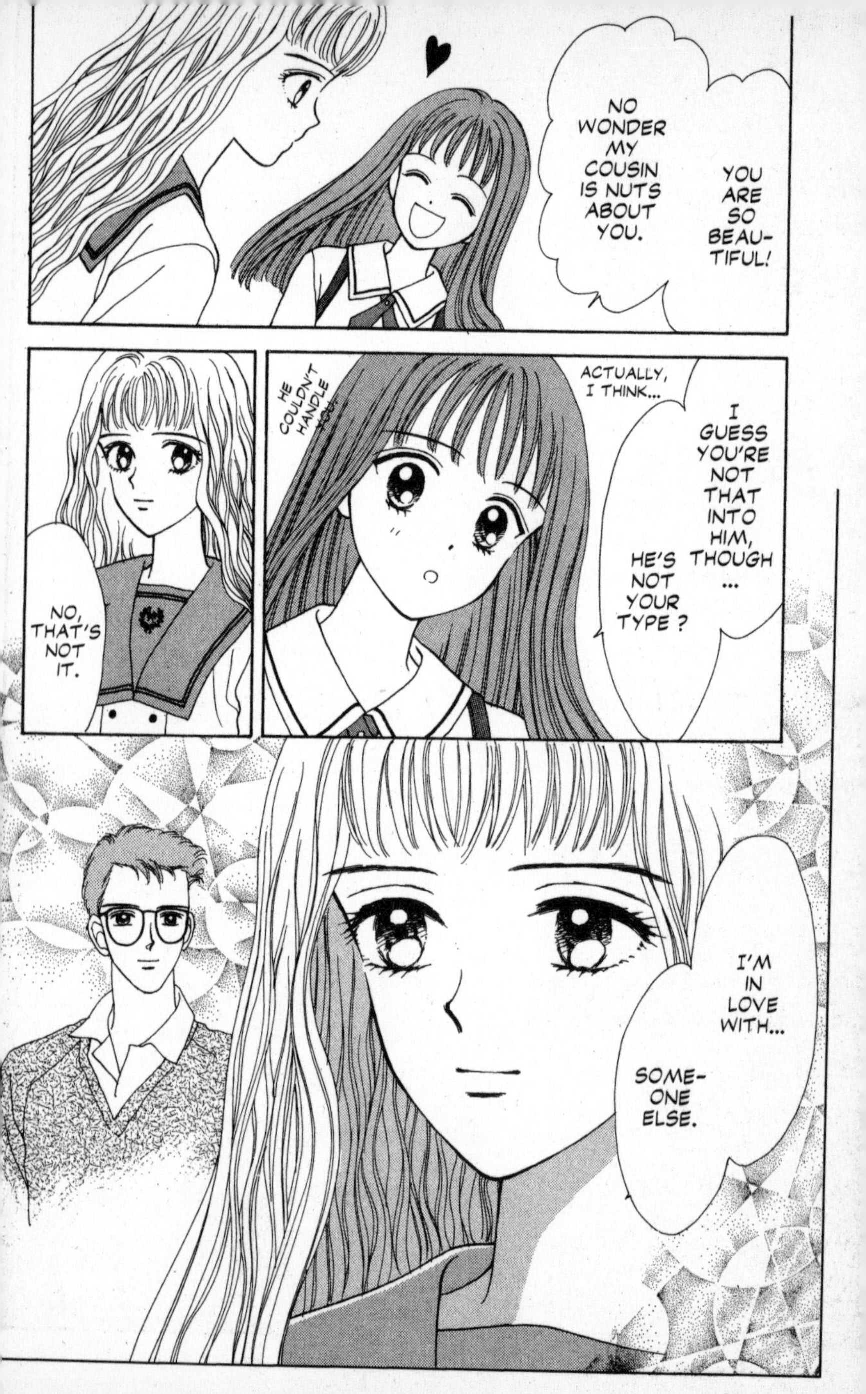
YOU ARE SO BEAU-TIFUL!
NO WONDER MY COUSIN IS NUTS ABOUT YOU.
I GUESS YOU'RE NOT THAT INTO HIM, THOUGH...
HE'S NOT YOUR TYPE?
ACTUALLY, I THINK...
HE COULDN'T HANDLE YOU.
NO, THAT'S NOT IT.
I'M IN LOVE WITH...
SOME-ONE ELSE.

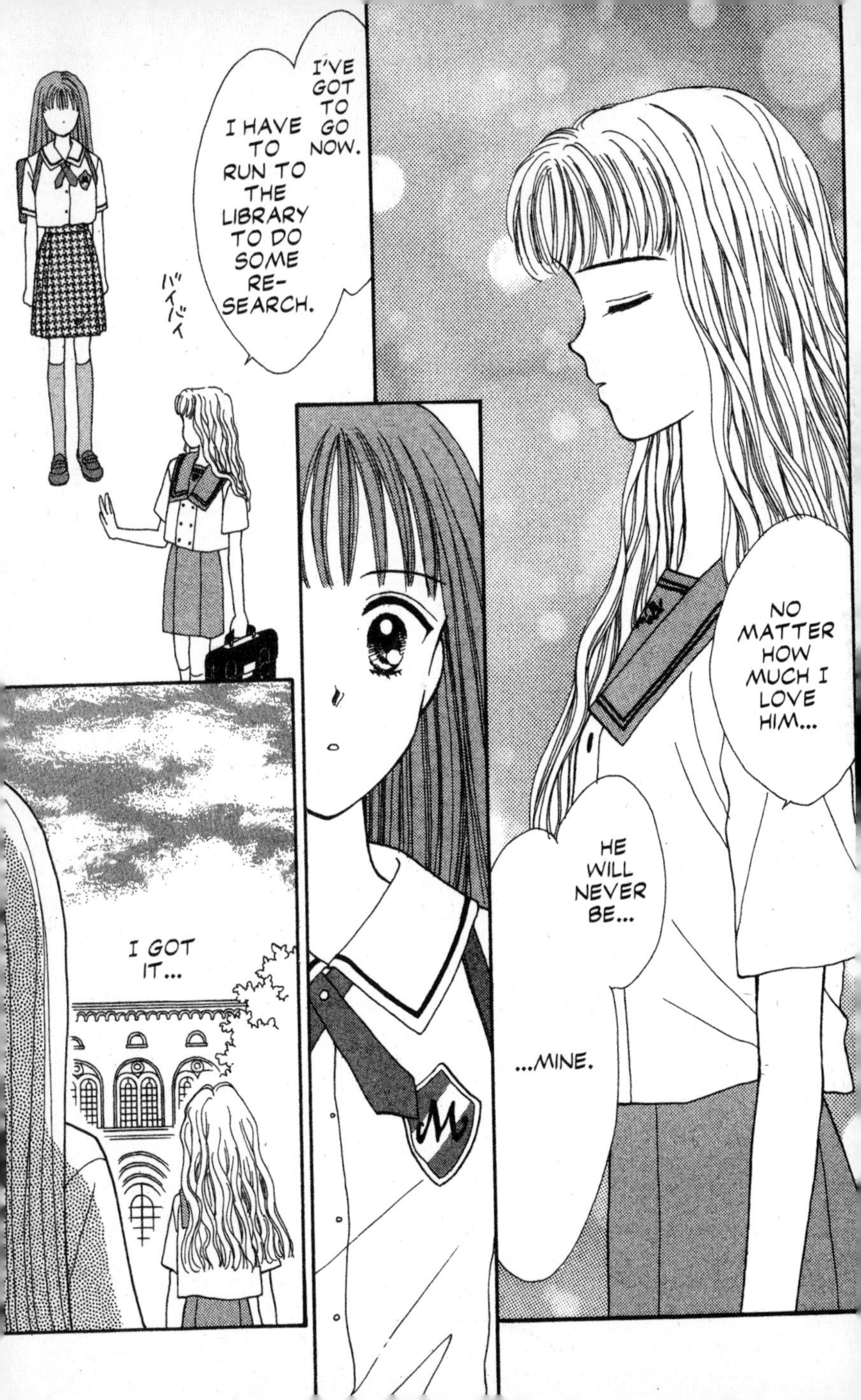
I'VE GOT TO GO NOW. I HAVE TO RUN TO THE LIBRARY TO DO SOME RE-SEARCH.
バイバイ
I GOT IT...
NO MATTER HOW MUCH I LOVE HIM...
HE WILL NEVER BE...
...MINE.

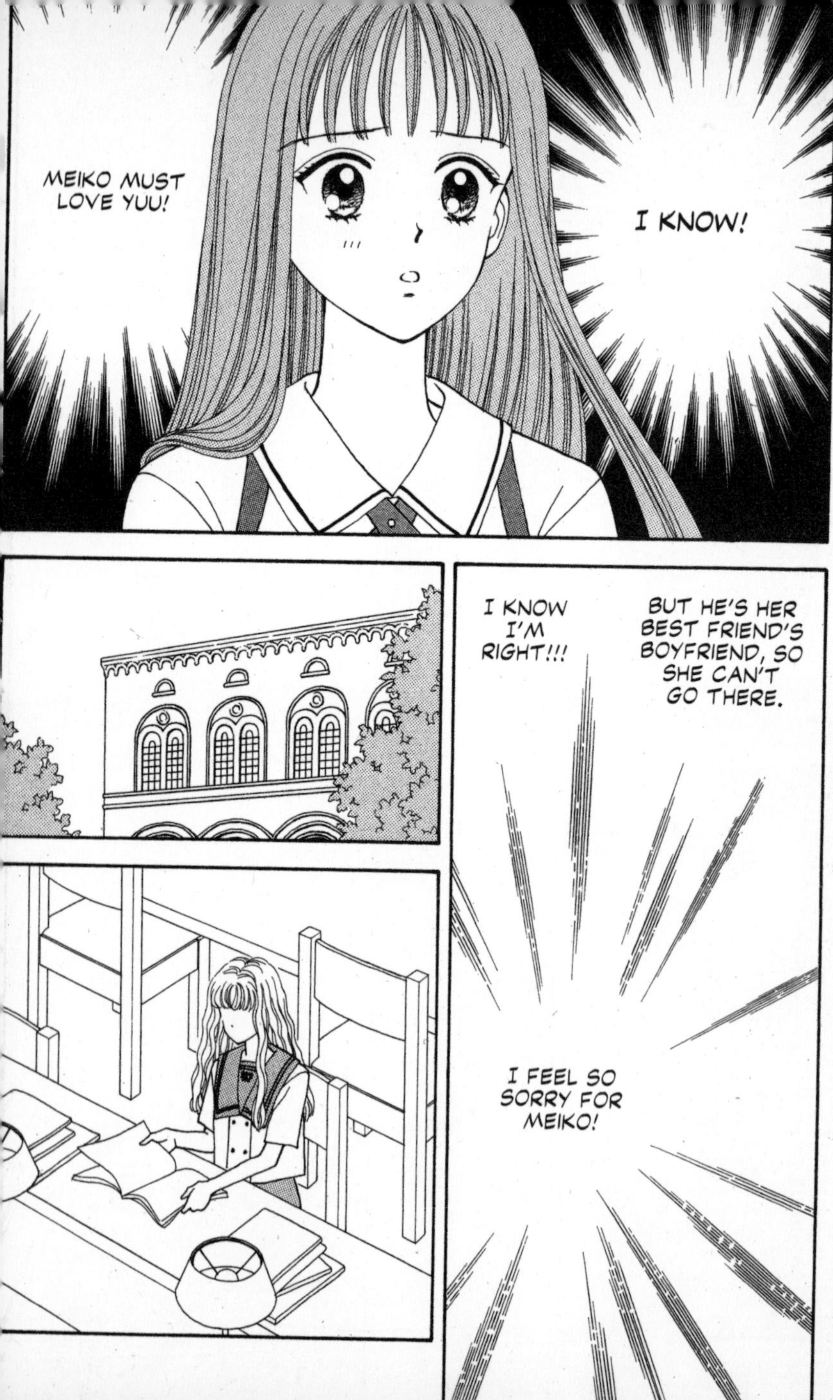
I KNOW!
MEIKO MUST LOVE YUU!
BUT HE'S HER BEST FRIEND'S BOYFRIEND, SO SHE CAN'T GO THERE.
I KNOW I'M RIGHT!!!
I FEEL SO SORRY FOR MEIKO!

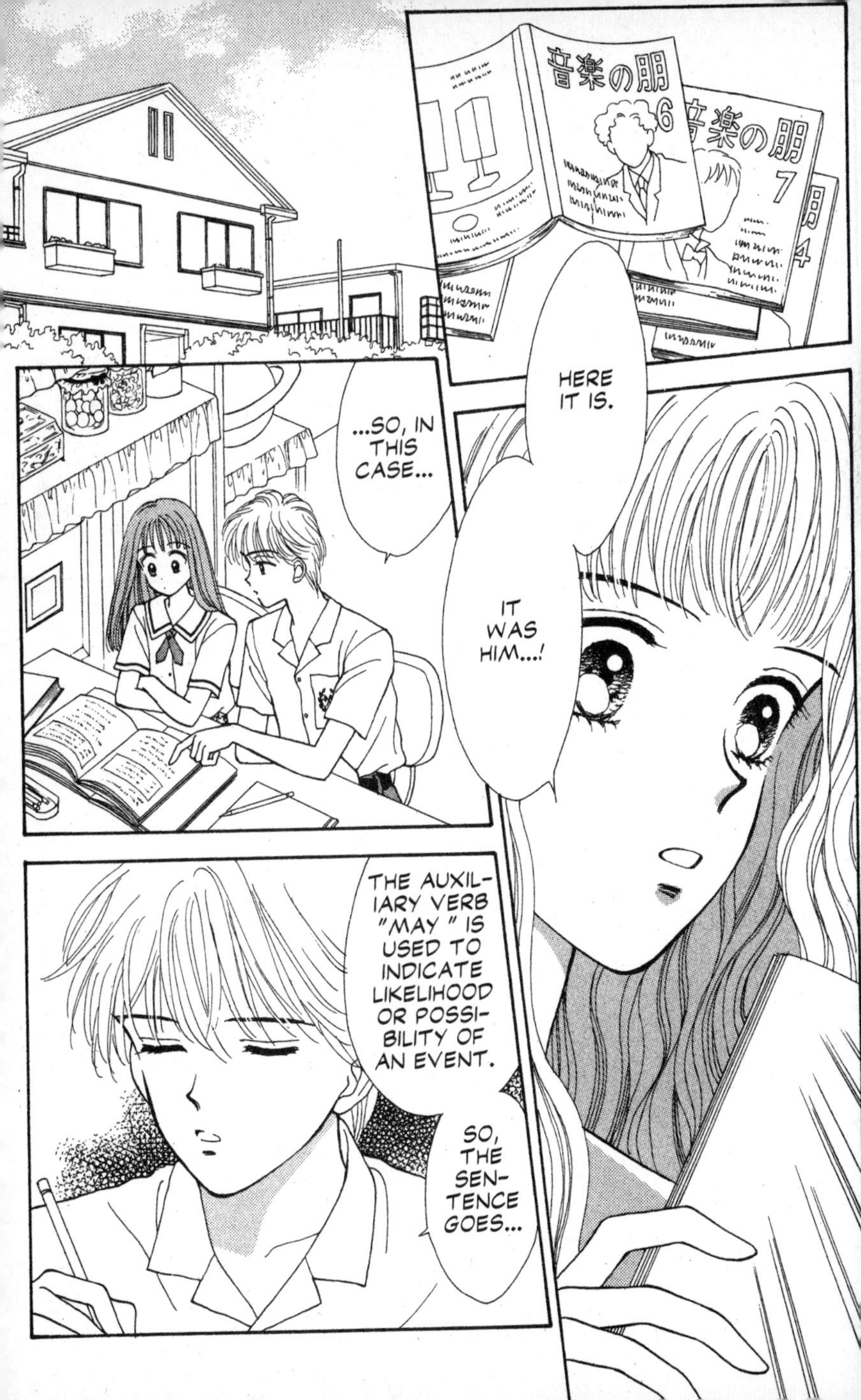
音楽の朋 6
音楽の朋 7
朋 4
HERE IT IS.
IT WAS HIM...!
...SO, IN THIS CASE...
THE AUXILIARY VERB "MAY" IS USED TO INDICATE LIKELIHOOD OR POSSIBILITY OF AN EVENT.
SO, THE SENTENCE GOES...

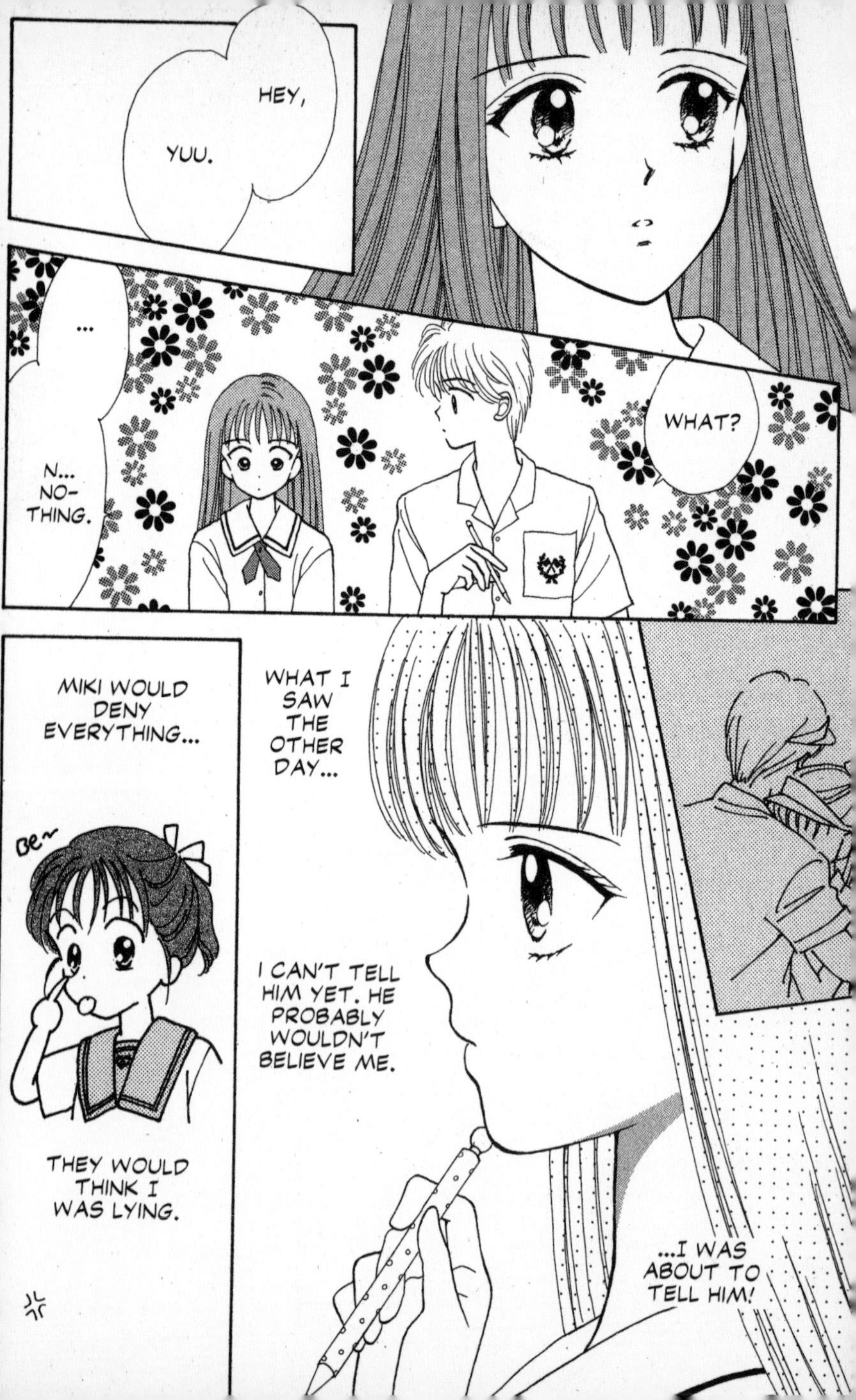
HEY, YUU.
WHAT?
...
N... NO-THING.
WHAT I SAW THE OTHER DAY...
...I WAS ABOUT TO TELL HIM!
I CAN'T TELL HIM YET. HE PROBABLY WOULDN'T BELIEVE ME.
MIKI WOULD DENY EVERYTHING...
Be~
THEY WOULD THINK I WAS LYING.

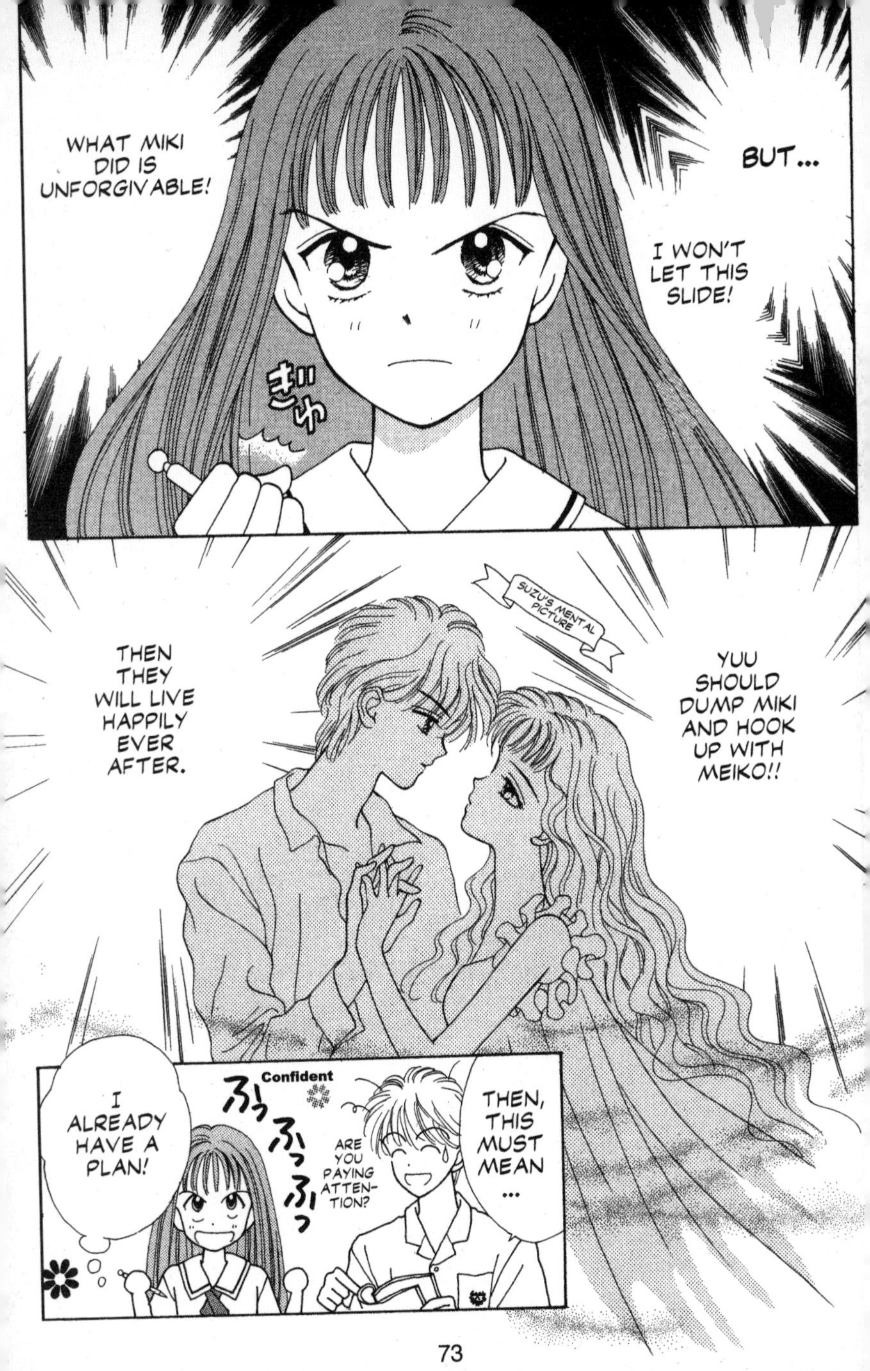
WHAT MIKI DID IS UNFORGIVABLE!
BUT...
I WON'T LET THIS SLIDE!
ぎゅ
SUZU'S MENTAL PICTURE
YUU SHOULD DUMP MIKI AND HOOK UP WITH MEIKO!!
THEN THEY WILL LIVE HAPPILY EVER AFTER.
THEN, THIS MUST MEAN ...
I ALREADY HAVE A PLAN!
Confident
ふっふっふっ
ARE YOU PAYING ATTEN-TION?

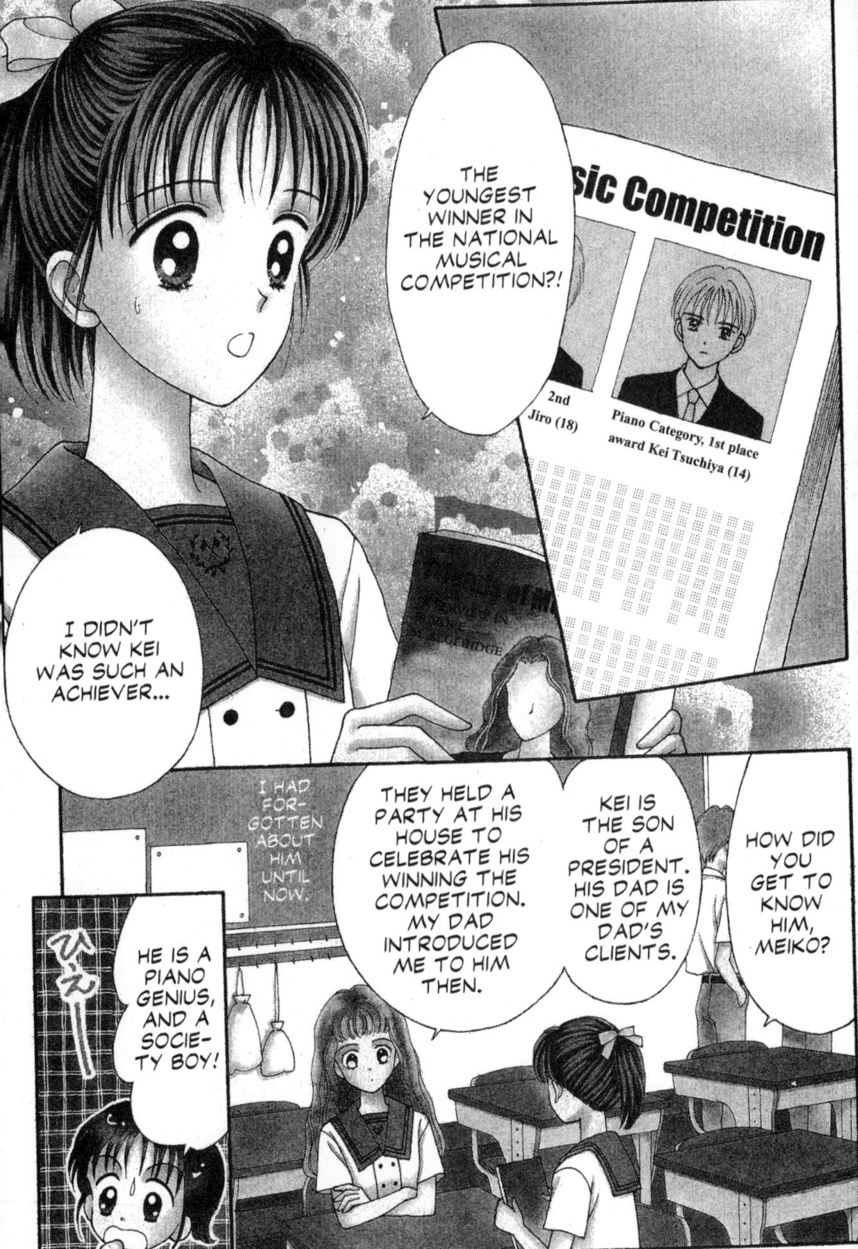
THE YOUNGEST WINNER IN THE NATIONAL MUSICAL COMPETITION?!
sic Competition
2nd
Jiro (18)
Piano Category, 1st place award Kei Tsuchiya (14)
I DIDN'T KNOW KEI WAS SUCH AN ACHIEVER...
HOW DID YOU GET TO KNOW HIM, MEIKO?
KEI IS THE SON OF A PRESIDENT. HIS DAD IS ONE OF MY DAD'S CLIENTS.
THEY HELD A PARTY AT HIS HOUSE TO CELEBRATE HIS WINNING THE COMPETITION. MY DAD INTRODUCED ME TO HIM THEN.
I HAD FOR-GOTTEN ABOUT HIM UNTIL NOW.
HE IS A PIANO GENIUS, AND A SOCIE-TY BOY!

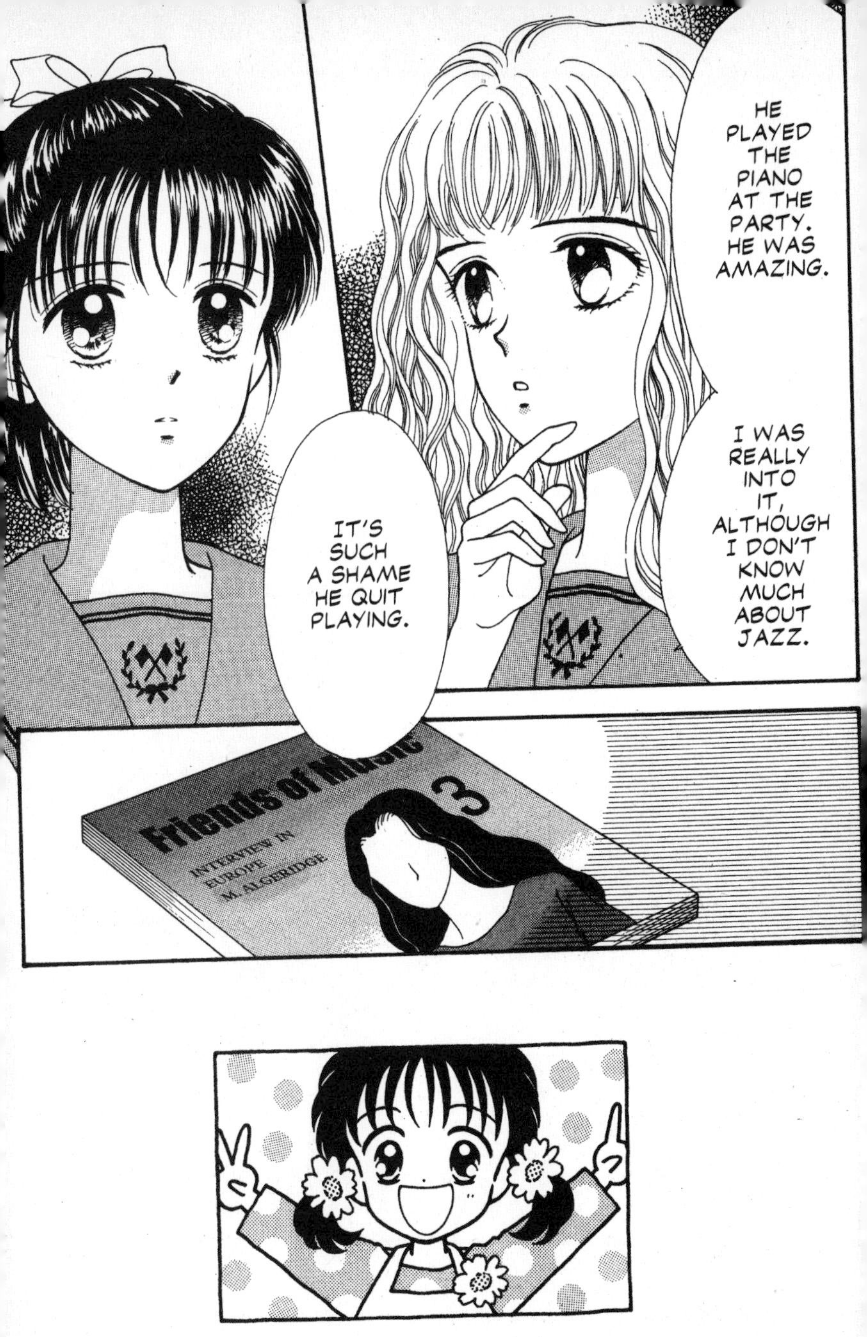
HE PLAYED THE PIANO AT THE PARTY. HE WAS AMAZING.
I WAS REALLY INTO IT, ALTHOUGH I DON'T KNOW MUCH ABOUT JAZZ.
IT'S SUCH A SHAME HE QUIT PLAYING.
Friends of Music
3
INTERVIEW IN EUROPE M. ALGERIDGE

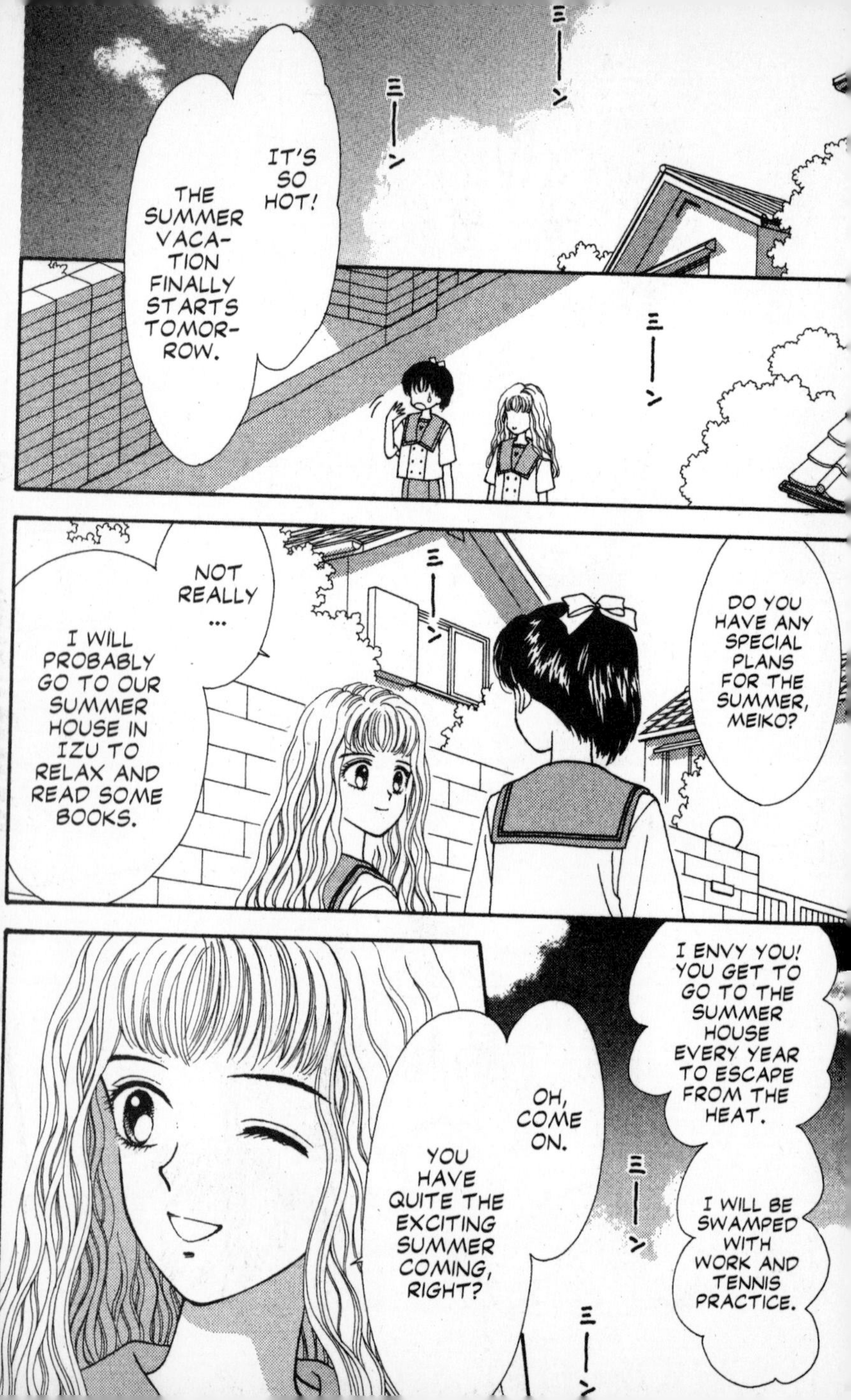
ミーン
ミーン
IT'S SO HOT! THE SUMMER VACATION FINALLY STARTS TOMORROW.
ミーン
ミーン
DO YOU HAVE ANY SPECIAL PLANS FOR THE SUMMER, MEIKO?
NOT REALLY ... I WILL PROBABLY GO TO OUR SUMMER HOUSE IN IZU TO RELAX AND READ SOME BOOKS.
I ENVY YOU! YOU GET TO GO TO THE SUMMER HOUSE EVERY YEAR TO ESCAPE FROM THE HEAT.
I WILL BE SWAMPED WITH WORK AND TENNIS PRACTICE.
ミーン
OH, COME ON. YOU HAVE QUITE THE EXCITING SUMMER COMING, RIGHT?
ミーン

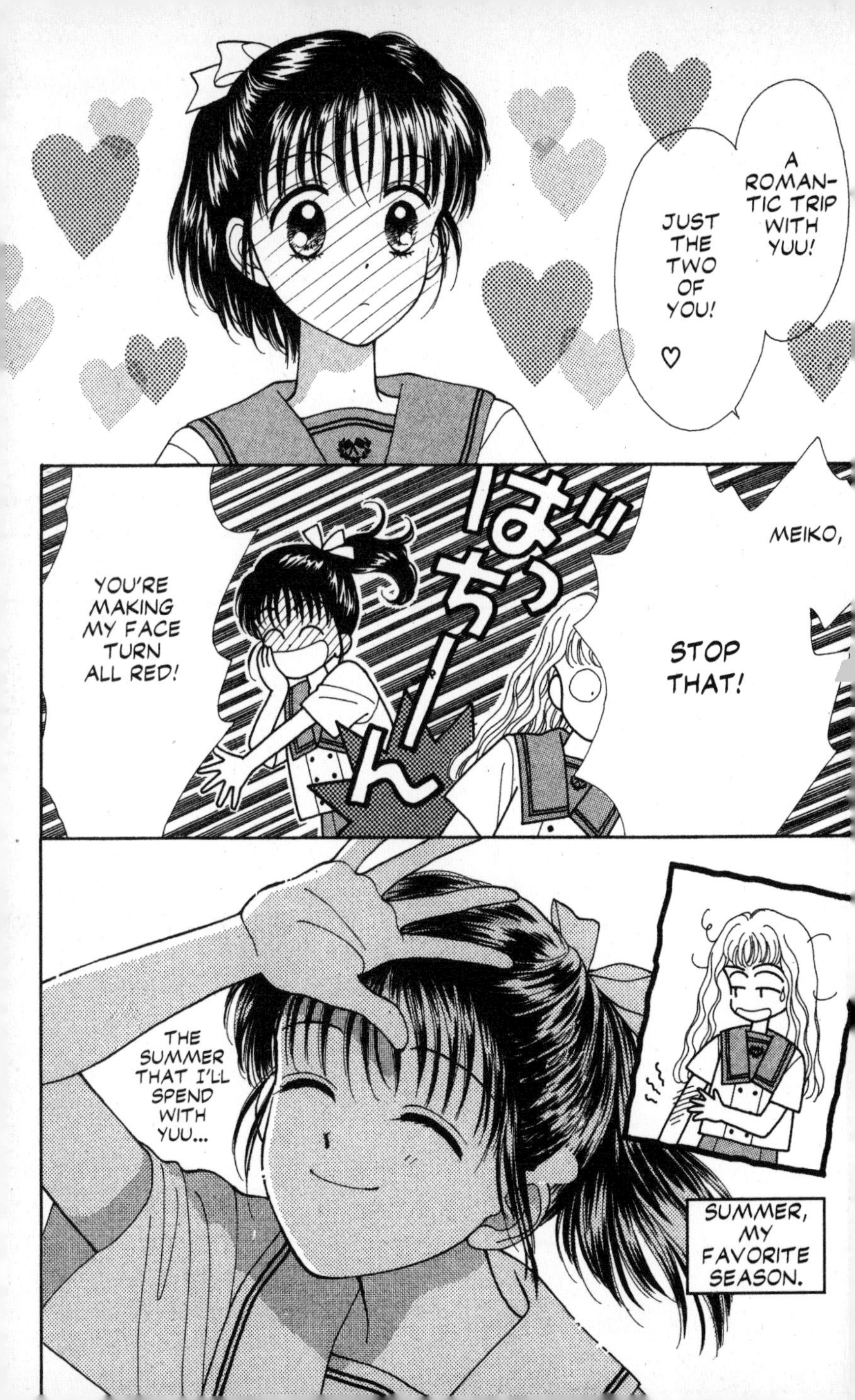
A ROMAN-TIC TRIP WITH YUU! JUST THE TWO OF YOU! ♡
MEIKO, STOP THAT!
ばっちーん
YOU'RE MAKING MY FACE TURN ALL RED!
THE SUMMER THAT I'LL SPEND WITH YUU...
SUMMER, MY FAVORITE SEASON.

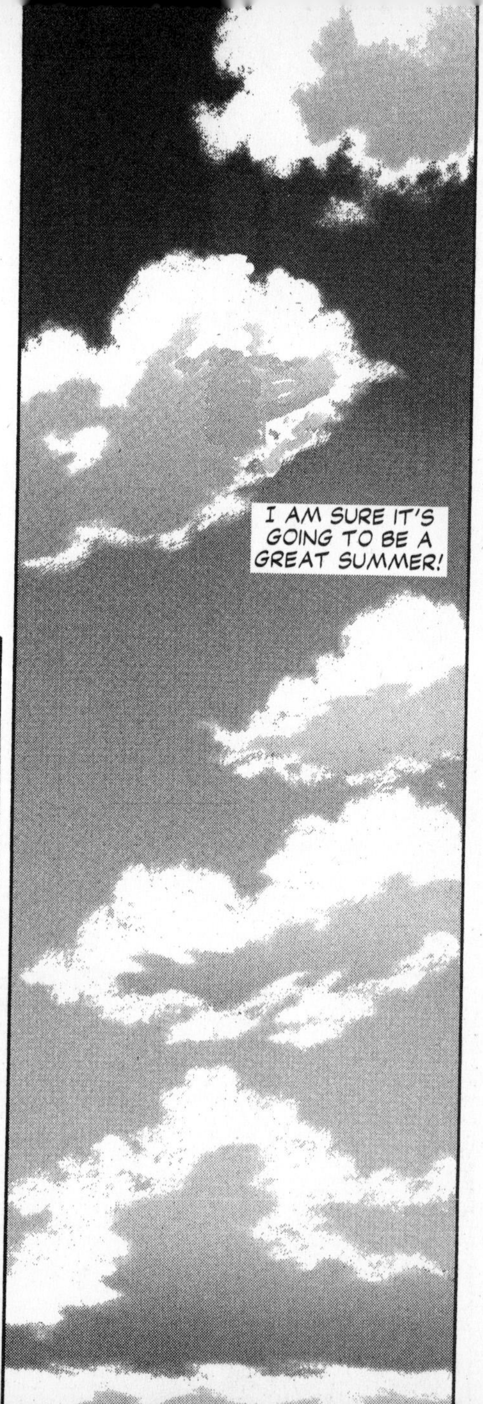
I AM SURE IT'S GOING TO BE A GREAT SUMMER!

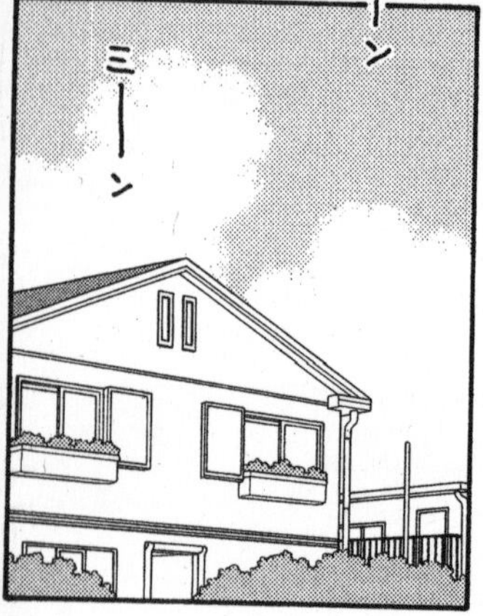
ーーン
ミーーン

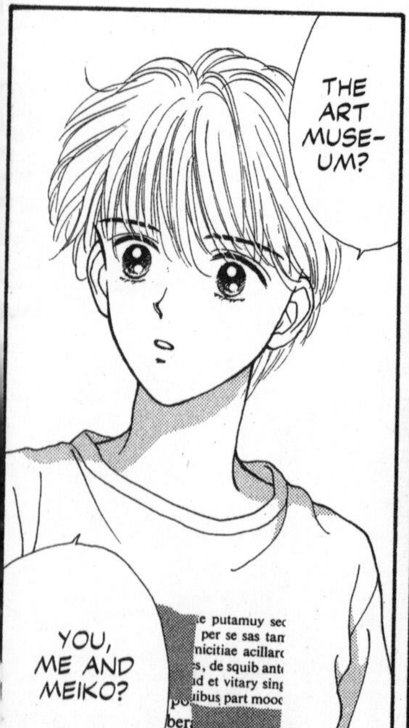
THE ART MUSE-UM?
YOU, ME AND MEIKO?

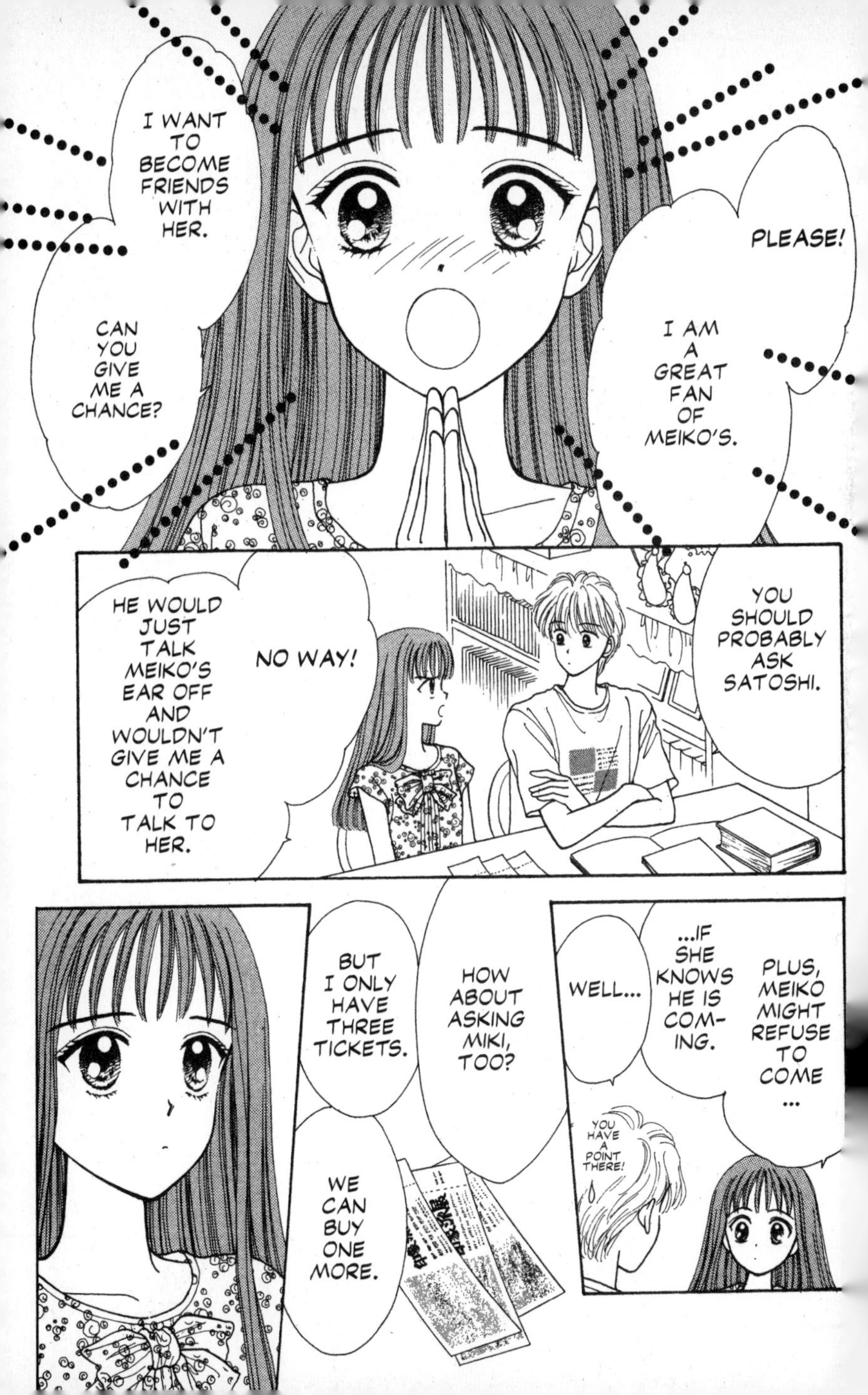
PLEASE!
I AM A GREAT FAN OF MEIKO'S.
I WANT TO BECOME FRIENDS WITH HER.
CAN YOU GIVE ME A CHANCE?
YOU SHOULD PROBABLY ASK SATOSHI.
NO WAY!
HE WOULD JUST TALK MEIKO'S EAR OFF AND WOULDN'T GIVE ME A CHANCE TO TALK TO HER.
PLUS, MEIKO MIGHT REFUSE TO COME ...
...IF SHE KNOWS HE IS COM-ING.
WELL...
YOU HAVE A POINT THERE!
HOW ABOUT ASKING MIKI, TOO?
BUT I ONLY HAVE THREE TICKETS.
WE CAN BUY ONE MORE.

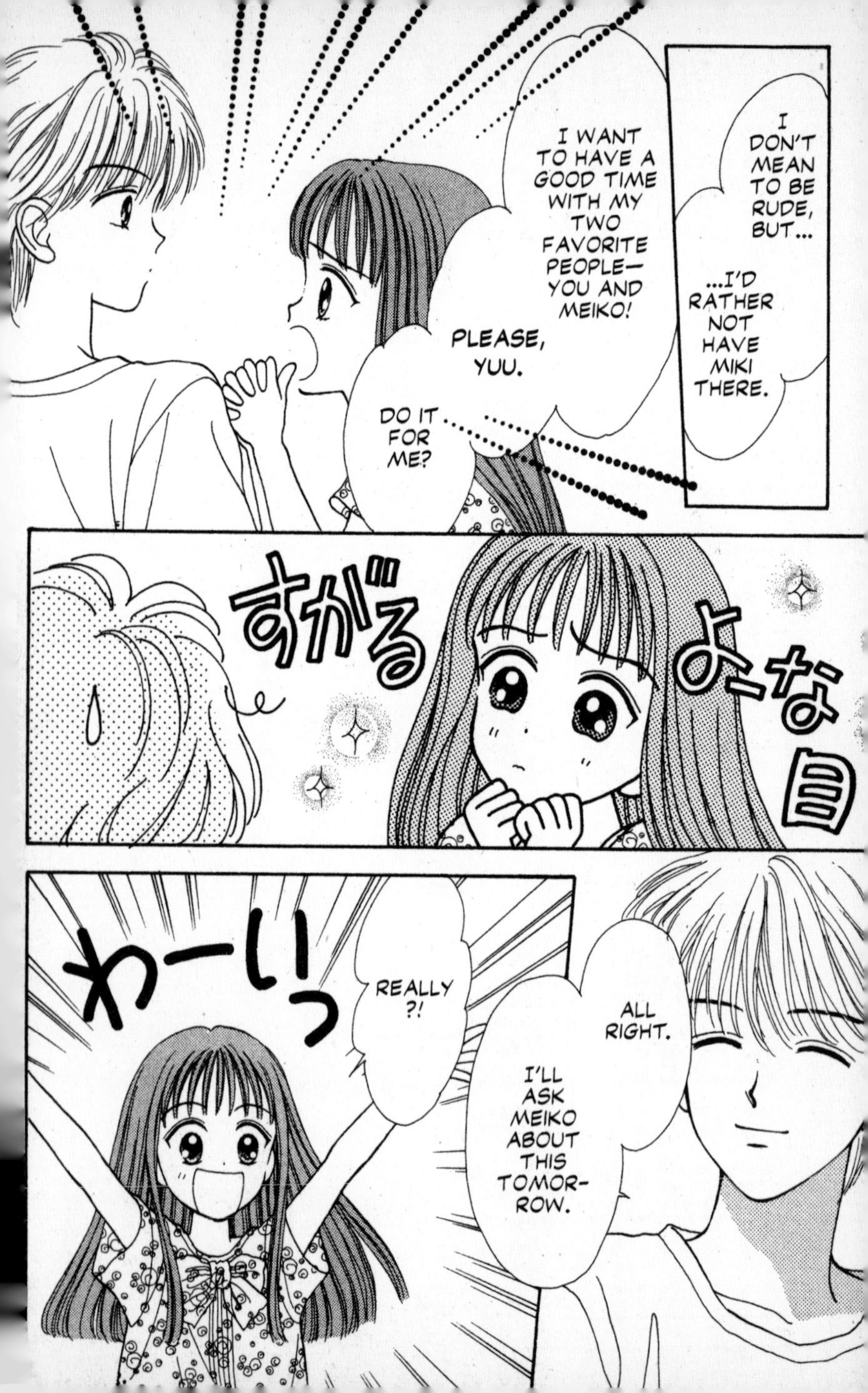
I DON'T MEAN TO BE RUDE, BUT...
...I'D RATHER NOT HAVE MIKI THERE.
I WANT TO HAVE A GOOD TIME WITH MY TWO FAVORITE PEOPLE—YOU AND MEIKO!
PLEASE, YUU.
DO IT FOR ME?
すがるよーな目
ALL RIGHT.
I'LL ASK MEIKO ABOUT THIS TOMOR-ROW.
REALLY?!
わーいっ

FREE TALK ⑦

There were some responses regarding the mispronunciation of "Nachan." Many viewers expected to hear NA-chan instead of Na-CHAN. I agree with the viewers. I asked the producer if he could fix the mis-take, but he said it was too late. I wonder if it's more natural to pro-nounce his name as Na-CHAN for people in the Kansai area. One more thing: I was expecting to hear Ko-ISHI-ka-wa for Koishikawa but they say Ko-I-SHI-KA-WA. This is such a subtle thing but it somehow sounds awkward. Ha ha!

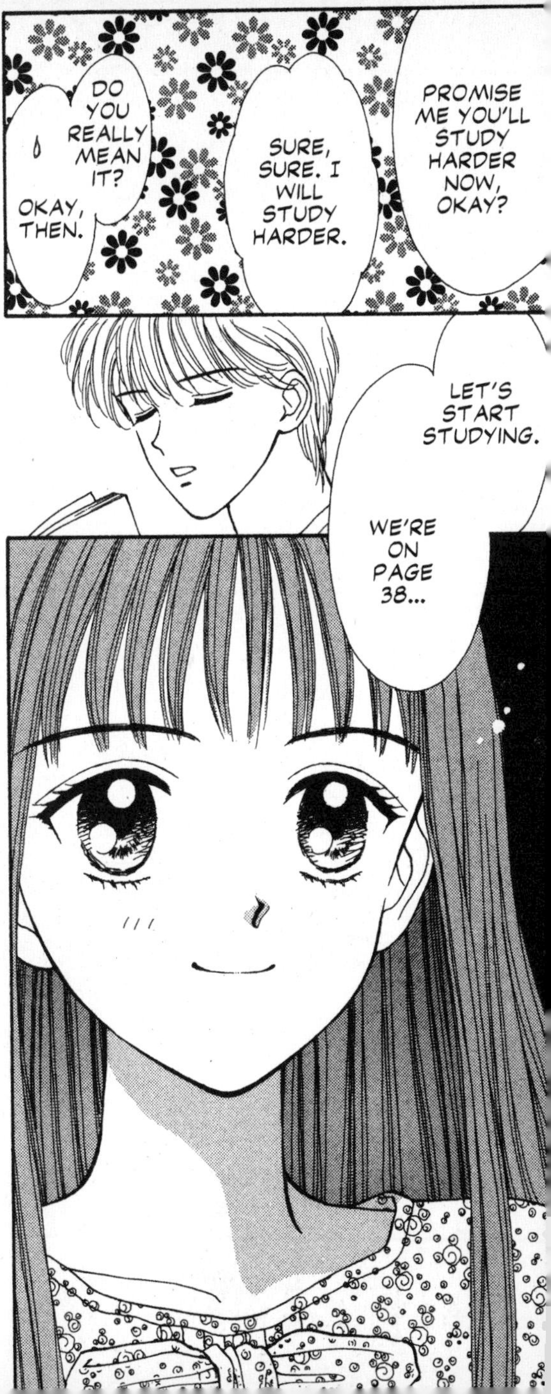
PROMISE ME YOU'LL STUDY HARDER NOW, OKAY?
SURE, SURE. I WILL STUDY HARDER.
DO YOU REALLY MEAN IT?
OKAY, THEN.
LET'S START STUDYING.
WE'RE ON PAGE 38...

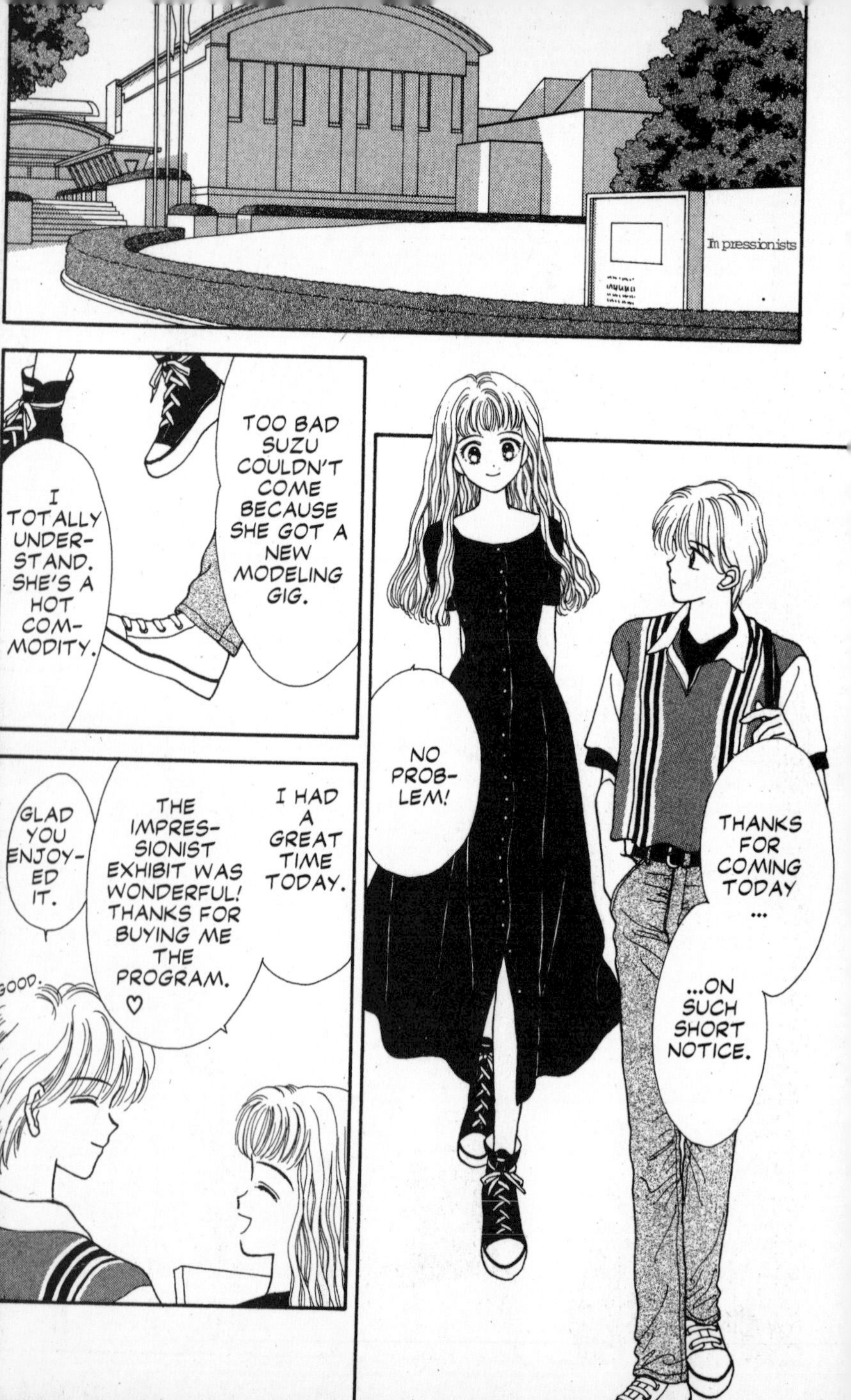
Impressionists
THANKS FOR COMING TODAY ...
...ON SUCH SHORT NOTICE.
NO PROB-LEM!
TOO BAD SUZU COULDN'T COME BECAUSE SHE GOT A NEW MODELING GIG.
I TOTALLY UNDER-STAND. SHE'S A HOT COM-MODITY.
I HAD A GREAT TIME TODAY.
THE IMPRES-SIONIST EXHIBIT WAS WONDERFUL! THANKS FOR BUYING ME THE PROGRAM. ♡
GLAD YOU ENJOY-ED IT.
GOOD.

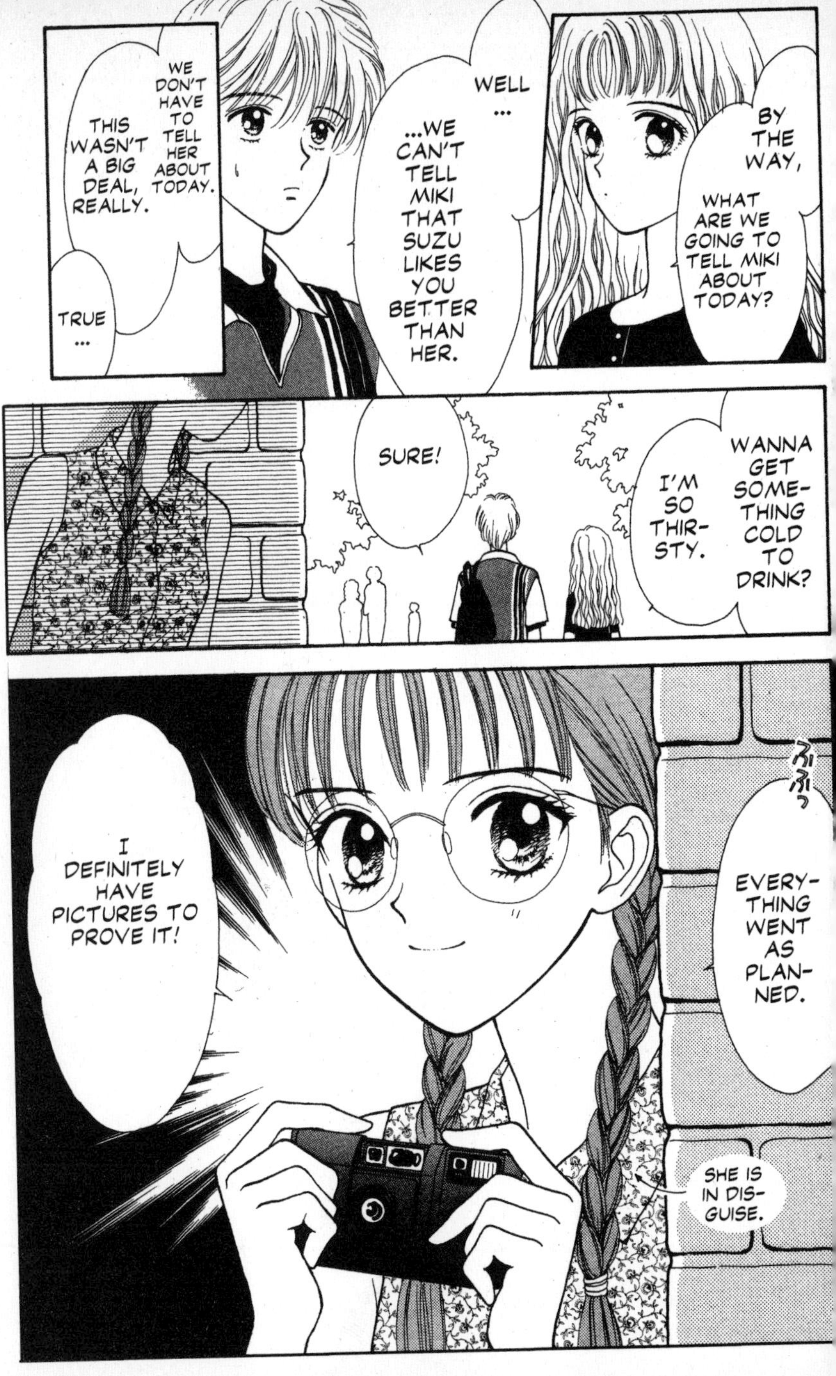
BY THE WAY,
WHAT ARE WE GOING TO TELL MIKI ABOUT TODAY?
WELL ...
...WE CAN'T TELL MIKI THAT SUZU LIKES YOU BETTER THAN HER.
WE DON'T HAVE TO TELL HER ABOUT TODAY.
THIS WASN'T A BIG DEAL, REALLY.
TRUE ...
WANNA GET SOMETHING COLD TO DRINK?
I'M SO THIRSTY.
SURE!
EVERYTHING WENT AS PLANNED.
I DEFINITELY HAVE PICTURES TO PROVE IT!
SHE IS IN DISGUISE.

Bobso
FINE BLENDED ICE CREA
SEE YOU TOMOR-ROW.
BYE!
ポーン
HI, KEI...
YO.
WHAT ARE YOU DOING HERE?
YOU'RE OFF TODAY, AREN'T YOU?
I'M ON MY WAY TO THE DRUG-STORE.
I LIVE IN THIS NEIGHBOR-HOOD.

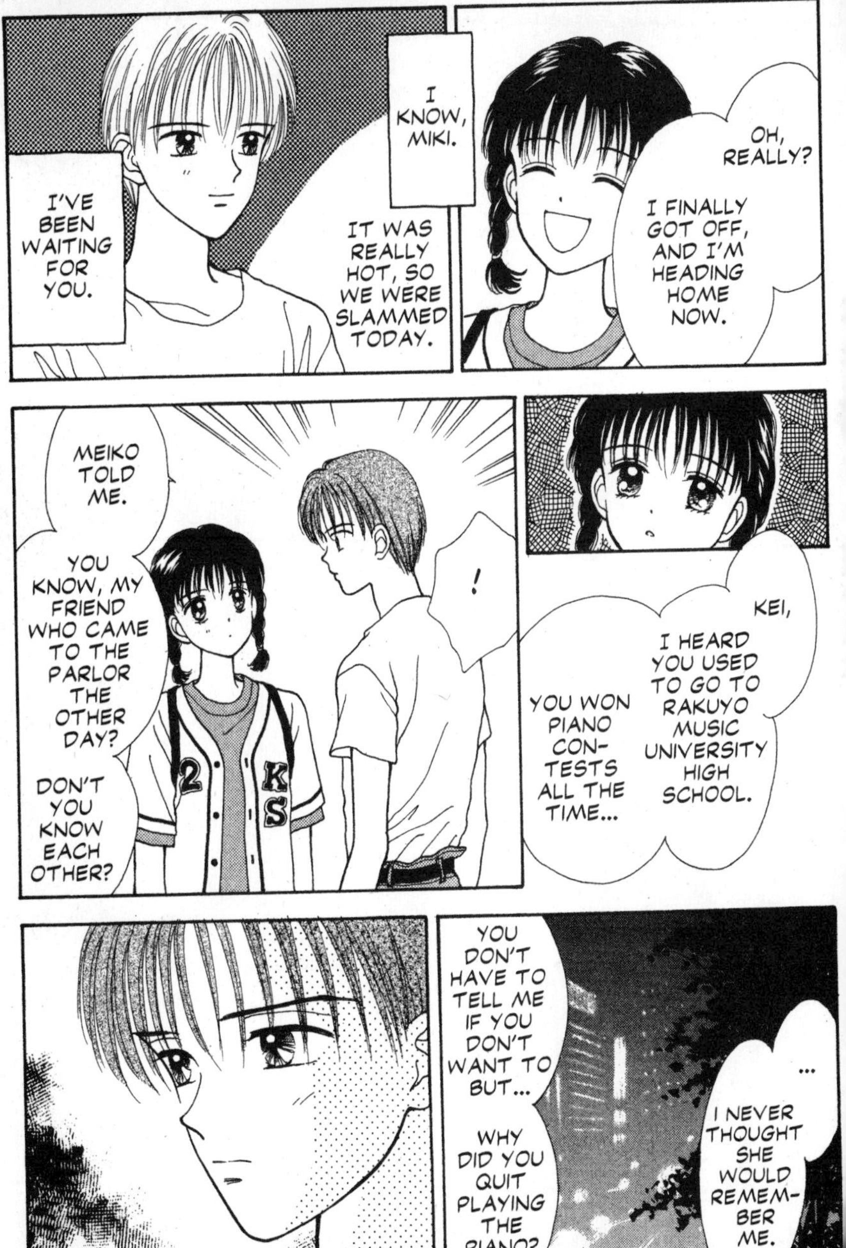
OH, REALLY?
I FINALLY GOT OFF, AND I'M HEADING HOME NOW.
I KNOW, MIKI.
IT WAS REALLY HOT, SO WE WERE SLAMMED TODAY.
I'VE BEEN WAITING FOR YOU.
KEI,
I HEARD YOU USED TO GO TO RAKUYO MUSIC UNIVERSITY HIGH SCHOOL.
YOU WON PIANO CON-TESTS ALL THE TIME...
!
MEIKO TOLD ME.
YOU KNOW, MY FRIEND WHO CAME TO THE PARLOR THE OTHER DAY?
DON'T YOU KNOW EACH OTHER?
YOU DON'T HAVE TO TELL ME IF YOU DON'T WANT TO BUT...
WHY DID YOU QUIT PLAYING THE PIANO?
...
I NEVER THOUGHT SHE WOULD REMEM-BER ME.

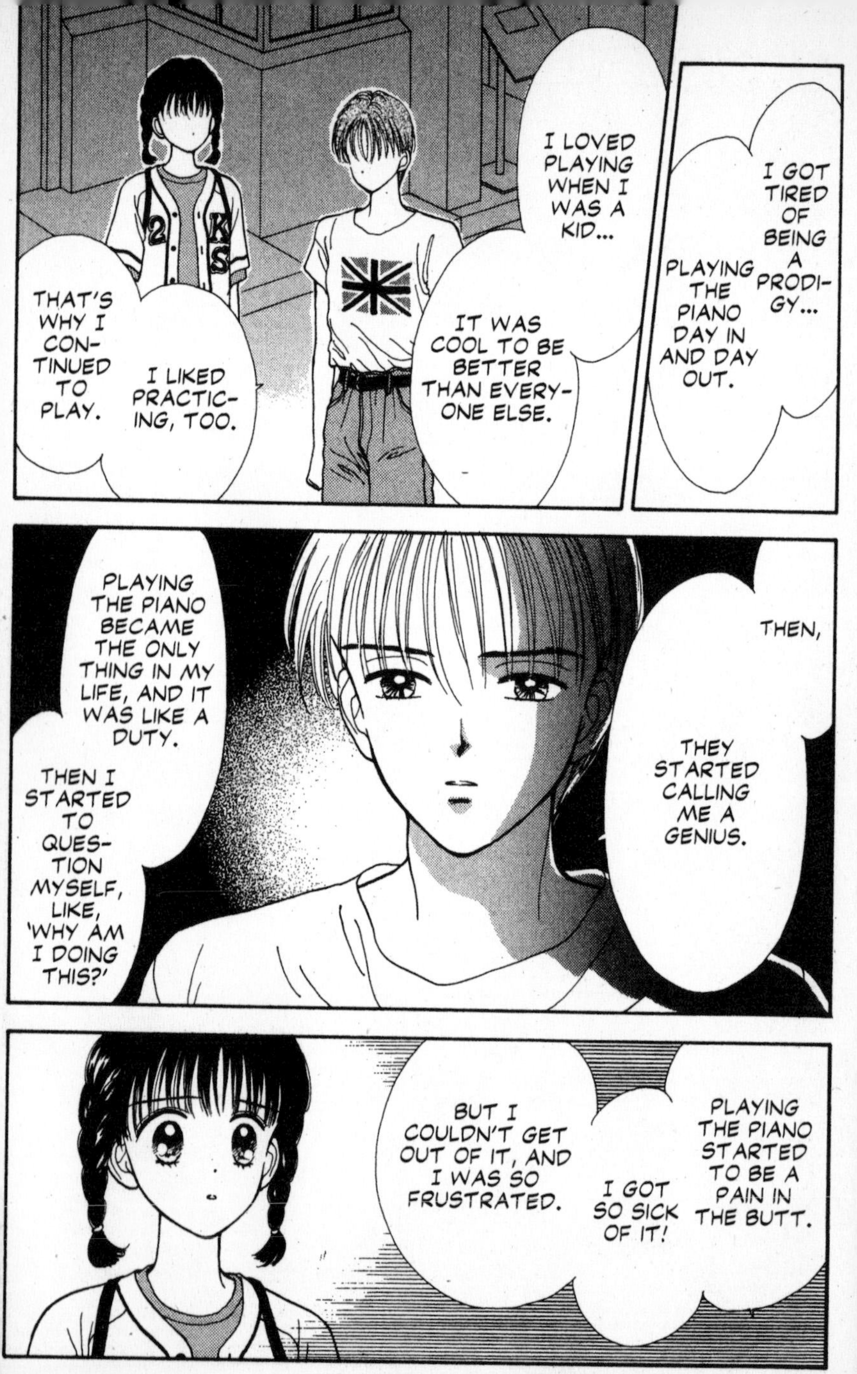
I GOT TIRED OF BEING A PRODIGY...
PLAYING THE PIANO DAY IN AND DAY OUT.
I LOVED PLAYING WHEN I WAS A KID...
IT WAS COOL TO BE BETTER THAN EVERYONE ELSE.
I LIKED PRACTICING, TOO.
THAT'S WHY I CONTINUED TO PLAY.
THEN,
THEY STARTED CALLING ME A GENIUS.
PLAYING THE PIANO BECAME THE ONLY THING IN MY LIFE, AND IT WAS LIKE A DUTY.
THEN I STARTED TO QUESTION MYSELF, LIKE, 'WHY AM I DOING THIS?'
PLAYING THE PIANO STARTED TO BE A PAIN IN THE BUTT.
I GOT SO SICK OF IT!
BUT I COULDN'T GET OUT OF IT, AND I WAS SO FRUSTRATED.

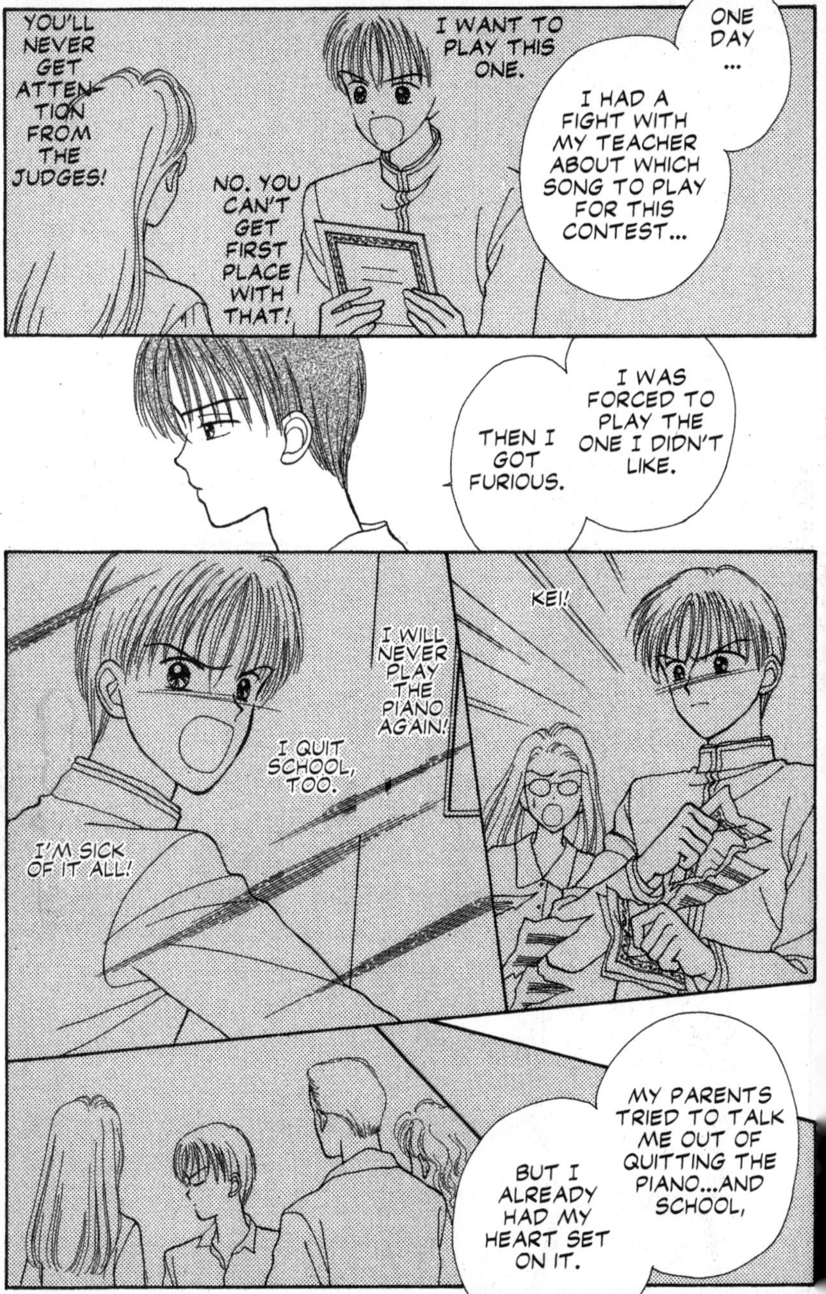
ONE DAY ...
I HAD A FIGHT WITH MY TEACHER ABOUT WHICH SONG TO PLAY FOR THIS CONTEST...
I WANT TO PLAY THIS ONE.
NO. YOU CAN'T GET FIRST PLACE WITH THAT!
YOU'LL NEVER GET ATTENTION FROM THE JUDGES!
I WAS FORCED TO PLAY THE ONE I DIDN'T LIKE.
THEN I GOT FURIOUS.
KEI!
I WILL NEVER PLAY THE PIANO AGAIN!
I QUIT SCHOOL, TOO.
I'M SICK OF IT ALL!
MY PARENTS TRIED TO TALK ME OUT OF QUITTING THE PIANO...AND SCHOOL,
BUT I ALREADY HAD MY HEART SET ON IT.

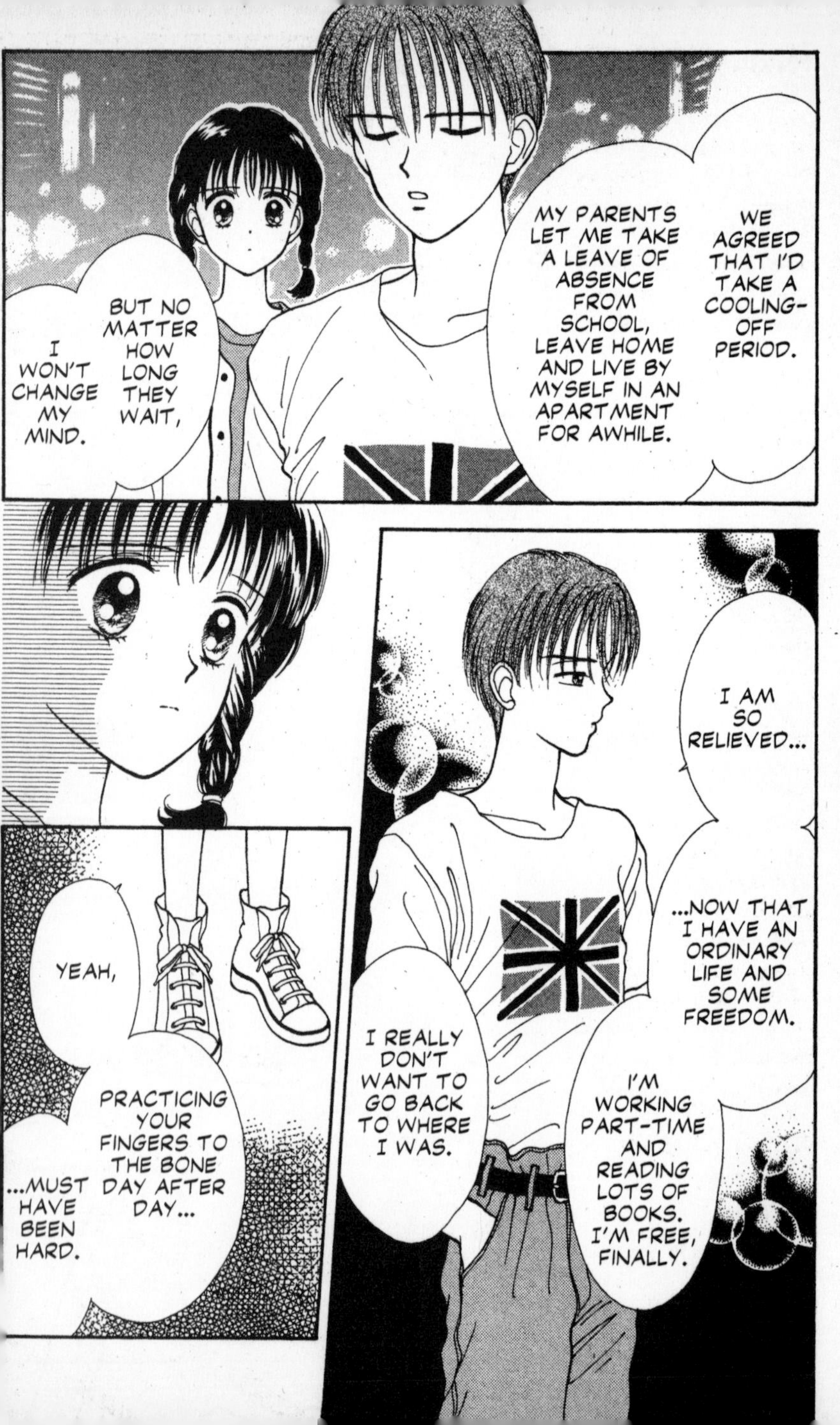
WE AGREED THAT I'D TAKE A COOLING-OFF PERIOD.
MY PARENTS LET ME TAKE A LEAVE OF ABSENCE FROM SCHOOL, LEAVE HOME AND LIVE BY MYSELF IN AN APARTMENT FOR AWHILE.
BUT NO MATTER HOW LONG THEY WAIT,
I WON'T CHANGE MY MIND.
I AM SO RELIEVED...
...NOW THAT I HAVE AN ORDINARY LIFE AND SOME FREEDOM.
I'M WORKING PART-TIME AND READING LOTS OF BOOKS. I'M FREE, FINALLY.
I REALLY DON'T WANT TO GO BACK TO WHERE I WAS.
YEAH,
PRACTICING YOUR FINGERS TO THE BONE DAY AFTER DAY...
...MUST HAVE BEEN HARD.

FREE TALK ⑧

The color of Arimi's hair also draws some attention from the animation viewers. According to the animation staff, green and purple can be used for hair and is considered acceptable, while pink is too weird. To me, all these colors appear unrealistic .They wanted to use green or brown for Arimi's hair. They chose green in the end because brown hair would make Arimi's image too cutesy. Green hair matches Arimi's cocky character. The first anime cel of Arimi (the one and only!) is right here with me. She looks so pretty. At first, the color of Rokutanda's hair was the same brown as Nachan's. No anime cels had been made for Nachan at that point. It was me who suggested that Rokudanda's hair didn't deserve to be brown. Let Nachan have brown hair, and use purple for Rokudanda's. Sorry, Rokudanda!

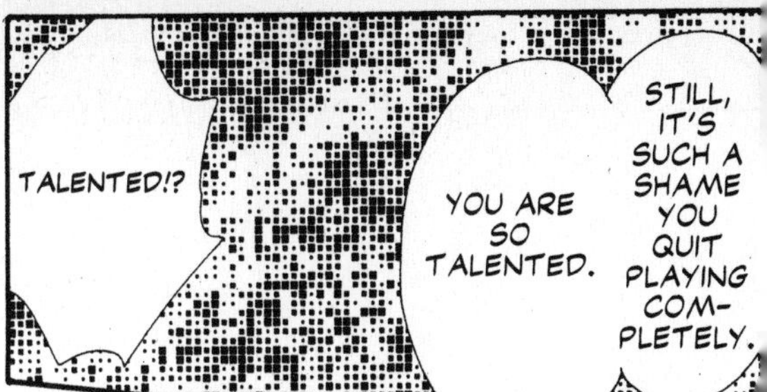
STILL, IT'S SUCH A SHAME YOU QUIT PLAYING COMPLETELY.
YOU ARE SO TALENTED.
TALENTED!?

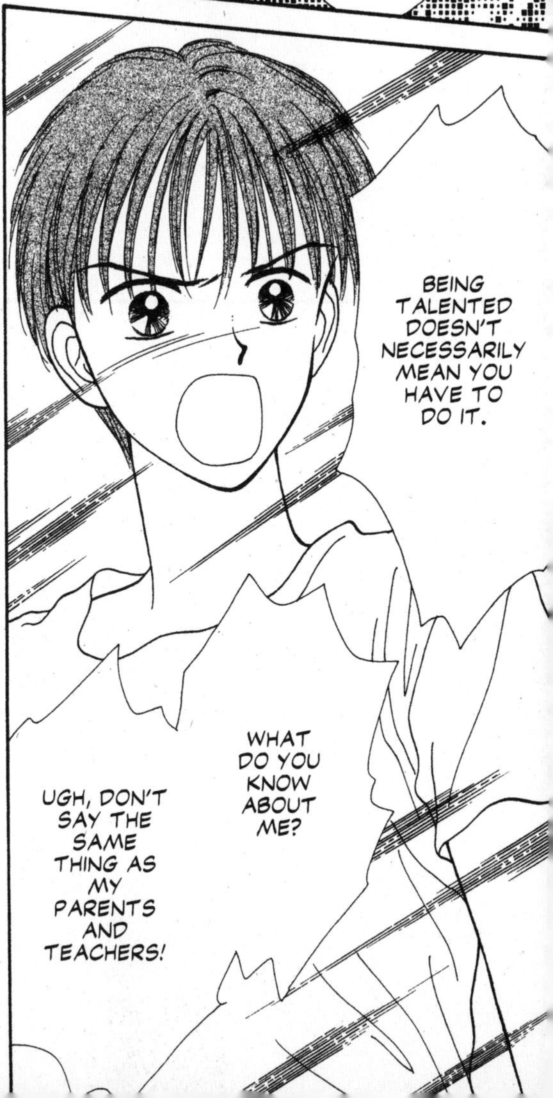
BEING TALENTED DOESN'T NECESSARILY MEAN YOU HAVE TO DO IT.
WHAT DO YOU KNOW ABOUT ME?
UGH, DON'T SAY THE SAME THING AS MY PARENTS AND TEACHERS!

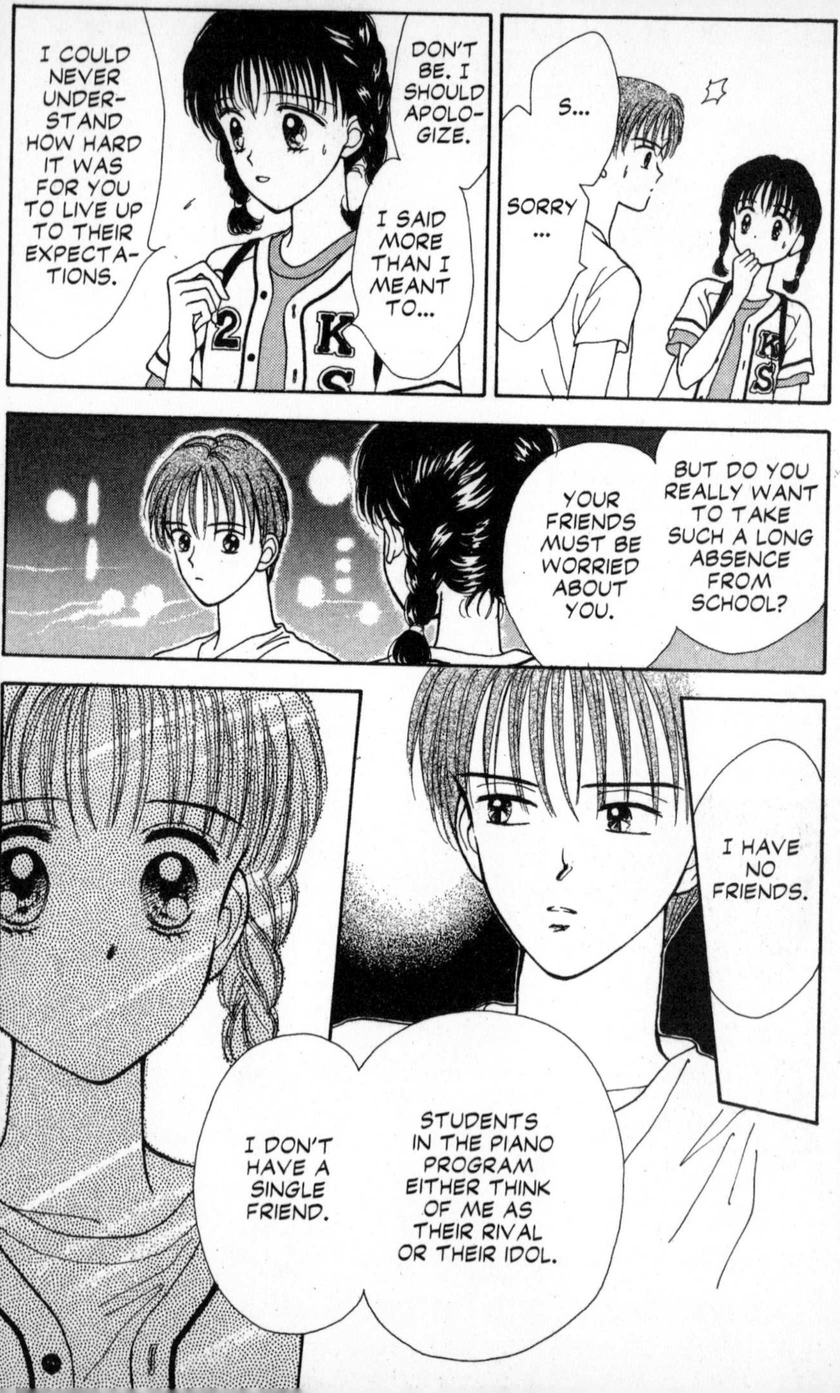
S...
SORRY...
DON'T BE. I SHOULD APOLOGIZE.
I SAID MORE THAN I MEANT TO...
I COULD NEVER UNDERSTAND HOW HARD IT WAS FOR YOU TO LIVE UP TO THEIR EXPECTATIONS.
BUT DO YOU REALLY WANT TO TAKE SUCH A LONG ABSENCE FROM SCHOOL?
YOUR FRIENDS MUST BE WORRIED ABOUT YOU.
I HAVE NO FRIENDS.
STUDENTS IN THE PIANO PROGRAM EITHER THINK OF ME AS THEIR RIVAL OR THEIR IDOL.
I DON'T HAVE A SINGLE FRIEND.

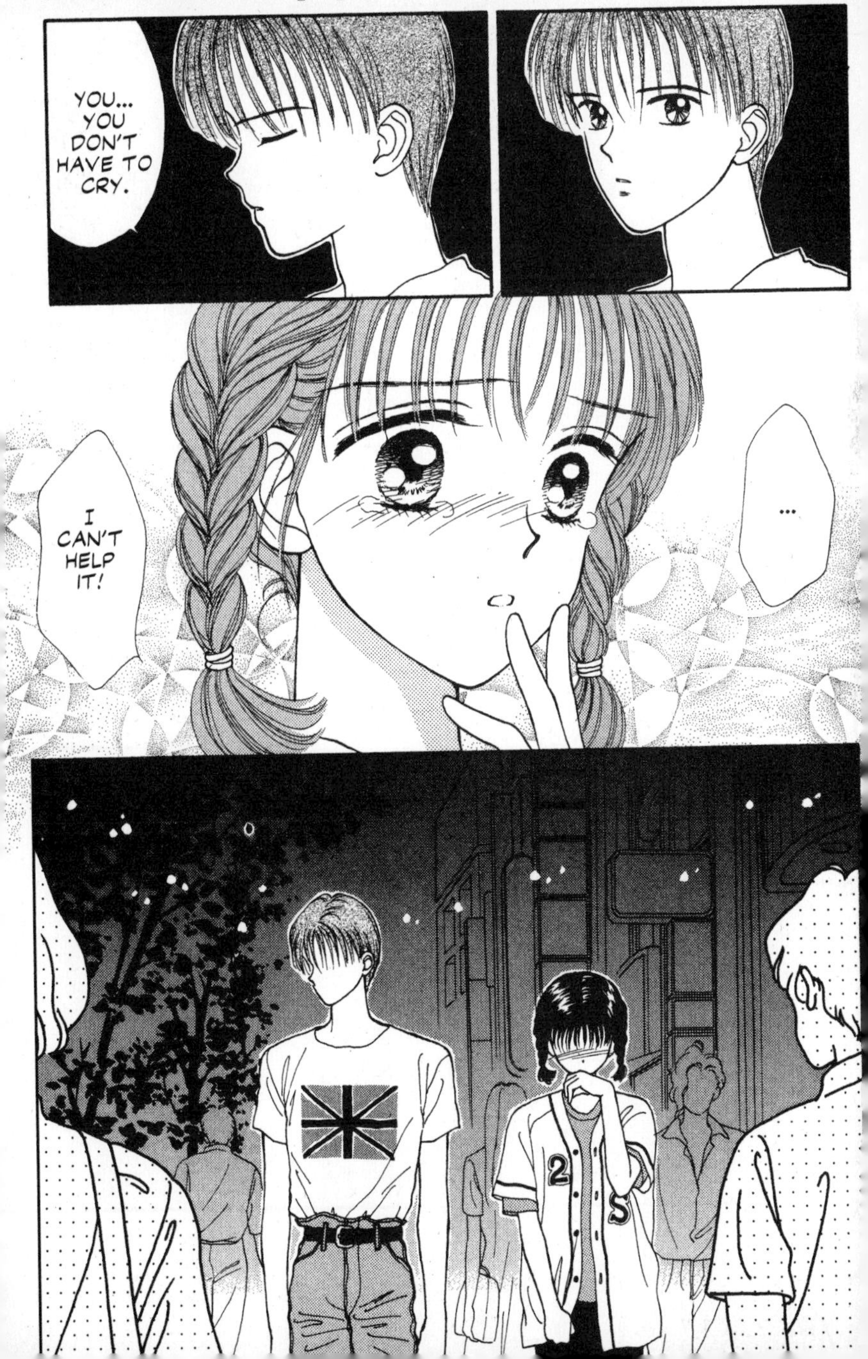
YOU... YOU DON'T HAVE TO CRY.
...
I CAN'T HELP IT!

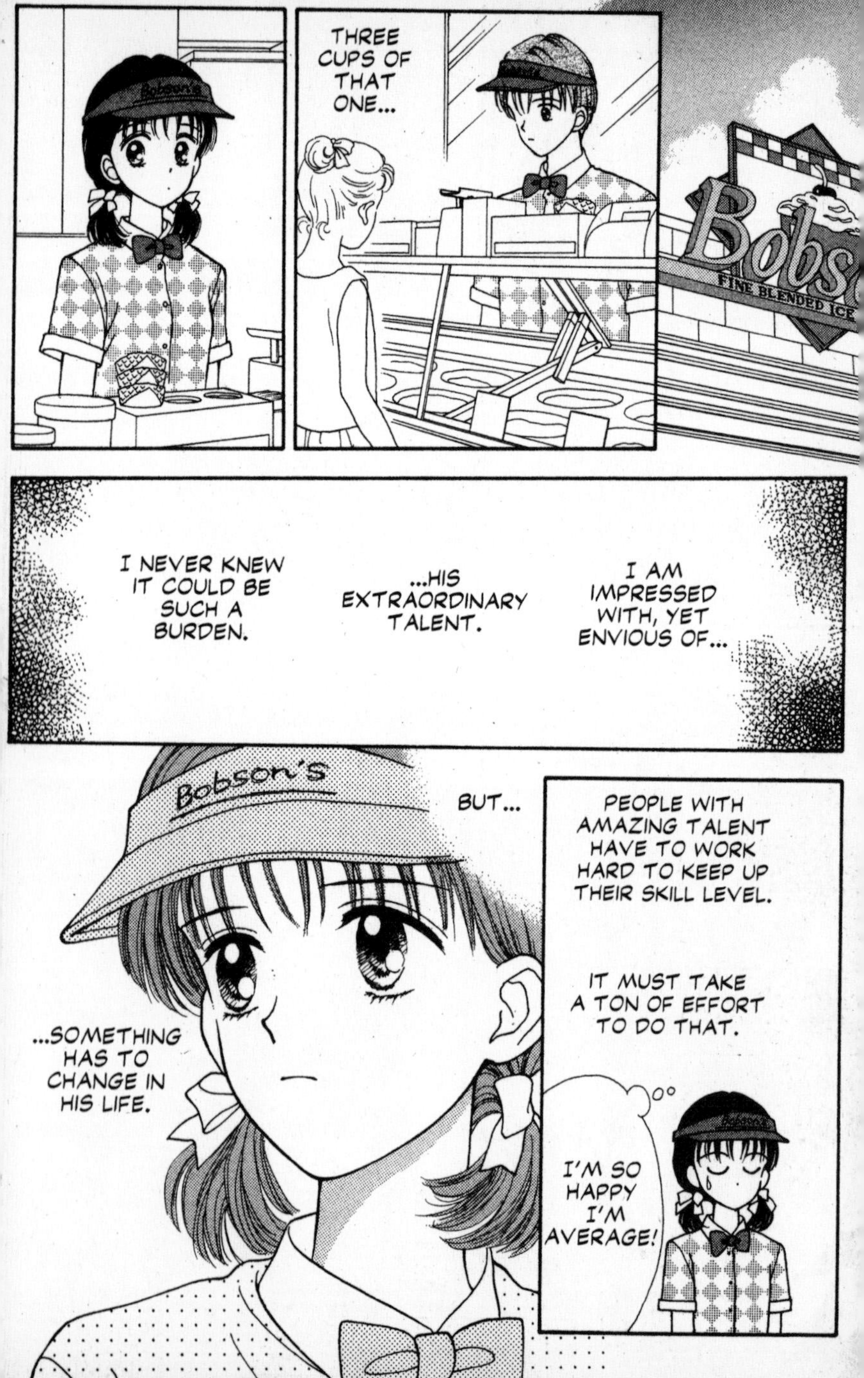
FINE BLENDED ICE
THREE CUPS OF THAT ONE...
I AM IMPRESSED WITH, YET ENVIOUS OF...
...HIS EXTRAORDINARY TALENT.
I NEVER KNEW IT COULD BE SUCH A BURDEN.
PEOPLE WITH AMAZING TALENT HAVE TO WORK HARD TO KEEP UP THEIR SKILL LEVEL.
IT MUST TAKE A TON OF EFFORT TO DO THAT.
I'M SO HAPPY I'M AVERAGE!
Bobson's
BUT...
...SOMETHING HAS TO CHANGE IN HIS LIFE.

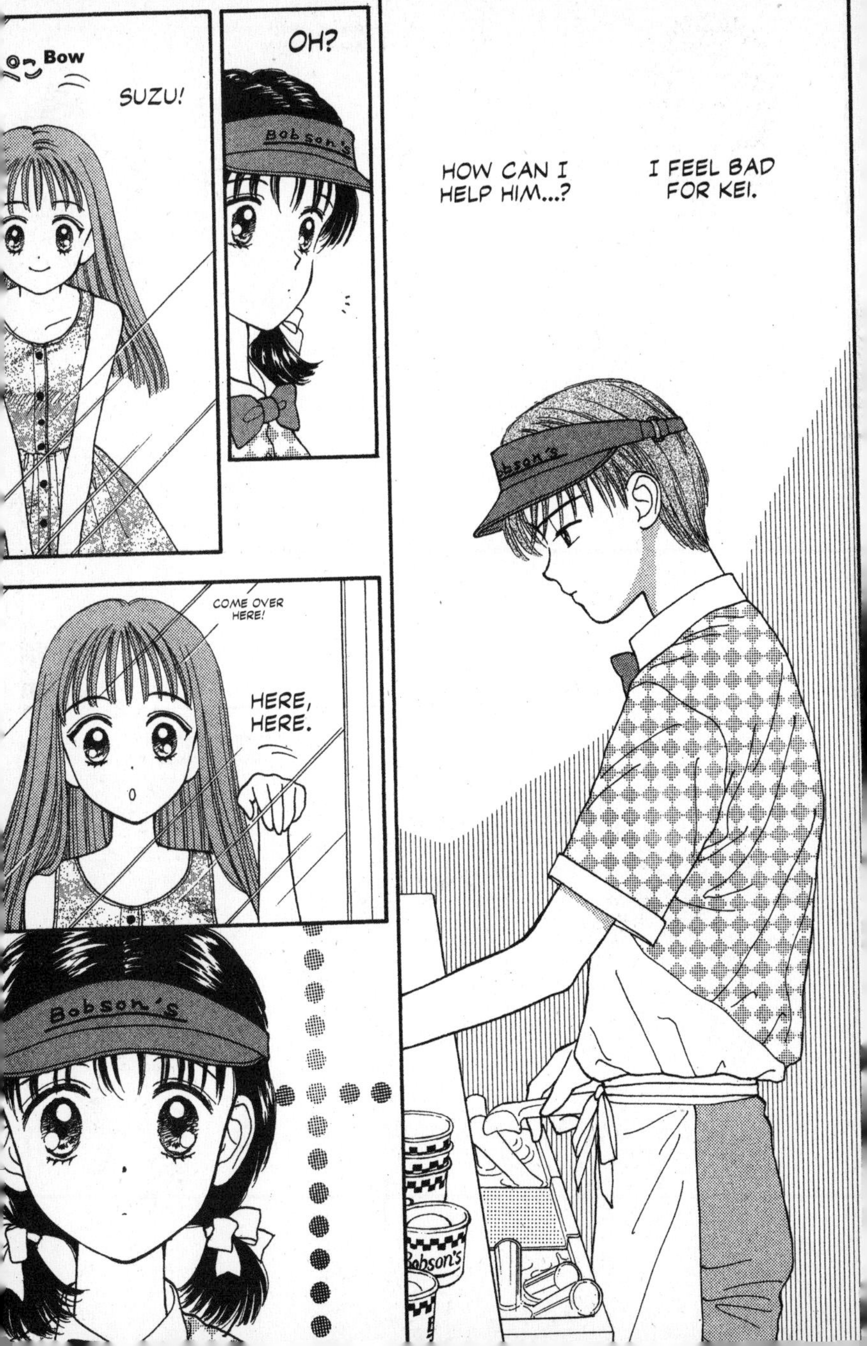
I FEEL BAD FOR KEI.
HOW CAN I HELP HIM...?
OH?
Bow
SUZU!
HERE, HERE.
COME OVER HERE!

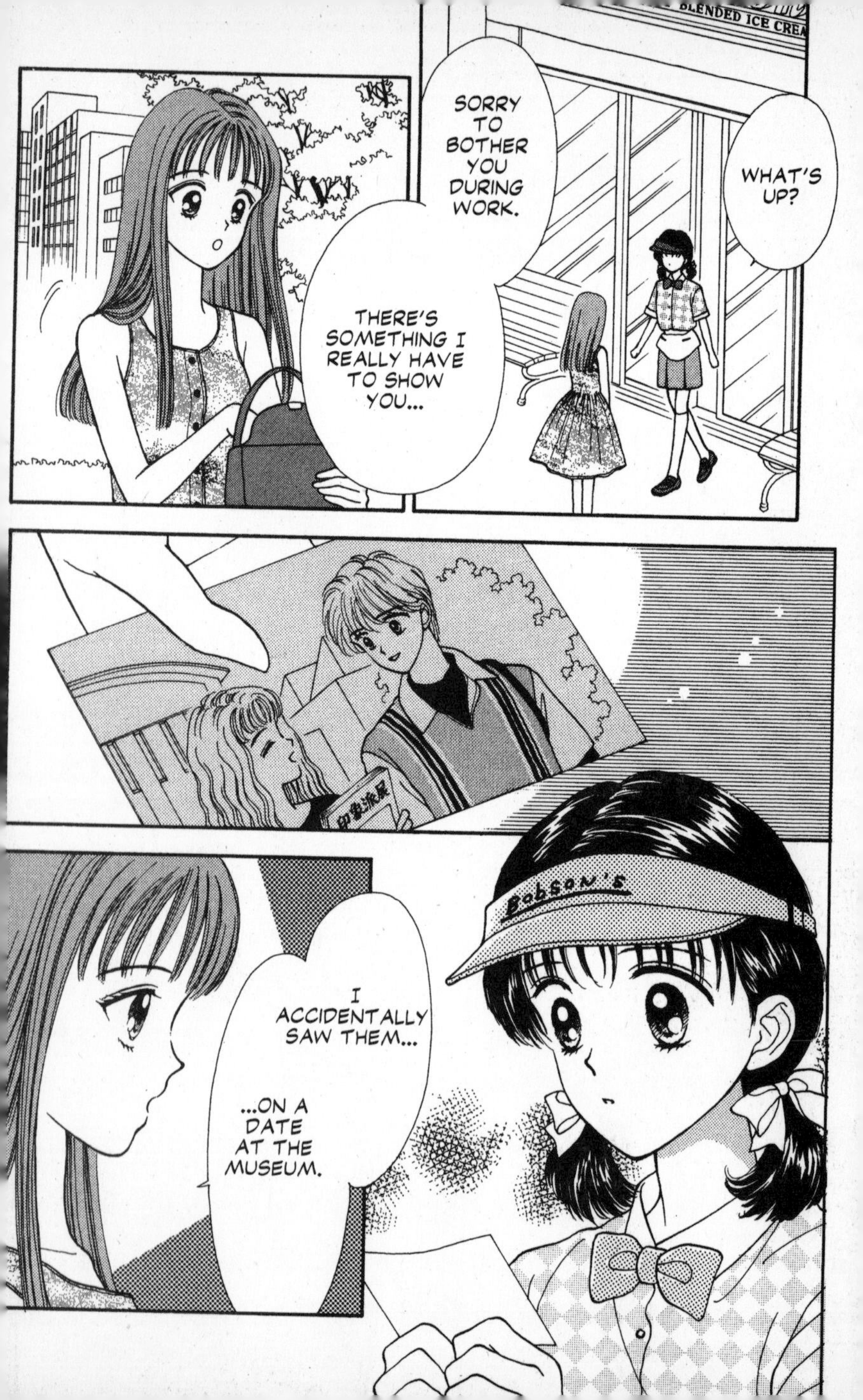
WHAT'S UP?
SORRY TO BOTHER YOU DURING WORK.
THERE'S SOMETHING I REALLY HAVE TO SHOW YOU...
BOBSON'S
I ACCIDENTALLY SAW THEM...
...ON A DATE AT THE MUSEUM.

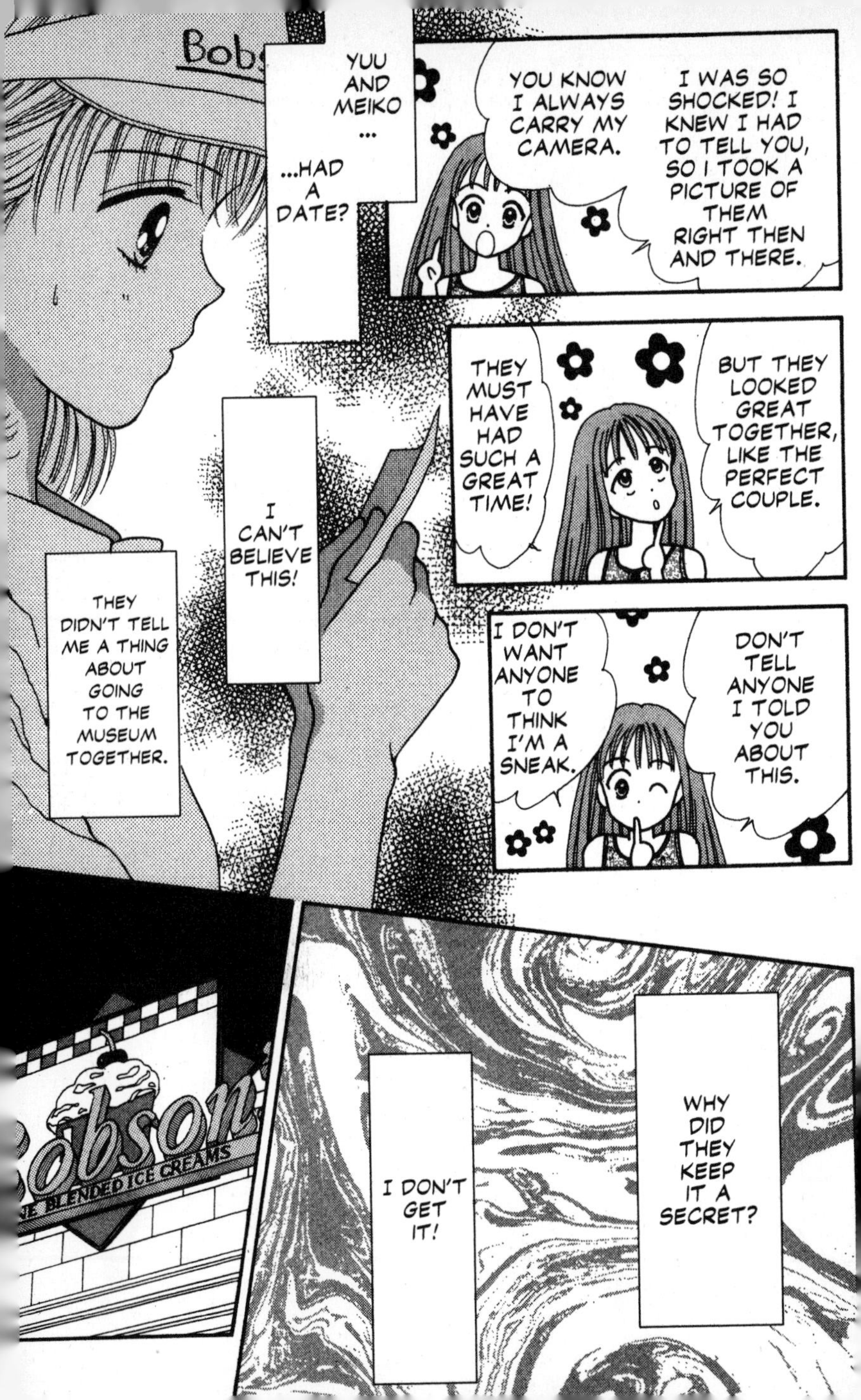
I WAS SO SHOCKED! I KNEW I HAD TO TELL YOU, SO I TOOK A PICTURE OF THEM RIGHT THEN AND THERE.
YOU KNOW I ALWAYS CARRY MY CAMERA.
BUT THEY LOOKED GREAT TOGETHER, LIKE THE PERFECT COUPLE.
THEY MUST HAVE HAD SUCH A GREAT TIME!
DON'T TELL ANYONE I TOLD YOU ABOUT THIS.
I DON'T WANT ANYONE TO THINK I'M A SNEAK.
YUU AND MEIKO ...
...HAD A DATE?
I CAN'T BELIEVE THIS!
THEY DIDN'T TELL ME A THING ABOUT GOING TO THE MUSEUM TOGETHER.
WHY DID THEY KEEP IT A SECRET?
I DON'T GET IT!
BLENDED ICE CREAMS

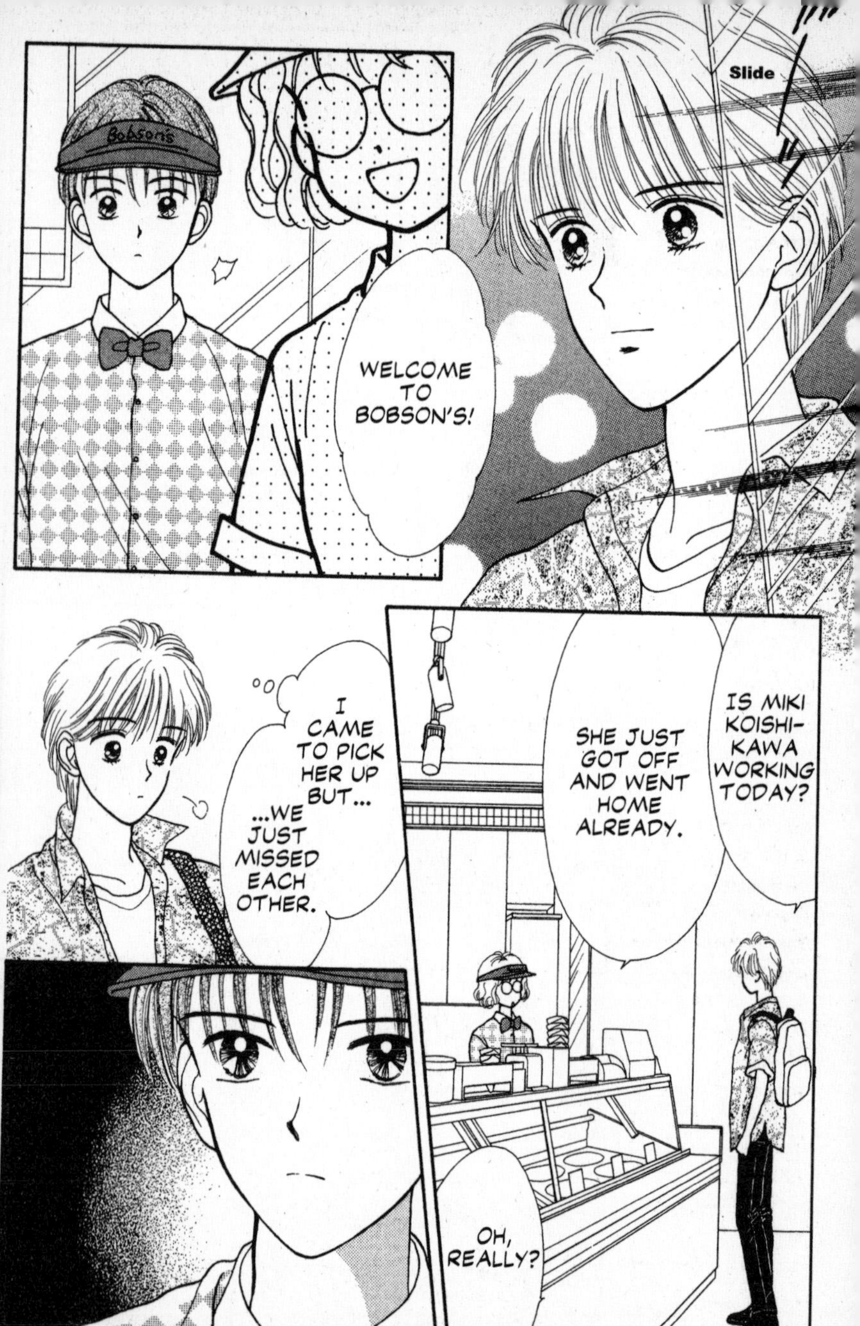
Slide
WELCOME TO BOBSON'S!
Bobson's
IS MIKI KOISHI-KAWA WORKING TODAY?
SHE JUST GOT OFF AND WENT HOME ALREADY.
I CAME TO PICK HER UP BUT...
...WE JUST MISSED EACH OTHER.
OH, REALLY?

FREE TALK⑨

The animation version of Marmalade Boy is produced by Toei Doga Motion Picture, Co., Ltd. The company produces animations. Although I am not involved in screenwriting or actual drawing, I created some additional characters as requested. I created Nachan in his high school years, Anju (and her uniform as well), Michael, Will, Jenny, Brian, Doris, and 3-toushin-sized* versions of various characters. That's all. Mr. Baba, who is in charge of character design, created Kyoko, Yayoi, Anju in her childhood, the principal and the vice-principal. Mr. Matsuda in the script writing department decided on the names of the characters who appear only in the animation version.

*In other words, these are scaled characters. The "3" refers to the ratio of body length to head length.

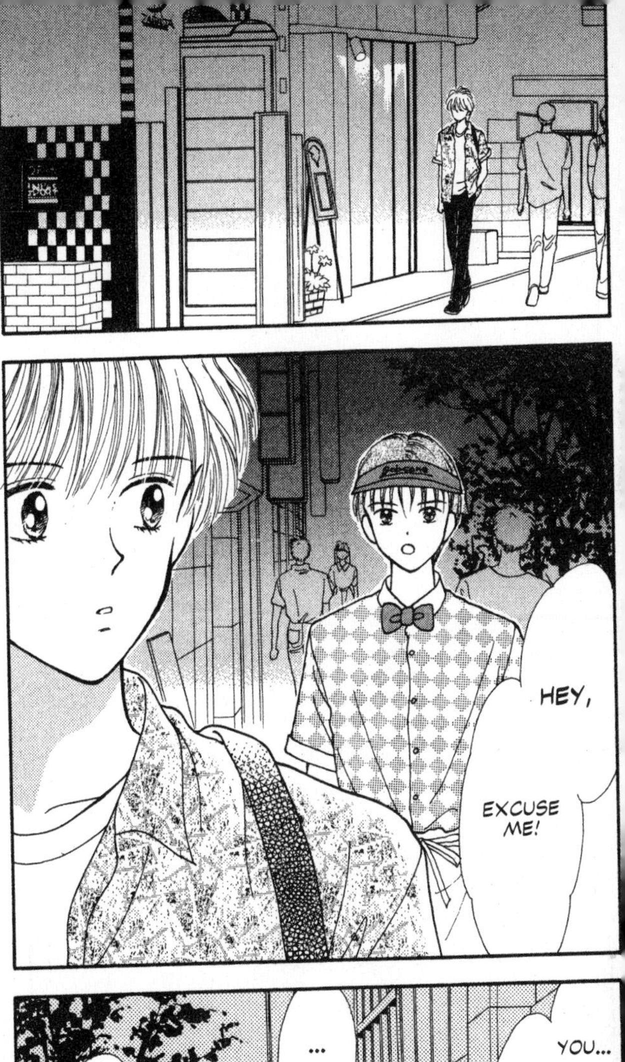
HEY,
EXCUSE ME!
YOU...
...MUST BE YUU!
...
YEAH,
BUT WHO ARE YOU?

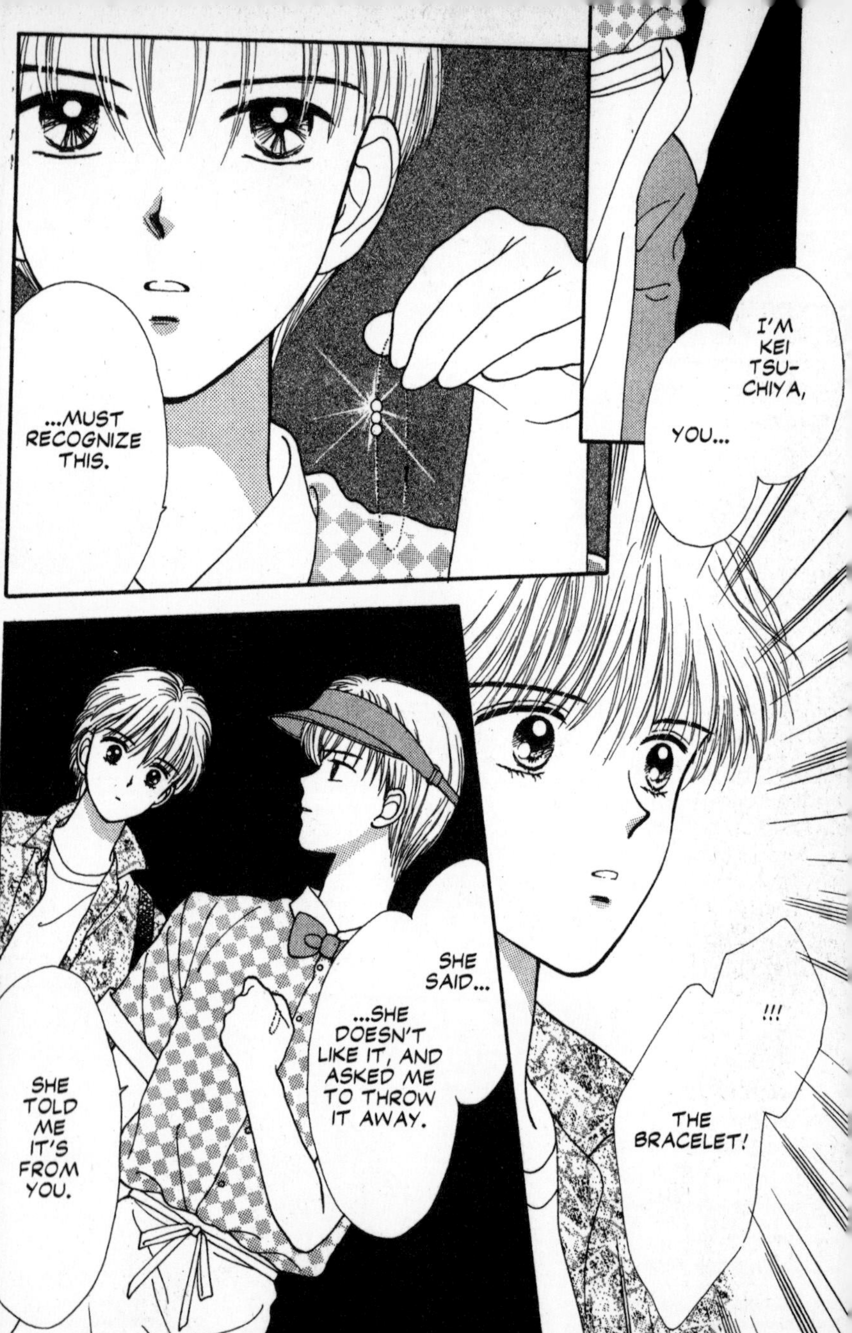
I'M KEI TSU-CHIYA, YOU...
...MUST RECOGNIZE THIS.
!!!
THE BRACELET!
SHE SAID...
...SHE DOESN'T LIKE IT, AND ASKED ME TO THROW IT AWAY.
SHE TOLD ME IT'S FROM YOU.

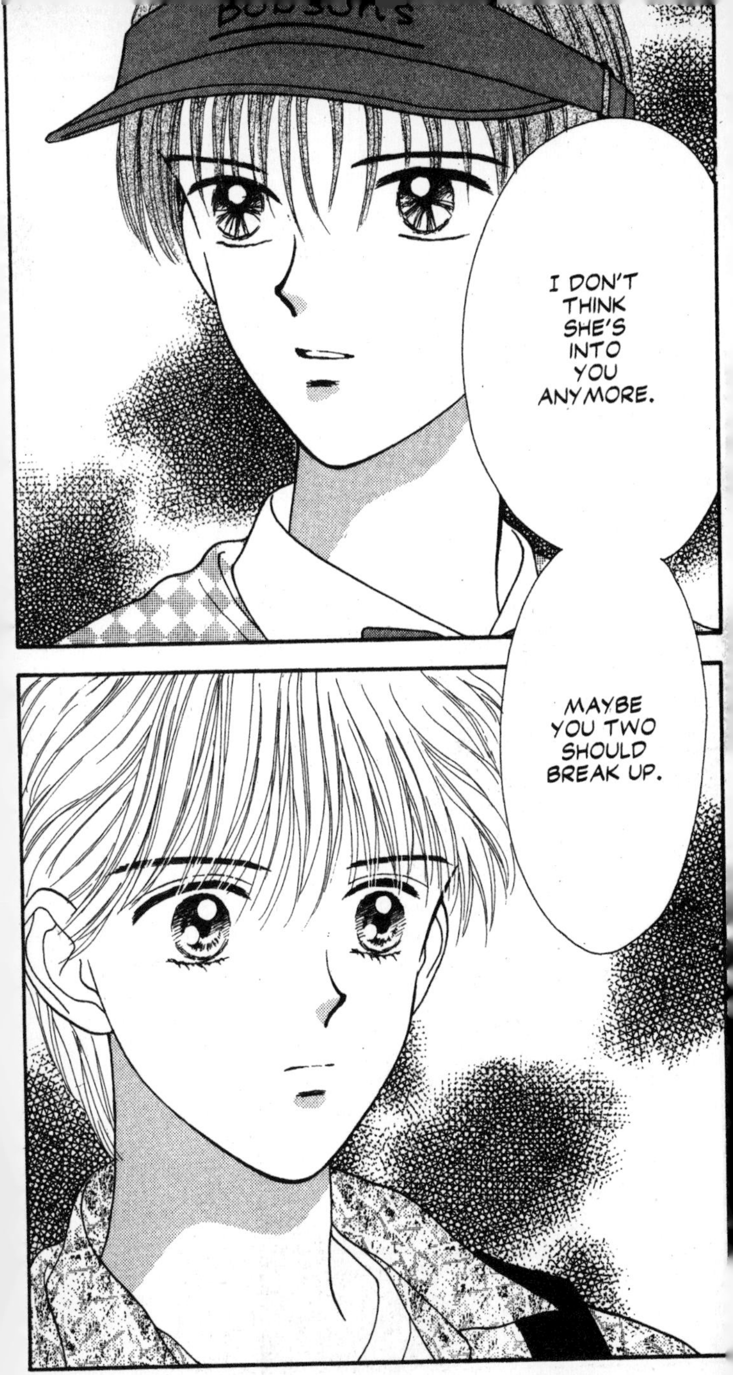
I DON'T THINK SHE'S INTO YOU ANYMORE.
MAYBE YOU TWO SHOULD BREAK UP.

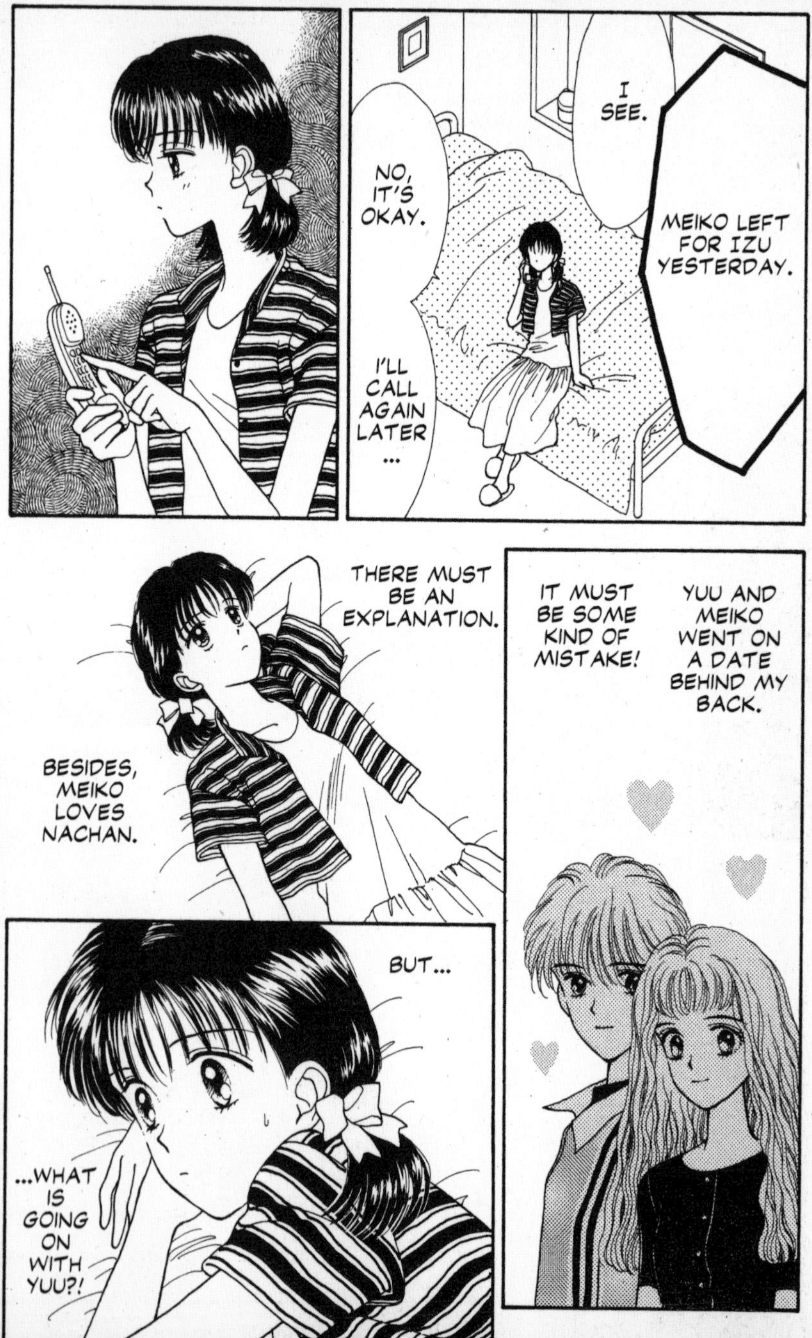
MEIKO LEFT FOR IZU YESTERDAY.
I SEE.
NO, IT'S OKAY.
I'LL CALL AGAIN LATER ...
YUU AND MEIKO WENT ON A DATE BEHIND MY BACK.
IT MUST BE SOME KIND OF MISTAKE!
THERE MUST BE AN EXPLANATION.
BESIDES, MEIKO LOVES NACHAN.
BUT...
...WHAT IS GOING ON WITH YUU?!

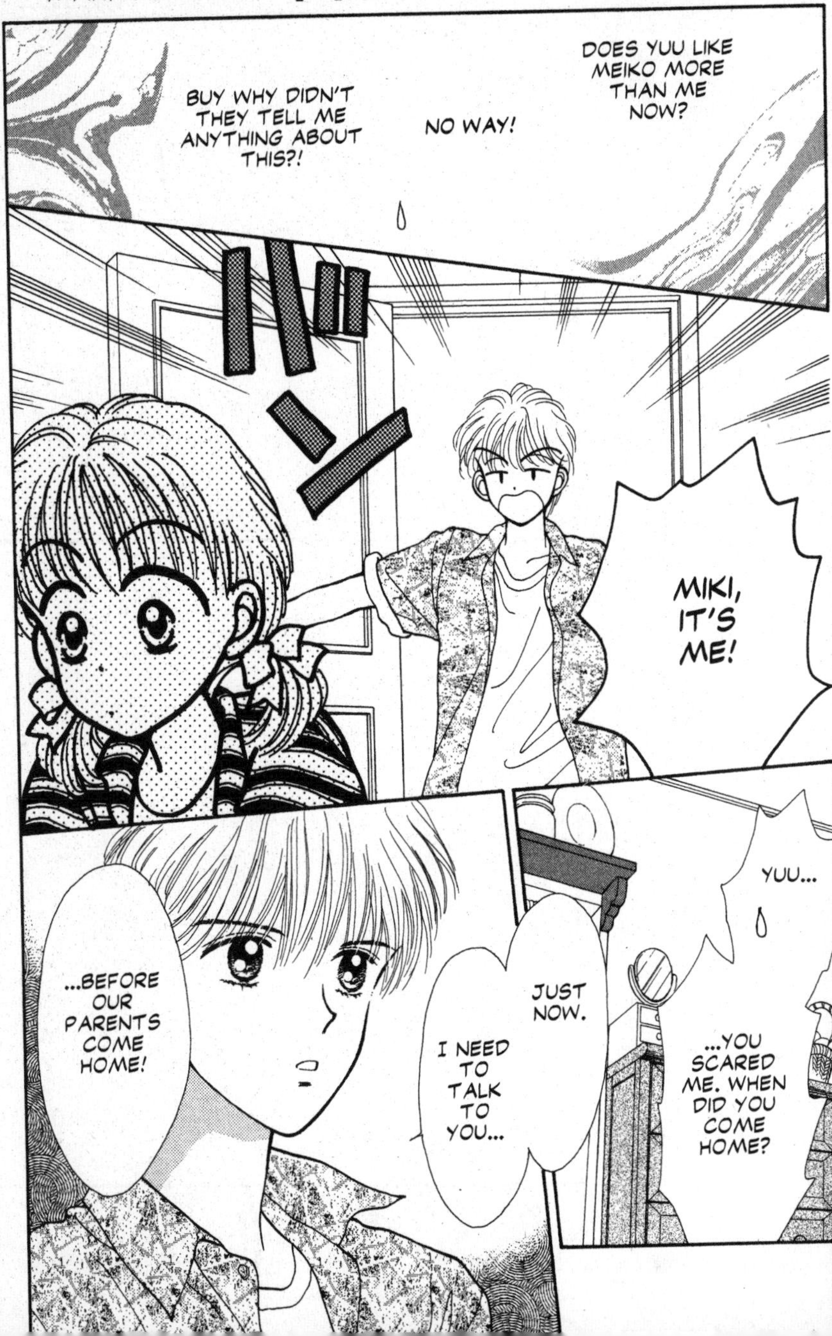
DOES YUU LIKE MEIKO MORE THAN ME NOW?
NO WAY!
BUY WHY DIDN'T THEY TELL ME ANYTHING ABOUT THIS?!
バン
MIKI, IT'S ME!
YUU...
...YOU SCARED ME. WHEN DID YOU COME HOME?
JUST NOW.
I NEED TO TALK TO YOU...
...BEFORE OUR PARENTS COME HOME!

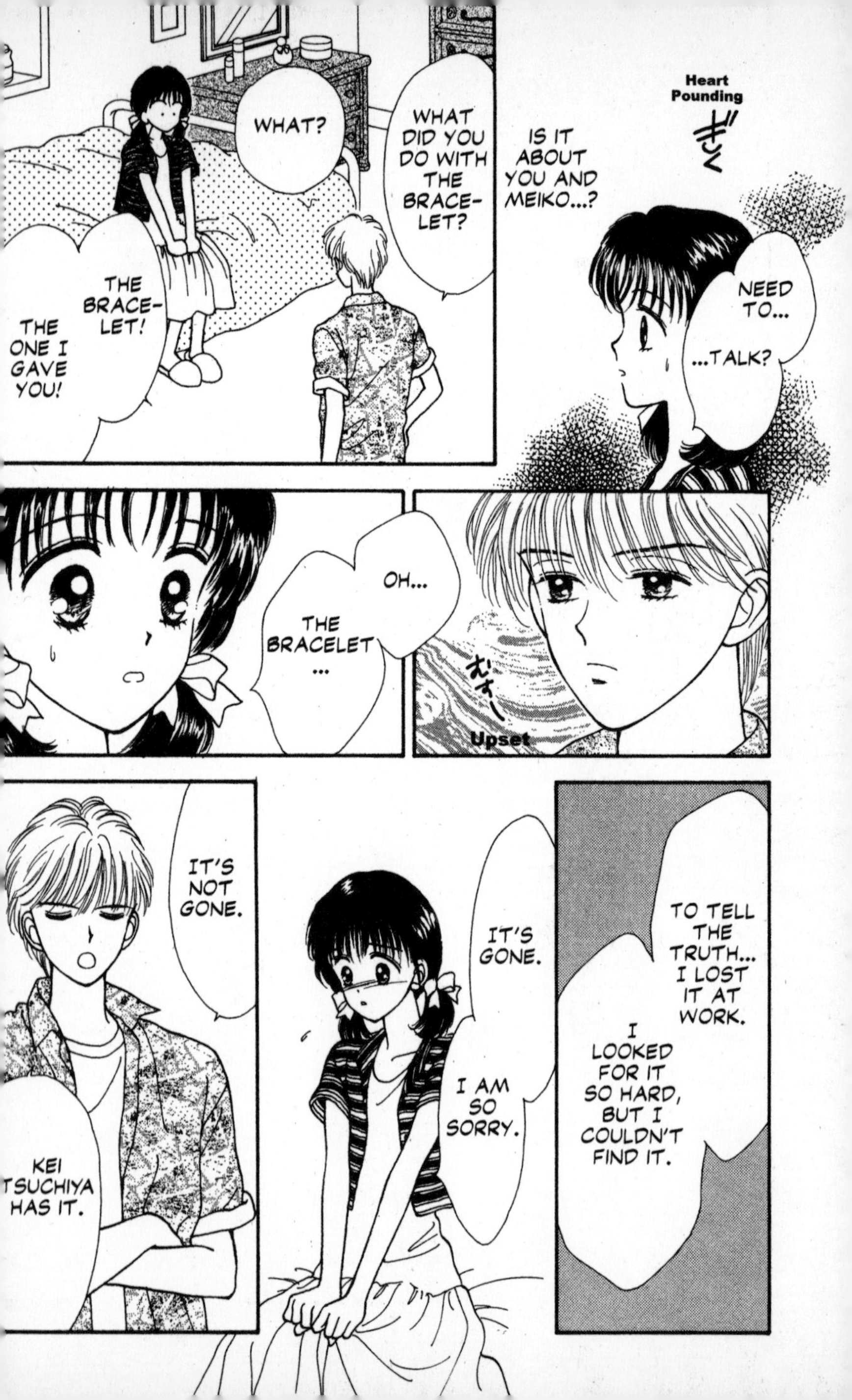
Heart Pounding
NEED TO... ...TALK?
IS IT ABOUT YOU AND MEIKO...?
WHAT DID YOU DO WITH THE BRACELET?
WHAT?
THE BRACELET!
THE ONE I GAVE YOU!
Upset
OH... THE BRACELET...
TO TELL THE TRUTH... I LOST IT AT WORK.
I LOOKED FOR IT SO HARD, BUT I COULDN'T FIND IT.
IT'S GONE.
I AM SO SORRY.
IT'S NOT GONE.
KEI TSUCHIYA HAS IT.

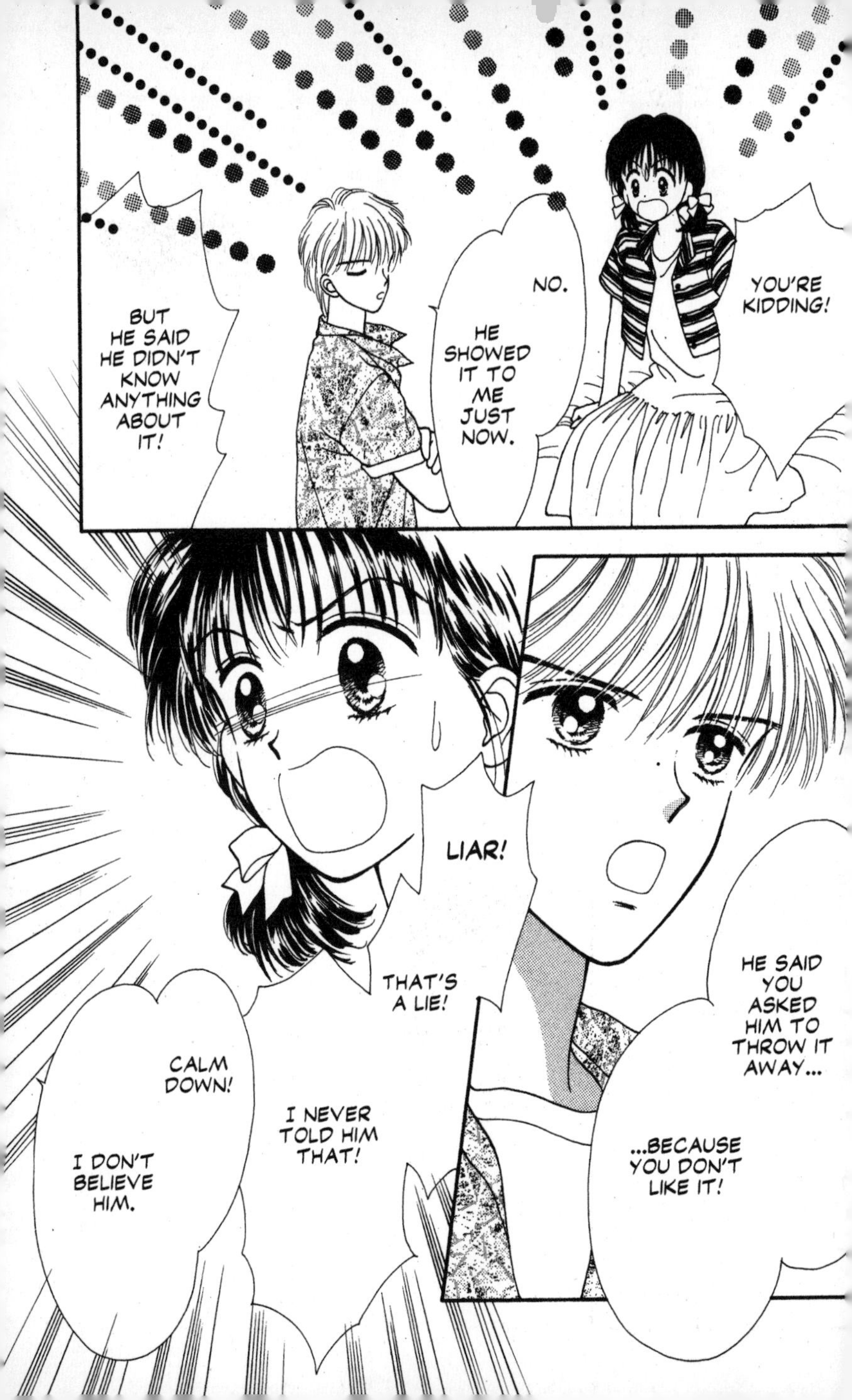
YOU'RE KIDDING!
NO.
HE SHOWED IT TO ME JUST NOW.
BUT HE SAID HE DIDN'T KNOW ANYTHING ABOUT IT!
HE SAID YOU ASKED HIM TO THROW IT AWAY...
...BECAUSE YOU DON'T LIKE IT!
LIAR!
THAT'S A LIE!
I NEVER TOLD HIM THAT!
CALM DOWN!
I DON'T BELIEVE HIM.

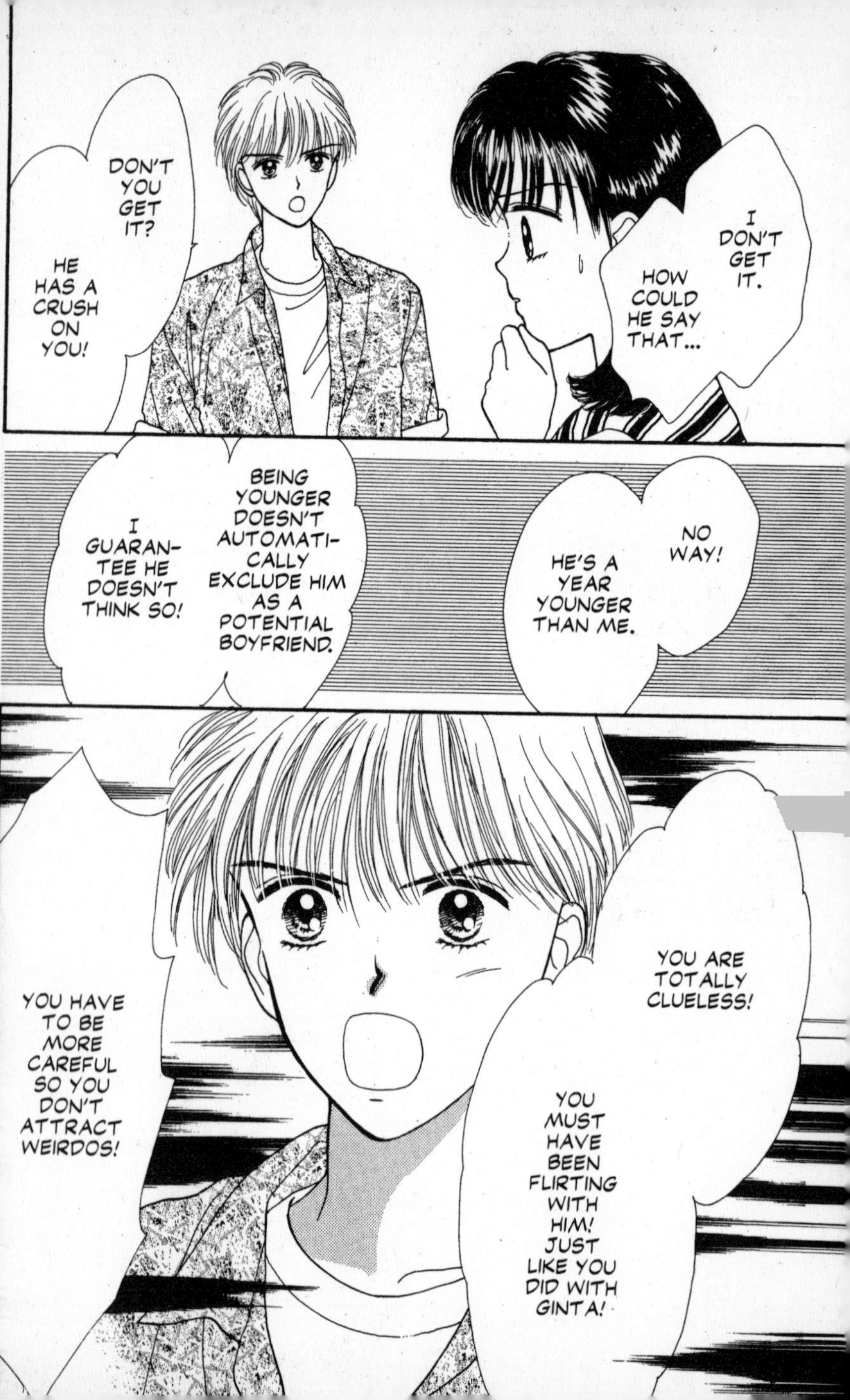
I DON'T GET IT.
HOW COULD HE SAY THAT...
DON'T YOU GET IT?
HE HAS A CRUSH ON YOU!
NO WAY!
HE'S A YEAR YOUNGER THAN ME.
BEING YOUNGER DOESN'T AUTOMATICALLY EXCLUDE HIM AS A POTENTIAL BOYFRIEND.
I GUARANTEE HE DOESN'T THINK SO!
YOU ARE TOTALLY CLUELESS!
YOU MUST HAVE BEEN FLIRTING WITH HIM! JUST LIKE YOU DID WITH GINTA!
YOU HAVE TO BE MORE CAREFUL SO YOU DON'T ATTRACT WEIRDOS!

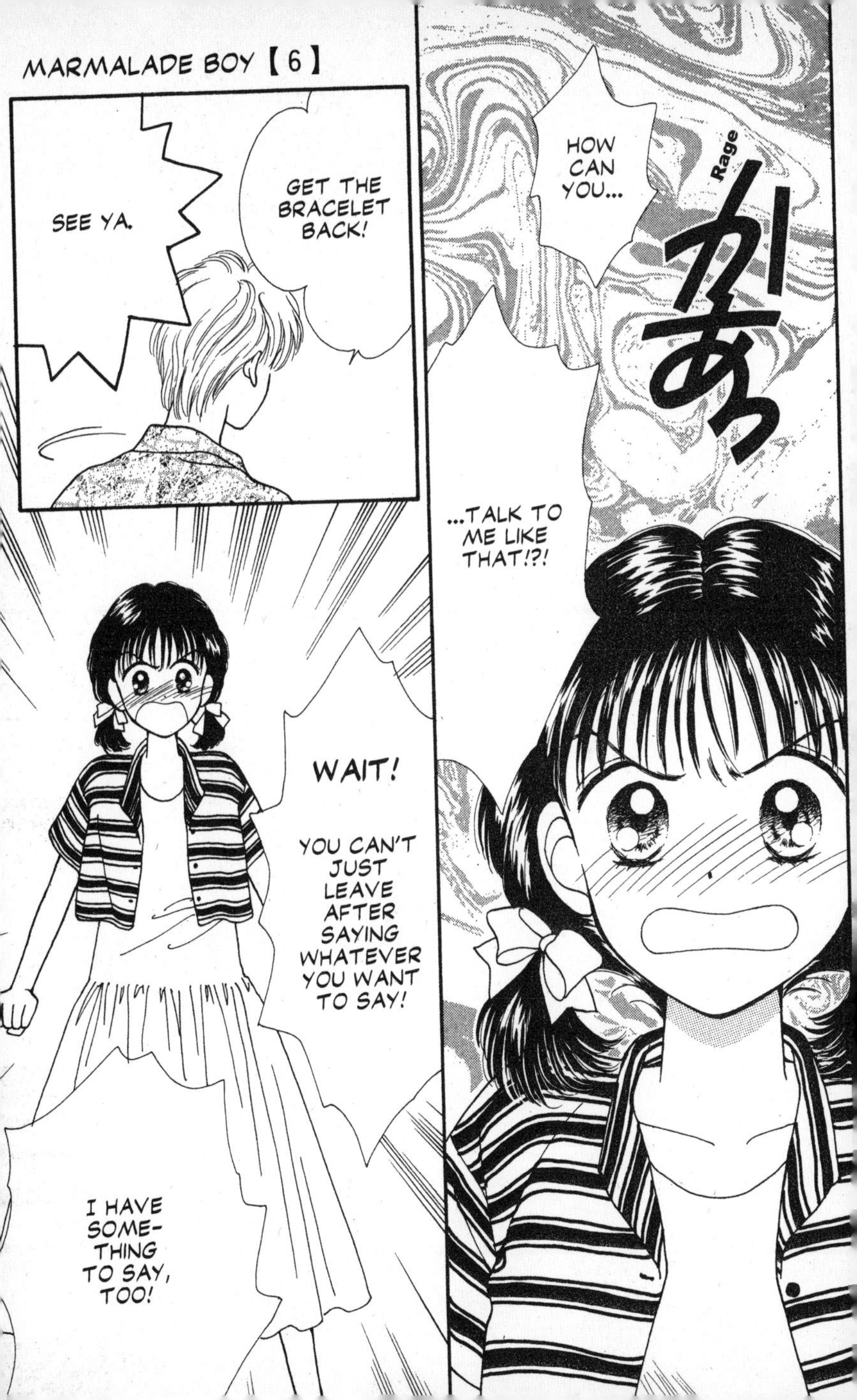
SEE YA.
GET THE BRACELET BACK!
WAIT!
YOU CAN'T JUST LEAVE AFTER SAYING WHATEVER YOU WANT TO SAY!
I HAVE SOME-THING TO SAY, TOO!
HOW CAN YOU...
Rage
かあっ
...TALK TO ME LIKE THAT!?!

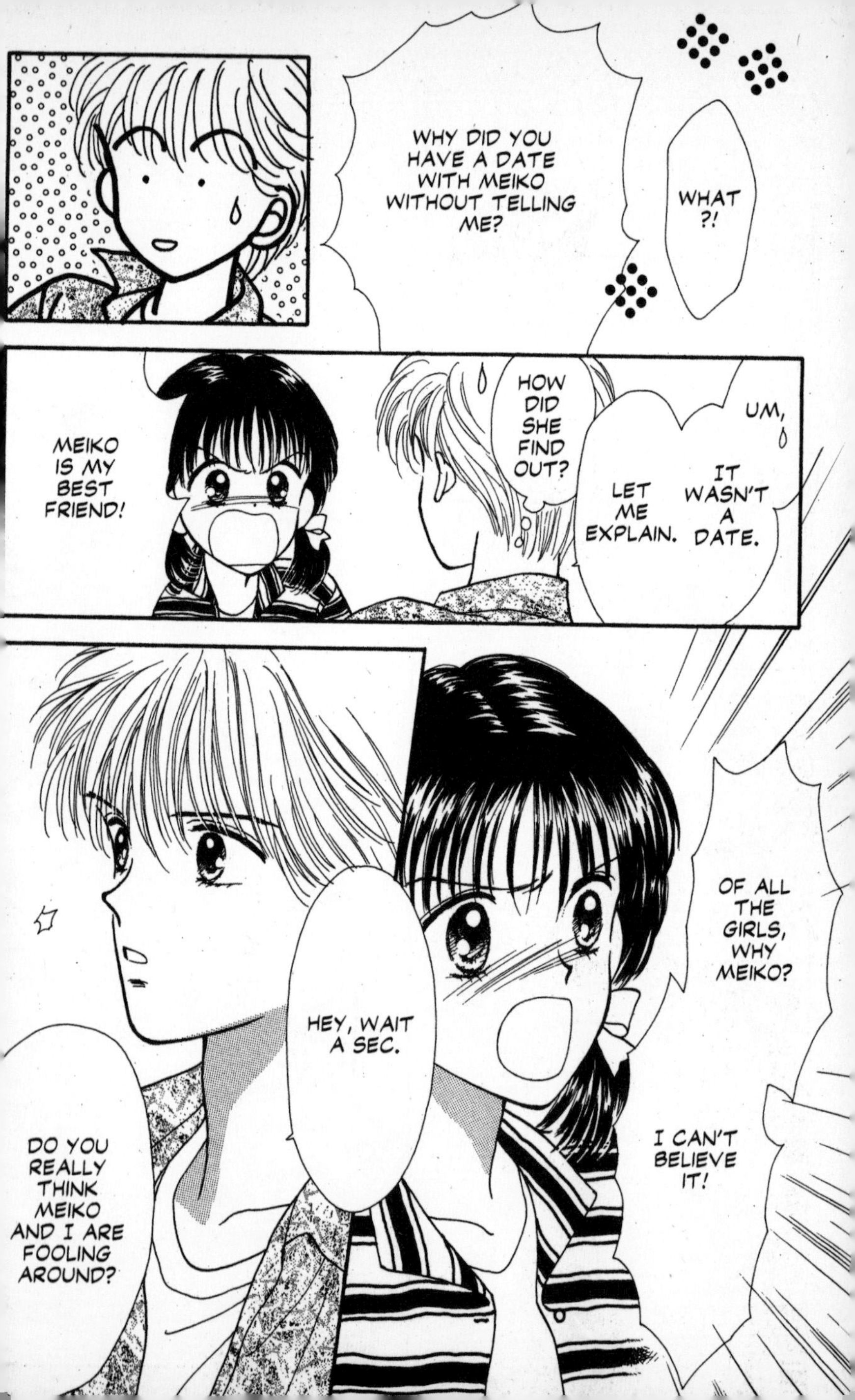
WHAT?!
WHY DID YOU HAVE A DATE WITH MEIKO WITHOUT TELLING ME?
HOW DID SHE FIND OUT?
UM, IT WASN'T A DATE.
LET ME EXPLAIN.
MEIKO IS MY BEST FRIEND!
OF ALL THE GIRLS, WHY MEIKO?
I CAN'T BELIEVE IT!
HEY, WAIT A SEC.
DO YOU REALLY THINK MEIKO AND I ARE FOOLING AROUND?

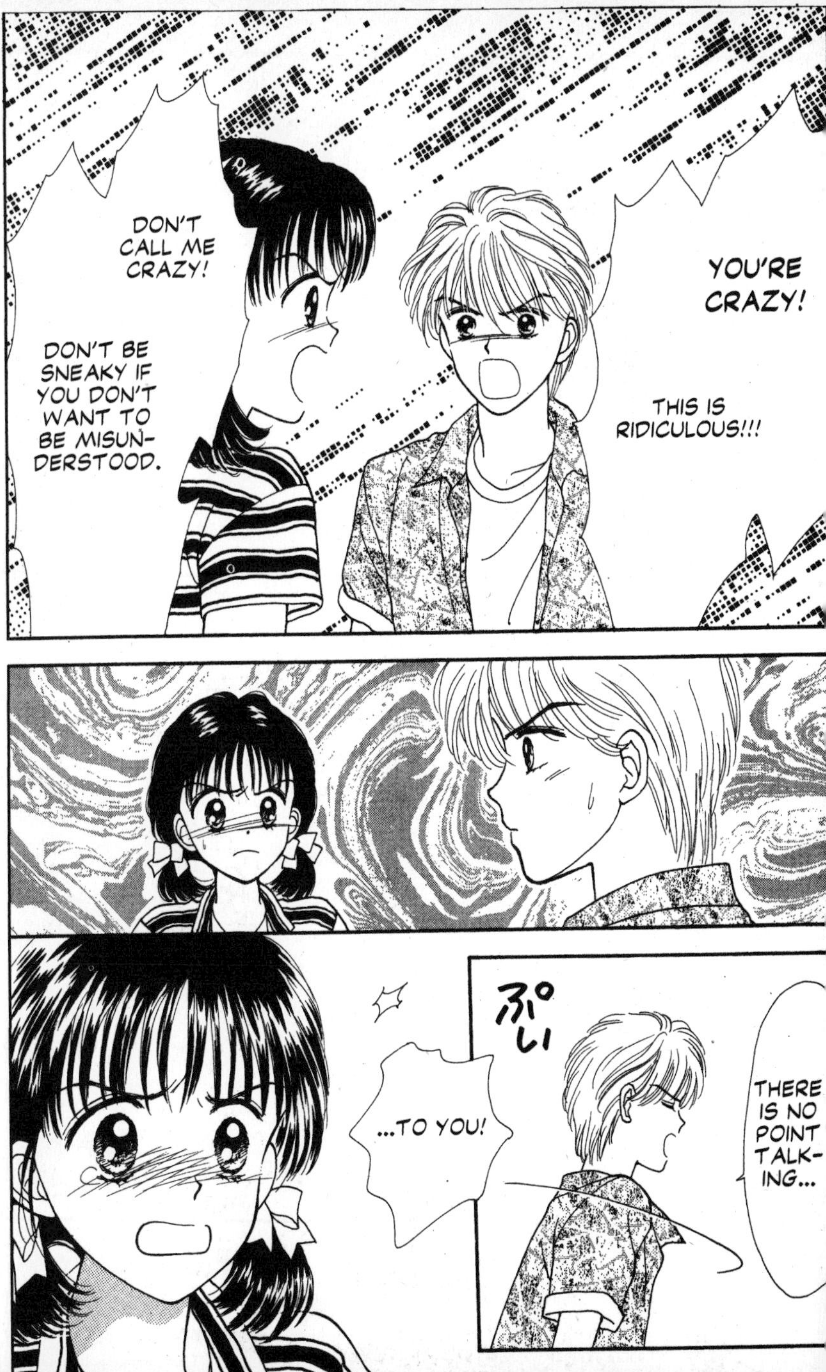
YOU'RE CRAZY!
THIS IS RIDICULOUS!!!
DON'T CALL ME CRAZY!
DON'T BE SNEAKY IF YOU DON'T WANT TO BE MISUNDERSTOOD.
ぷい
THERE IS NO POINT TALKING...
...TO YOU!

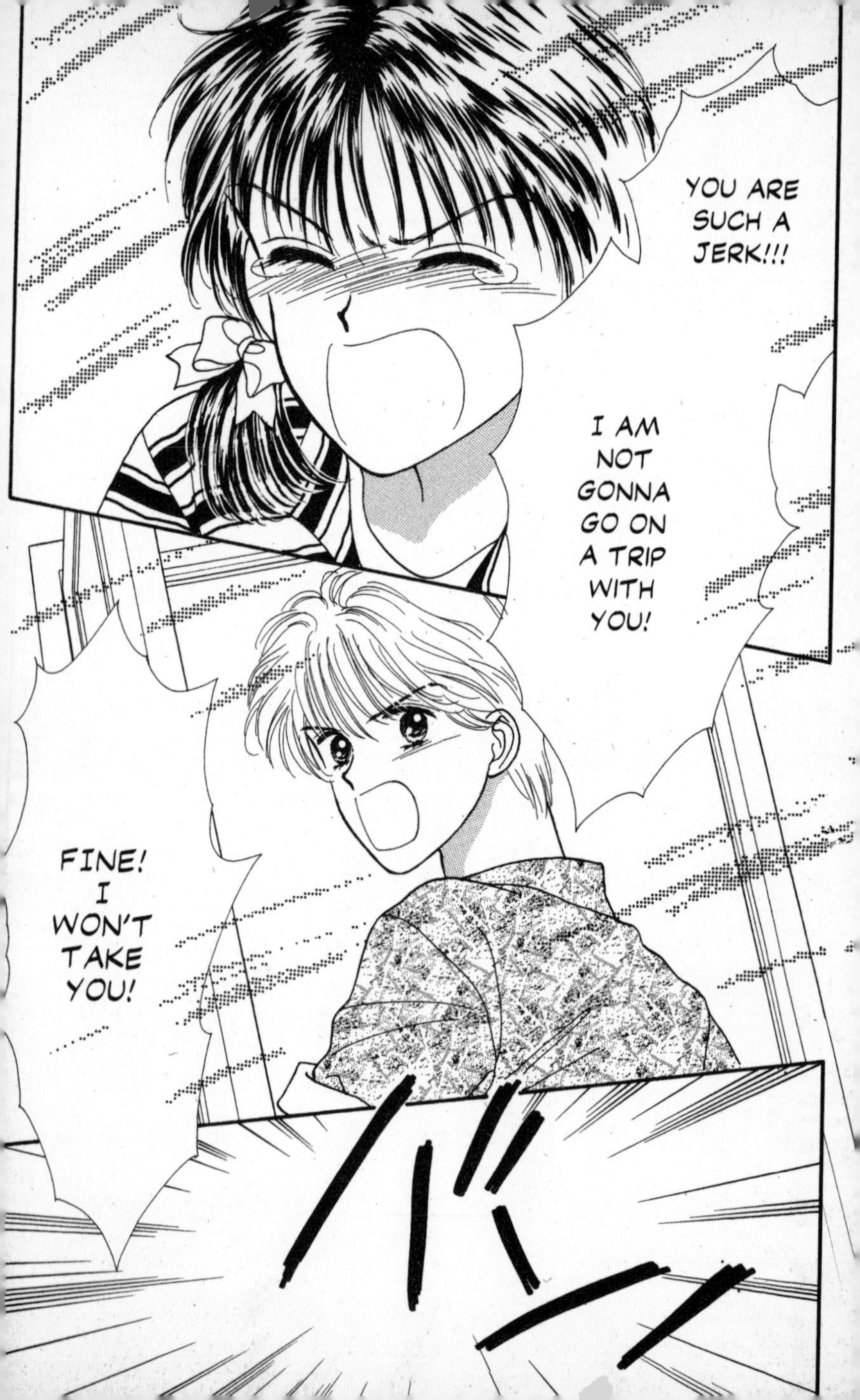
YOU ARE SUCH A JERK!!!
I AM NOT GONNA GO ON A TRIP WITH YOU!
FINE! I WON'T TAKE YOU!

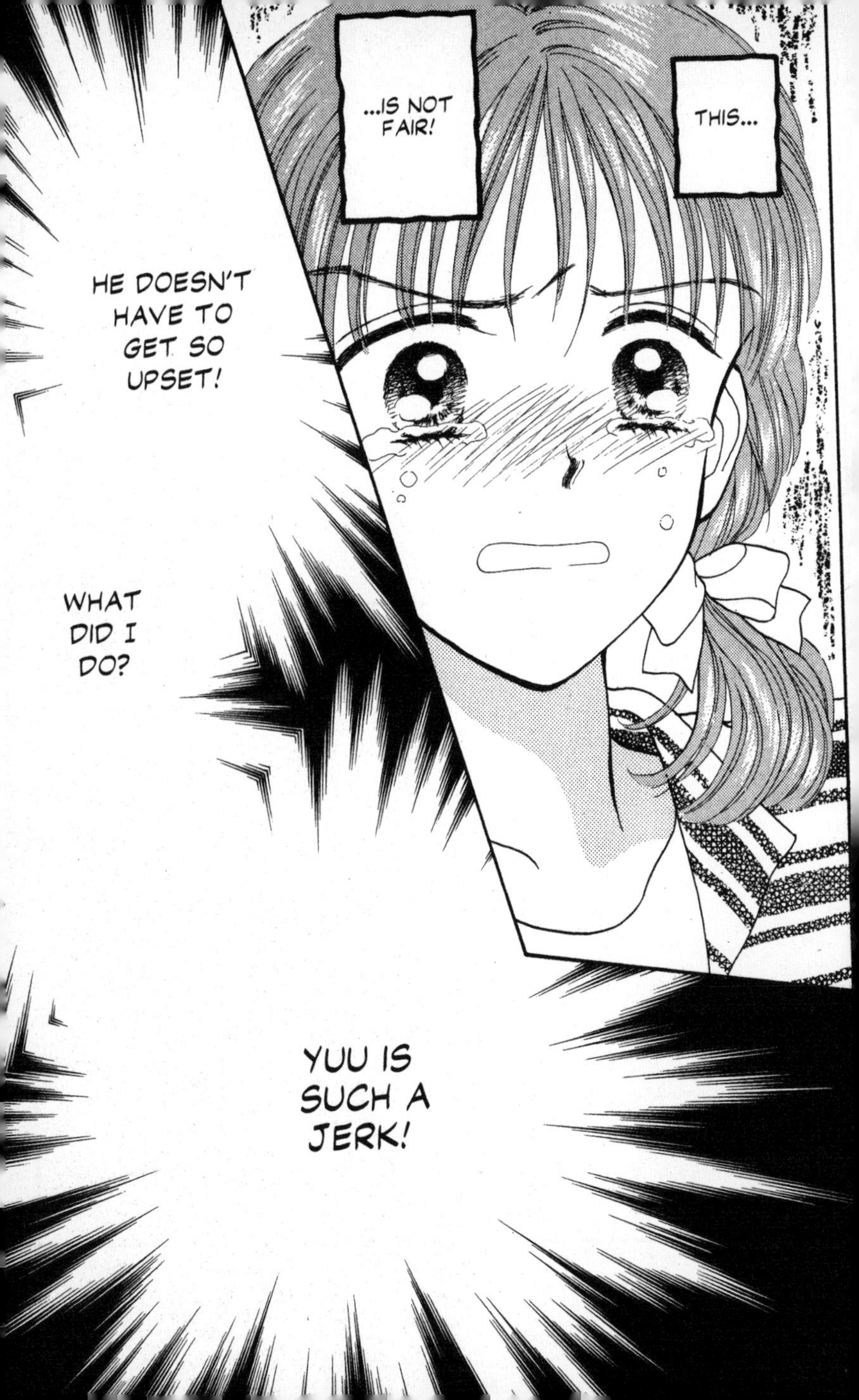
THIS...
...IS NOT FAIR!
HE DOESN'T HAVE TO GET SO UPSET!
WHAT DID I DO?
YUU IS SUCH A JERK!

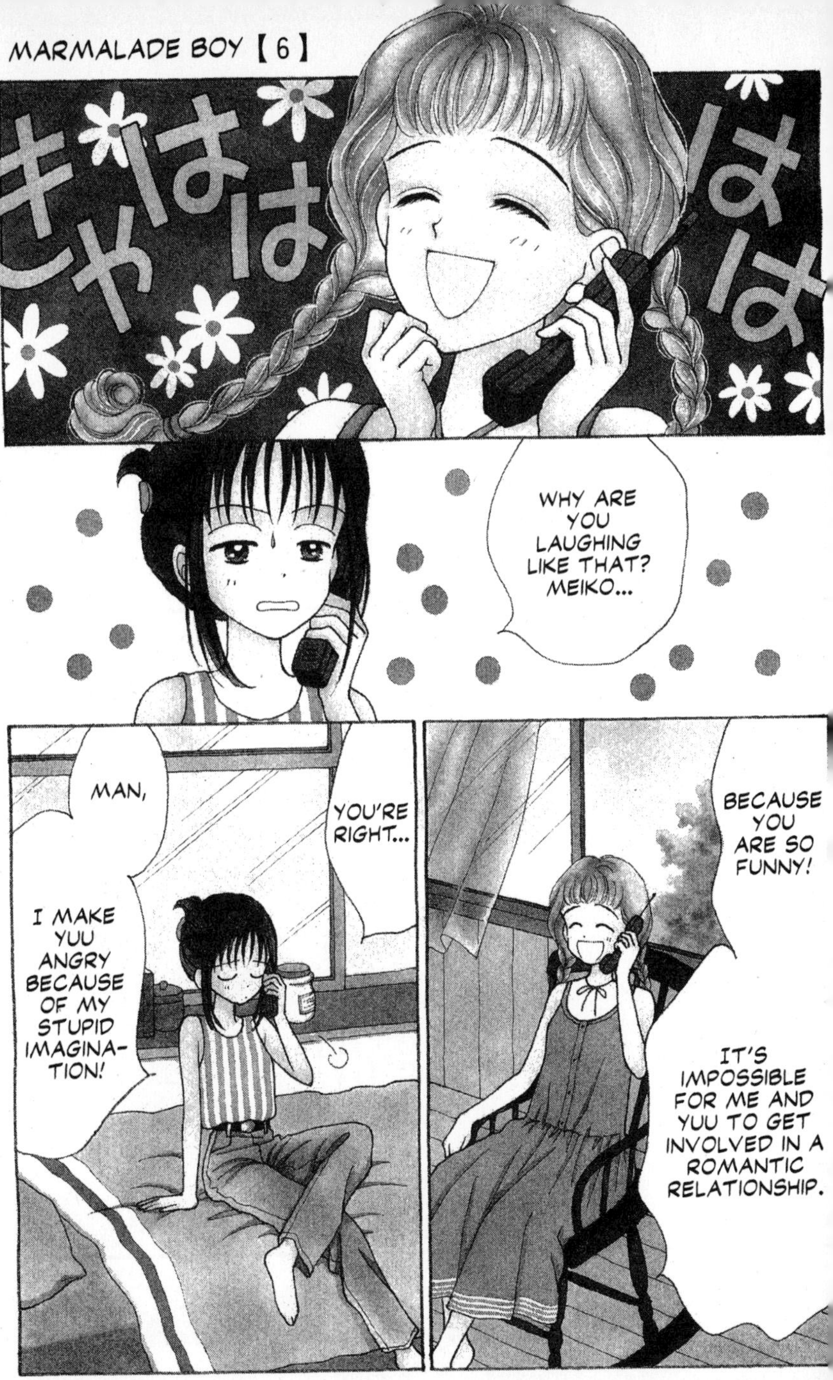
きゃはははは
WHY ARE YOU LAUGHING LIKE THAT? MEIKO...
BECAUSE YOU ARE SO FUNNY!
IT'S IMPOSSIBLE FOR ME AND YUU TO GET INVOLVED IN A ROMANTIC RELATIONSHIP.
YOU'RE RIGHT...
MAN, I MAKE YUU ANGRY BECAUSE OF MY STUPID IMAGINA-TION!

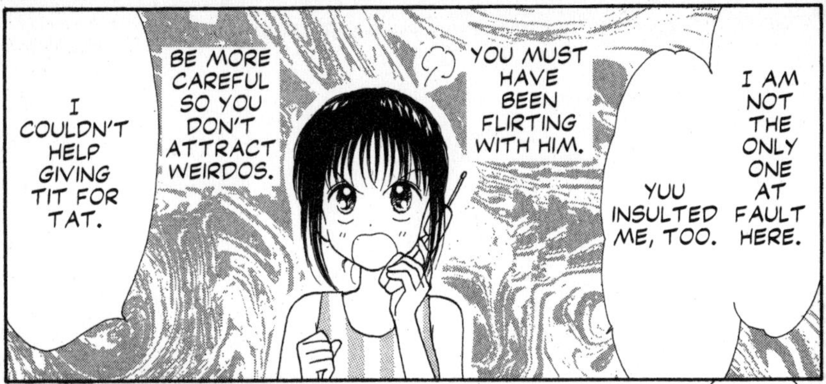
I AM NOT THE ONLY ONE AT FAULT HERE.
YUU INSULTED ME, TOO.
YOU MUST HAVE BEEN FLIRTING WITH HIM.
BE MORE CAREFUL SO YOU DON'T ATTRACT WEIRDOS.
I COULDN'T HELP GIVING TIT FOR TAT.

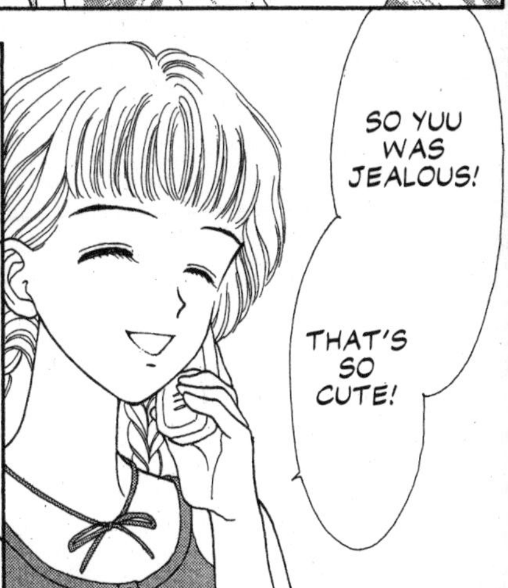
SO YUU WAS JEALOUS!
THAT'S SO CUTE!

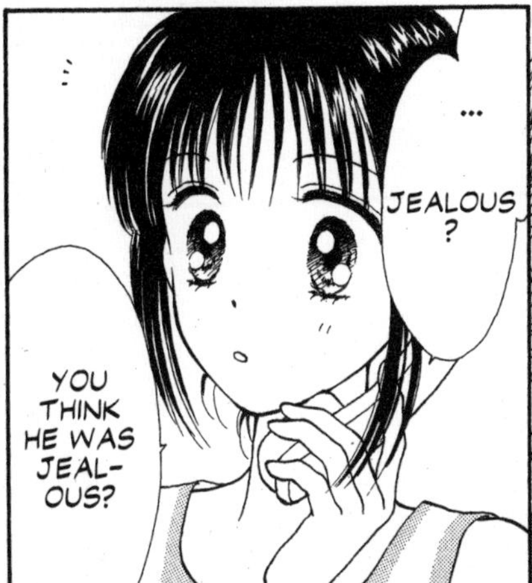
...
JEALOUS?
YOU THINK HE WAS JEALOUS?

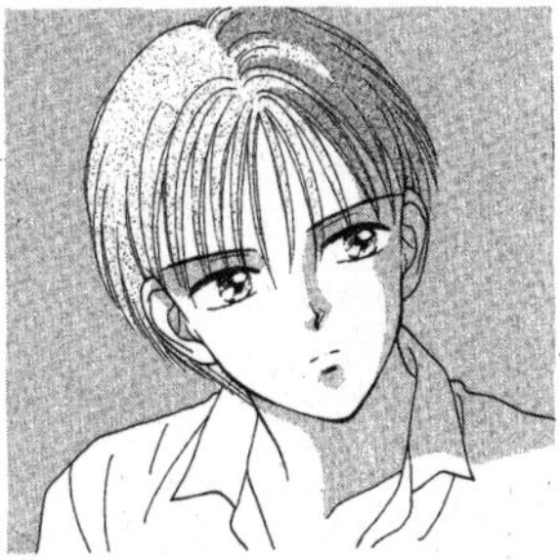

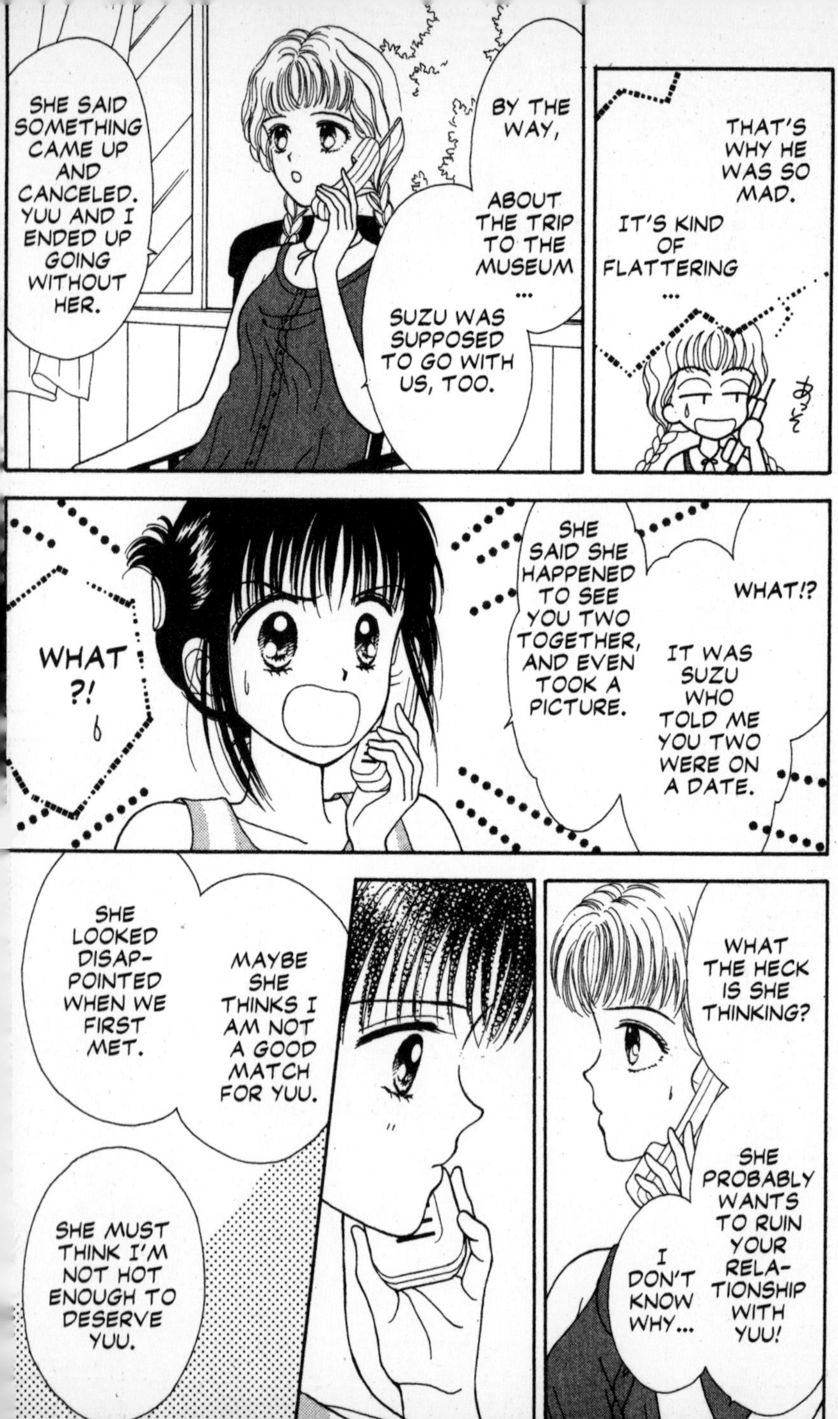
THAT'S WHY HE WAS SO MAD.
IT'S KIND OF FLATTERING ...
BY THE WAY,
ABOUT THE TRIP TO THE MUSEUM ...
SUZU WAS SUPPOSED TO GO WITH US, TOO.
SHE SAID SOMETHING CAME UP AND CANCELED. YUU AND I ENDED UP GOING WITHOUT HER.
WHAT!?
IT WAS SUZU WHO TOLD ME YOU TWO WERE ON A DATE.
SHE SAID SHE HAPPENED TO SEE YOU TWO TOGETHER, AND EVEN TOOK A PICTURE.
WHAT ?!
WHAT THE HECK IS SHE THINKING?
SHE PROBABLY WANTS TO RUIN YOUR RELATIONSHIP WITH YUU!
I DON'T KNOW WHY...
MAYBE SHE THINKS I AM NOT A GOOD MATCH FOR YUU.
SHE LOOKED DISAPPOINTED WHEN WE FIRST MET.
SHE MUST THINK I'M NOT HOT ENOUGH TO DESERVE YUU.

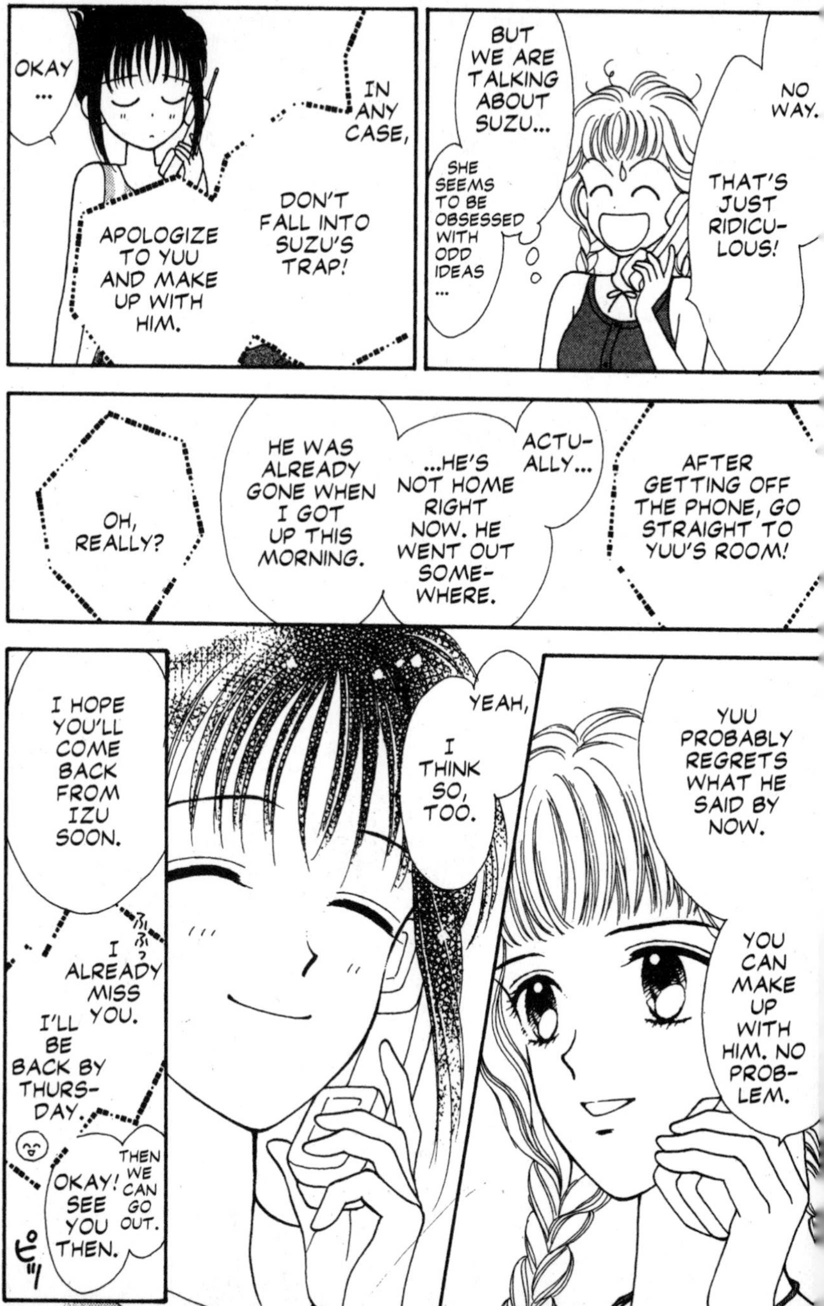
NO WAY.
THAT'S JUST RIDICULOUS!
BUT WE ARE TALKING ABOUT SUZU...
SHE SEEMS TO BE OBSESSED WITH ODD IDEAS ...
IN ANY CASE,
DON'T FALL INTO SUZU'S TRAP!
APOLOGIZE TO YUU AND MAKE UP WITH HIM.
OKAY ...
AFTER GETTING OFF THE PHONE, GO STRAIGHT TO YUU'S ROOM!
ACTUALLY...
...HE'S NOT HOME RIGHT NOW. HE WENT OUT SOMEWHERE.
HE WAS ALREADY GONE WHEN I GOT UP THIS MORNING.
OH, REALLY?
YUU PROBABLY REGRETS WHAT HE SAID BY NOW.
YOU CAN MAKE UP WITH HIM. NO PROBLEM.
YEAH, I THINK SO, TOO.
I HOPE YOU'LL COME BACK FROM IZU SOON.
I ALREADY MISS YOU.
I'LL BE BACK BY THURSDAY.
THEN WE CAN GO OUT.
OKAY! SEE YOU THEN.

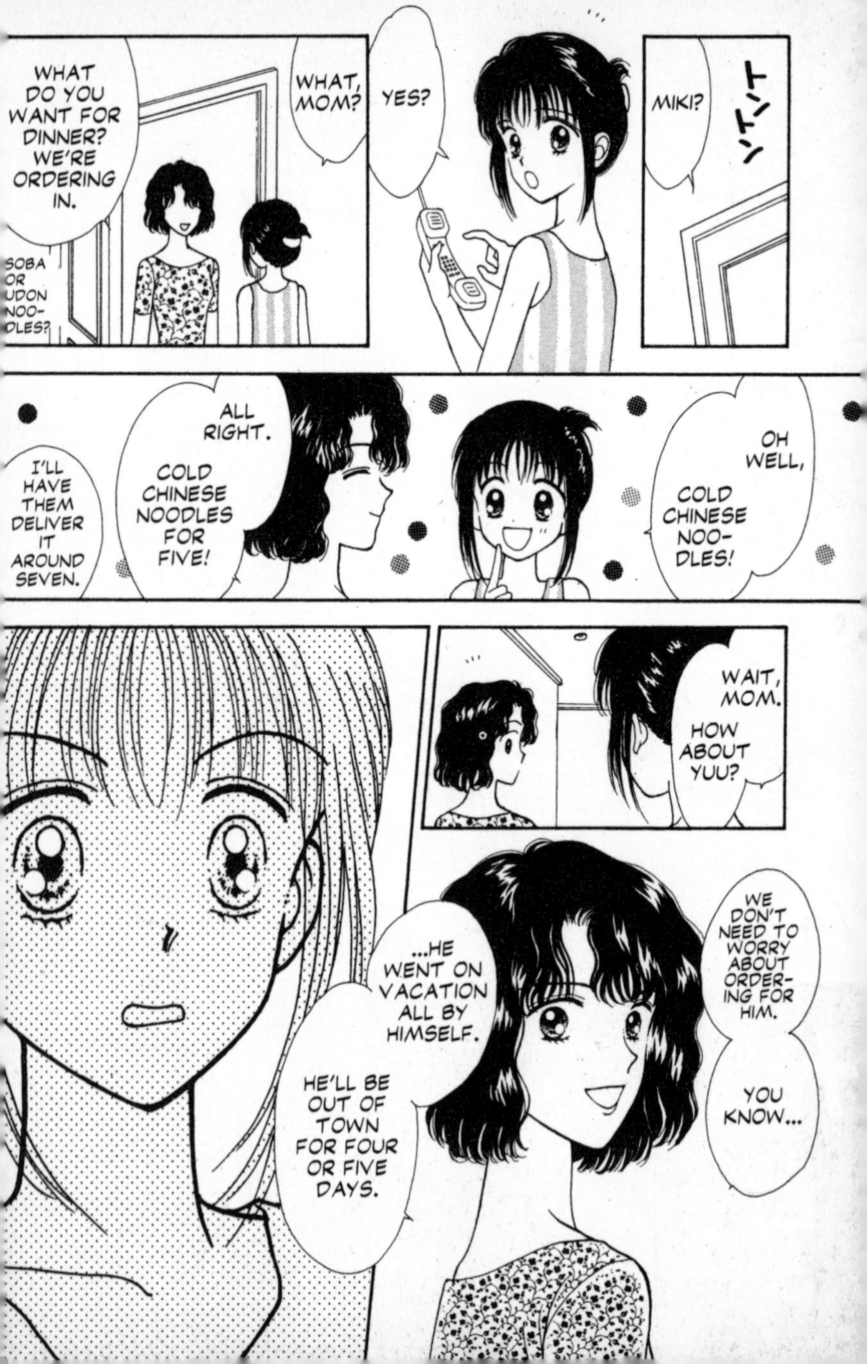
MIKI?
トントン
YES?
WHAT, MOM?
WHAT DO YOU WANT FOR DINNER? WE'RE ORDERING IN.
SOBA OR UDON NOODLES?
OH WELL,
COLD CHINESE NOODLES!
ALL RIGHT.
COLD CHINESE NOODLES FOR FIVE!
I'LL HAVE THEM DELIVER IT AROUND SEVEN.
WAIT, MOM.
HOW ABOUT YUU?
WE DON'T NEED TO WORRY ABOUT ORDERING FOR HIM.
YOU KNOW...
...HE WENT ON VACATION ALL BY HIMSELF.
HE'LL BE OUT OF TOWN FOR FOUR OR FIVE DAYS.

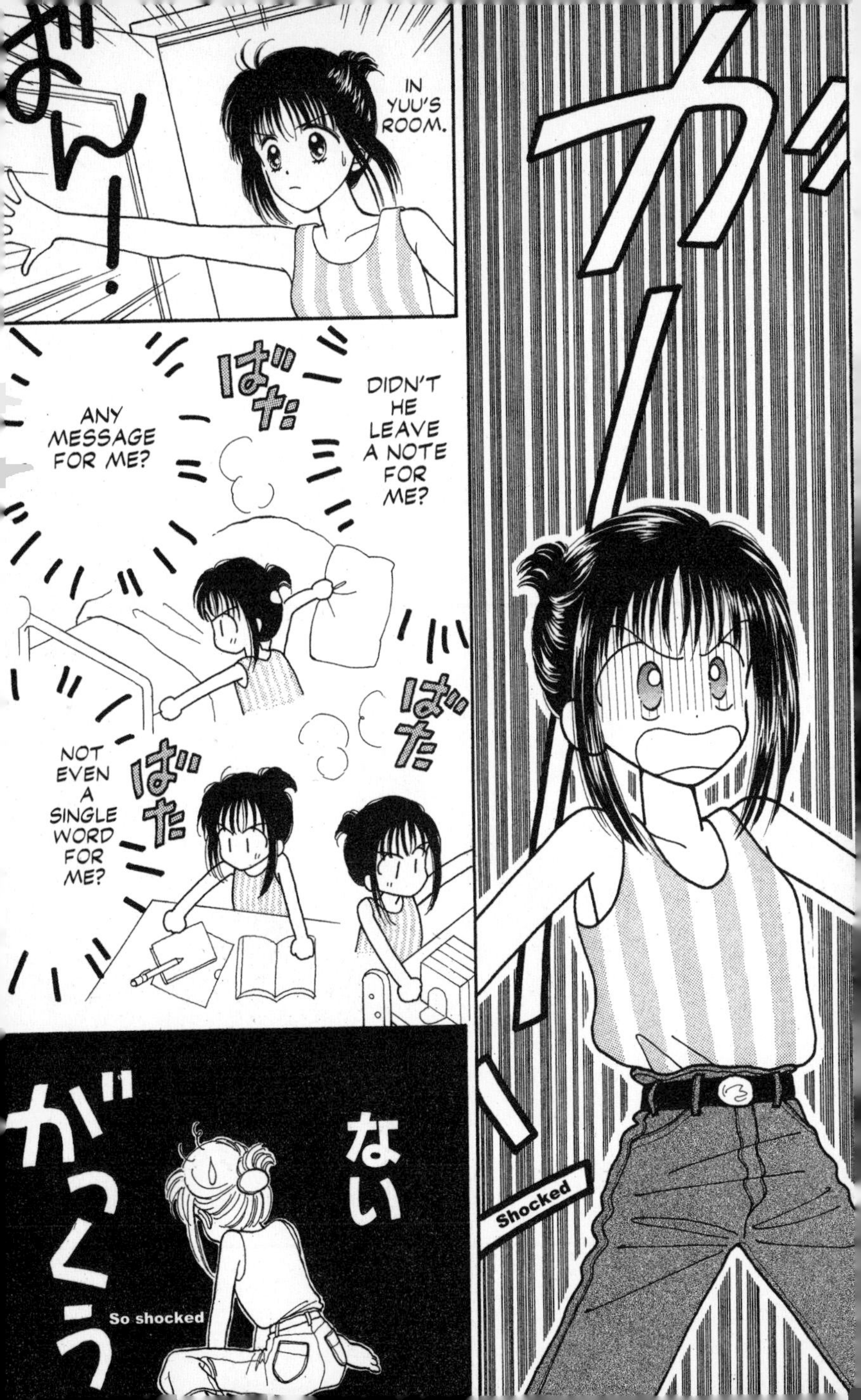
Shocked
IN YUU'S ROOM.
DIDN'T HE LEAVE A NOTE FOR ME?
ANY MESSAGE FOR ME?
ばた
NOT EVEN A SINGLE WORD FOR ME?
ばた
ない
So shocked

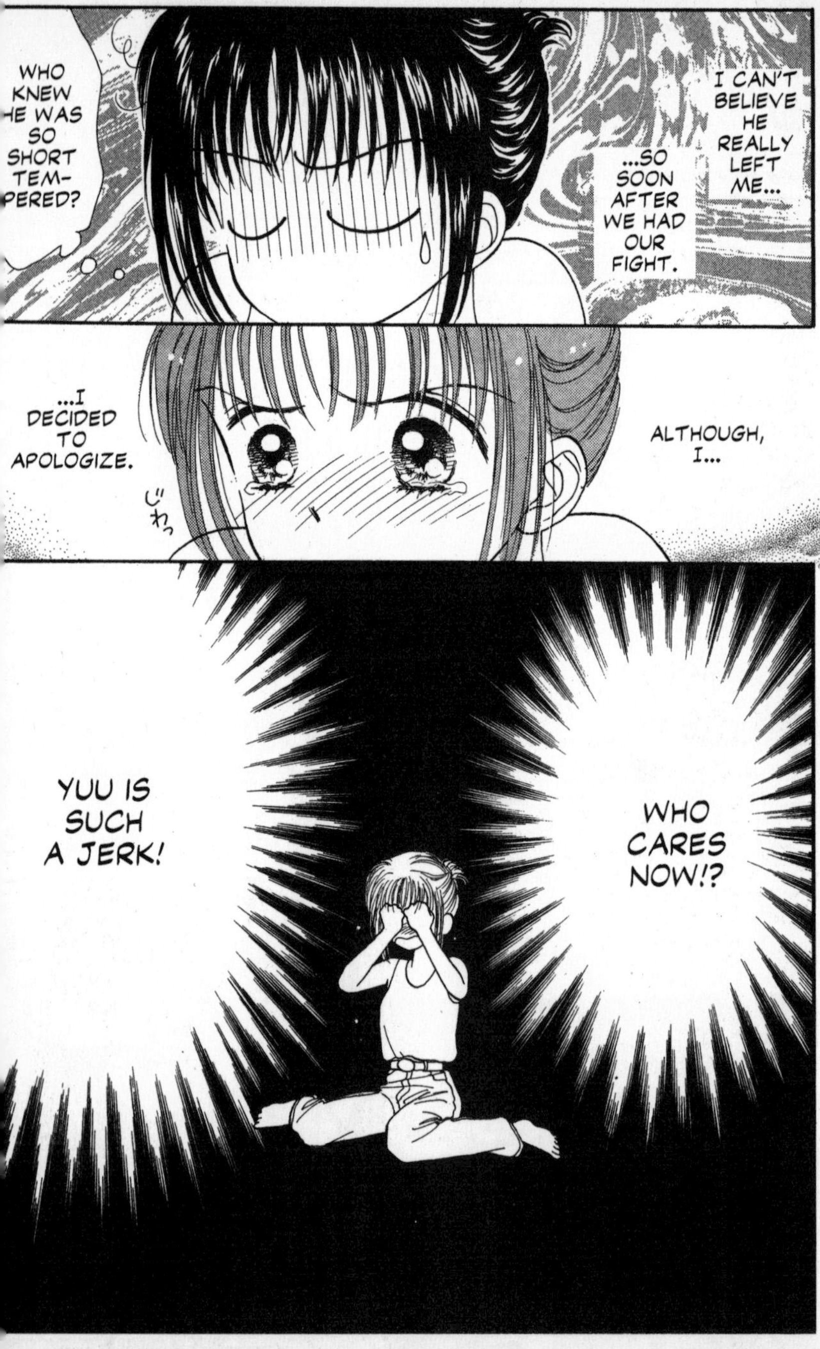
I CAN'T BELIEVE HE REALLY LEFT ME...
...SO SOON AFTER WE HAD OUR FIGHT.
WHO KNEW HE WAS SO SHORT TEM-PERED?
ALTHOUGH, I...
...I DECIDED TO APOLOGIZE.
じわっ
WHO CARES NOW!?
YUU IS SUCH A JERK!

FREE TALK ⑩

I would like to talk more about Marmalade Boy goods that I mentioned in volume 4. New products come out every month, and I enjoy looking at the samples they send me. My favorite are the 3-toushin-sized figures. They come with clothes, hats, and bags for you to change their outfits. I try various outfits for the figures and put them on the shelves. One of the title pages (from Ribon; February, 1995) has photos of those figures.

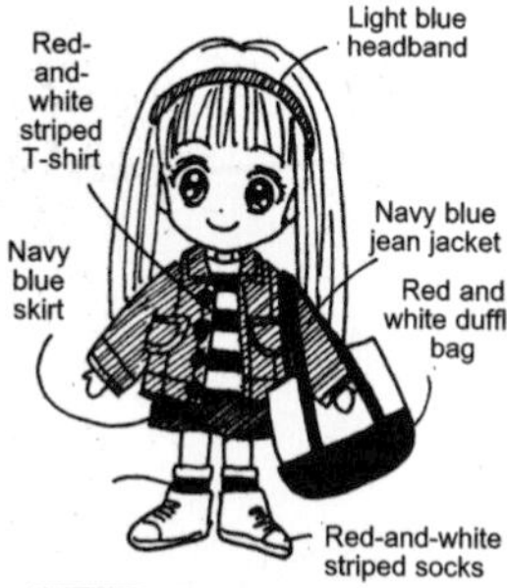
Light blue headband
Red-and-white striped T-shirt
Navy blue jean jacket
Navy blue skirt
Red and white duffle bag
Red-and-white striped socks

My favorite outfit for Suzu

You can choose your own favorite outfits with the tops, jackets, pants, and skirts. It's nothing like simply putting a one-piece dress on the figure—you need to be a good dresser to come up with a nice outfit. I hope many girls who love dressing up will enjoy playing with the clothes. The figures are all less than 10 centimeters tall and they don't take up too much room. I highly recommend them!

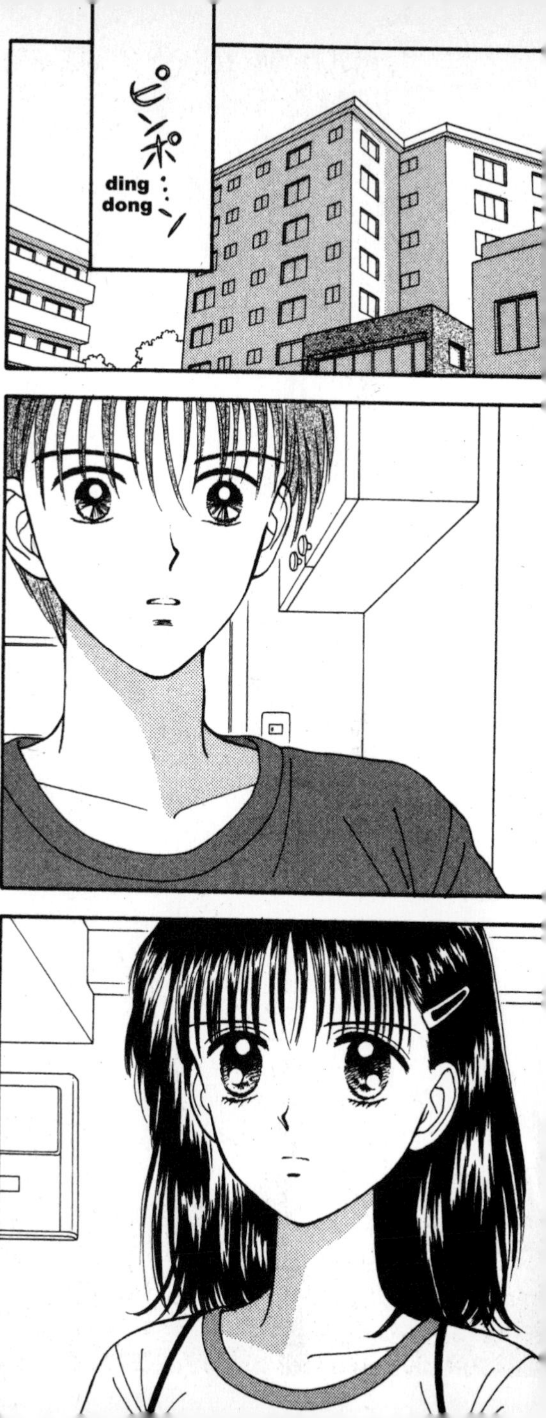
ピンポ…ン
ding dong

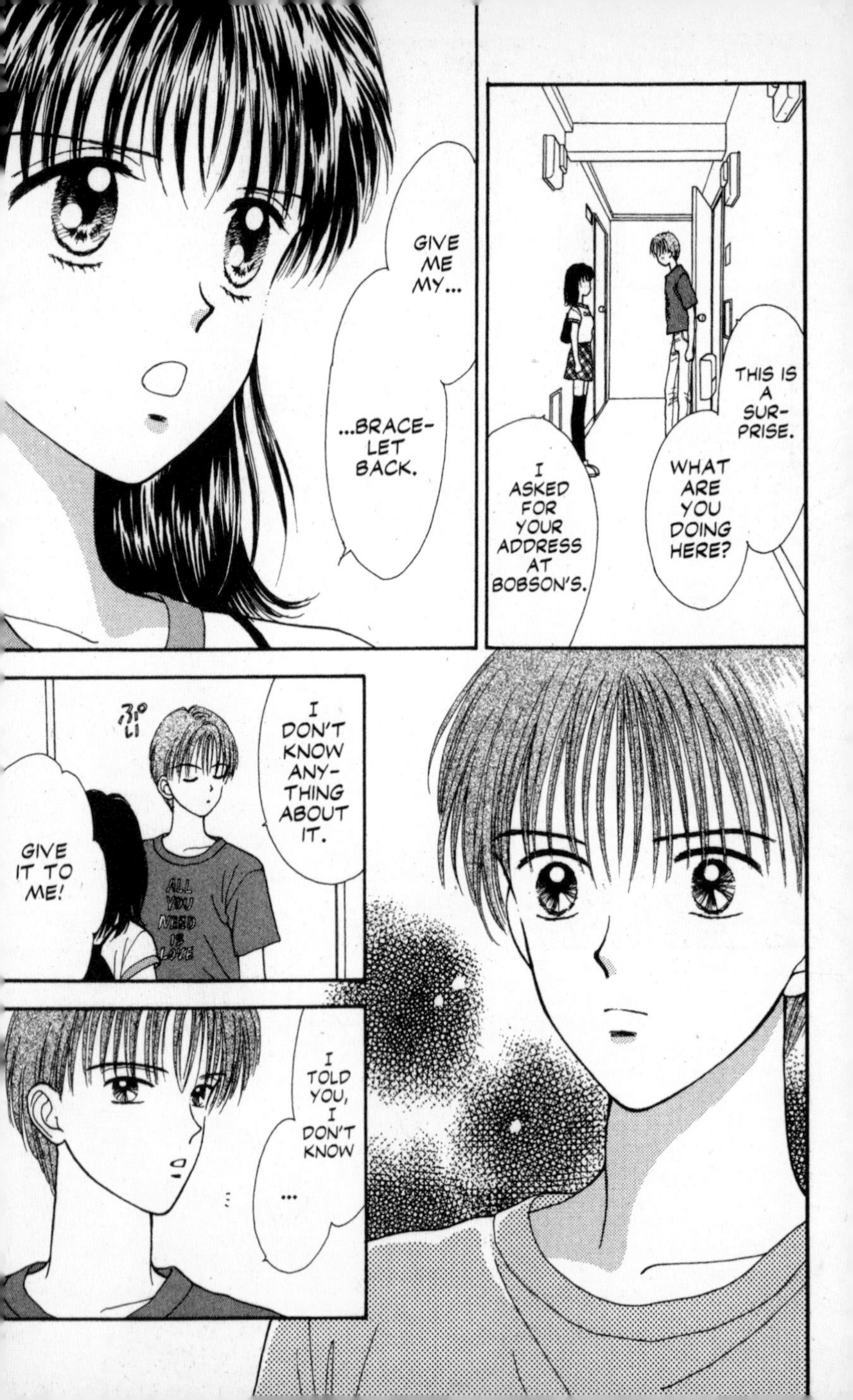
THIS IS A SURPRISE.
WHAT ARE YOU DOING HERE?
I ASKED FOR YOUR ADDRESS AT BOBSON'S.
GIVE ME MY...
...BRACELET BACK.
I DON'T KNOW ANYTHING ABOUT IT.
GIVE IT TO ME!
I TOLD YOU, I DON'T KNOW
...

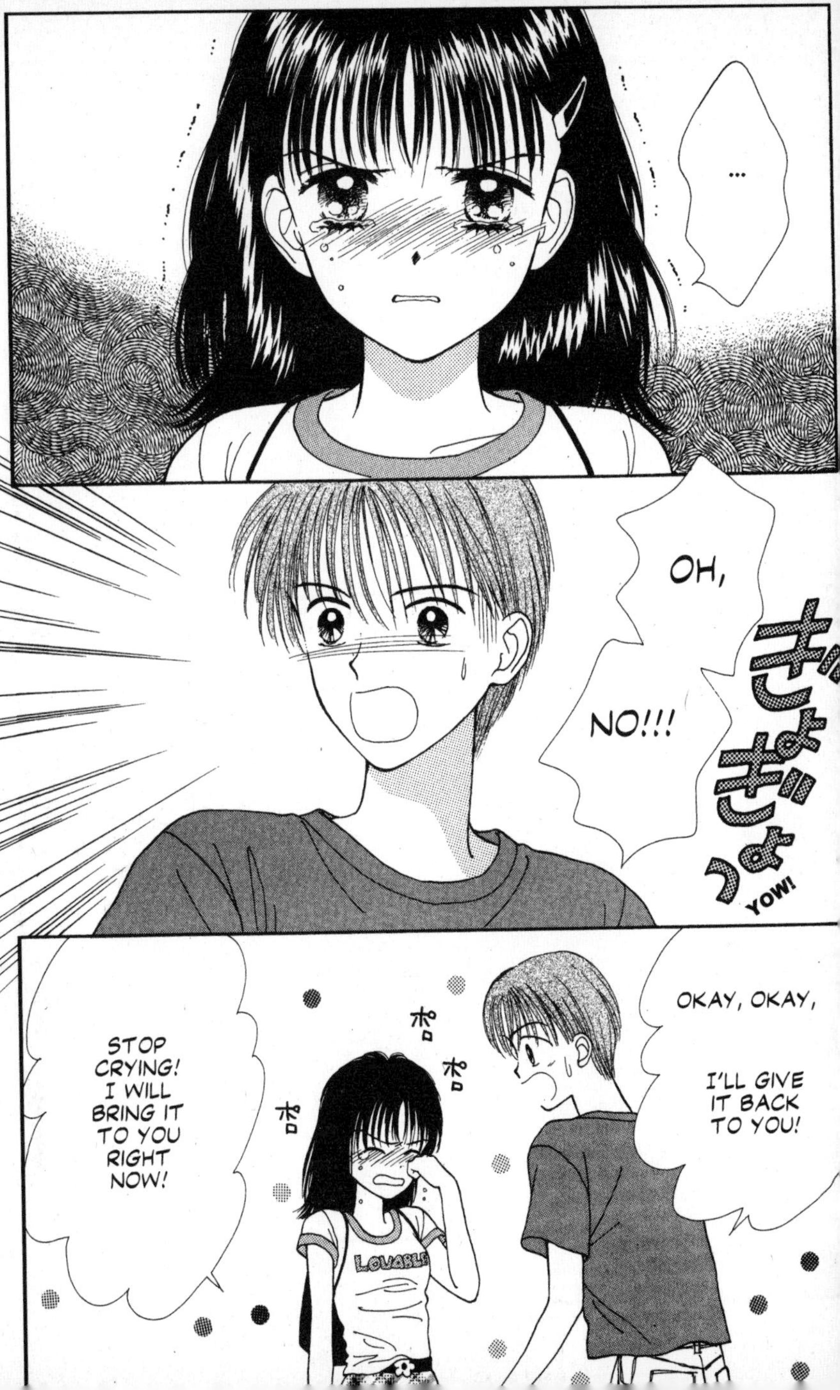
...
OH, NO!!!
ぎょぎょっ
YOW!
OKAY, OKAY, I'LL GIVE IT BACK TO YOU!
ポロ
ポロ
ポロ
STOP CRYING! I WILL BRING IT TO YOU RIGHT NOW!

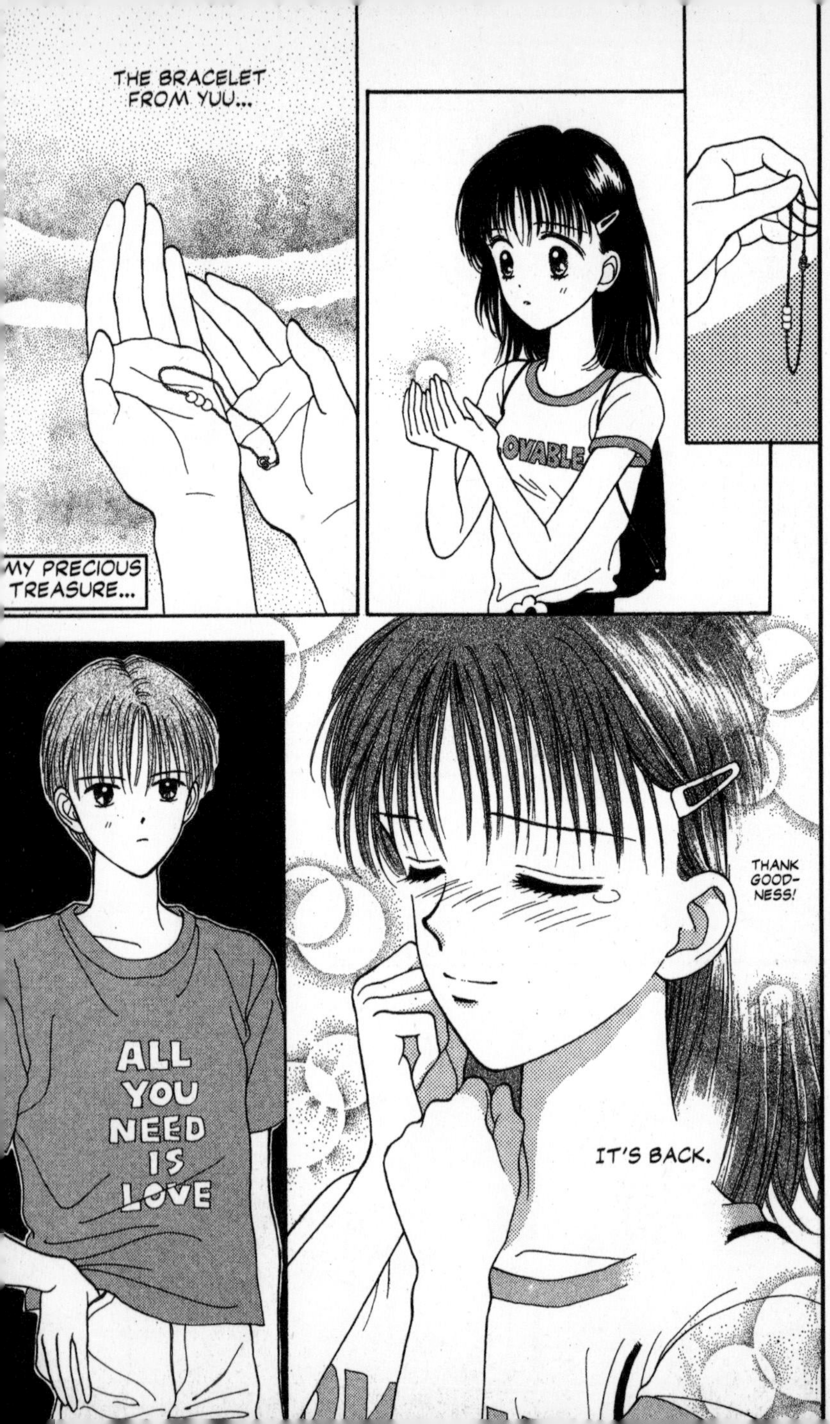
THE BRACELET FROM YUU...
MY PRECIOUS TREASURE...
THANK GOODNESS!
IT'S BACK.
ALL YOU NEED IS LOVE

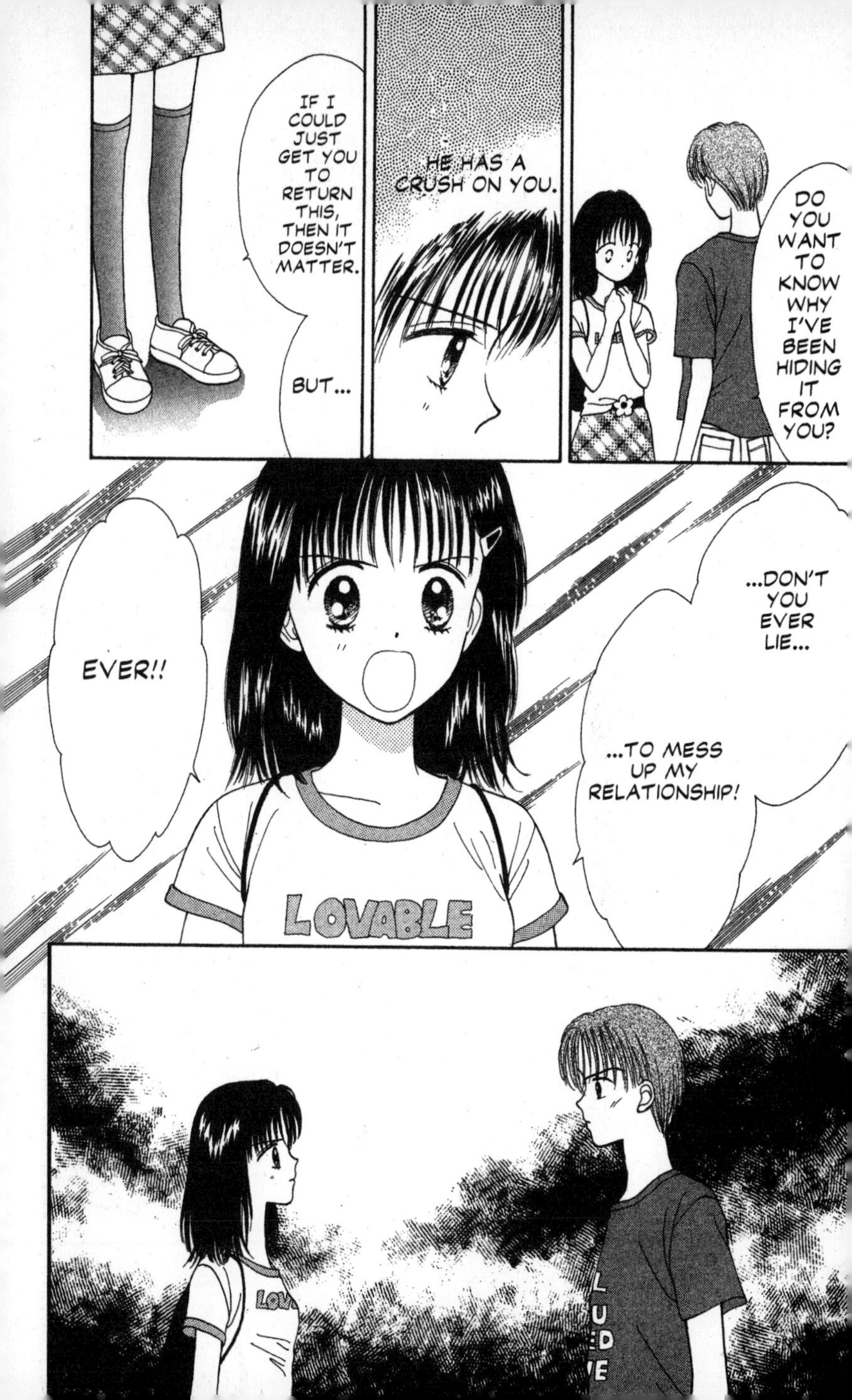
DO YOU WANT TO KNOW WHY I'VE BEEN HIDING IT FROM YOU?
HE HAS A CRUSH ON YOU.
IF I COULD JUST GET YOU TO RETURN THIS, THEN IT DOESN'T MATTER.
BUT...
...DON'T YOU EVER LIE...
...TO MESS UP MY RELATIONSHIP!
EVER!!
LOVABLE

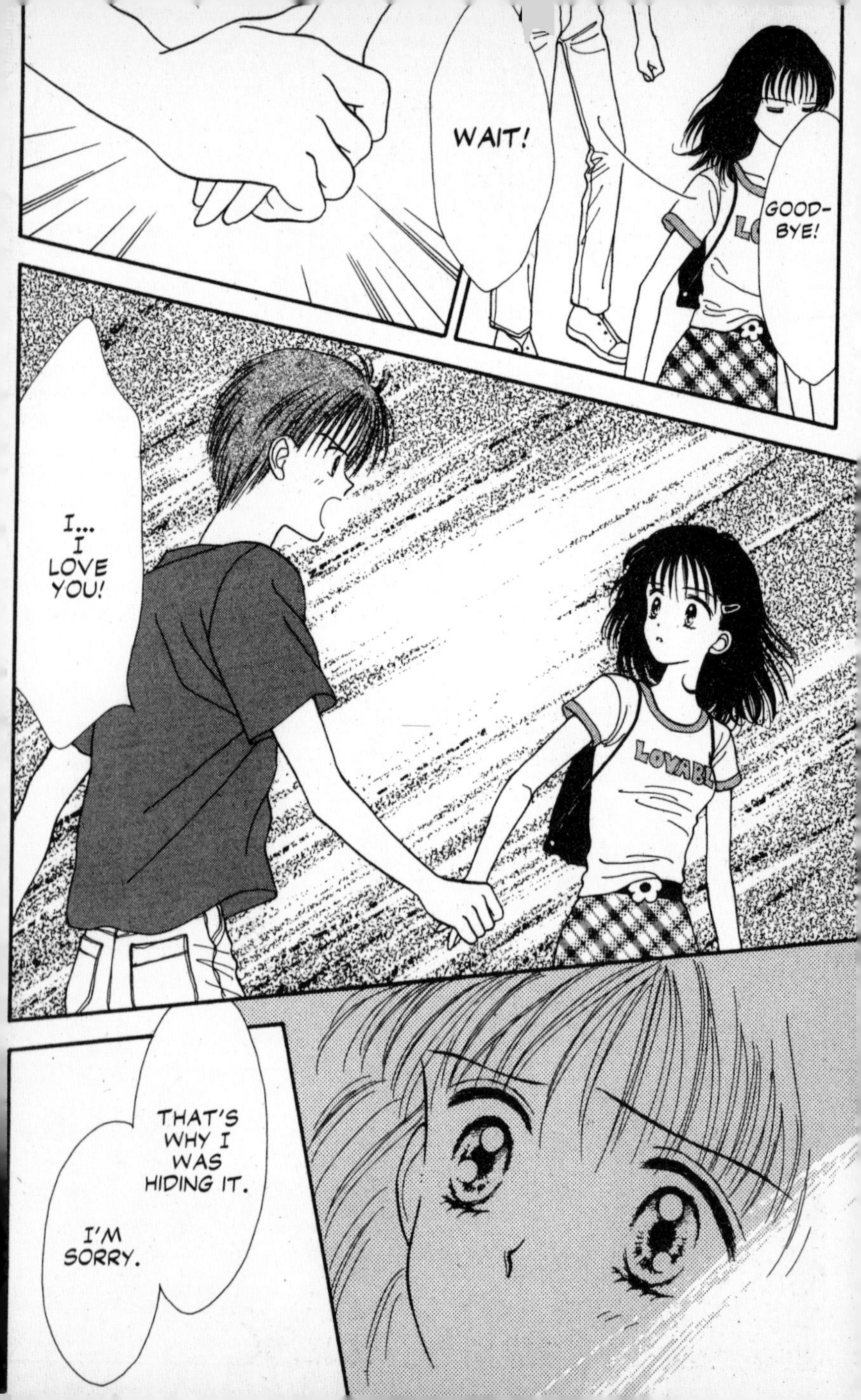
GOOD-BYE!
WAIT!
I... I LOVE YOU!
THAT'S WHY I WAS HIDING IT.
I'M SORRY.

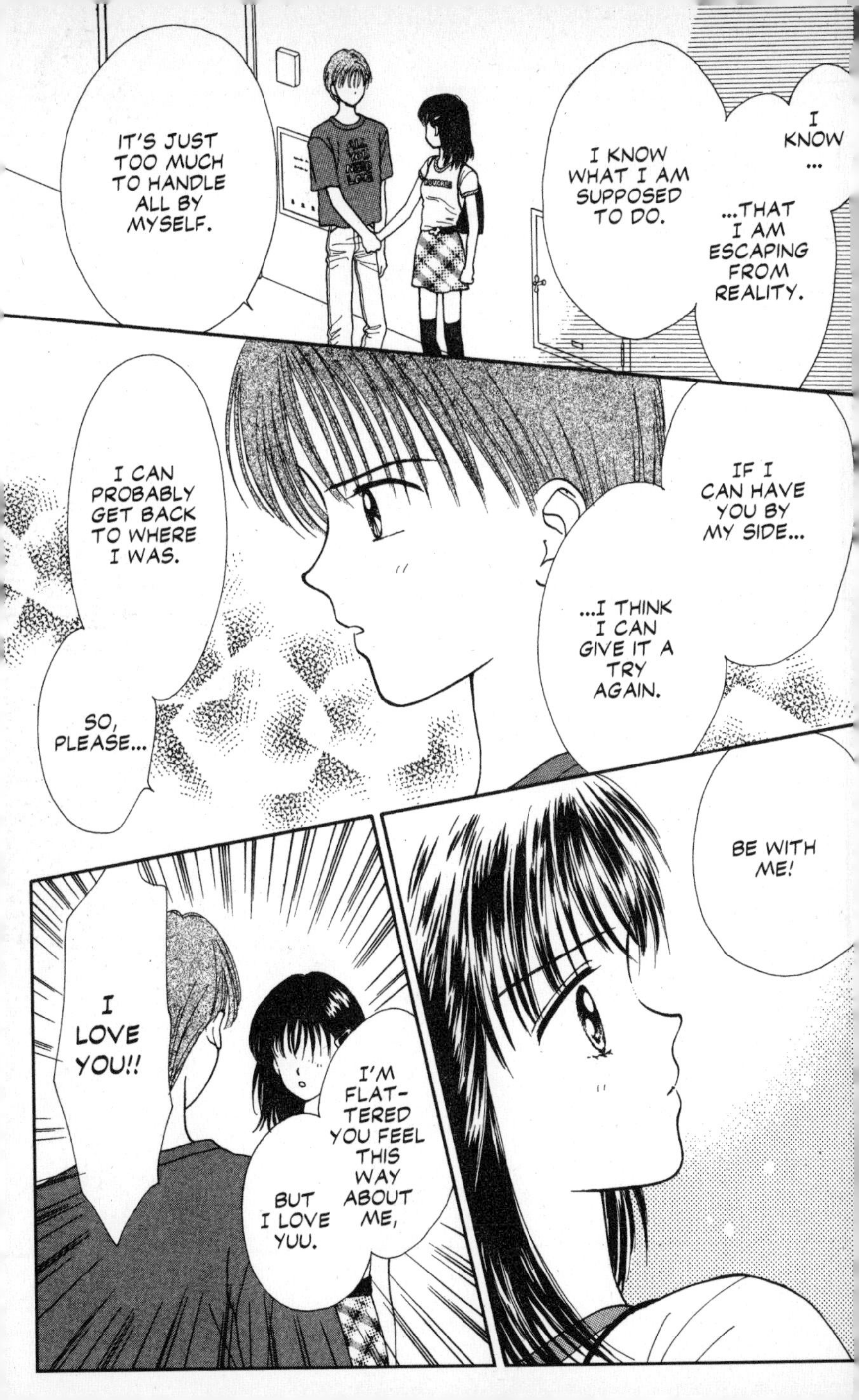
I KNOW ...
...THAT I AM ESCAPING FROM REALITY.
I KNOW WHAT I AM SUPPOSED TO DO.
IT'S JUST TOO MUCH TO HANDLE ALL BY MYSELF.
IF I CAN HAVE YOU BY MY SIDE...
...I THINK I CAN GIVE IT A TRY AGAIN.
I CAN PROBABLY GET BACK TO WHERE I WAS.
SO, PLEASE...
BE WITH ME!
I LOVE YOU!!
I'M FLAT-TERED YOU FEEL THIS WAY ABOUT ME,
BUT I LOVE YUU.

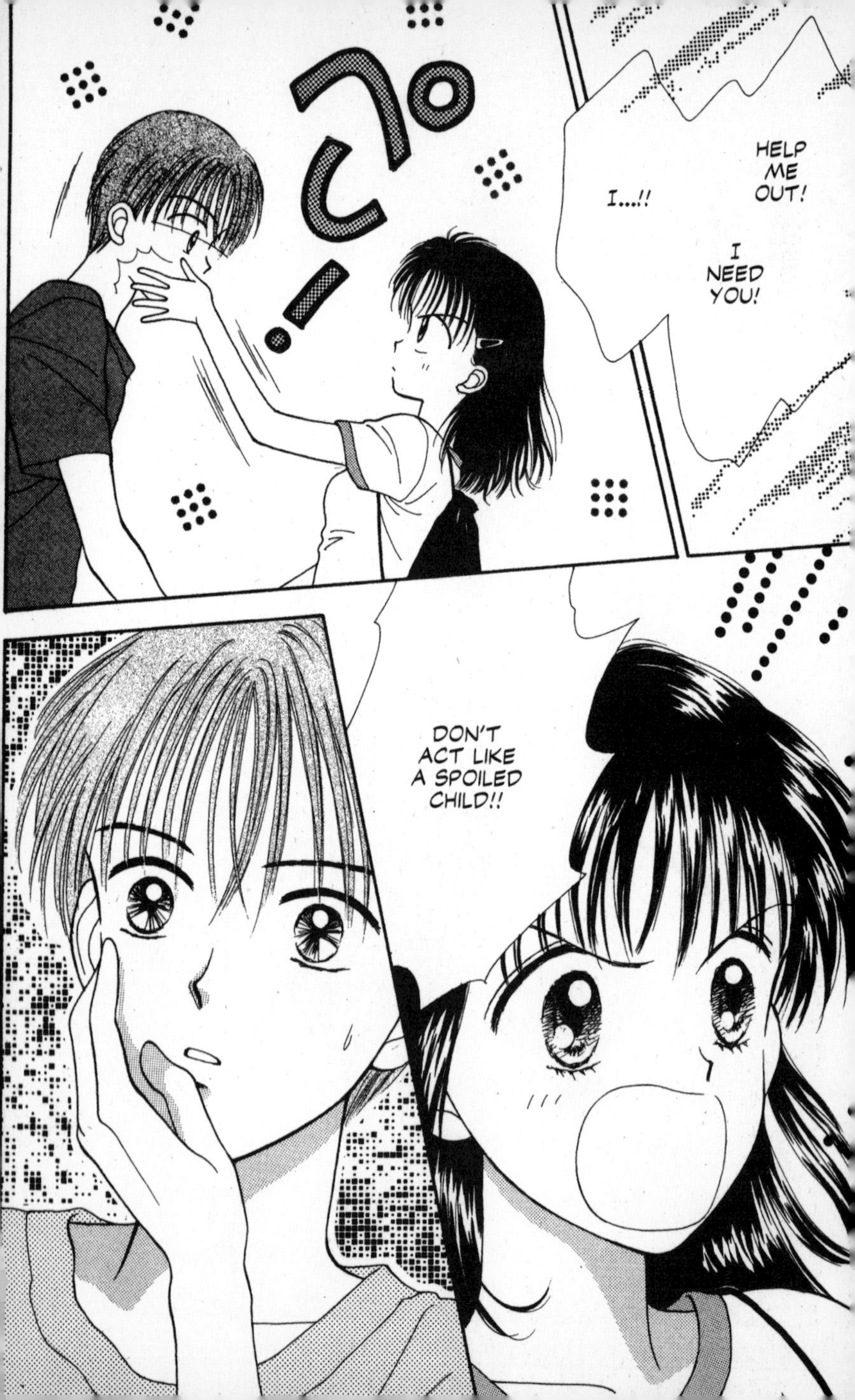
HELP ME OUT!
I NEED YOU!
I...!!
ぺし!
DON'T ACT LIKE A SPOILED CHILD!!

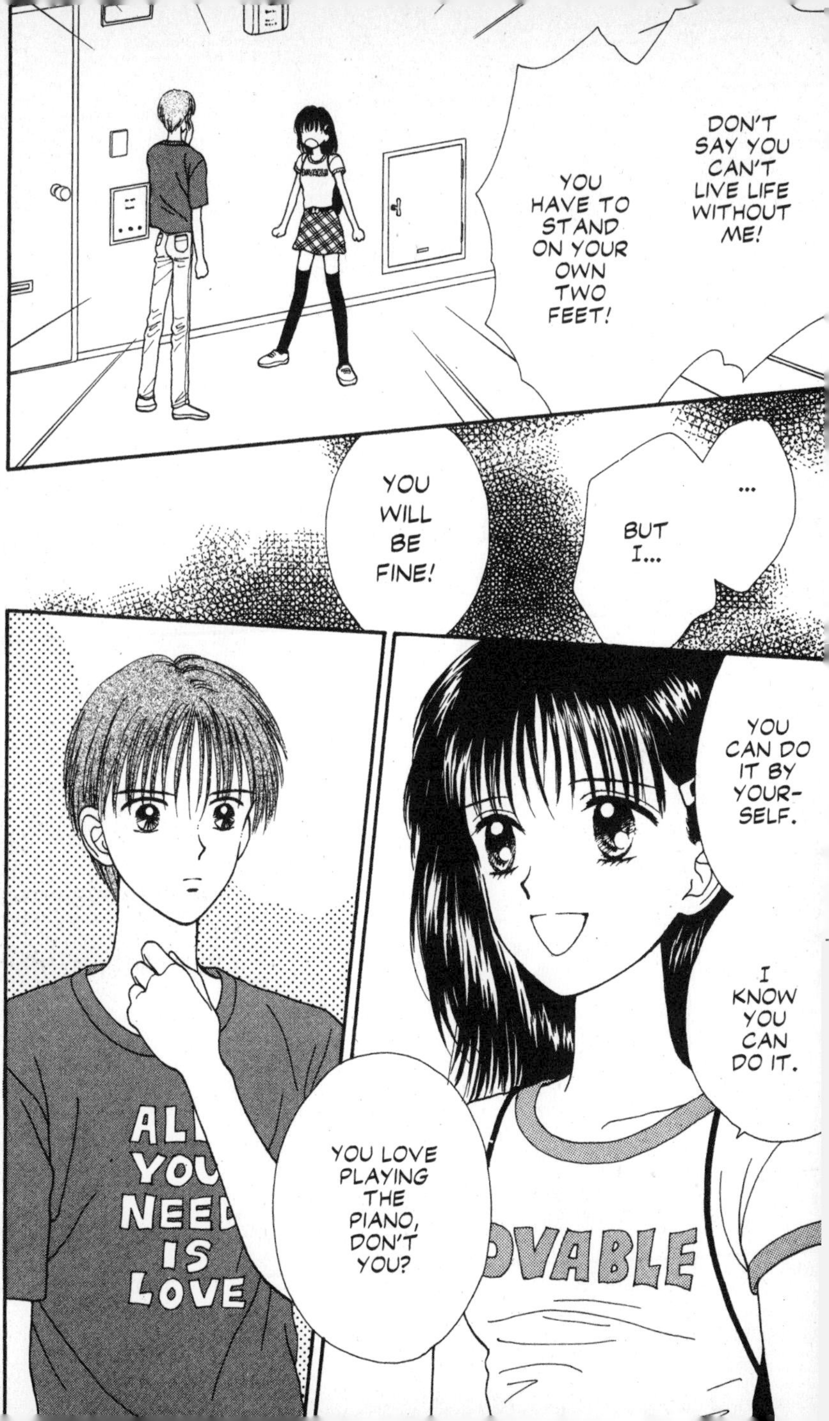
DON'T SAY YOU CAN'T LIVE LIFE WITHOUT ME!
YOU HAVE TO STAND ON YOUR OWN TWO FEET!
...
BUT I...
YOU WILL BE FINE!
YOU CAN DO IT BY YOUR-SELF.
I KNOW YOU CAN DO IT.
YOU LOVE PLAYING THE PIANO, DON'T YOU?

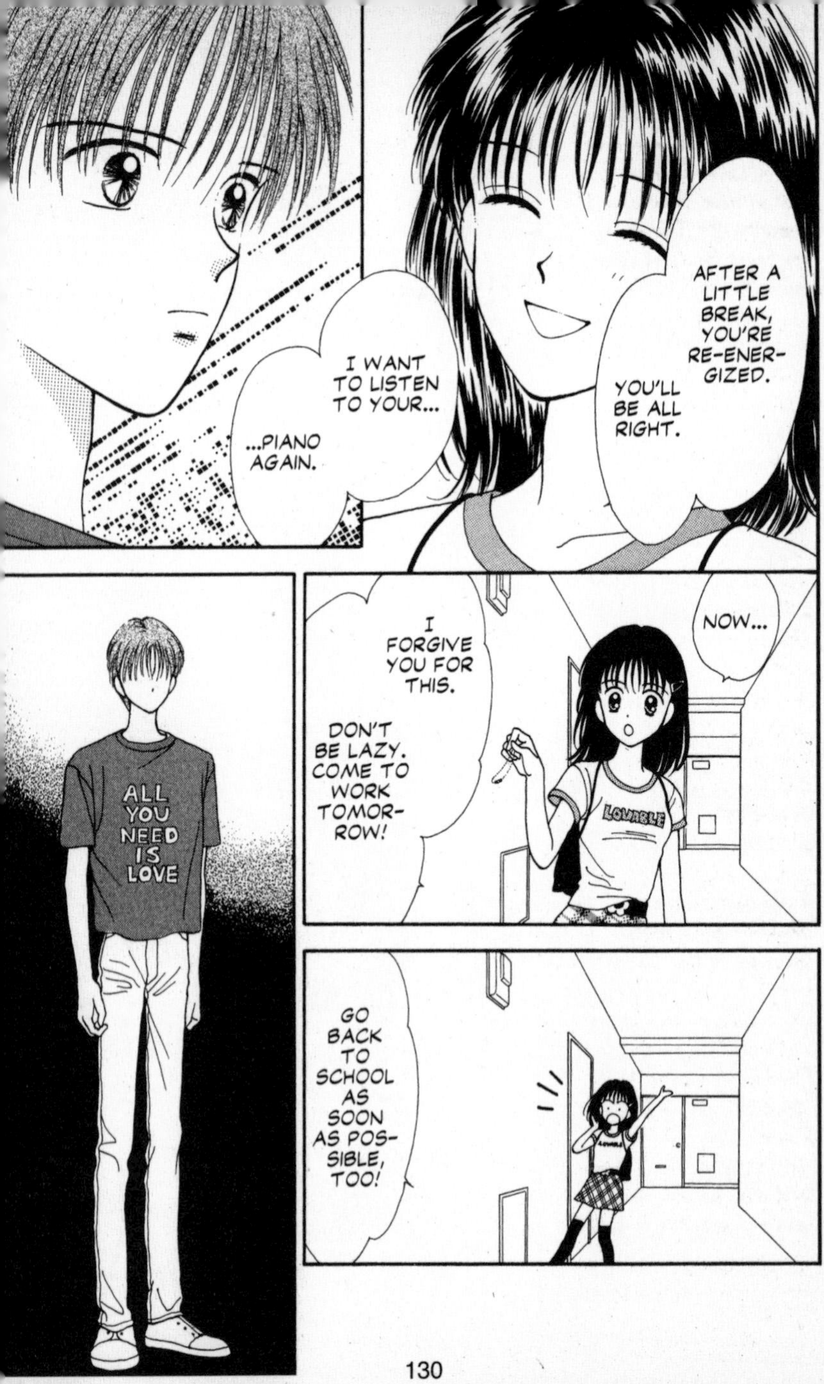
AFTER A LITTLE BREAK, YOU'RE RE-ENERGIZED.
YOU'LL BE ALL RIGHT.
I WANT TO LISTEN TO YOUR...
...PIANO AGAIN.
NOW...
I FORGIVE YOU FOR THIS.
DON'T BE LAZY. COME TO WORK TOMORROW!
GO BACK TO SCHOOL AS SOON AS POSSIBLE, TOO!
ALL YOU NEED IS LOVE

FREE TALK ⑪

Another Marmalade Boy item I can recommend is the "Love Diary," second edition. How can I describe it? The diary contains loads of relationship advice, love spells, incantations, fortunes, and so forth. You can use it as an kokan-nikki* with a friend. This diary comes with an interesting CD. The CD not only contains theme songs including "Moment," but also includes voices of Miki (Mariko Kouda) and Yuu (Ryutaro Okiayu) giving messages and advice to the listener. Miki's talk on the CD is quite funny. She says things such as, " You are always pretty" and ""Boys will be attracted to you" and "Hope you will see your loved one in your dream—good night". I listened to the CD at home and it cracked me up. According to Mr. Seki, the producer, Mr. Okiayu was a bit shy about recording the CD. I can't blame him. Ha ha! Fans of Mr. Okiayu and Ms. Kouda should really check out this CD.

*Kokan-nikki - This is an exchange diary that you write in with your friends.

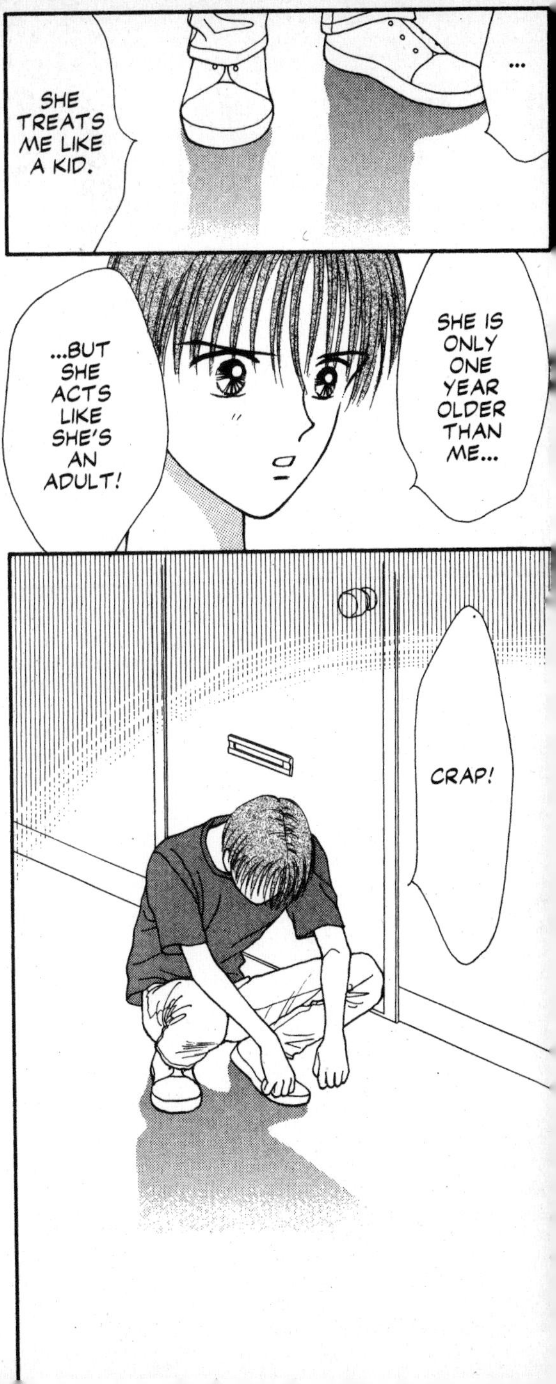
...
SHE TREATS ME LIKE A KID.
SHE IS ONLY ONE YEAR OLDER THAN ME...
...BUT SHE ACTS LIKE SHE'S AN ADULT!
CRAP!

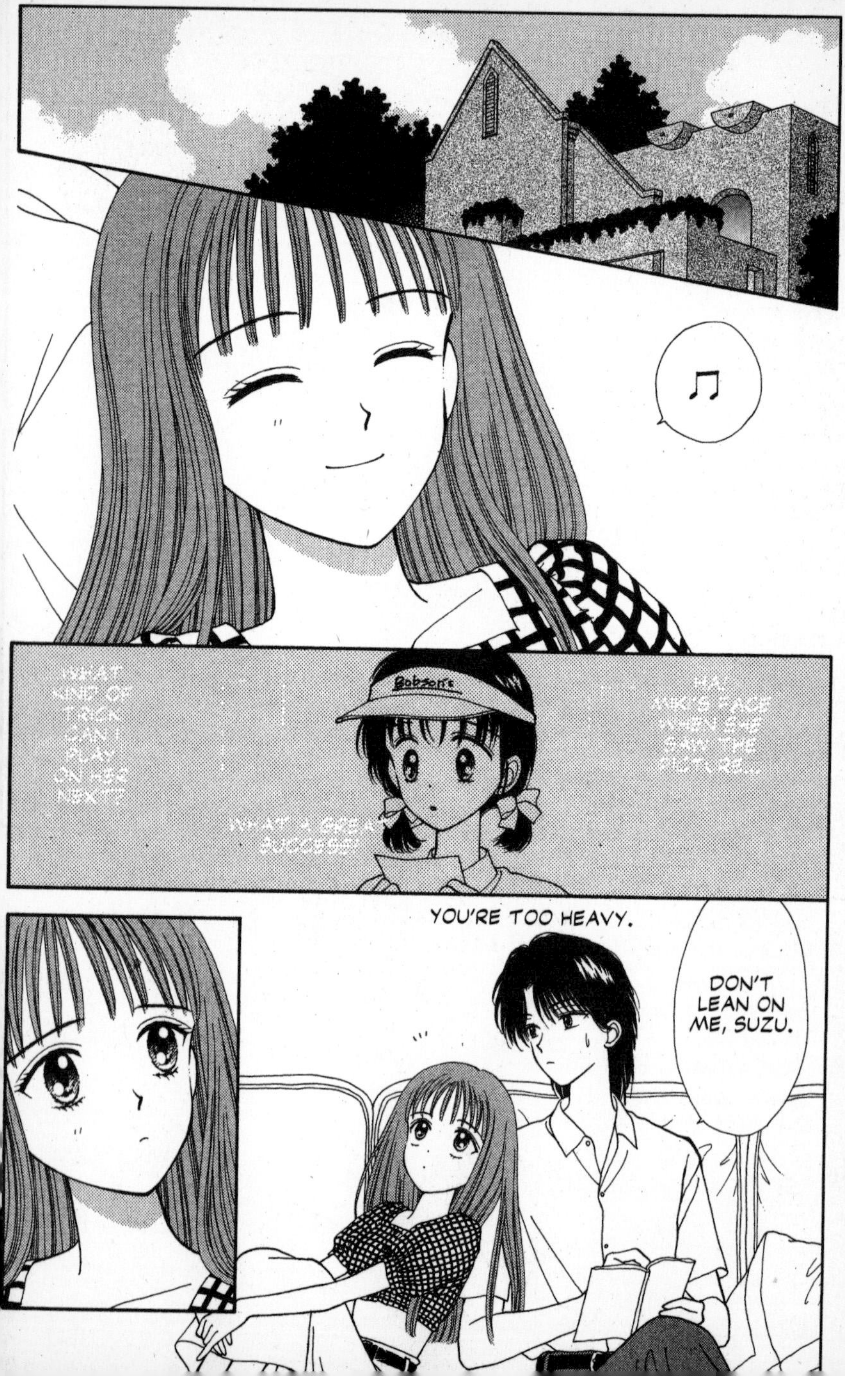
♫
HA. MIKI'S FACE WHEN SHE SAW THE PICTURE...
WHAT A GREAT SUCCESS!
WHAT KIND OF TRICK CAN I PLAY ON HER NEXT?
DON'T LEAN ON ME, SUZU.
YOU'RE TOO HEAVY.

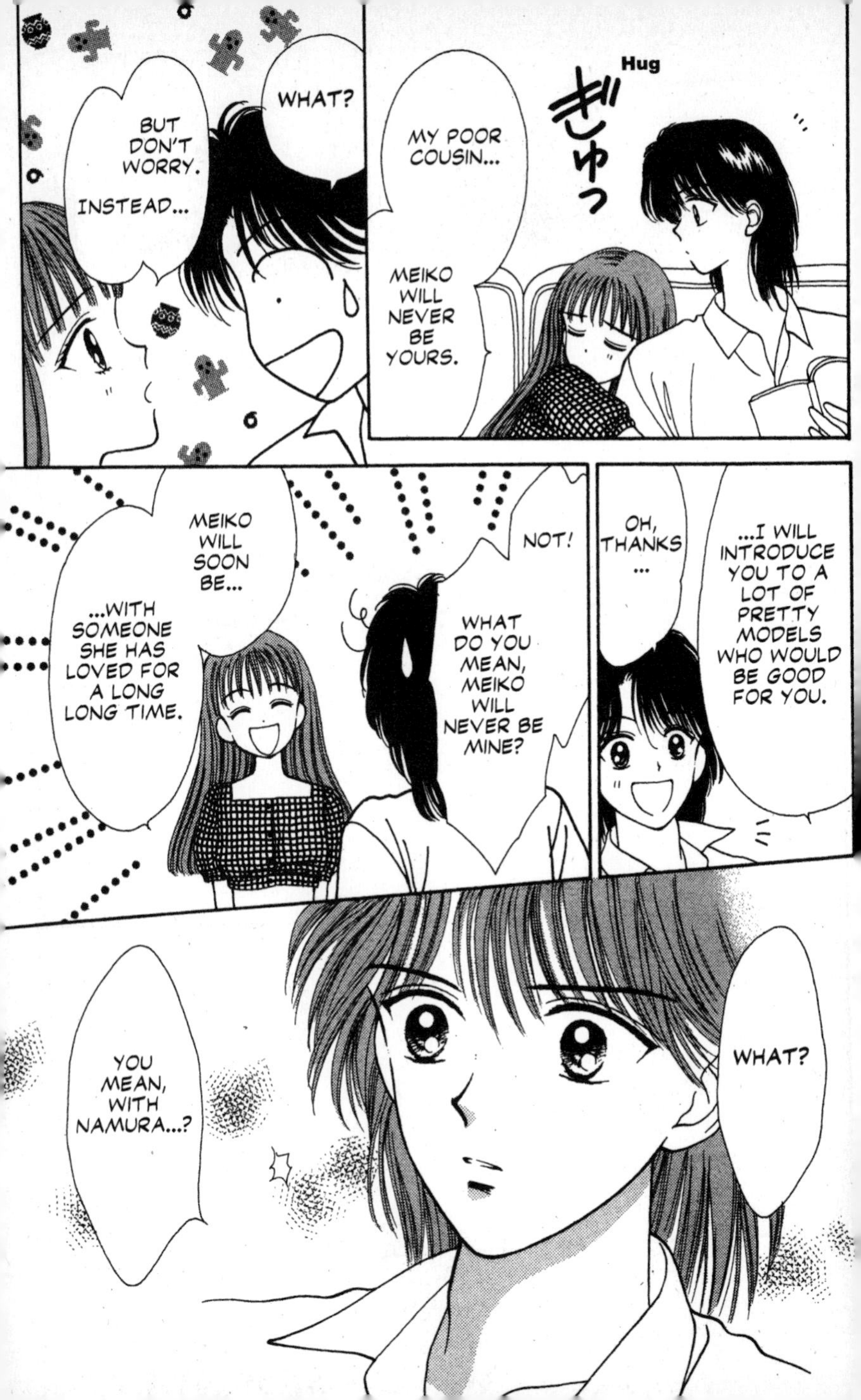
Hug
ぎゅっ
MY POOR COUSIN...
MEIKO WILL NEVER BE YOURS.
WHAT?
BUT DON'T WORRY.
INSTEAD...
...I WILL INTRODUCE YOU TO A LOT OF PRETTY MODELS WHO WOULD BE GOOD FOR YOU.
OH, THANKS...
NOT!
WHAT DO YOU MEAN, MEIKO WILL NEVER BE MINE?
MEIKO WILL SOON BE...
...WITH SOMEONE SHE HAS LOVED FOR A LONG LONG TIME.
WHAT?
YOU MEAN, WITH NAMURA...?

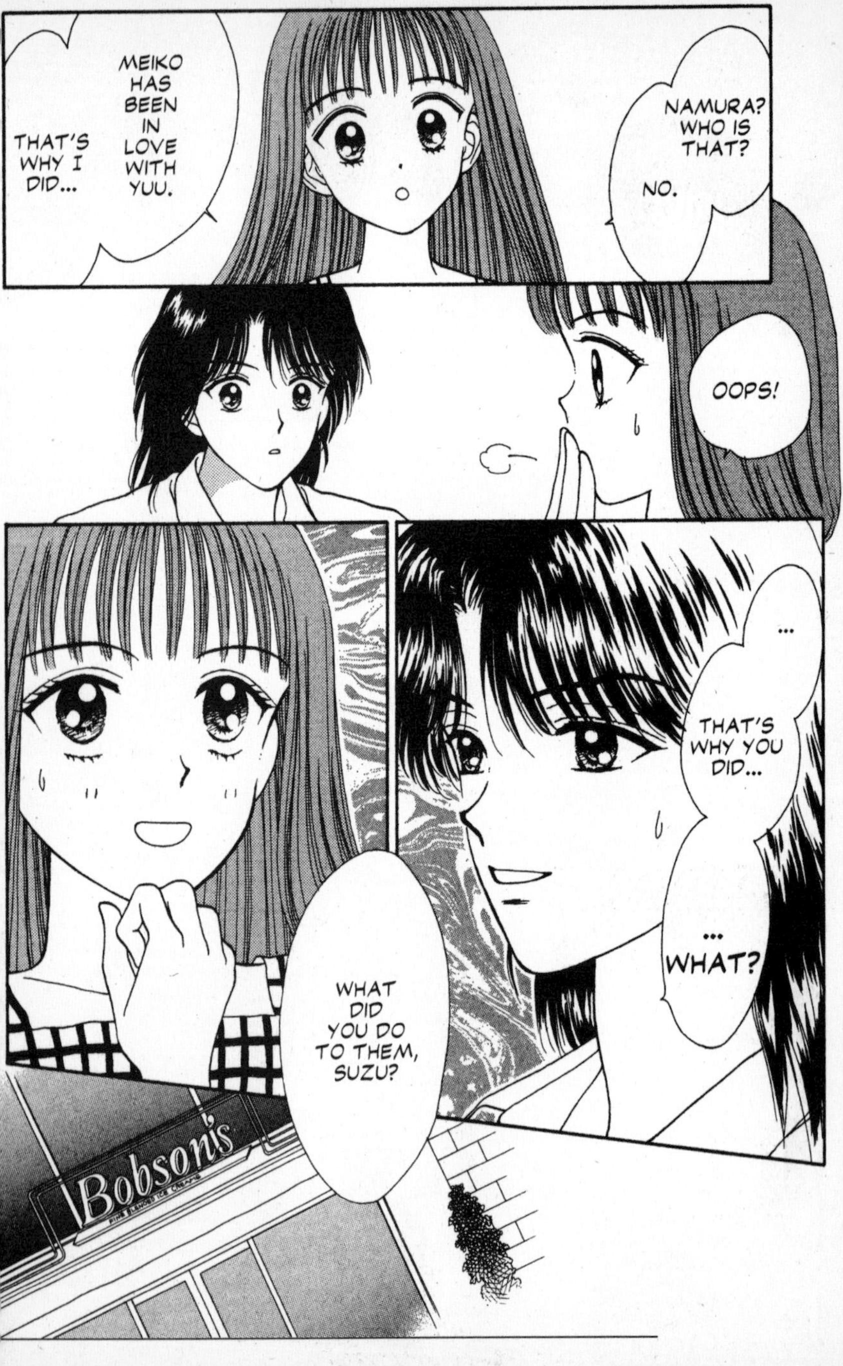
NAMURA? WHO IS THAT?
NO.
MEIKO HAS BEEN IN LOVE WITH YUU.
THAT'S WHY I DID...
OOPS!
...
THAT'S WHY YOU DID...
... WHAT?
WHAT DID YOU DO TO THEM, SUZU?
Bobson's
FINE BLENDED ICE CREAMS

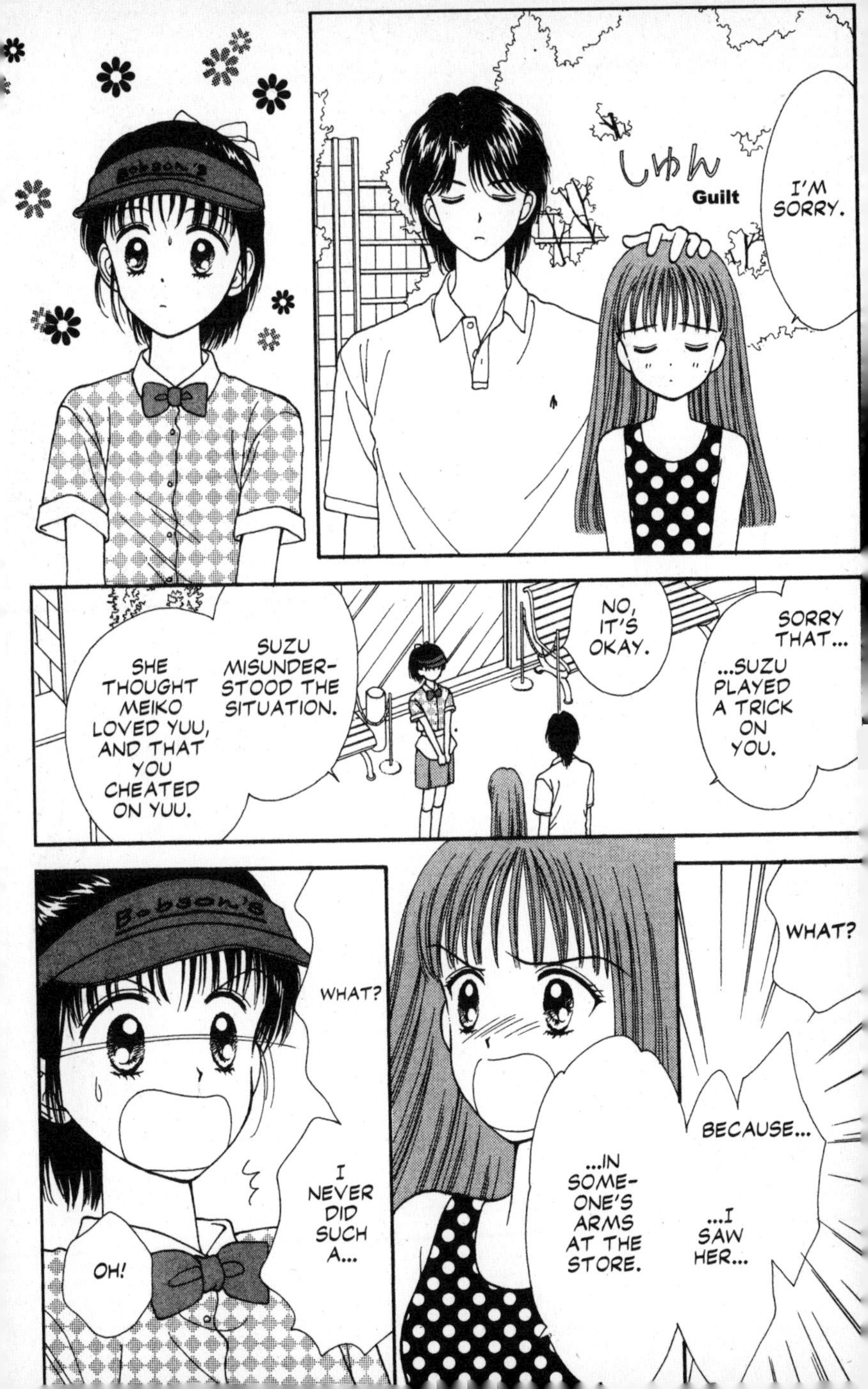
しゅん
Guilt
I'M SORRY.
SORRY THAT...
...SUZU PLAYED A TRICK ON YOU.
NO, IT'S OKAY.
SUZU MISUNDERSTOOD THE SITUATION.
SHE THOUGHT MEIKO LOVED YUU, AND THAT YOU CHEATED ON YUU.
WHAT?
BECAUSE...
...I SAW HER...
...IN SOMEONE'S ARMS AT THE STORE.
WHAT?
I NEVER DID SUCH A...
OH!

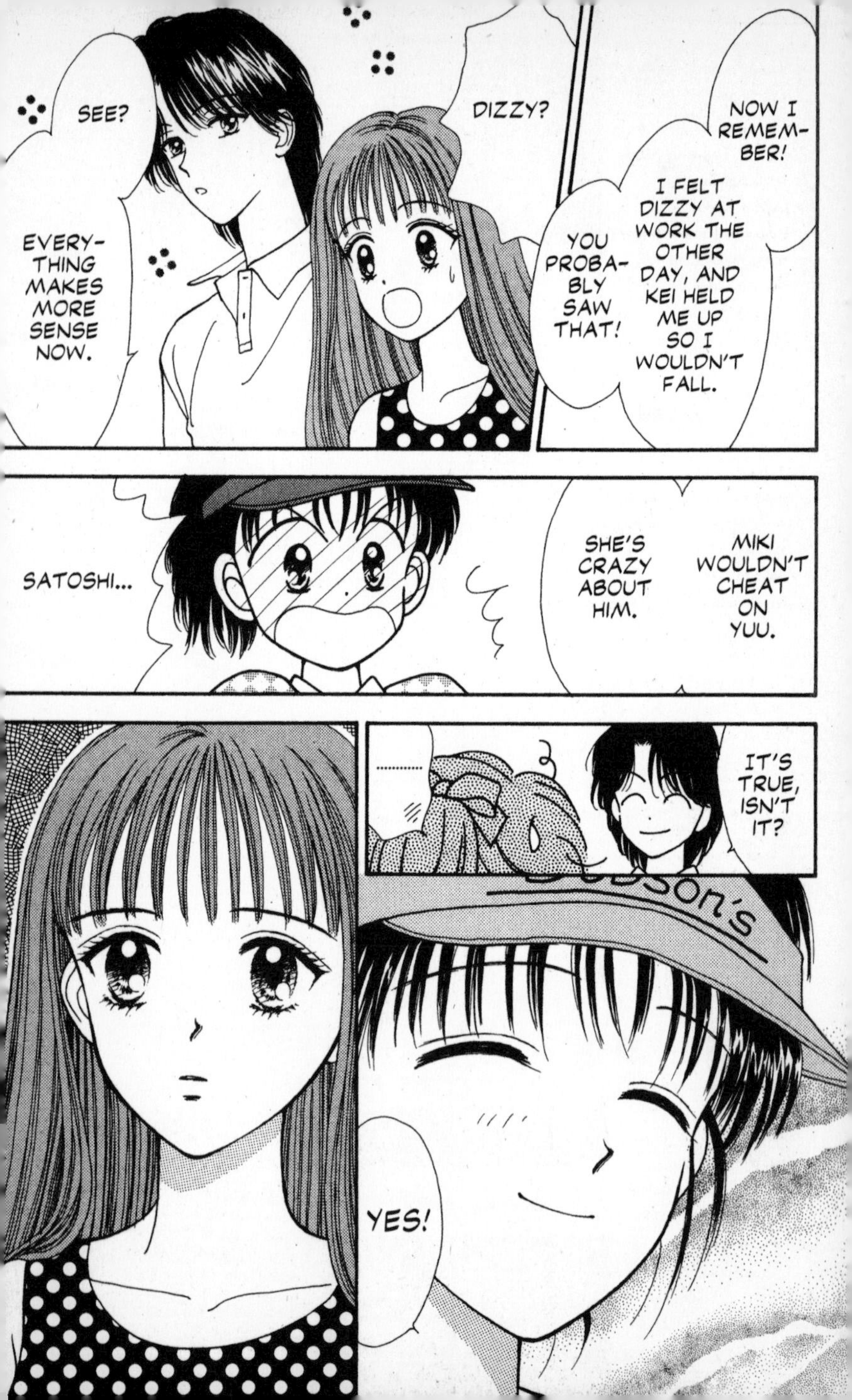
NOW I REMEM-BER!
I FELT DIZZY AT WORK THE OTHER DAY, AND KEI HELD ME UP SO I WOULDN'T FALL.
YOU PROBA-BLY SAW THAT!
DIZZY?
SEE?
EVERY-THING MAKES MORE SENSE NOW.
MIKI WOULDN'T CHEAT ON YUU.
SHE'S CRAZY ABOUT HIM.
SATOSHI...
IT'S TRUE, ISN'T IT?
....
YES!

FREE TALK ⑫

Okay, back to the Marmalade Boy goods! The bag, wallet, and watch I talked about in Volume 4 were never mass-produced for the general public. I wonder if that's because those items didn't have any Marmalade Boy characters on them. I liked the samples, though. Instead, bags in various sizes with 3-toushin-sized versions of Miki and Yuu are now for sale. They are all very cute. I hope you can get them at a local store. I am going to use the bags, too.

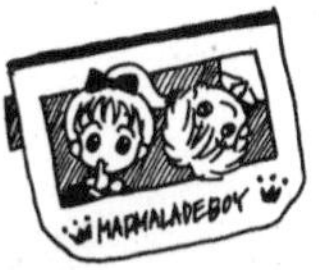
MARMALADEBOY

One of them looks like this one above. Also the manicure sets are cute. The motorized nail shiner is excellent but the more traditional nail compact is just as good. They come in a light-blue case with a golden crown mark. They're also fun for adults.

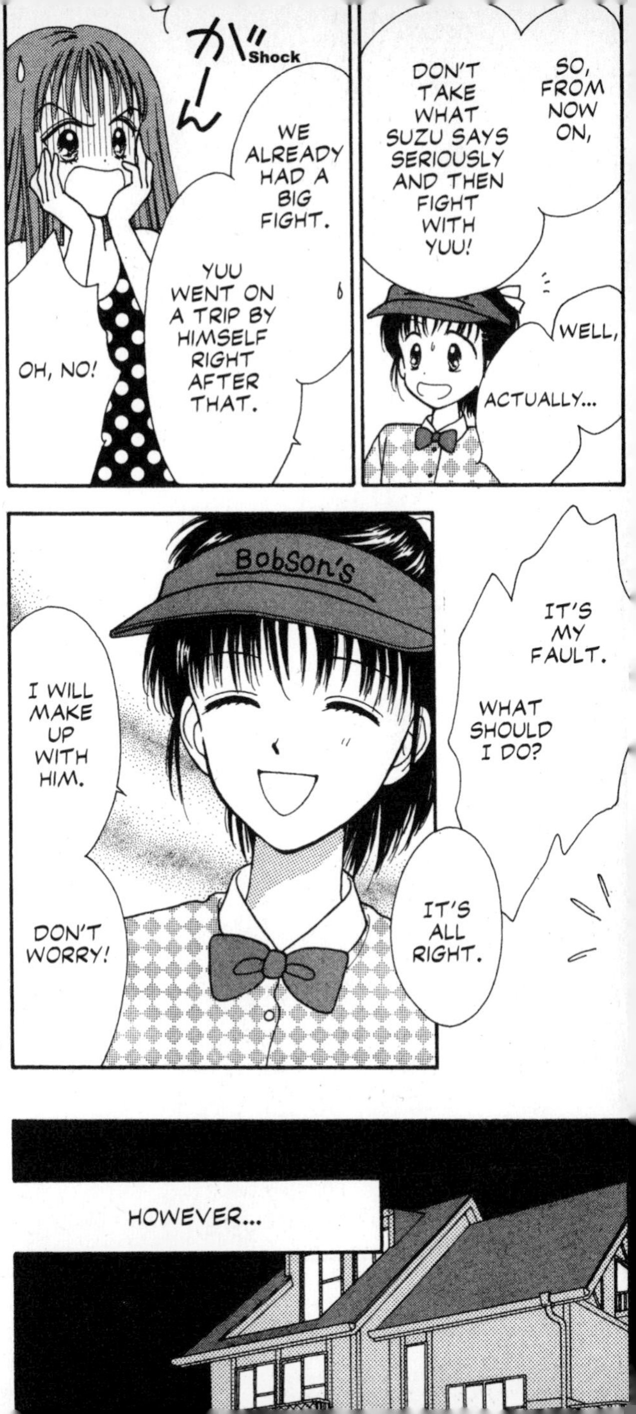
SO, FROM NOW ON,
DON'T TAKE WHAT SUZU SAYS SERIOUSLY AND THEN FIGHT WITH YUU!
WELL,
ACTUALLY...
WE ALREADY HAD A BIG FIGHT.
YUU WENT ON A TRIP BY HIMSELF RIGHT AFTER THAT.
がーん Shock
OH, NO!
Bobson's
IT'S MY FAULT.
WHAT SHOULD I DO?
IT'S ALL RIGHT.
DON'T WORRY!
I WILL MAKE UP WITH HIM.
HOWEVER...

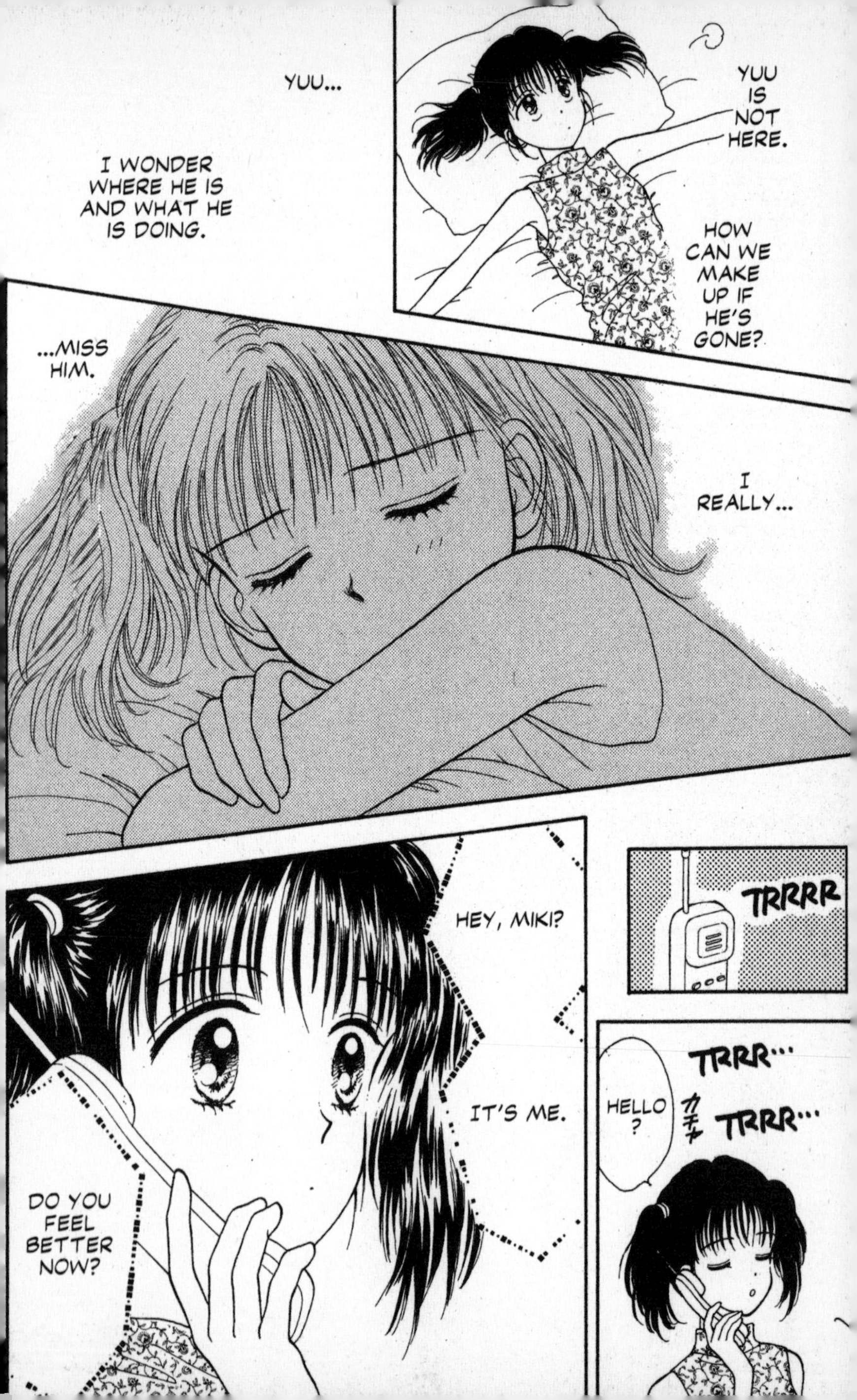
YUU IS NOT HERE.
HOW CAN WE MAKE UP IF HE'S GONE?
YUU...
I WONDER WHERE HE IS AND WHAT HE IS DOING.
I REALLY...
...MISS HIM.
TRRRR
TRRR...
カチャ
TRRR...
HELLO?
HEY, MIKI?
IT'S ME.
DO YOU FEEL BETTER NOW?

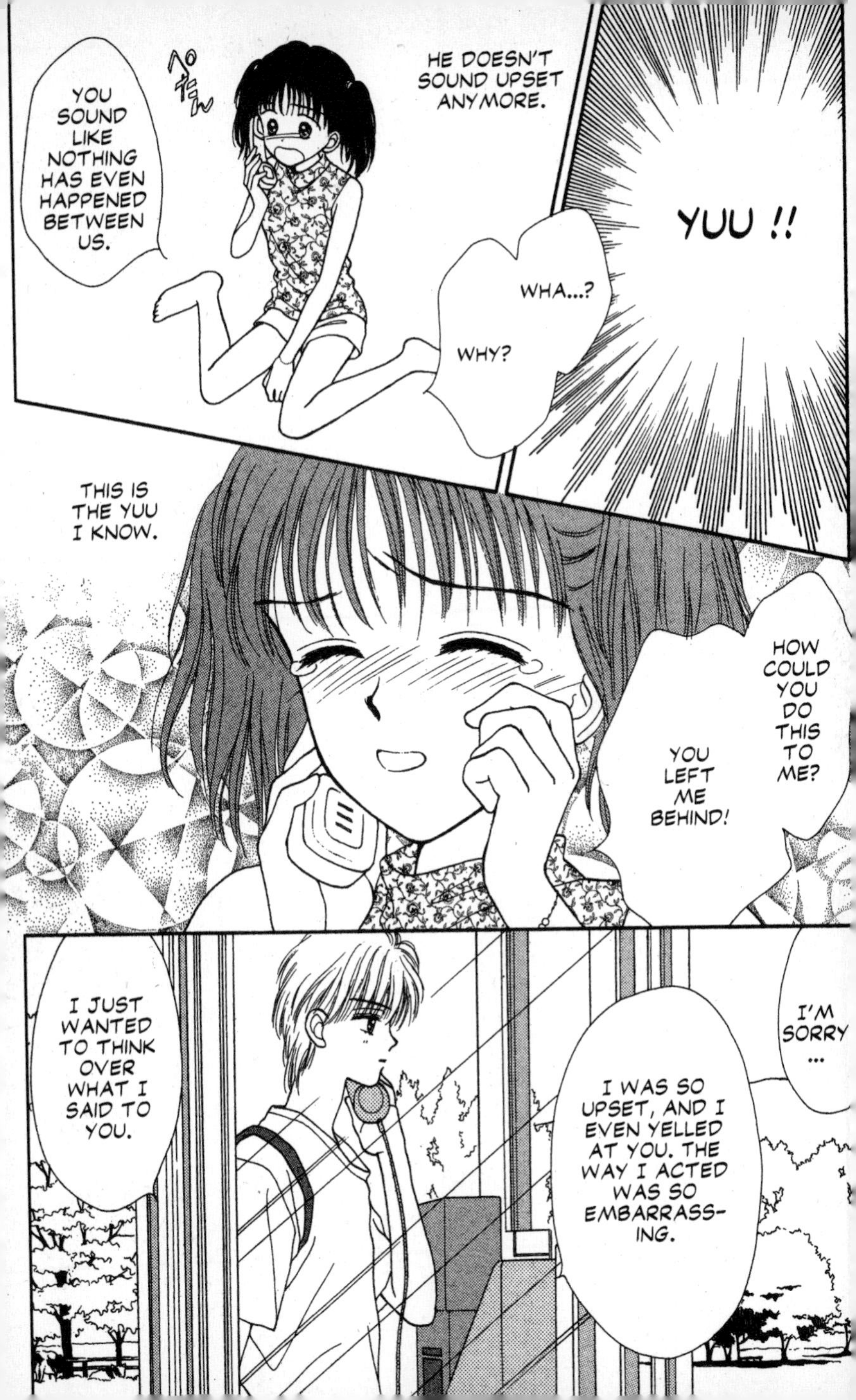
YUU !!
WHA...?
WHY?
HE DOESN'T SOUND UPSET ANYMORE.
YOU SOUND LIKE NOTHING HAS EVEN HAPPENED BETWEEN US.
THIS IS THE YUU I KNOW.
HOW COULD YOU DO THIS TO ME?
YOU LEFT ME BEHIND!
I'M SORRY...
I WAS SO UPSET, AND I EVEN YELLED AT YOU. THE WAY I ACTED WAS SO EMBARRASS-ING.
I JUST WANTED TO THINK OVER WHAT I SAID TO YOU.

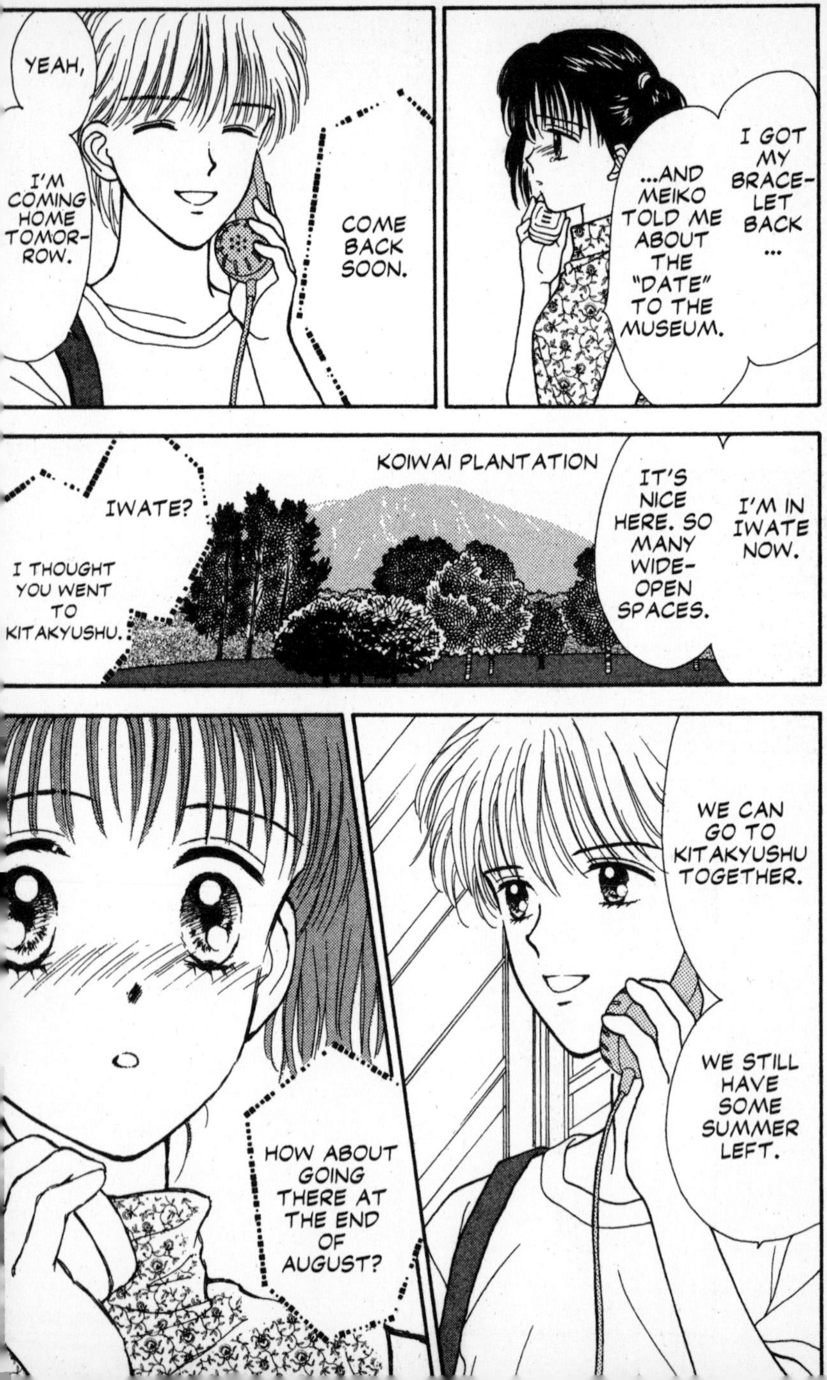
I GOT MY BRACELET BACK...
...AND MEIKO TOLD ME ABOUT THE "DATE" TO THE MUSEUM.
COME BACK SOON.
YEAH,
I'M COMING HOME TOMORROW.
I'M IN IWATE NOW.
IT'S NICE HERE. SO MANY WIDE-OPEN SPACES.
KOIWAI PLANTATION
IWATE?
I THOUGHT YOU WENT TO KITAKYUSHU.
WE CAN GO TO KITAKYUSHU TOGETHER.
WE STILL HAVE SOME SUMMER LEFT.
HOW ABOUT GOING THERE AT THE END OF AUGUST?

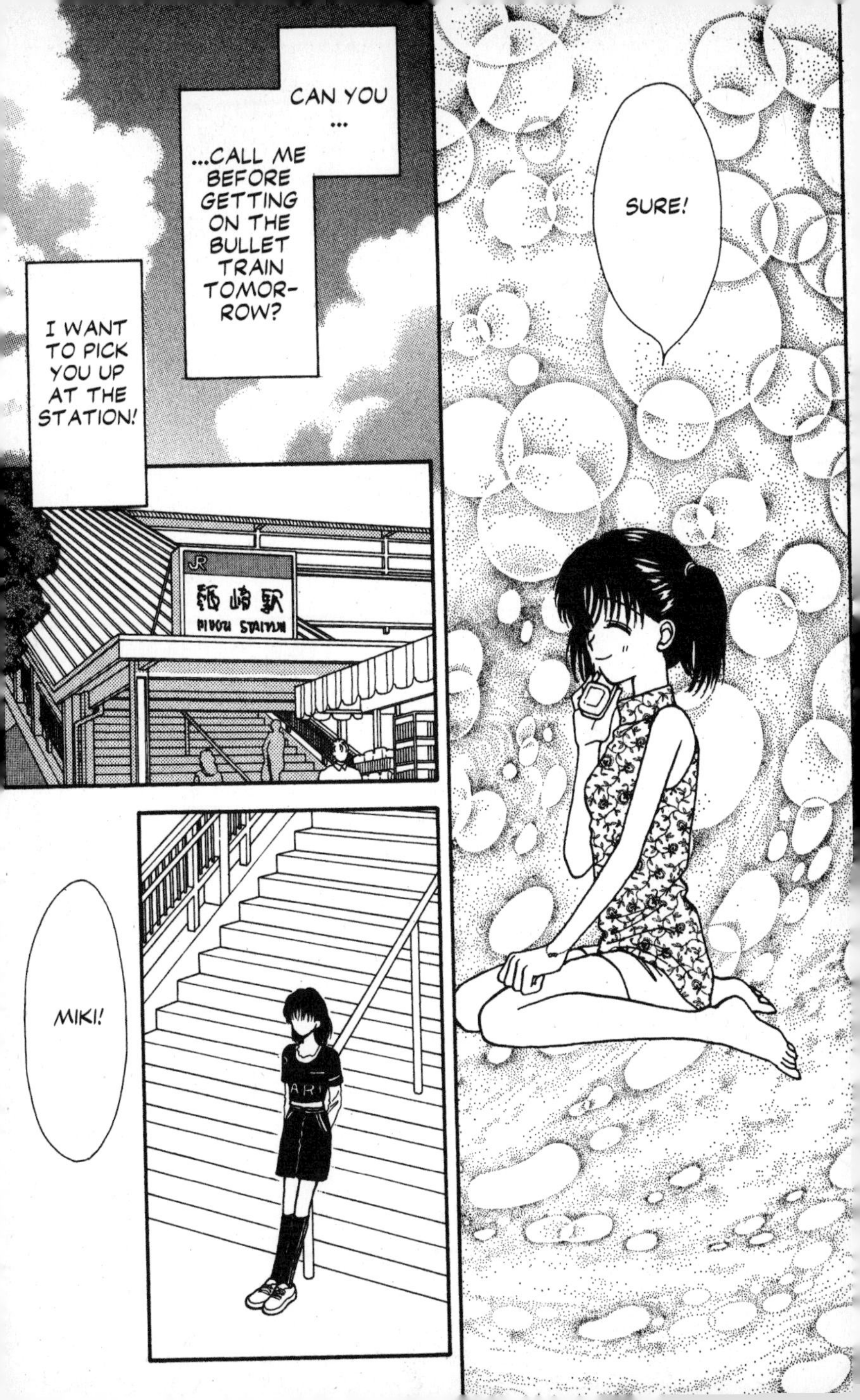
CAN YOU ... ...CALL ME BEFORE GETTING ON THE BULLET TRAIN TOMORROW?
I WANT TO PICK YOU UP AT THE STATION!
SURE!
MIKI!

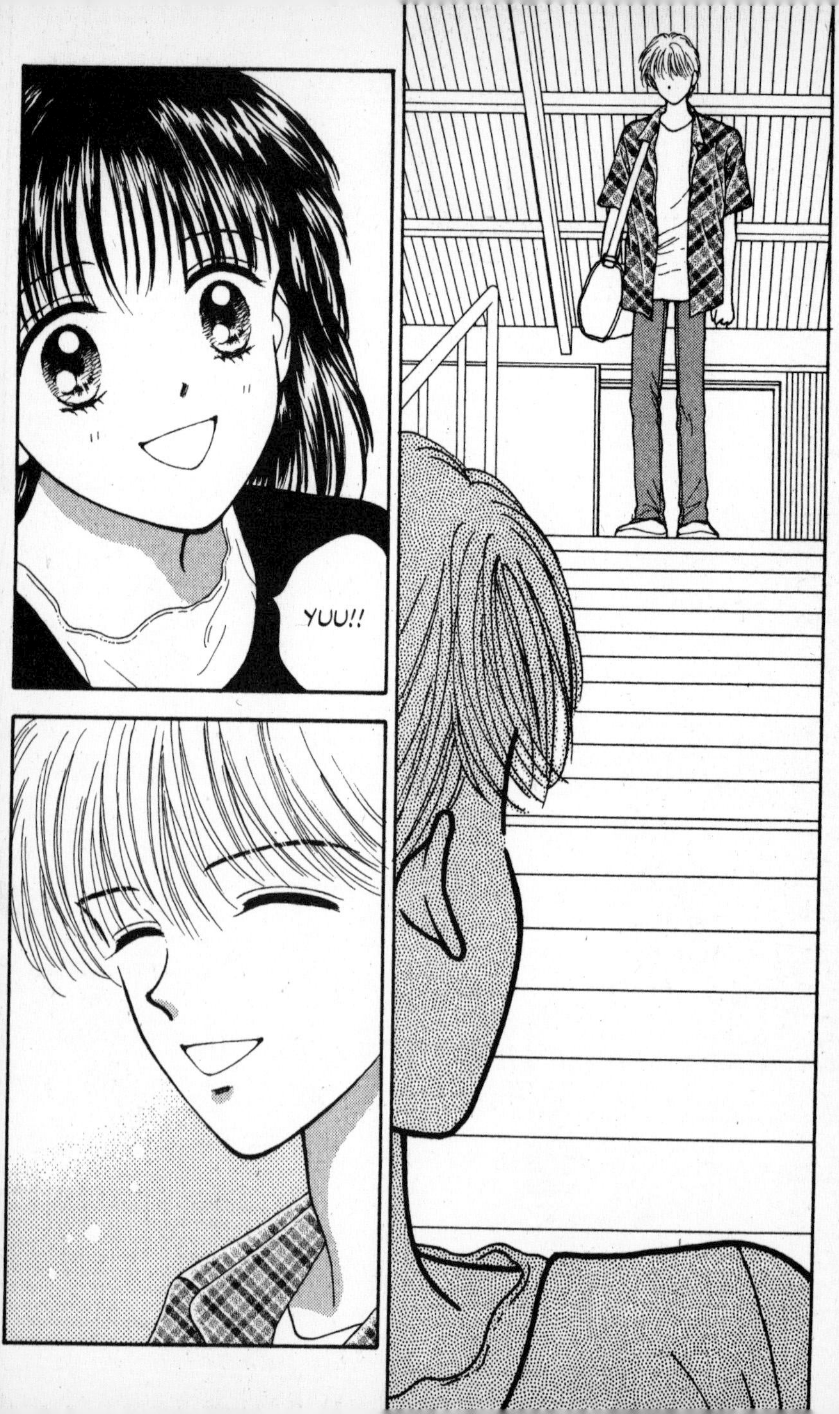
YUU!!

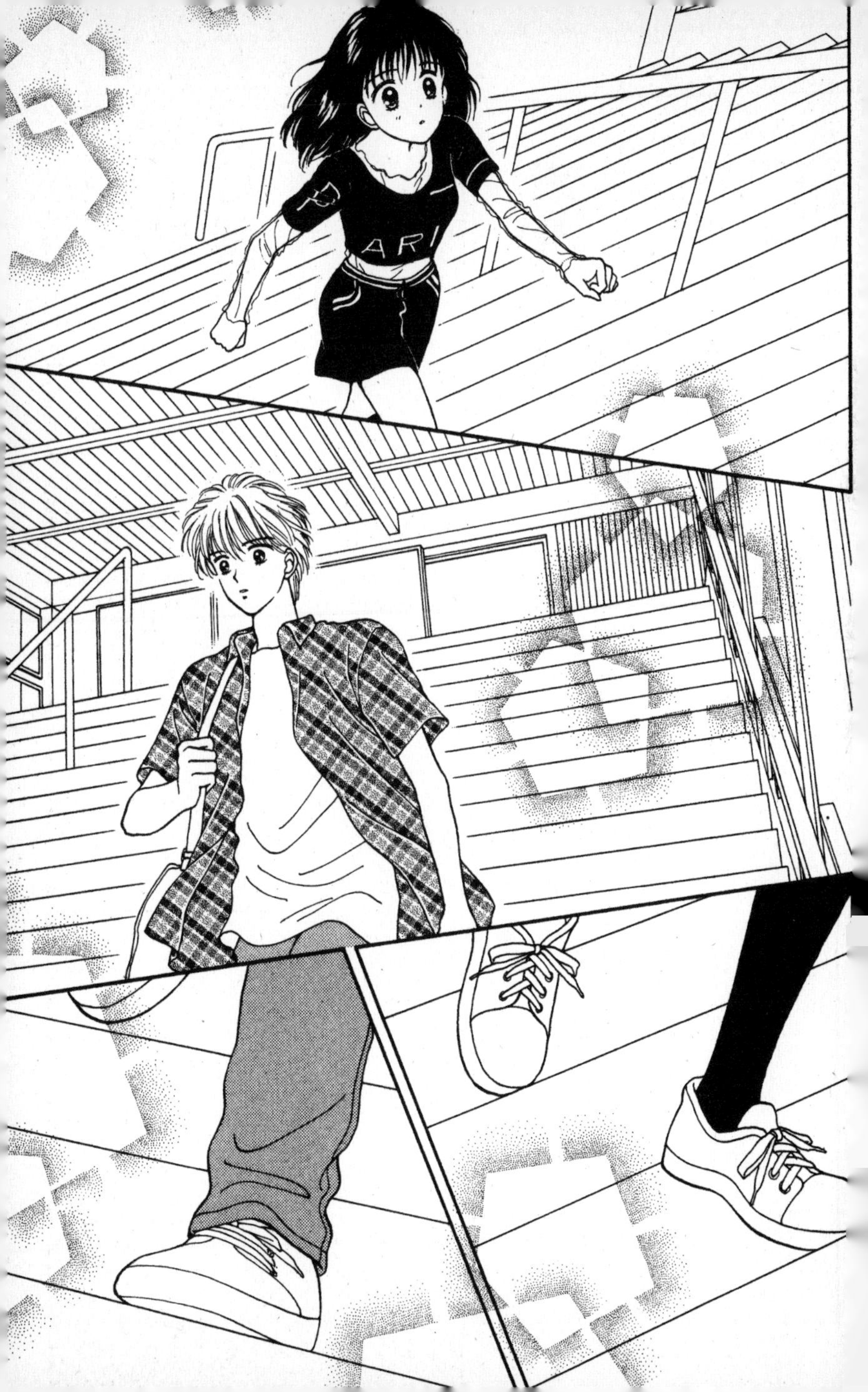

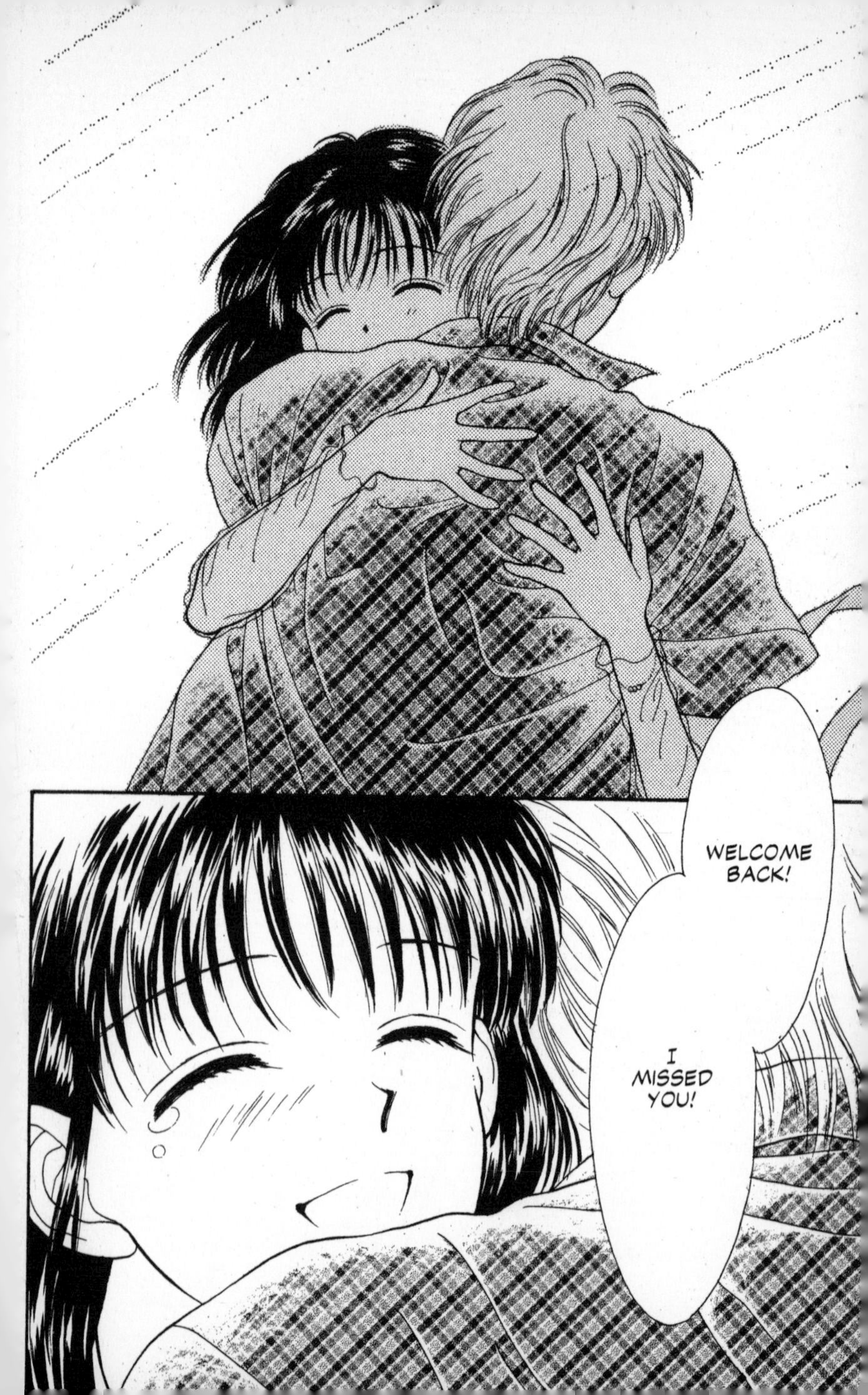
WELCOME BACK!
I MISSED YOU!

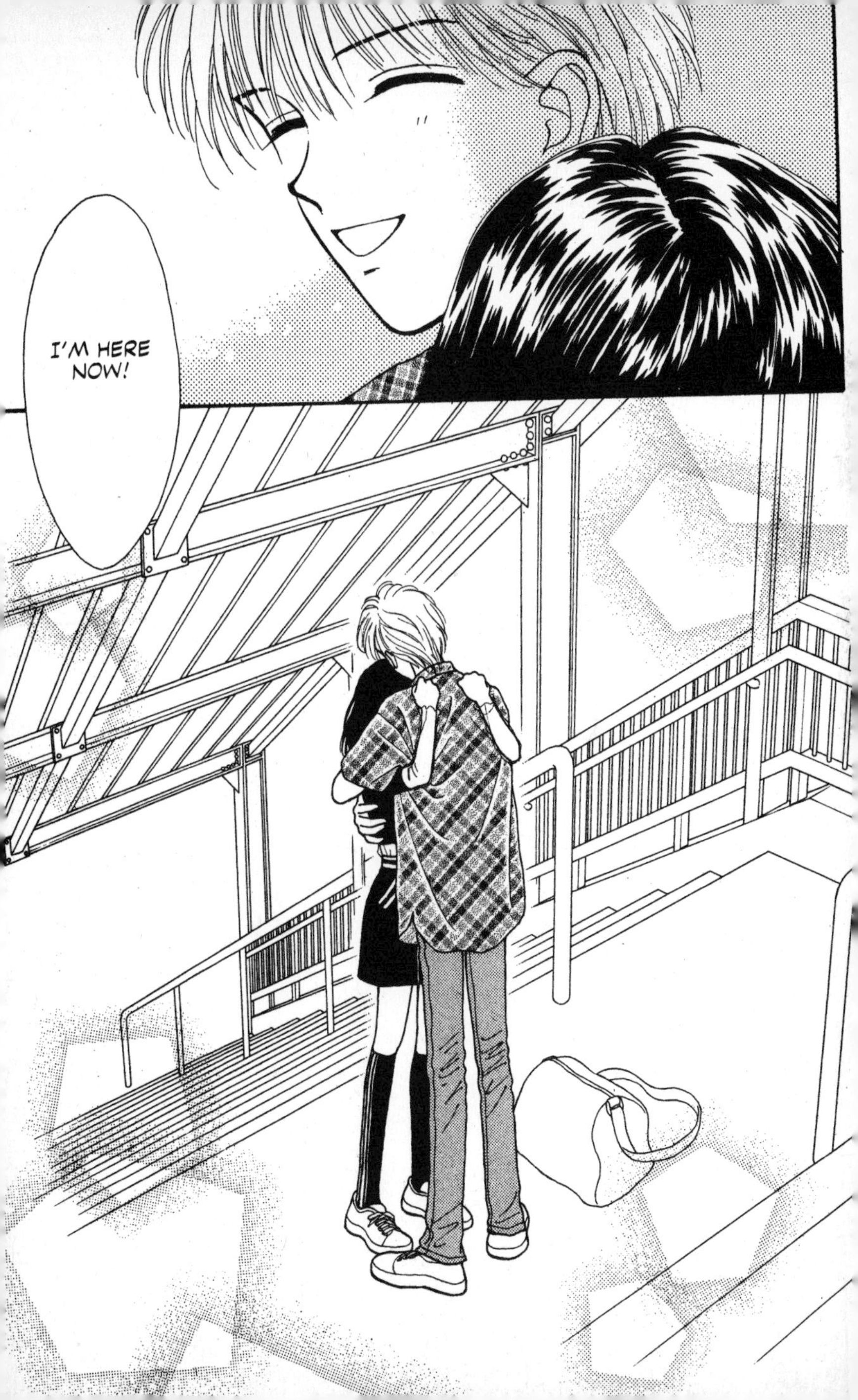
I'M HERE NOW!

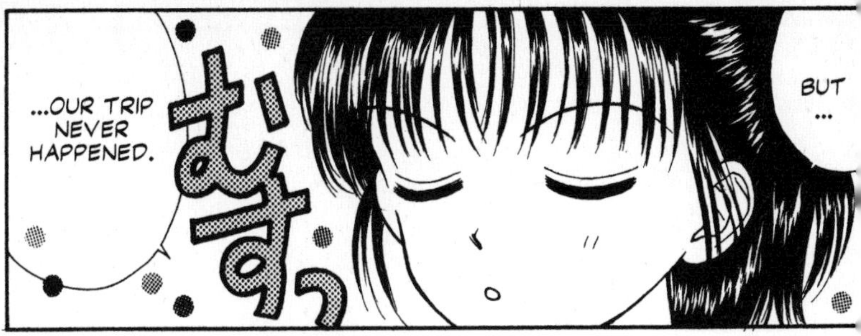
BUT ...
むすっ
...OUR TRIP NEVER HAPPENED.

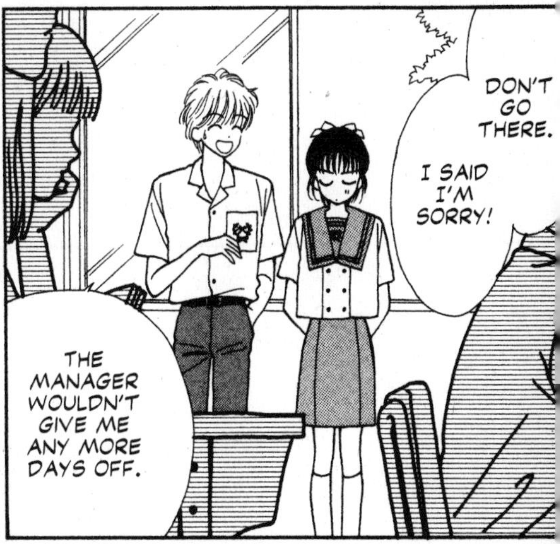
DON'T GO THERE.
I SAID I'M SORRY!
THE MANAGER WOULDN'T GIVE ME ANY MORE DAYS OFF.

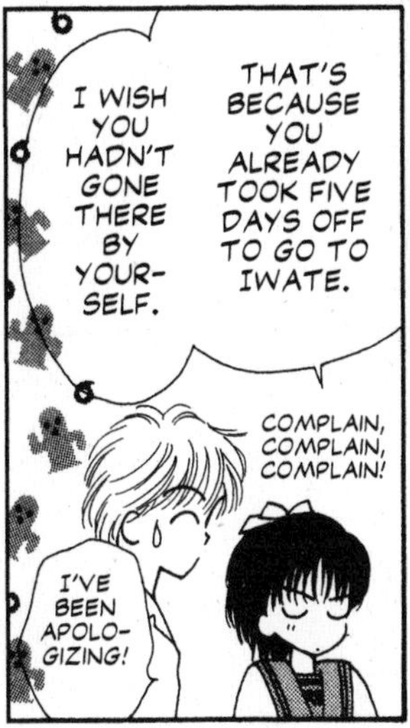
THAT'S BECAUSE YOU ALREADY TOOK FIVE DAYS OFF TO GO TO IWATE.
I WISH YOU HADN'T GONE THERE BY YOUR-SELF.
COMPLAIN, COMPLAIN, COMPLAIN!
I'VE BEEN APOLO-GIZING!

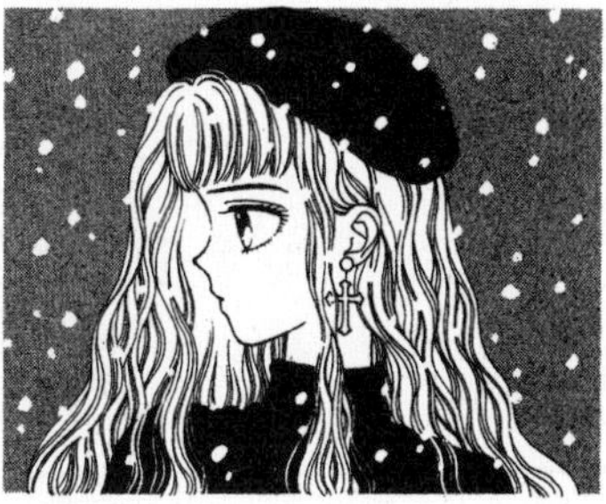

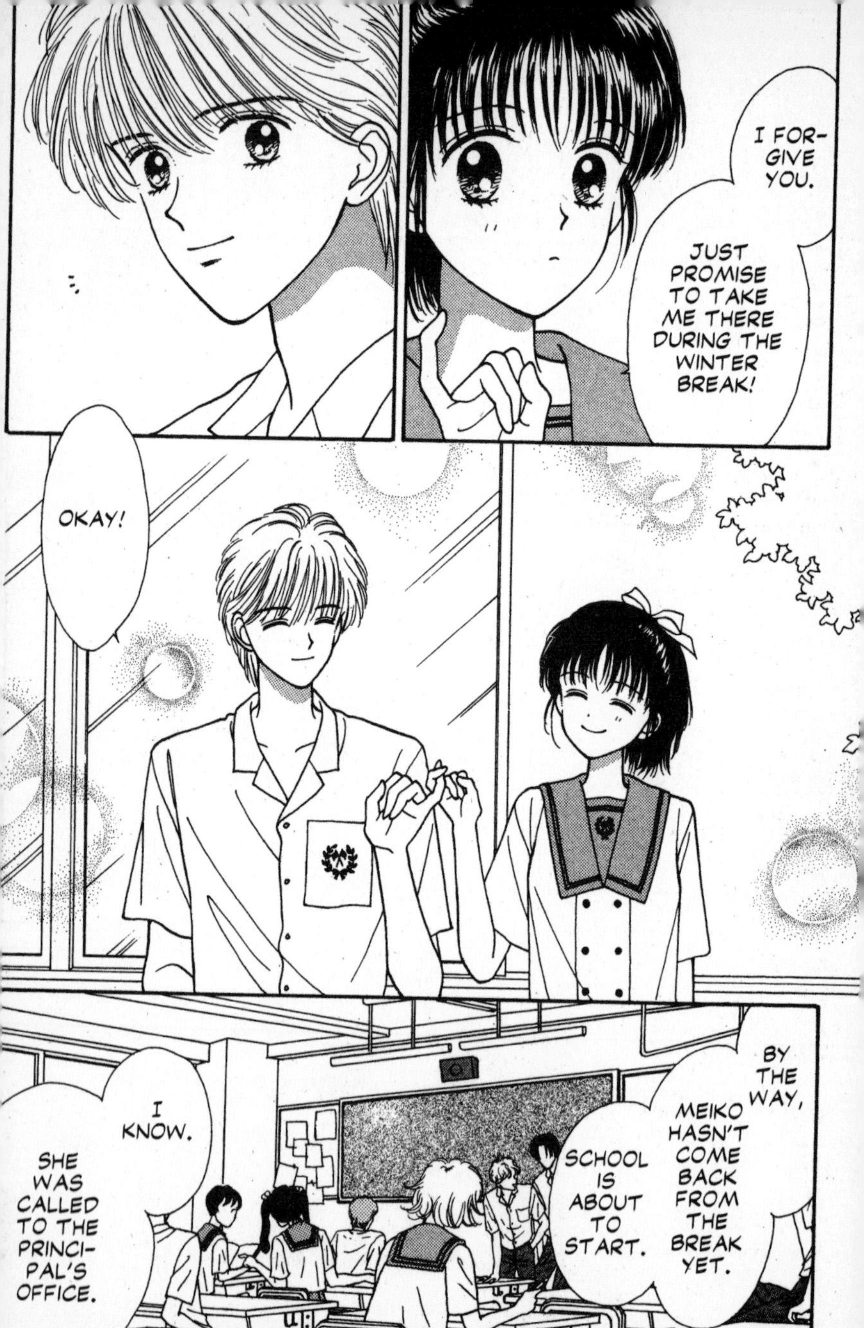
I FOR-GIVE YOU.
JUST PROMISE TO TAKE ME THERE DURING THE WINTER BREAK!
OKAY!
BY THE WAY,
MEIKO HASN'T COME BACK FROM THE BREAK YET.
SCHOOL IS ABOUT TO START.
I KNOW.
SHE WAS CALLED TO THE PRINCI-PAL'S OFFICE.

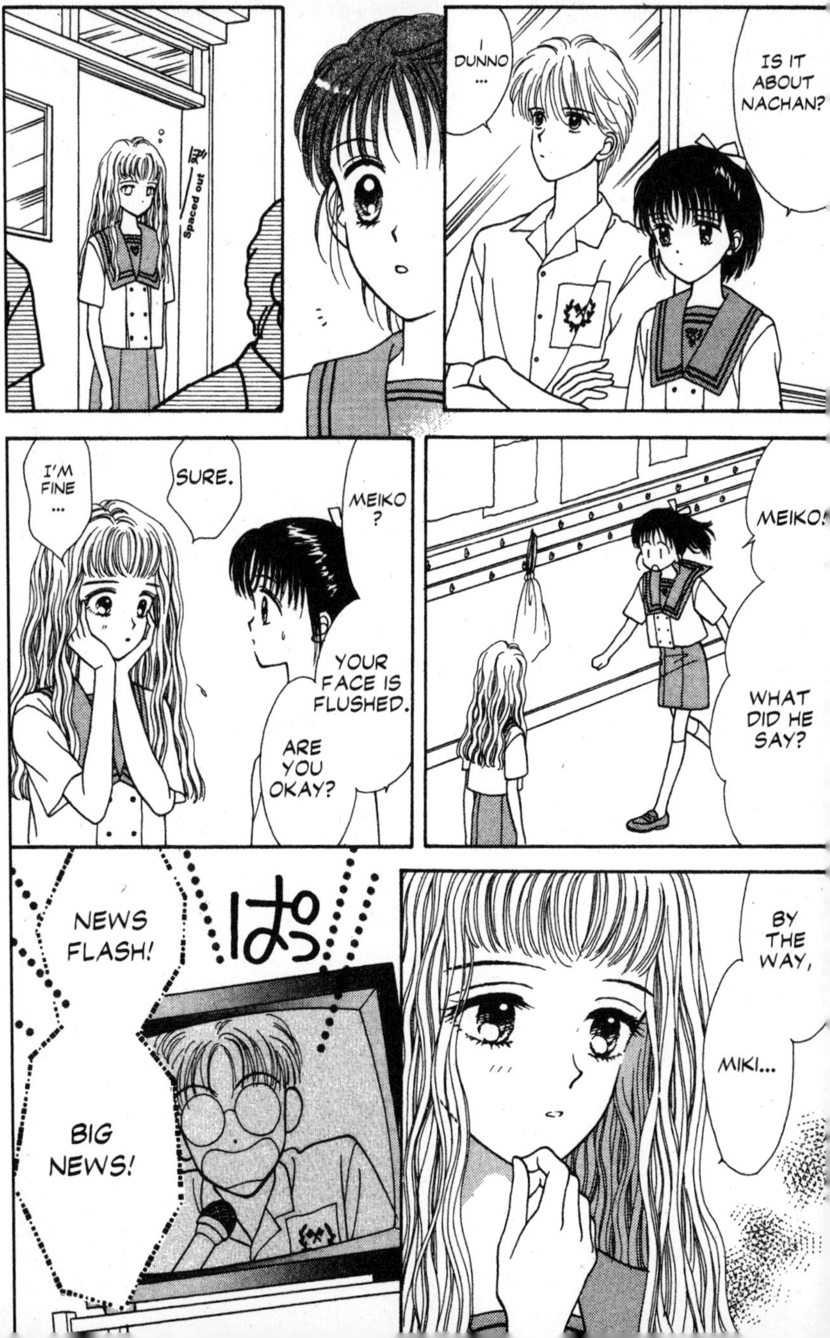
IS IT ABOUT NACHAN?
I DUNNO ...
Spaced out
MEIKO!
WHAT DID HE SAY?
MEIKO?
YOUR FACE IS FLUSHED.
ARE YOU OKAY?
I'M FINE ...
SURE.
BY THE WAY,
MIKI...
ぱっ
NEWS FLASH!
BIG NEWS!

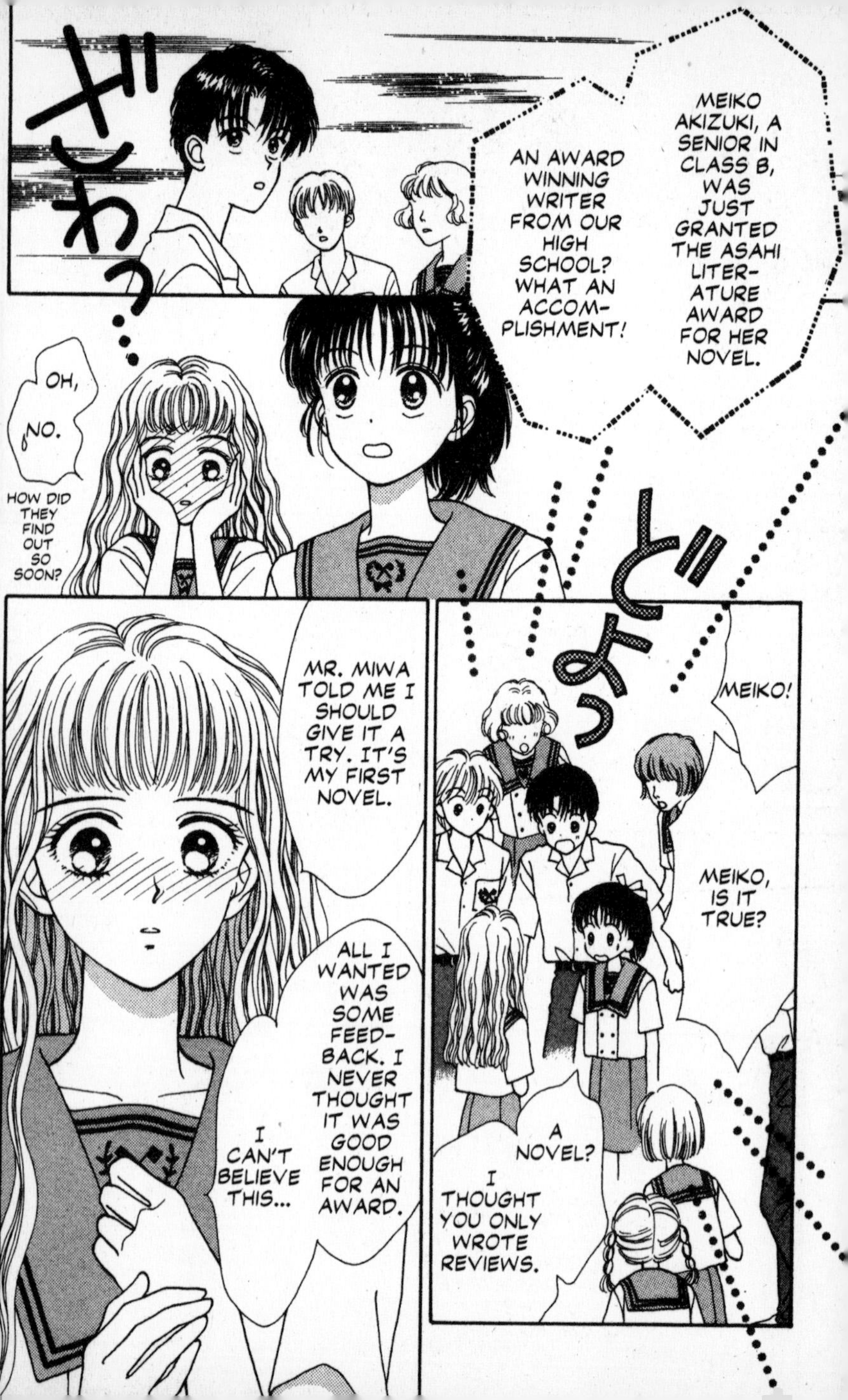
ざわっ
MEIKO AKIZUKI, A SENIOR IN CLASS B, WAS JUST GRANTED THE ASAHI LITER-ATURE AWARD FOR HER NOVEL.
AN AWARD WINNING WRITER FROM OUR HIGH SCHOOL? WHAT AN ACCOM-PLISHMENT!
どよっ
OH, NO.
HOW DID THEY FIND OUT SO SOON?
MEIKO!
MEIKO, IS IT TRUE?
A NOVEL?
I THOUGHT YOU ONLY WROTE REVIEWS.
MR. MIWA TOLD ME I SHOULD GIVE IT A TRY. IT'S MY FIRST NOVEL.
ALL I WANTED WAS SOME FEED-BACK. I NEVER THOUGHT IT WAS GOOD ENOUGH FOR AN AWARD.
I CAN'T BELIEVE THIS...

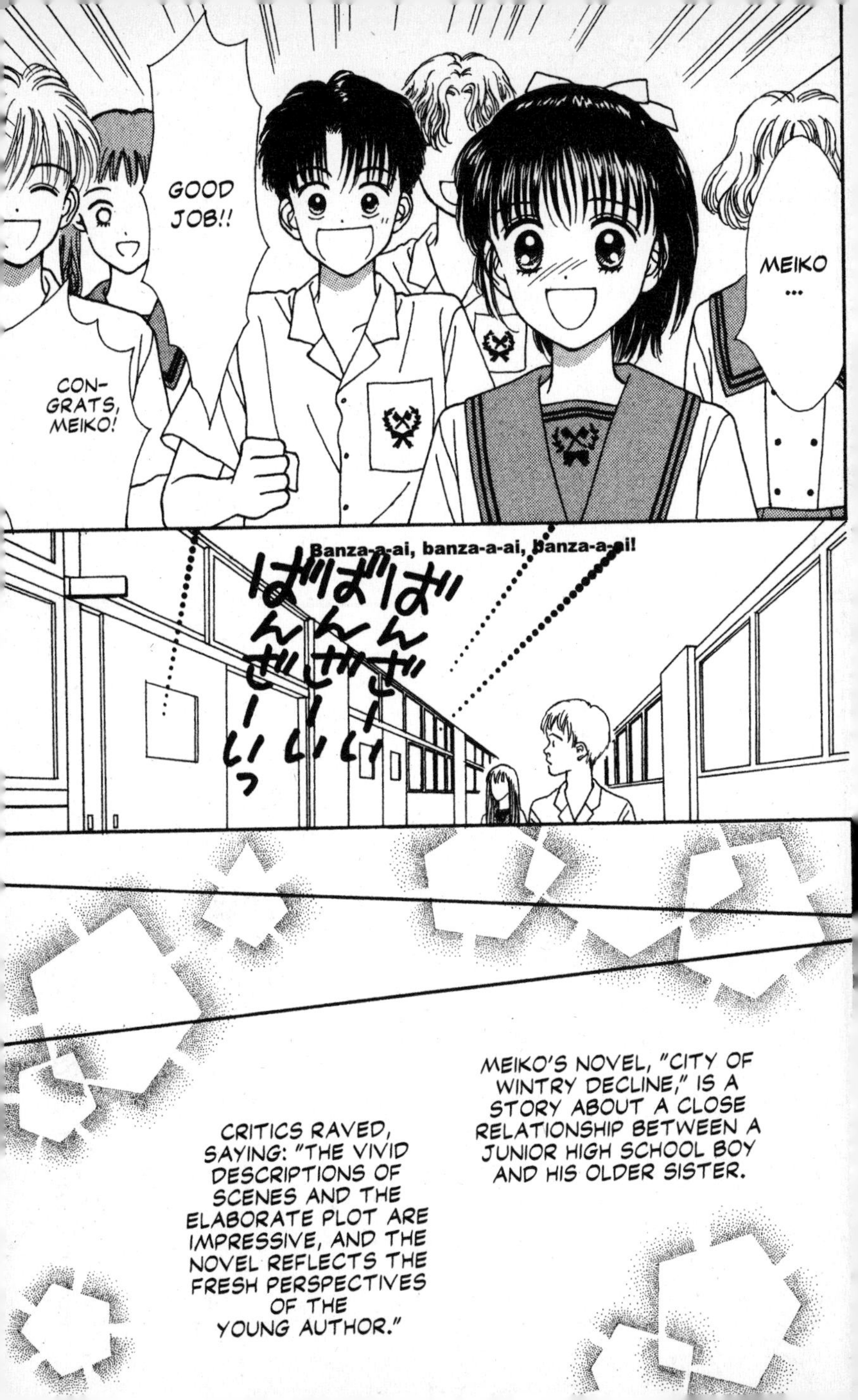
MEIKO ...
GOOD JOB!!
CON-GRATS, MEIKO!
Banza-a-ai, banza-a-ai, banza-a-ai!
ばんざーい ばんざーい ばんざーいっ
MEIKO'S NOVEL, "CITY OF WINTRY DECLINE," IS A STORY ABOUT A CLOSE RELATIONSHIP BETWEEN A JUNIOR HIGH SCHOOL BOY AND HIS OLDER SISTER.
CRITICS RAVED, SAYING: "THE VIVID DESCRIPTIONS OF SCENES AND THE ELABORATE PLOT ARE IMPRESSIVE, AND THE NOVEL REFLECTS THE FRESH PERSPECTIVES OF THE YOUNG AUTHOR."

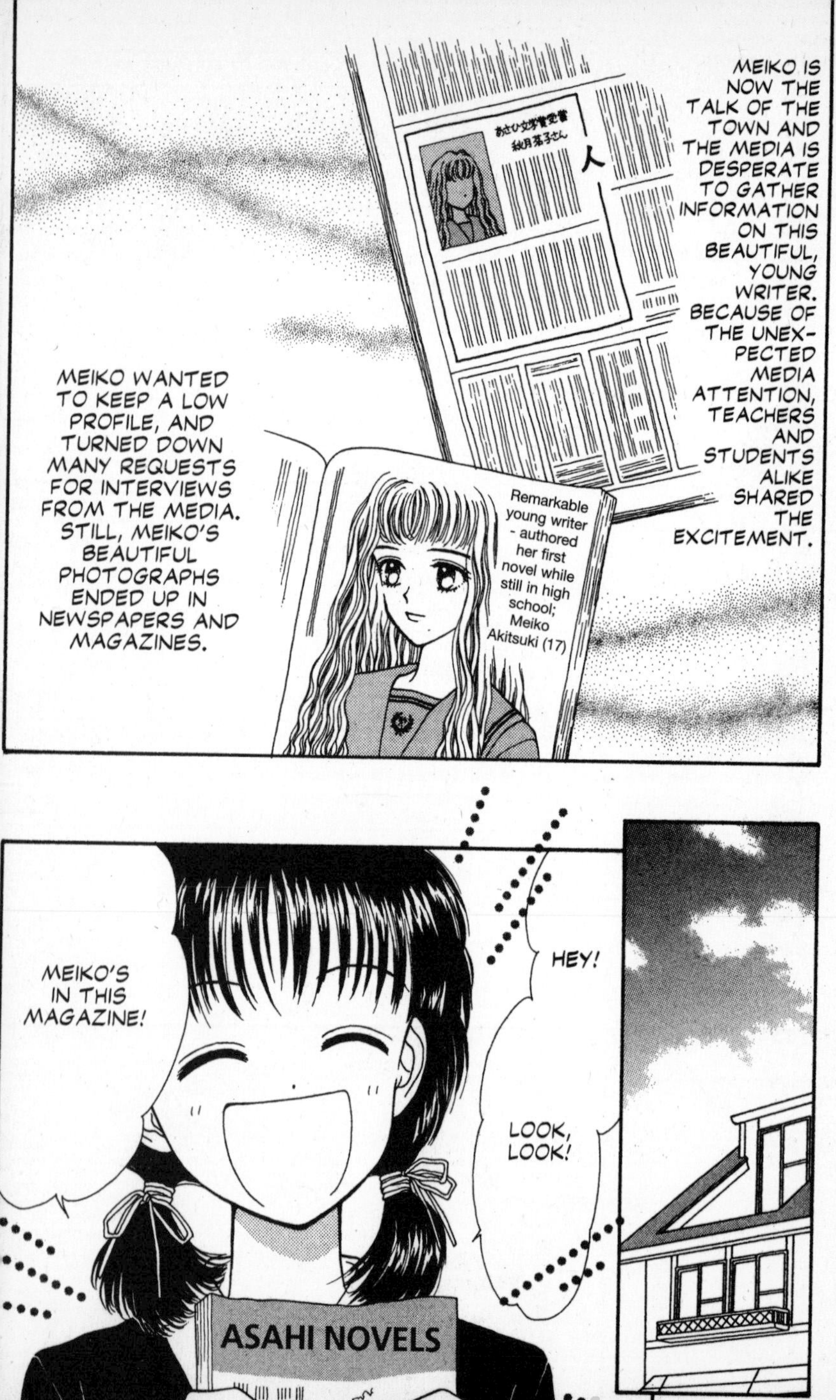

MEIKO IS NOW THE TALK OF THE TOWN AND THE MEDIA IS DESPERATE TO GATHER INFORMATION ON THIS BEAUTIFUL, YOUNG WRITER. BECAUSE OF THE UNEXPECTED MEDIA ATTENTION, TEACHERS AND STUDENTS ALIKE SHARED THE EXCITEMENT.
人
あさひ文学賞受賞
秋月茗子さん
MEIKO WANTED TO KEEP A LOW PROFILE, AND TURNED DOWN MANY REQUESTS FOR INTERVIEWS FROM THE MEDIA. STILL, MEIKO'S BEAUTIFUL PHOTOGRAPHS ENDED UP IN NEWSPAPERS AND MAGAZINES.
Remarkable young writer - authored her first novel while still in high school; Meiko Akitsuki (17)
HEY!
LOOK, LOOK!
MEIKO'S IN THIS MAGAZINE!
ASAHI NOVELS

FREE TALK ⑬

Marmalade Boy the movie is coming up in March. It will be shown along with Dragon Ball Z and Slamdunk. While Dragon Ball Z and Slamdunk are full-length movies, Marmalade Boy is a short movie lasting only 30 minutes. I can't wait to go see it on a big screen. Mr. Babakoshi directed it and it turned out to be a beautiful movie. Hope everyone will see it! The movie covers the first episode of Marmalade Boy. Yuu happens to see Miki before the first dinner together with Miki and their parents. Four CDs, a CD book and a novel of Marmalade Boy have been released (and four CDs are for sale as of December, 1994). I hope you will enjoy them all as well as the comic books.

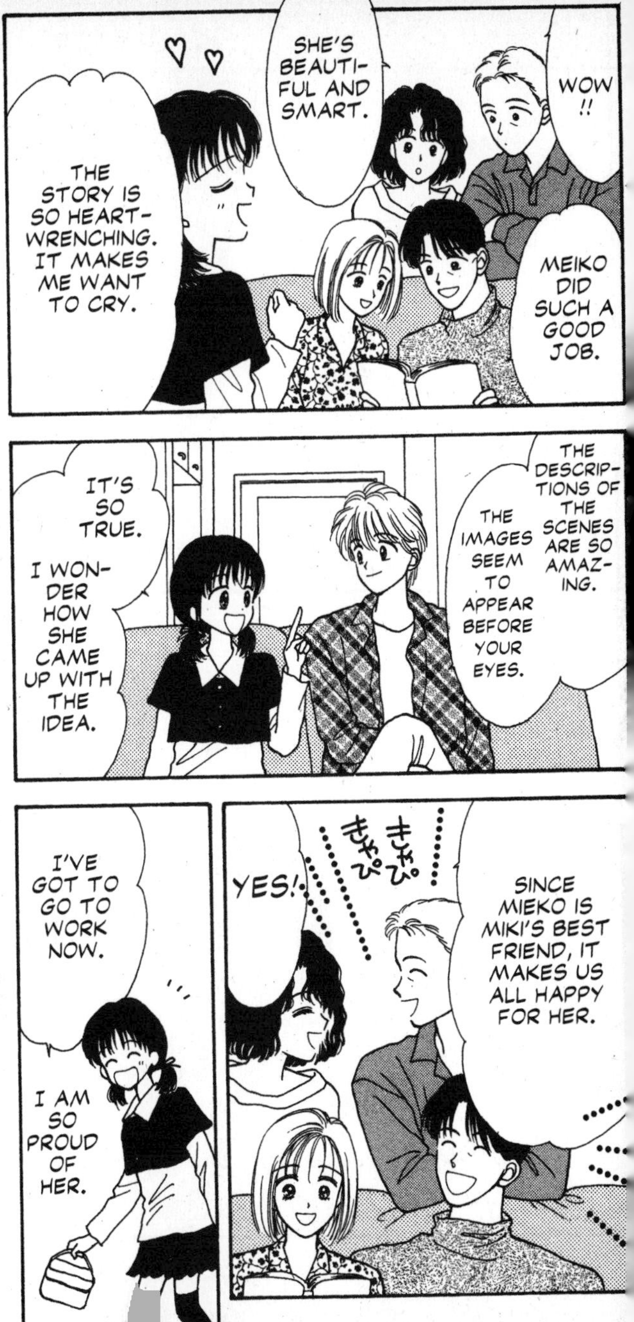
WOW !!
SHE'S BEAUTIFUL AND SMART.
MEIKO DID SUCH A GOOD JOB.
THE STORY IS SO HEART-WRENCHING. IT MAKES ME WANT TO CRY.
THE DESCRIPTIONS OF THE SCENES ARE SO AMAZING.
THE IMAGES SEEM TO APPEAR BEFORE YOUR EYES.
IT'S SO TRUE.
I WONDER HOW SHE CAME UP WITH THE IDEA.
SINCE MIEKO IS MIKI'S BEST FRIEND, IT MAKES US ALL HAPPY FOR HER.
きゃぴきゃぴ
YES!
I'VE GOT TO GO TO WORK NOW.
I AM SO PROUD OF HER.

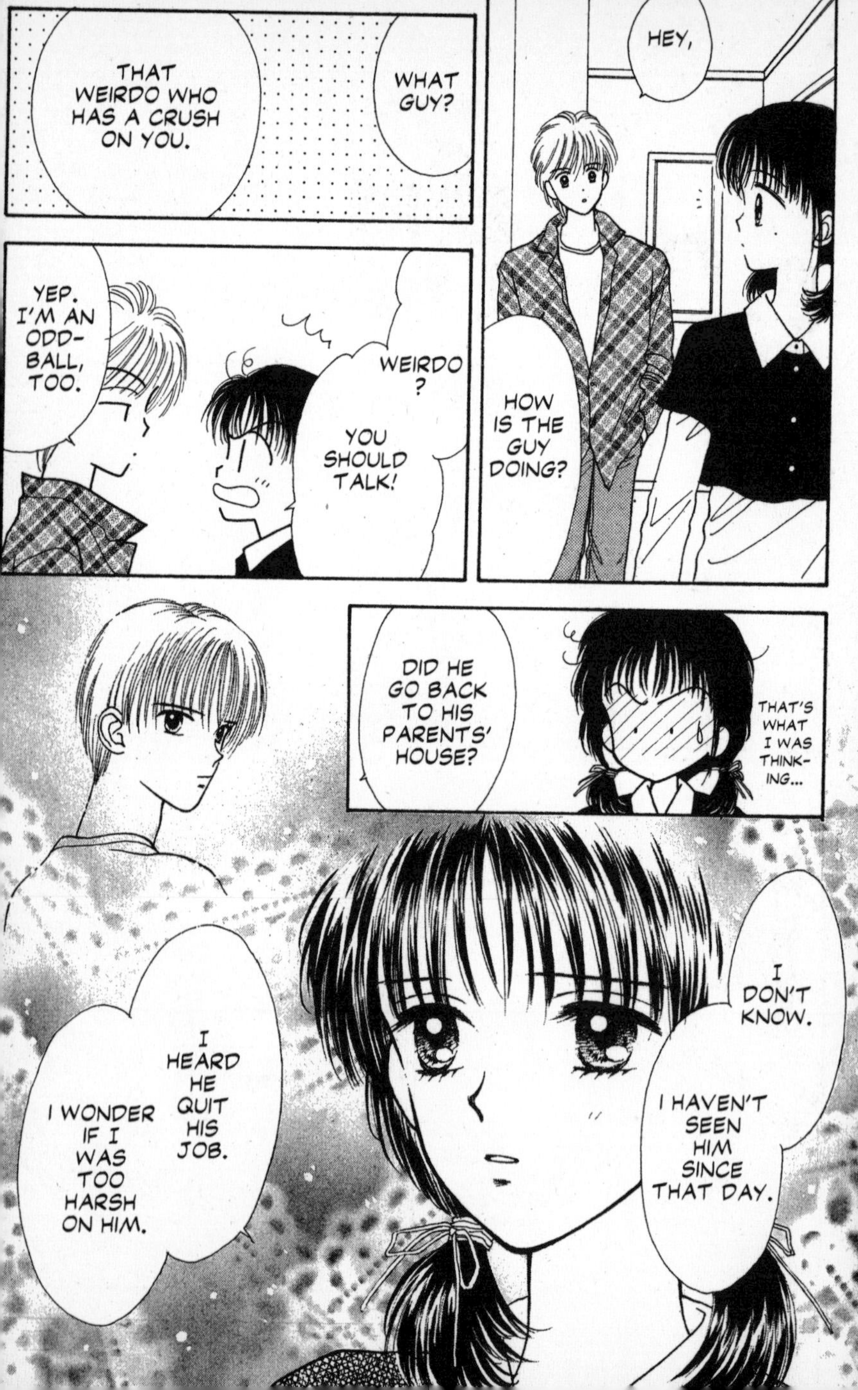
HEY,
HOW IS THE GUY DOING?
WHAT GUY?
THAT WEIRDO WHO HAS A CRUSH ON YOU.
WEIRDO? YOU SHOULD TALK!
YEP. I'M AN ODD-BALL, TOO.
DID HE GO BACK TO HIS PARENTS' HOUSE?
THAT'S WHAT I WAS THINK-ING...
I DON'T KNOW.
I HAVEN'T SEEN HIM SINCE THAT DAY.
I HEARD HE QUIT HIS JOB.
I WONDER IF I WAS TOO HARSH ON HIM.

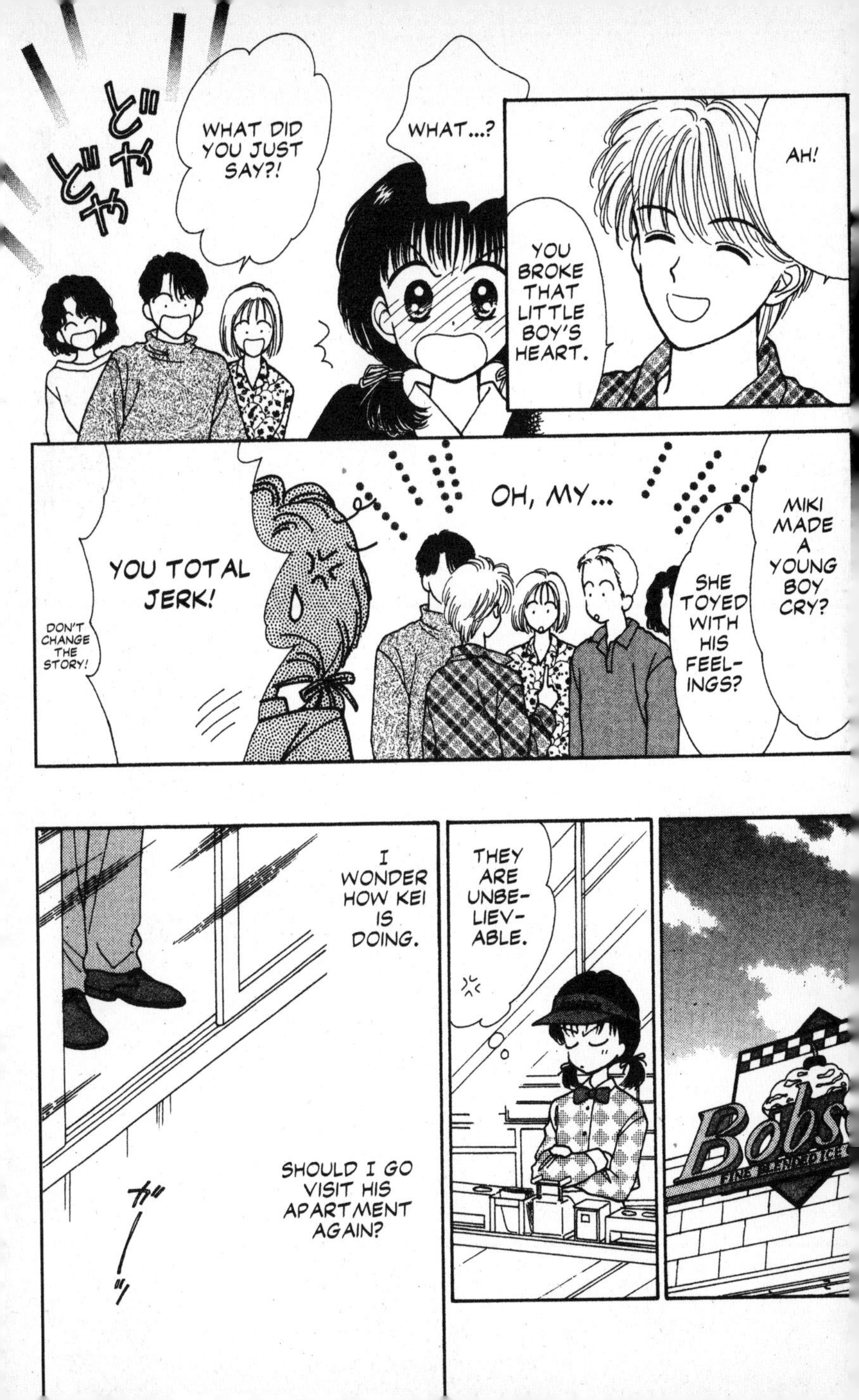
AH!
YOU BROKE THAT LITTLE BOY'S HEART.
WHAT...?
WHAT DID YOU JUST SAY?!
どやどや
MIKI MADE A YOUNG BOY CRY?
SHE TOYED WITH HIS FEELINGS?
OH, MY...
YOU TOTAL JERK!
DON'T CHANGE THE STORY!
THEY ARE UNBE-LIEV-ABLE.
I WONDER HOW KEI IS DOING.
SHOULD I GO VISIT HIS APARTMENT AGAIN?

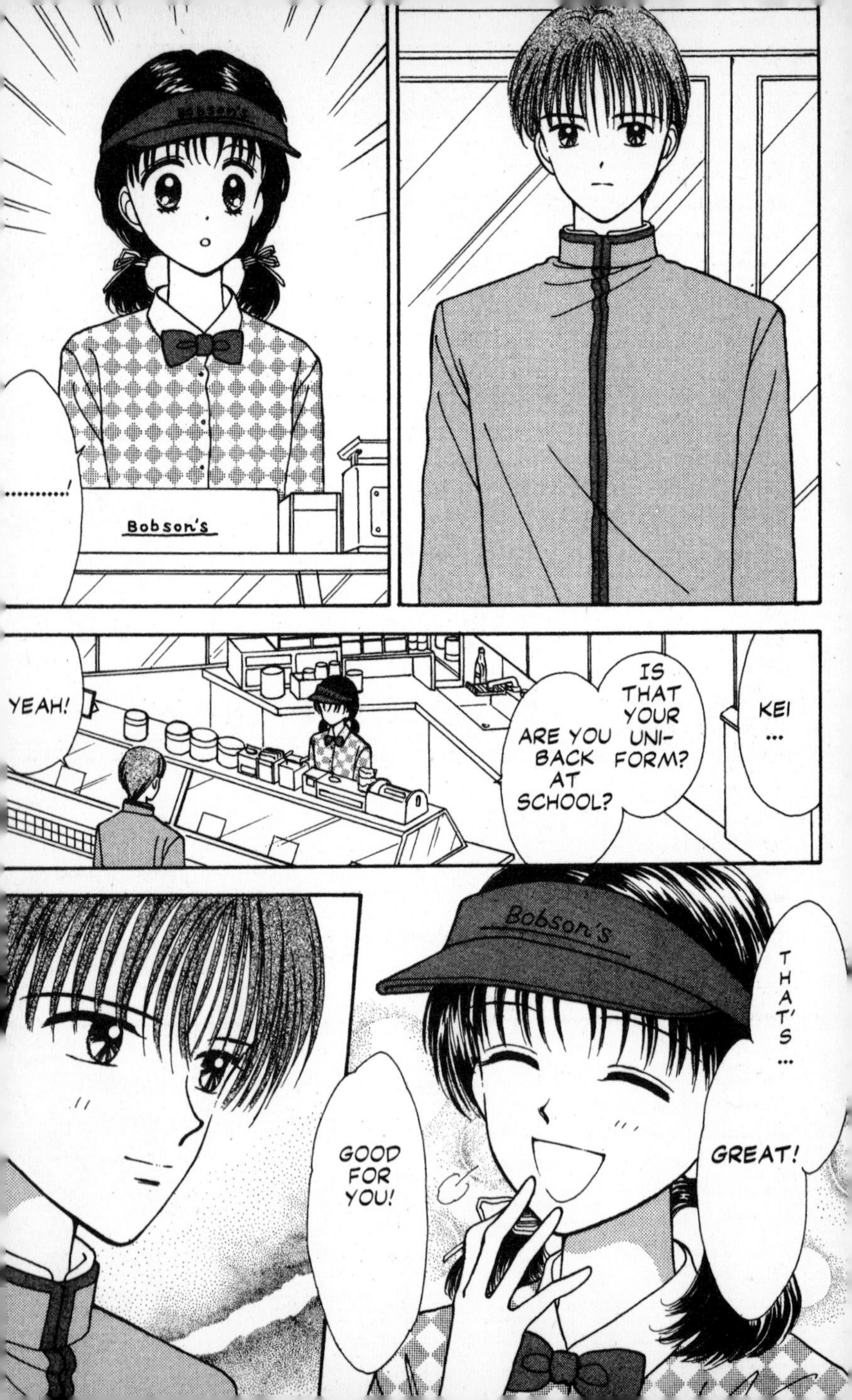
Bobson's
............!
Bobson's
KEI ...
IS THAT YOUR UNI-FORM?
ARE YOU BACK AT SCHOOL?
YEAH!
Bobson's
THAT'S ...
GREAT!
GOOD FOR YOU!

FREE TALK ⑭

My illustration book was finally published on January 25th. I always wanted to share this with the public, so I am very happy! I had a really tight deadline, and I wish I had more time to put in more stuff. But I am happy that the book came out beautifully. The book is entitled "Marmalade Boy," but it includes many drawings of characters in "Handsome Girl" as well as in "Marmalade Boy." The "project pages" include rough sketches from my sketch books and comments on my works. I wanted to throw in more sketches in the book but the number of pages were limited. I tried to write positive things about my work. However, I had trouble expressing myself. Later, when I reviewed my comments, I found myself having different feelings toward some drawings than what I had written. Still, I hope everyone will enjoy the book.

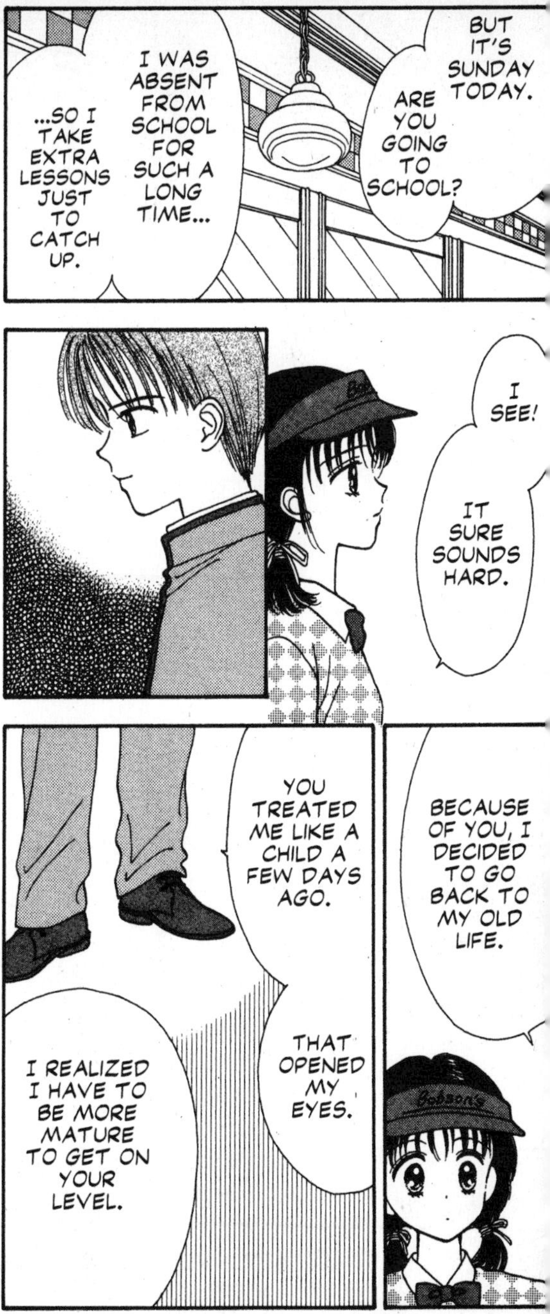
BUT IT'S SUNDAY TODAY.
ARE YOU GOING TO SCHOOL?
I WAS ABSENT FROM SCHOOL FOR SUCH A LONG TIME...
...SO I TAKE EXTRA LESSONS JUST TO CATCH UP.
I SEE!
IT SURE SOUNDS HARD.
BECAUSE OF YOU, I DECIDED TO GO BACK TO MY OLD LIFE.
YOU TREATED ME LIKE A CHILD A FEW DAYS AGO.
THAT OPENED MY EYES.
I REALIZED I HAVE TO BE MORE MATURE TO GET ON YOUR LEVEL.

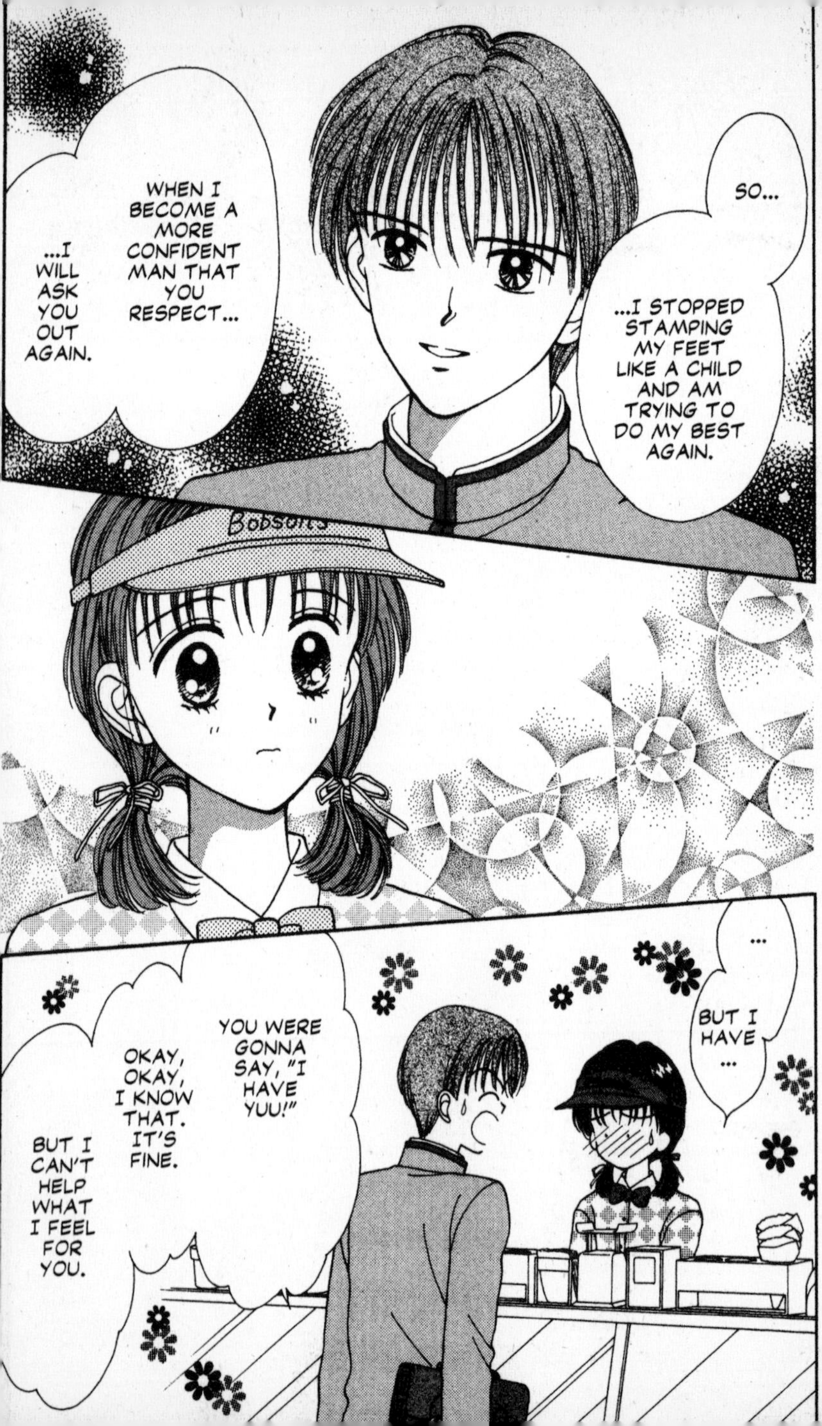
SO...
...I STOPPED STAMPING MY FEET LIKE A CHILD AND AM TRYING TO DO MY BEST AGAIN.
WHEN I BECOME A MORE CONFIDENT MAN THAT YOU RESPECT...
...I WILL ASK YOU OUT AGAIN.
...
BUT I HAVE ...
YOU WERE GONNA SAY, "I HAVE YUU!"
OKAY, OKAY, I KNOW THAT. IT'S FINE.
BUT I CAN'T HELP WHAT I FEEL FOR YOU.

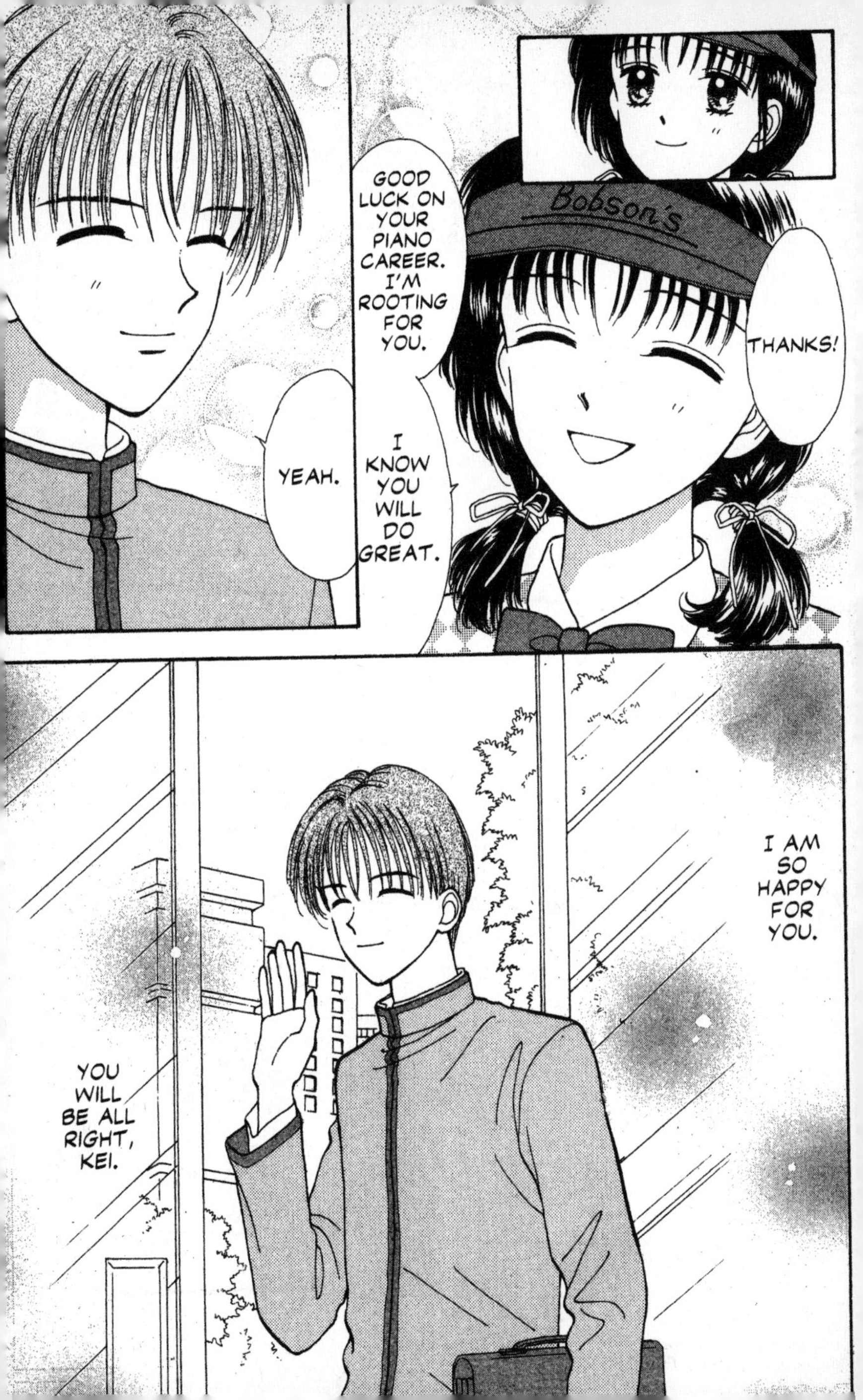
Bobson's
THANKS!
GOOD LUCK ON YOUR PIANO CAREER. I'M ROOTING FOR YOU.
I KNOW YOU WILL DO GREAT.
YEAH.
I AM SO HAPPY FOR YOU.
YOU WILL BE ALL RIGHT, KEI.

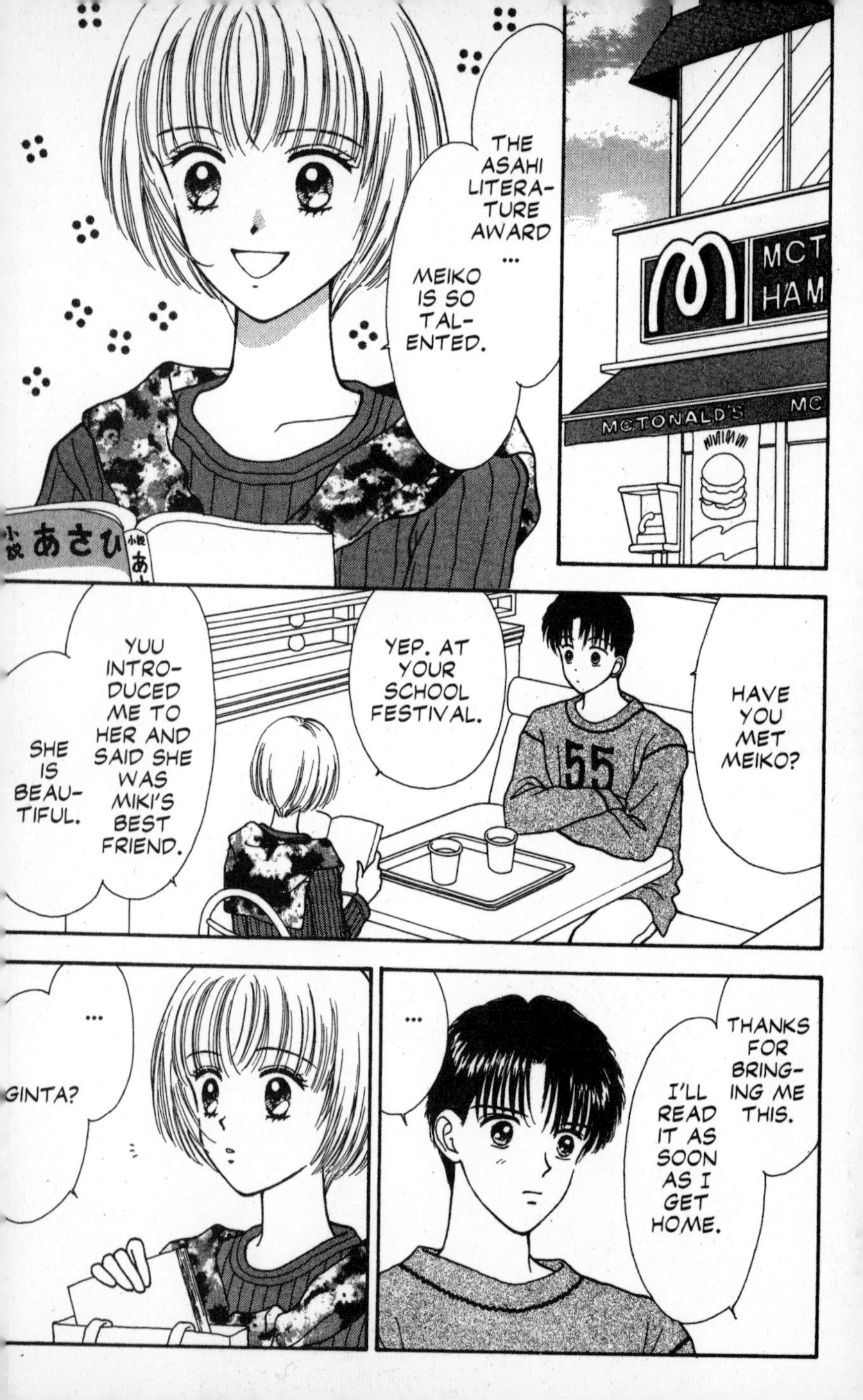
MCT
HAM
MCTONALD'S
MC
THE ASAHI LITERATURE AWARD ...
MEIKO IS SO TALENTED.
小説あさひ
HAVE YOU MET MEIKO?
YEP. AT YOUR SCHOOL FESTIVAL.
YUU INTRODUCED ME TO HER AND SAID SHE WAS MIKI'S BEST FRIEND.
SHE IS BEAUTIFUL.
THANKS FOR BRINGING ME THIS.
I'LL READ IT AS SOON AS I GET HOME.
...
...
GINTA?

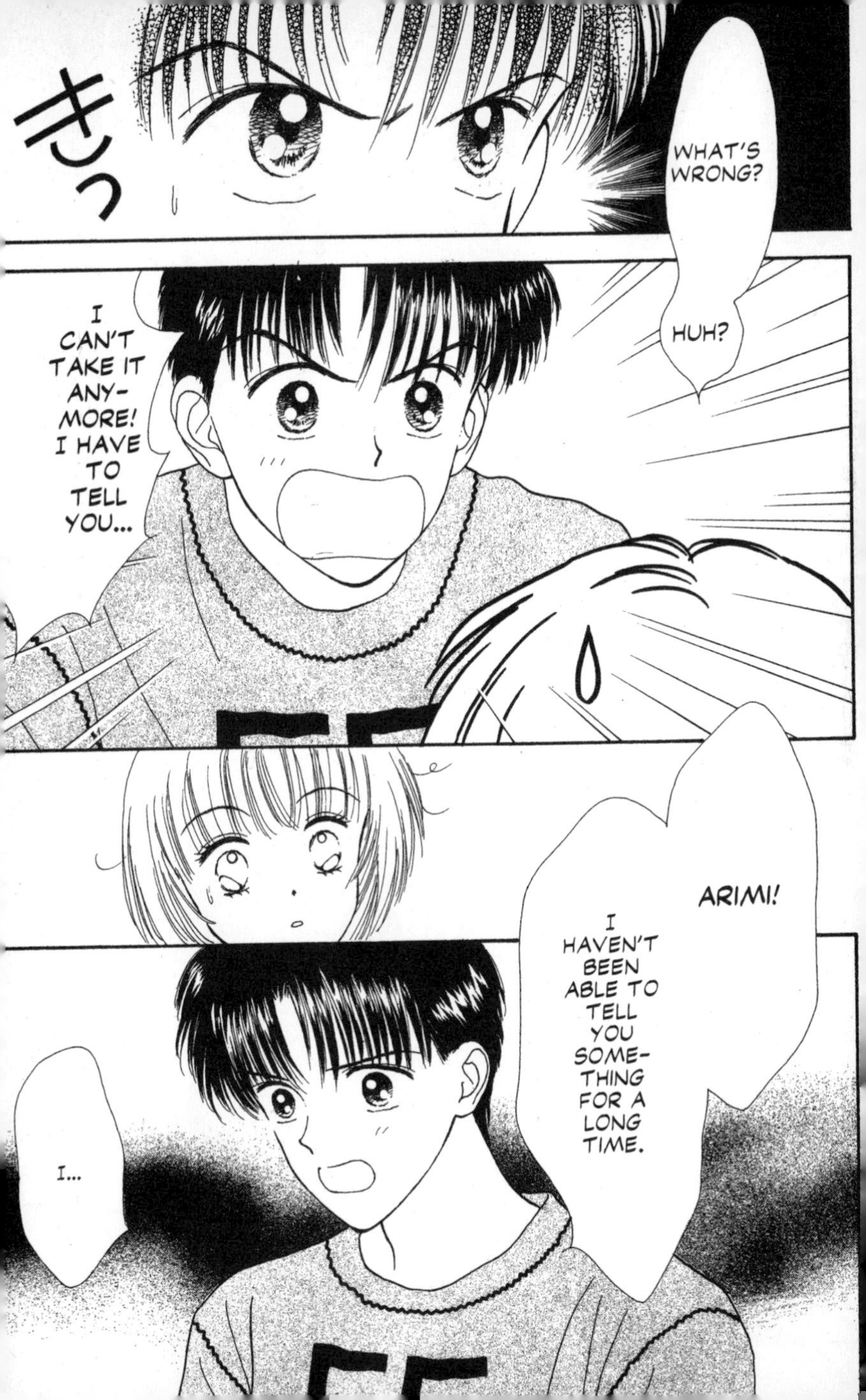

WHAT'S WRONG?
きっ
HUH?
I CAN'T TAKE IT ANYMORE! I HAVE TO TELL YOU...
ARIMI!
I HAVEN'T BEEN ABLE TO TELL YOU SOMETHING FOR A LONG TIME.
I...

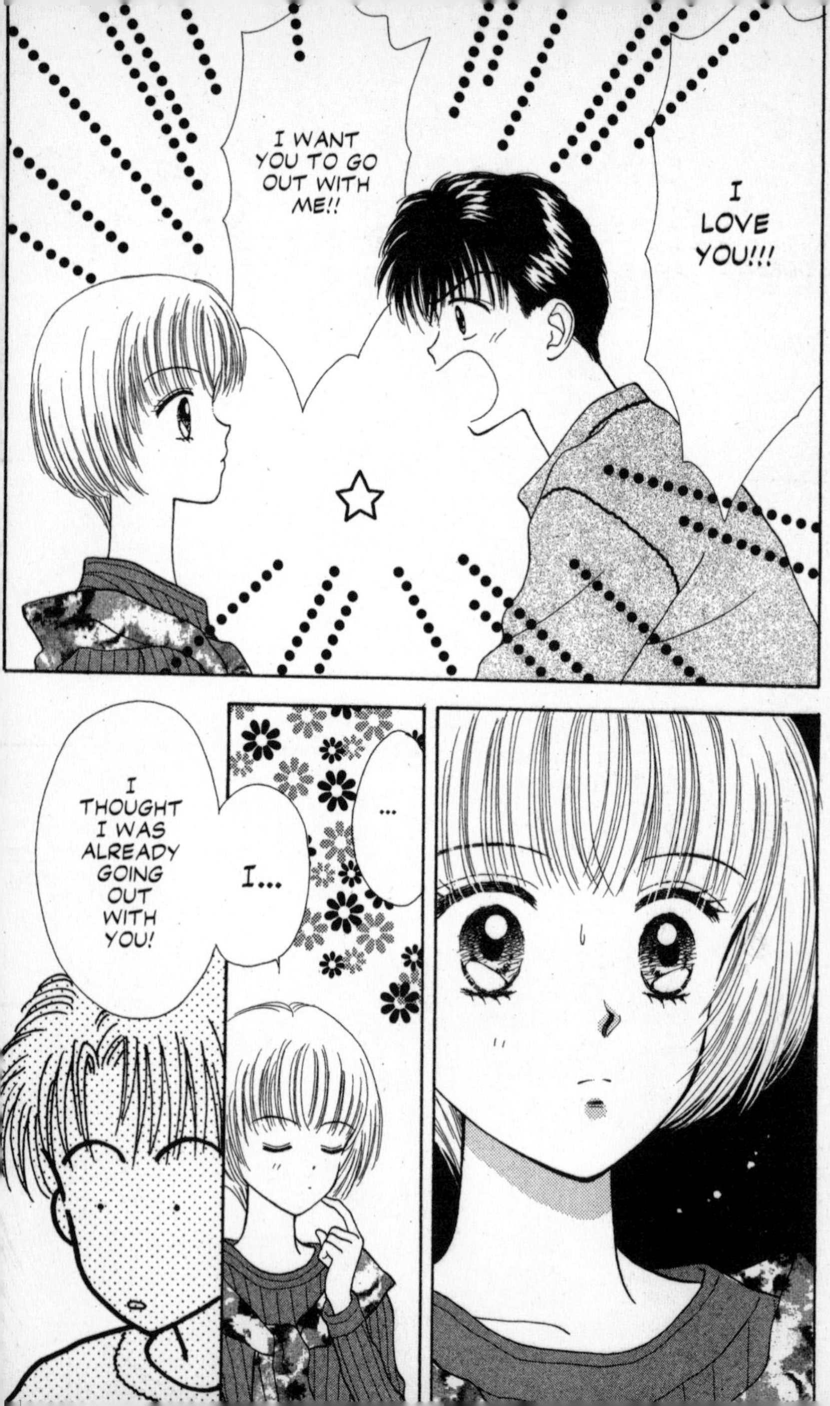
I LOVE YOU!!!
I WANT YOU TO GO OUT WITH ME!!
...
I...
I THOUGHT I WAS ALREADY GOING OUT WITH YOU!

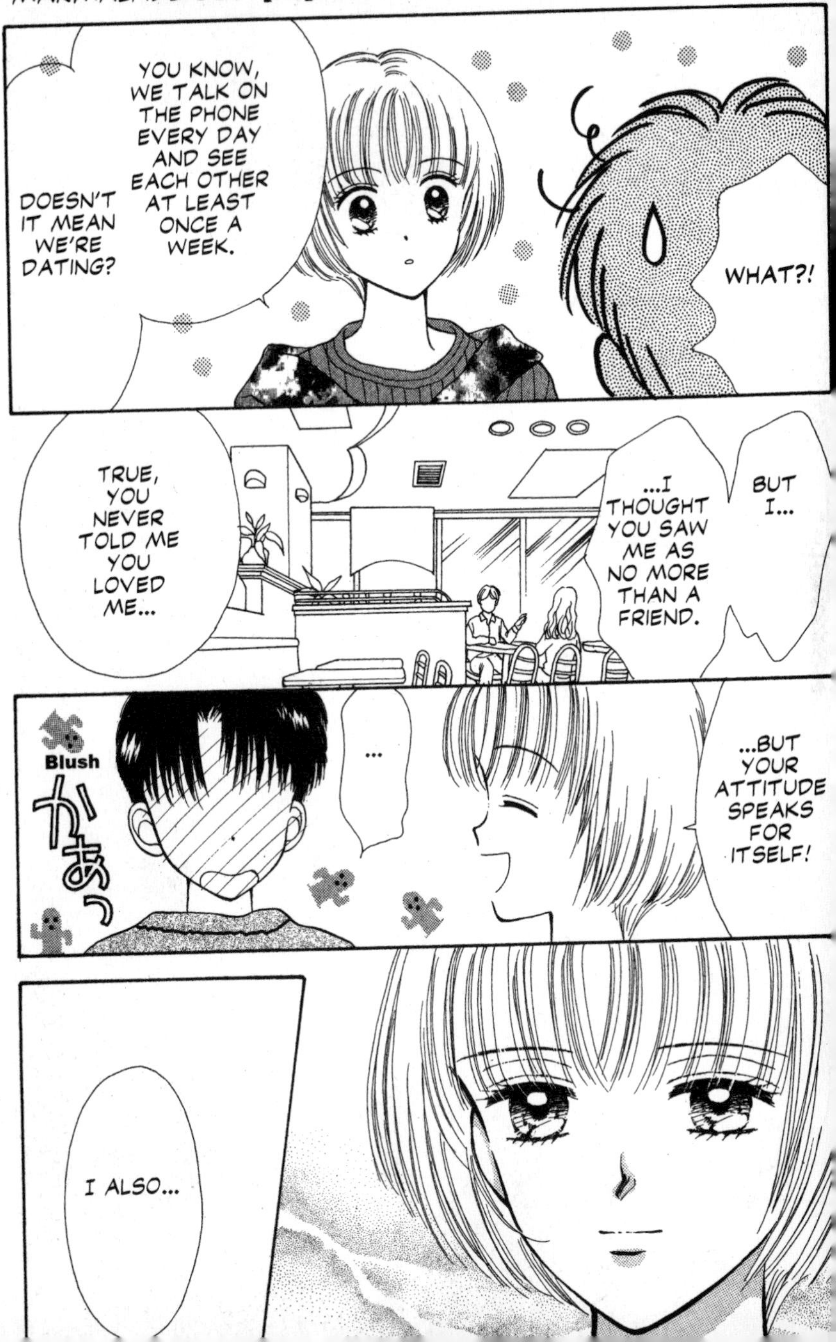
YOU KNOW, WE TALK ON THE PHONE EVERY DAY AND SEE EACH OTHER AT LEAST ONCE A WEEK.
DOESN'T IT MEAN WE'RE DATING?
WHAT?!
BUT I...
...I THOUGHT YOU SAW ME AS NO MORE THAN A FRIEND.
TRUE, YOU NEVER TOLD ME YOU LOVED ME...
...BUT YOUR ATTITUDE SPEAKS FOR ITSELF!
...
Blush
かあっ
I ALSO...

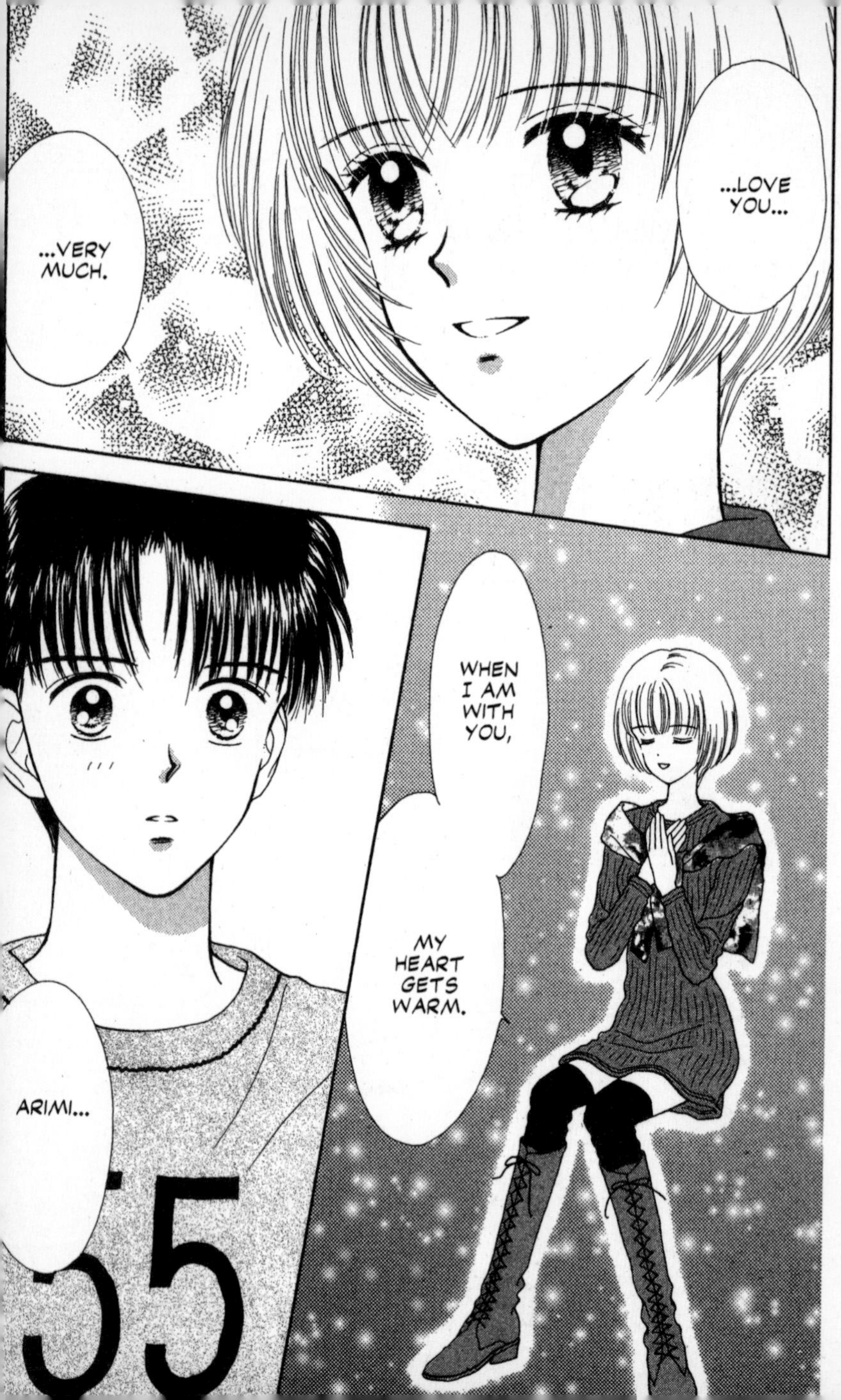
...LOVE YOU...
...VERY MUCH.
WHEN I AM WITH YOU,
MY HEART GETS WARM.
ARIMI...

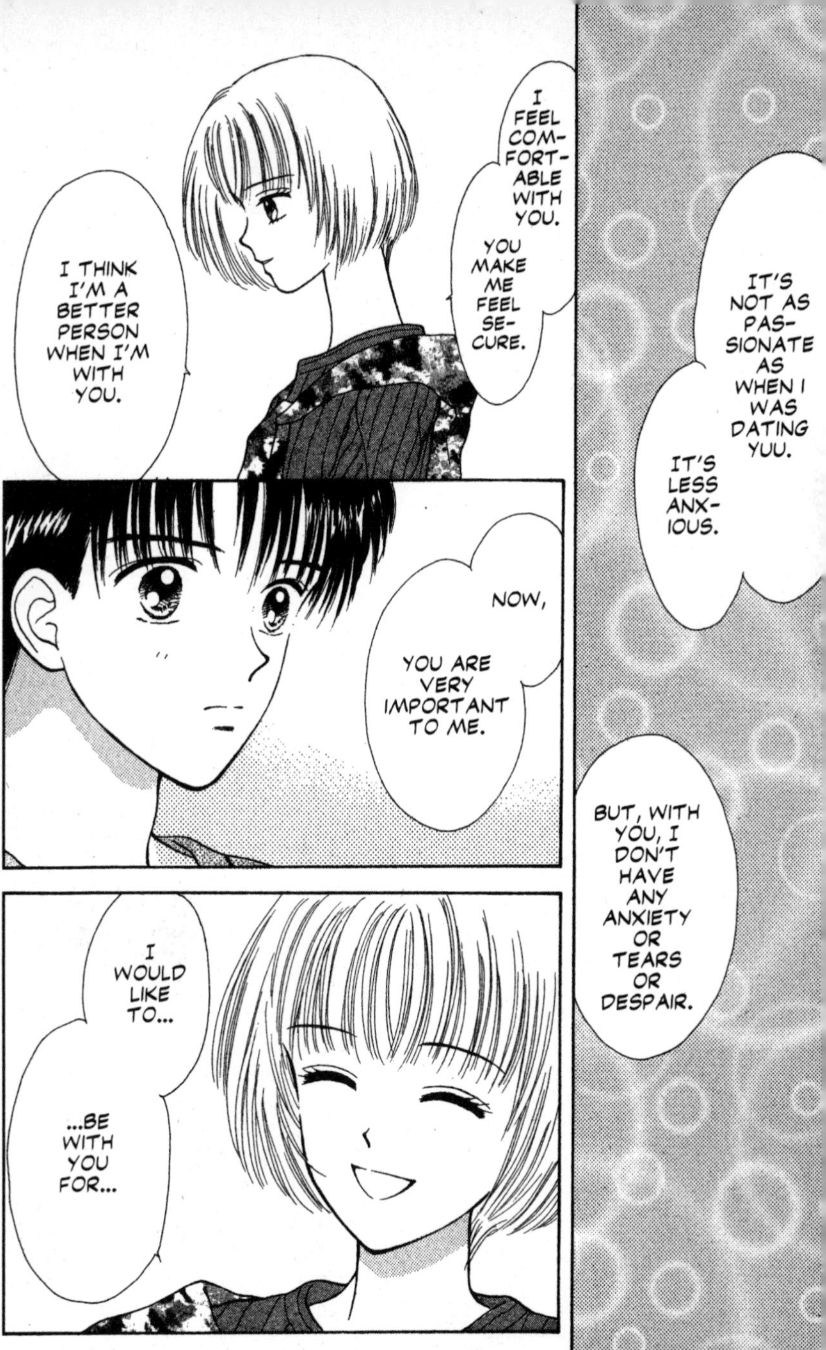
IT'S NOT AS PAS-SIONATE AS WHEN I WAS DATING YUU.
IT'S LESS ANX-IOUS.
BUT, WITH YOU, I DON'T HAVE ANY ANXIETY OR TEARS OR DESPAIR.
I FEEL COM-FORT-ABLE WITH YOU.
YOU MAKE ME FEEL SE-CURE.
I THINK I'M A BETTER PERSON WHEN I'M WITH YOU.
NOW,
YOU ARE VERY IMPORTANT TO ME.
I WOULD LIKE TO...
...BE WITH YOU FOR...

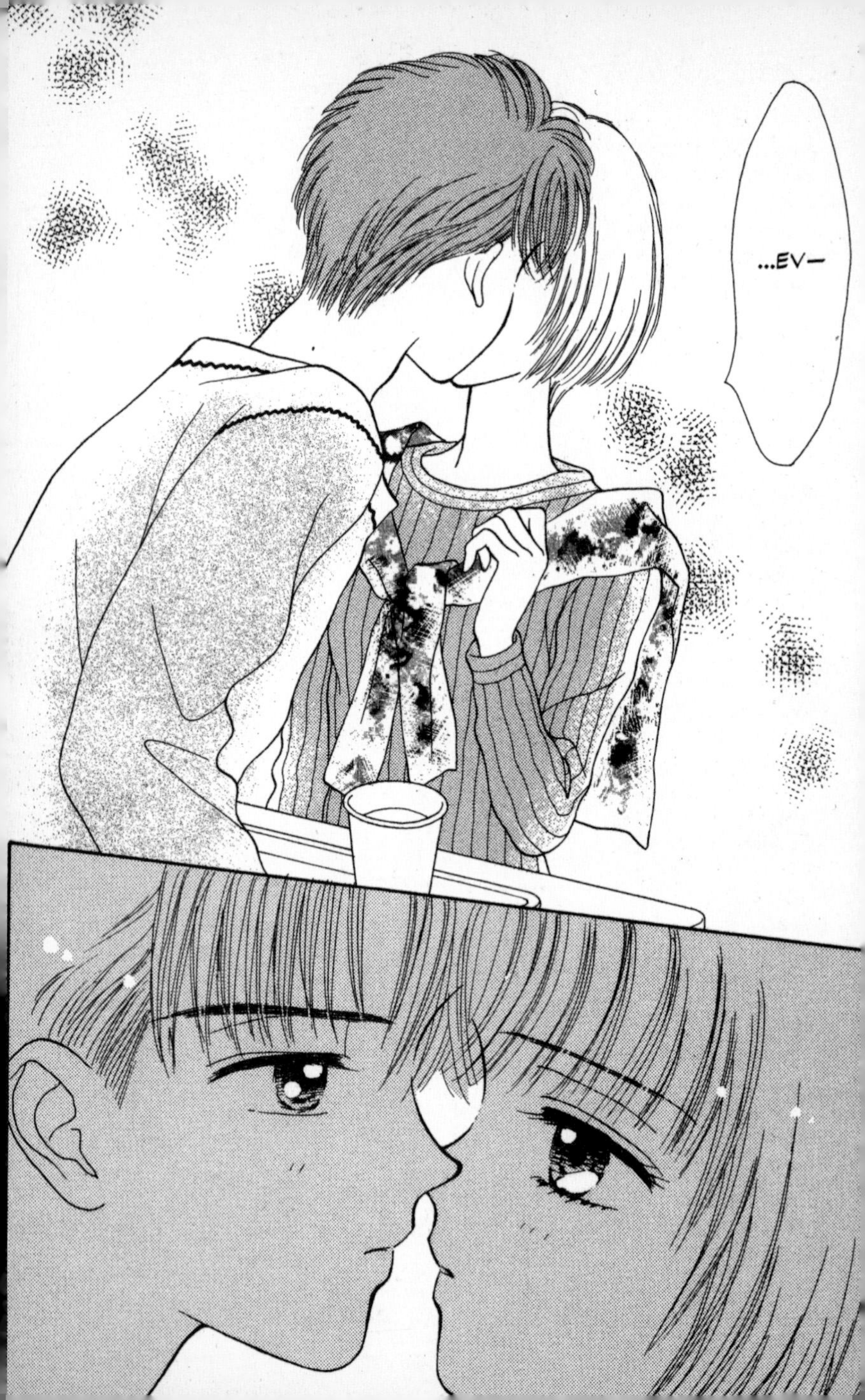
...EV—

FREE TALK ⑮

Many readers tell me they enjoy the illustrations on the title pages. However, I don't have a clue which illustrations they like the best. So please give me more opinions! The illustration book has a bonus poster enclosed. It's a double-sided poster, and I drew the pictures especially for it. The front side features Yuu and Ginta. The idea came from a Marmalade Boy doujinshi that an editor gave me which included a drawing of Yuu and Ginta in a homosexual relationship. I realized some people enjoy those kind of things so I did the drawing of the two together. I myself don't have much interest in the homosexual culture, but I thought whoever drew Yuu and Ginta as homosexuals must like Marmalade Boy very much. That makes me happy, so I really enjoyed reading the doujinshi magazine, too. I would love to see drawings with different perspectives and would like to read more issues of the magazine. The back side of the poster features Suzu. The book costs 15 dollars. It's a bit expensive, but I hope you will buy one. Okay?*

To be continued in volume 7.

* Doujinshi - Japanese fan comics

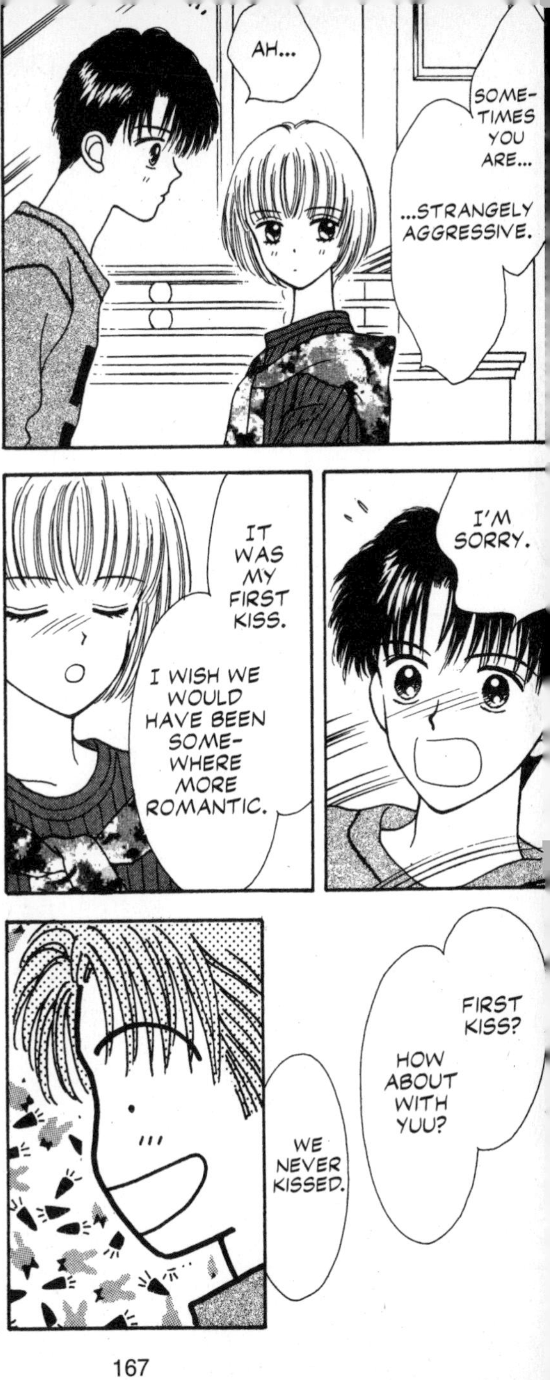
AH...
SOMETIMES YOU ARE... ...STRANGELY AGGRESSIVE.
I'M SORRY.
IT WAS MY FIRST KISS.
I WISH WE WOULD HAVE BEEN SOMEWHERE MORE ROMANTIC.
FIRST KISS? HOW ABOUT WITH YUU?
WE NEVER KISSED.

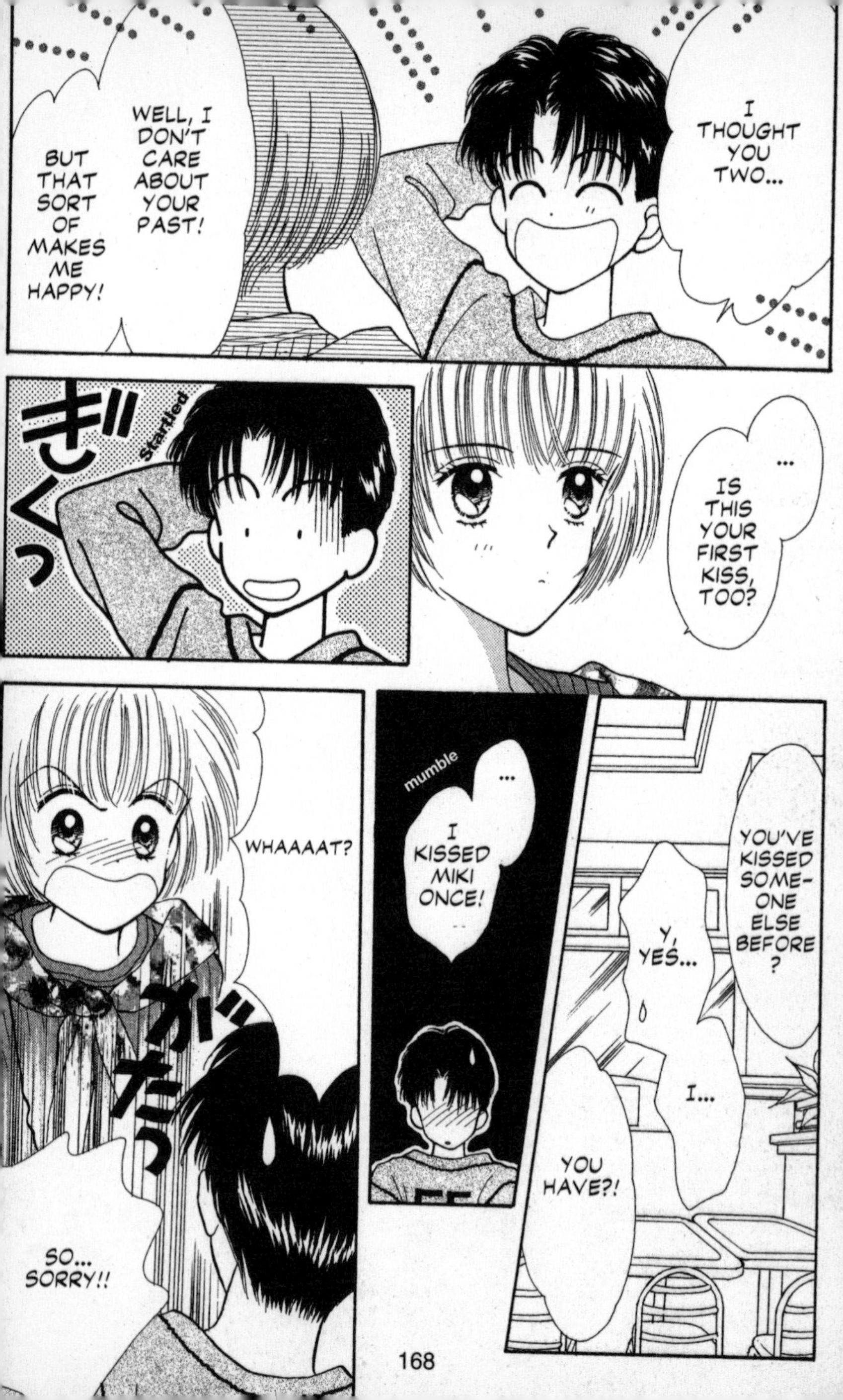
I THOUGHT YOU TWO...
WELL, I DON'T CARE ABOUT YOUR PAST!
BUT THAT SORT OF MAKES ME HAPPY!
... IS THIS YOUR FIRST KISS, TOO?
ぎくっ
Startled
YOU'VE KISSED SOME-ONE ELSE BEFORE?
Y, YES...
I...
YOU HAVE?!
mumble
... I KISSED MIKI ONCE!
WHAAAAT?
ガたっ
SO... SORRY!!

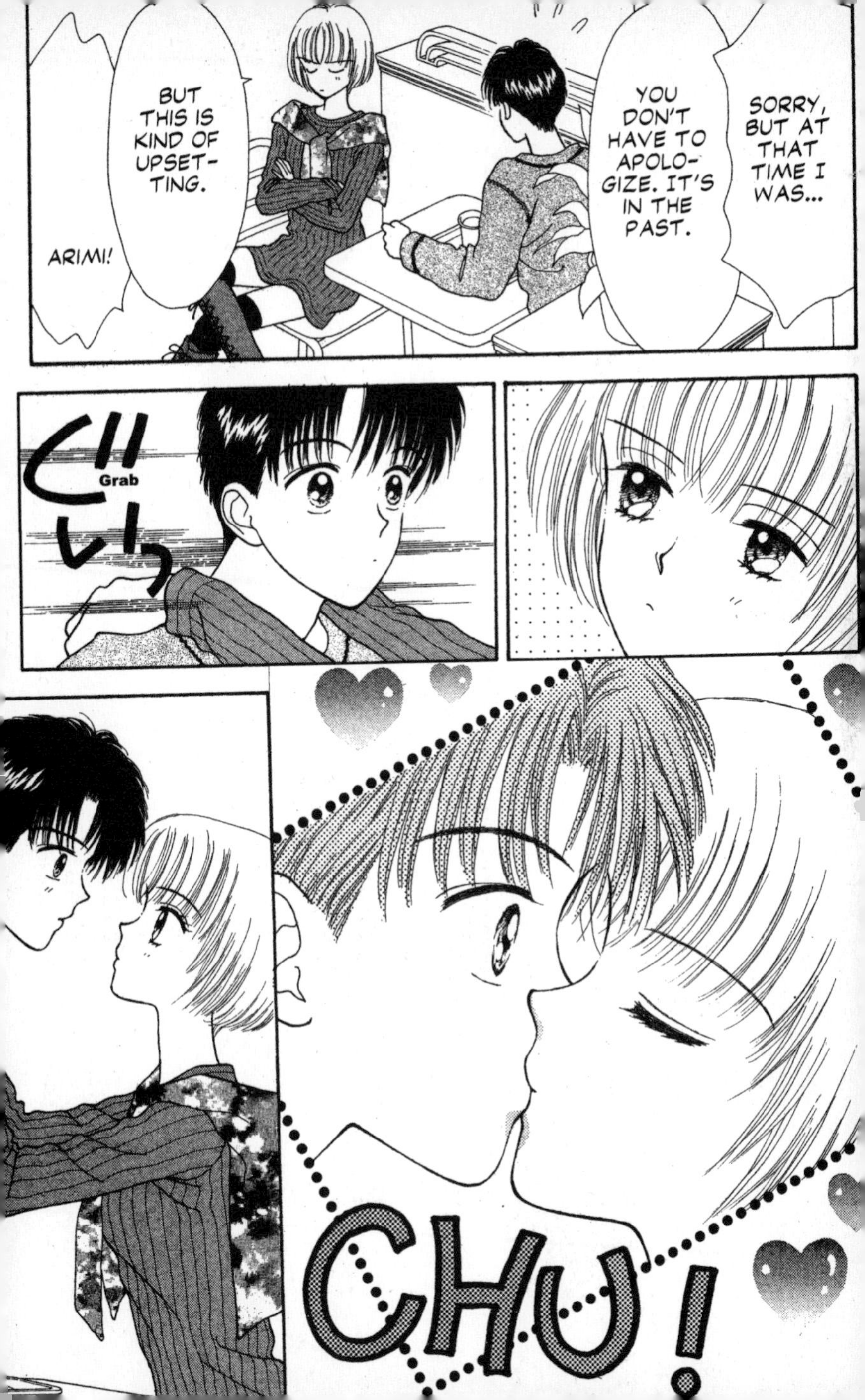
SORRY, BUT AT THAT TIME I WAS...
YOU DON'T HAVE TO APOLOGIZE. IT'S IN THE PAST.
BUT THIS IS KIND OF UPSET-TING.
ARIMI!
ぐいっ
Grab
CHU!

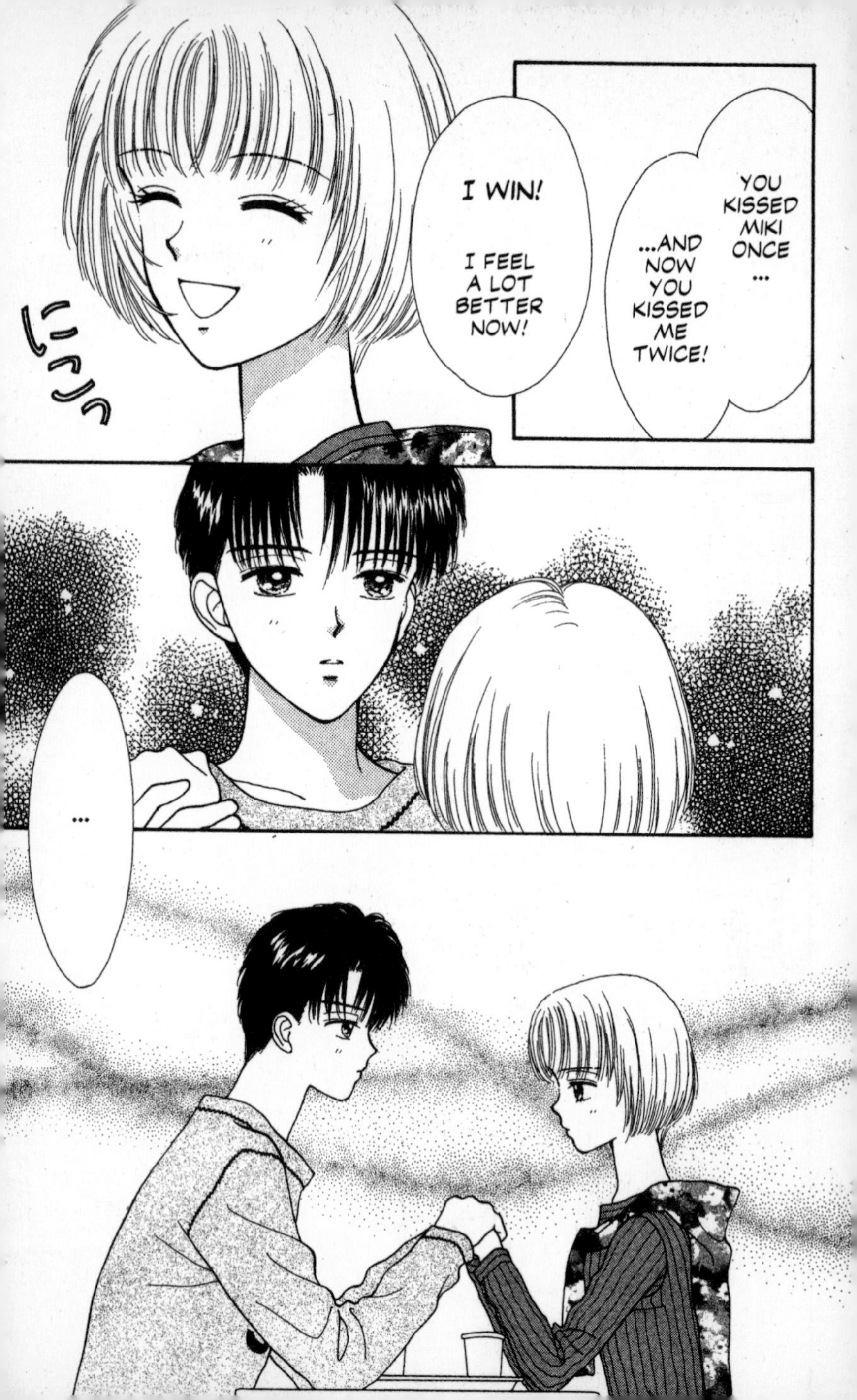
YOU KISSED MIKI ONCE ...
...AND NOW YOU KISSED ME TWICE!
I WIN!
I FEEL A LOT BETTER NOW!
...

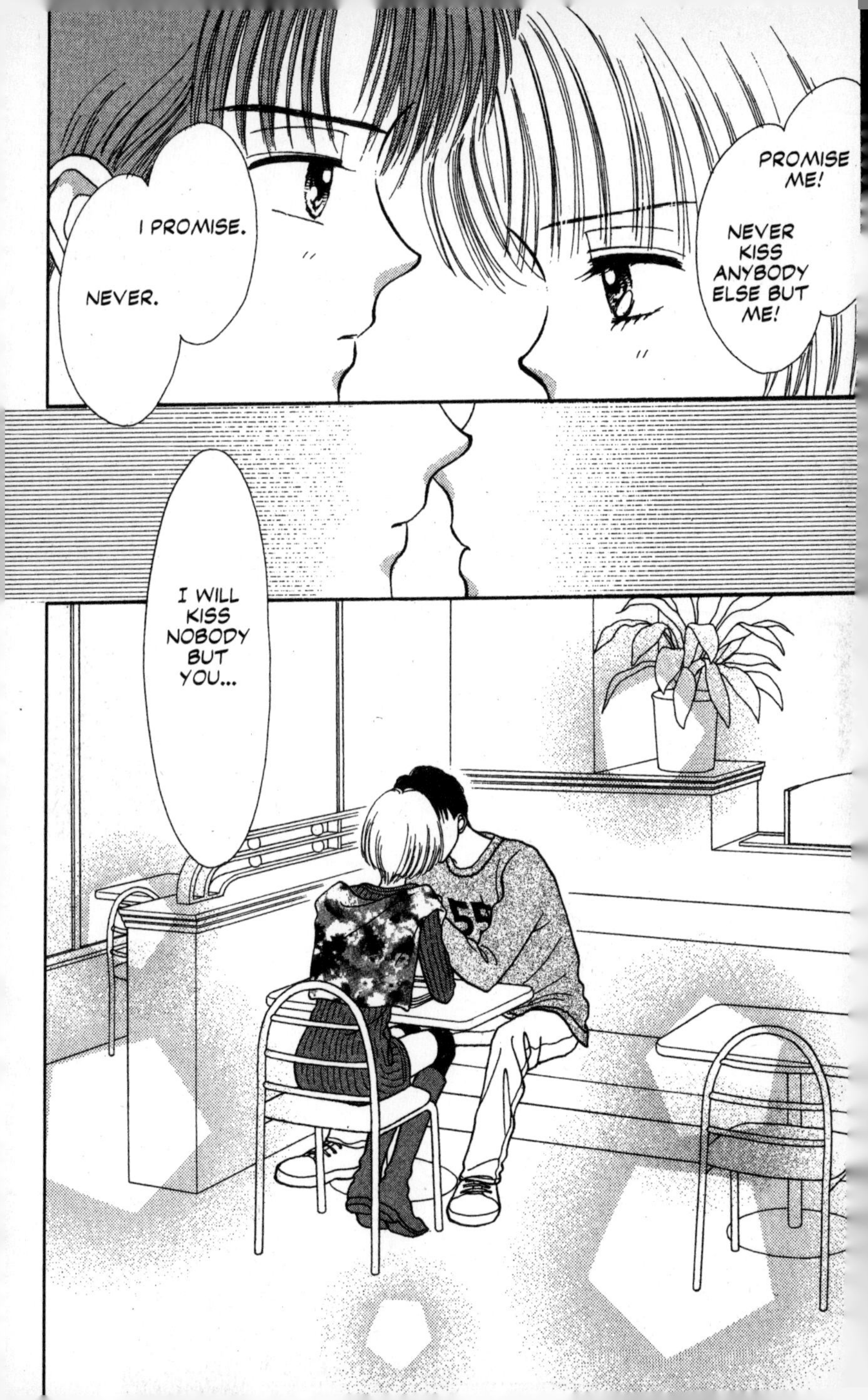
PROMISE ME!
NEVER KISS ANYBODY ELSE BUT ME!
I PROMISE.
NEVER.
I WILL KISS NOBODY BUT YOU...

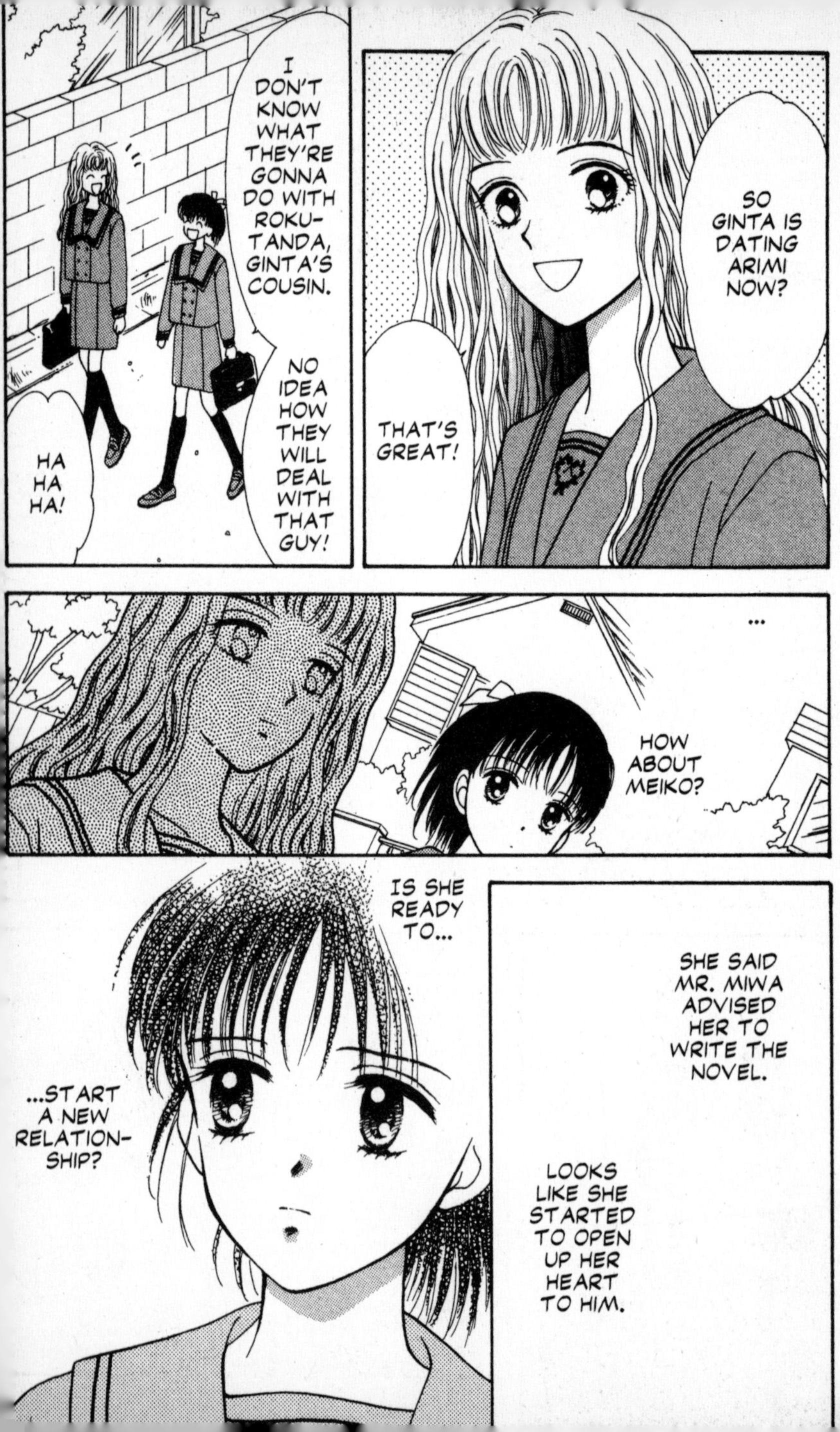
SO GINTA IS DATING ARIMI NOW?
THAT'S GREAT!
I DON'T KNOW WHAT THEY'RE GONNA DO WITH ROKU-TANDA, GINTA'S COUSIN.
NO IDEA HOW THEY WILL DEAL WITH THAT GUY!
HA HA HA!
...
HOW ABOUT MEIKO?
SHE SAID MR. MIWA ADVISED HER TO WRITE THE NOVEL.
LOOKS LIKE SHE STARTED TO OPEN UP HER HEART TO HIM.
IS SHE READY TO...
...START A NEW RELATION-SHIP?

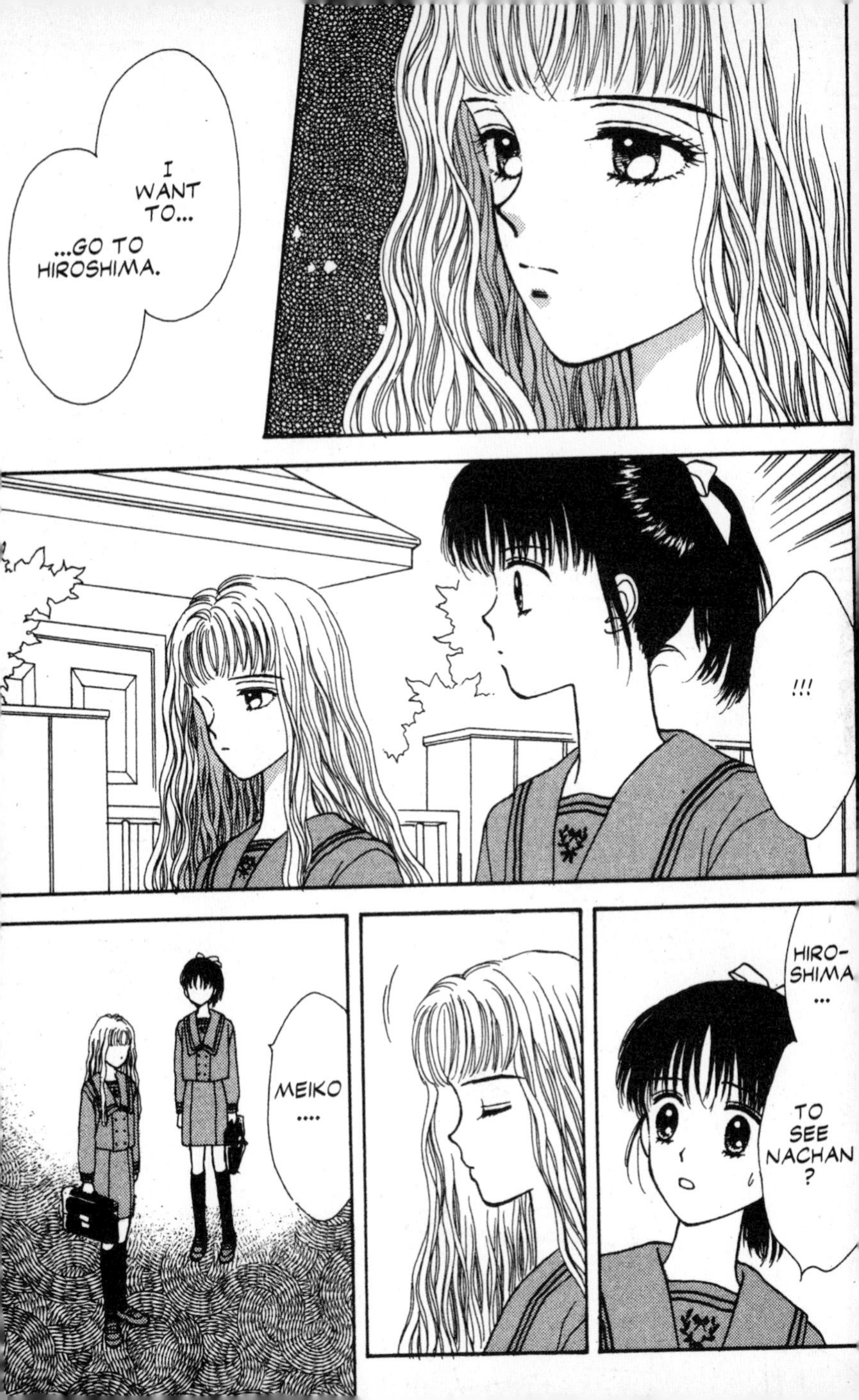
I WANT TO... ...GO TO HIROSHIMA.
!!!
HIRO-SHIMA ...
TO SEE NACHAN ?
MEIKO ....

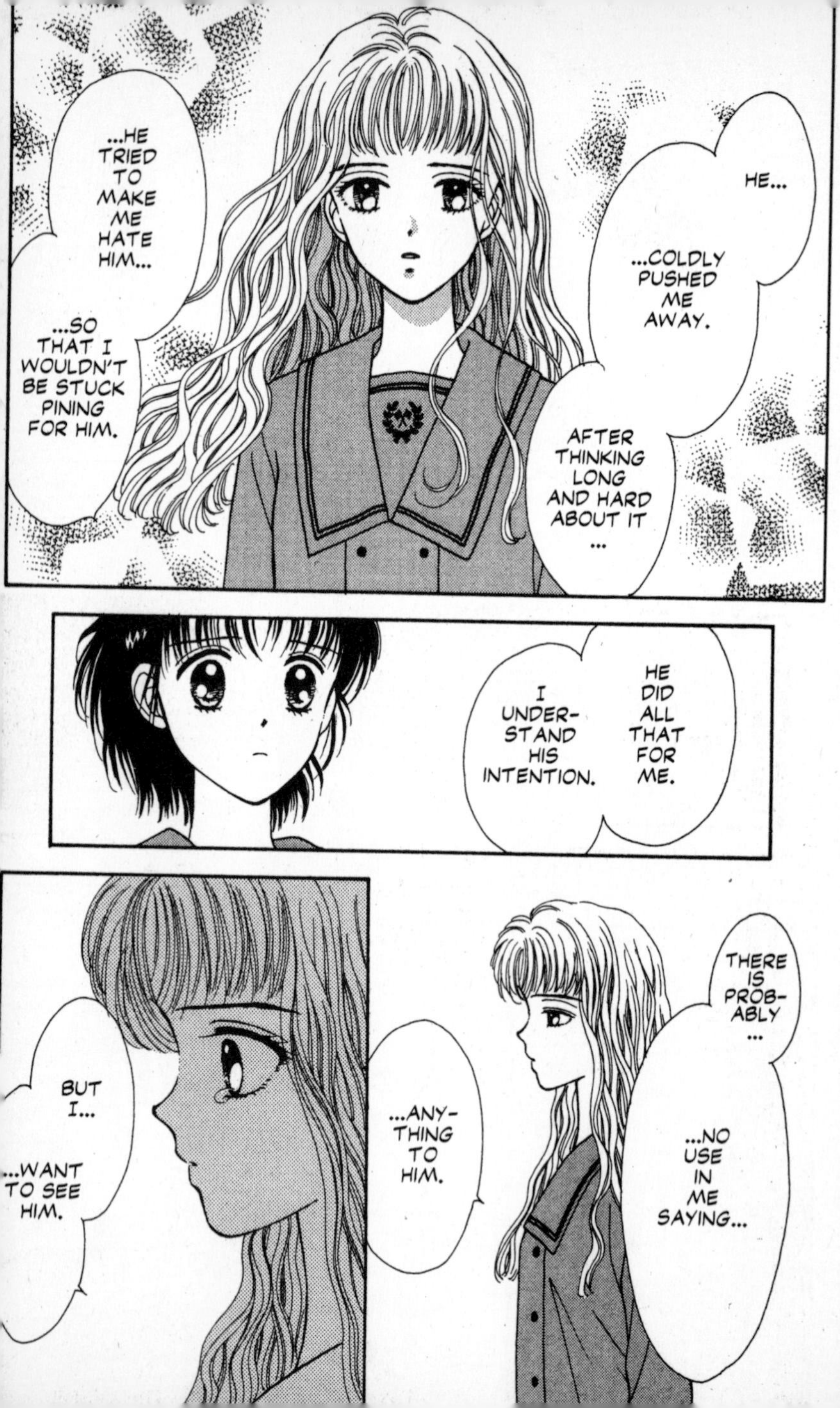
HE...
...COLDLY PUSHED ME AWAY.
AFTER THINKING LONG AND HARD ABOUT IT ...
...HE TRIED TO MAKE ME HATE HIM...
...SO THAT I WOULDN'T BE STUCK PINING FOR HIM.
HE DID ALL THAT FOR ME.
I UNDER-STAND HIS INTENTION.
THERE IS PROB-ABLY ...
...NO USE IN ME SAYING...
...ANY-THING TO HIM.
BUT I...
...WANT TO SEE HIM.

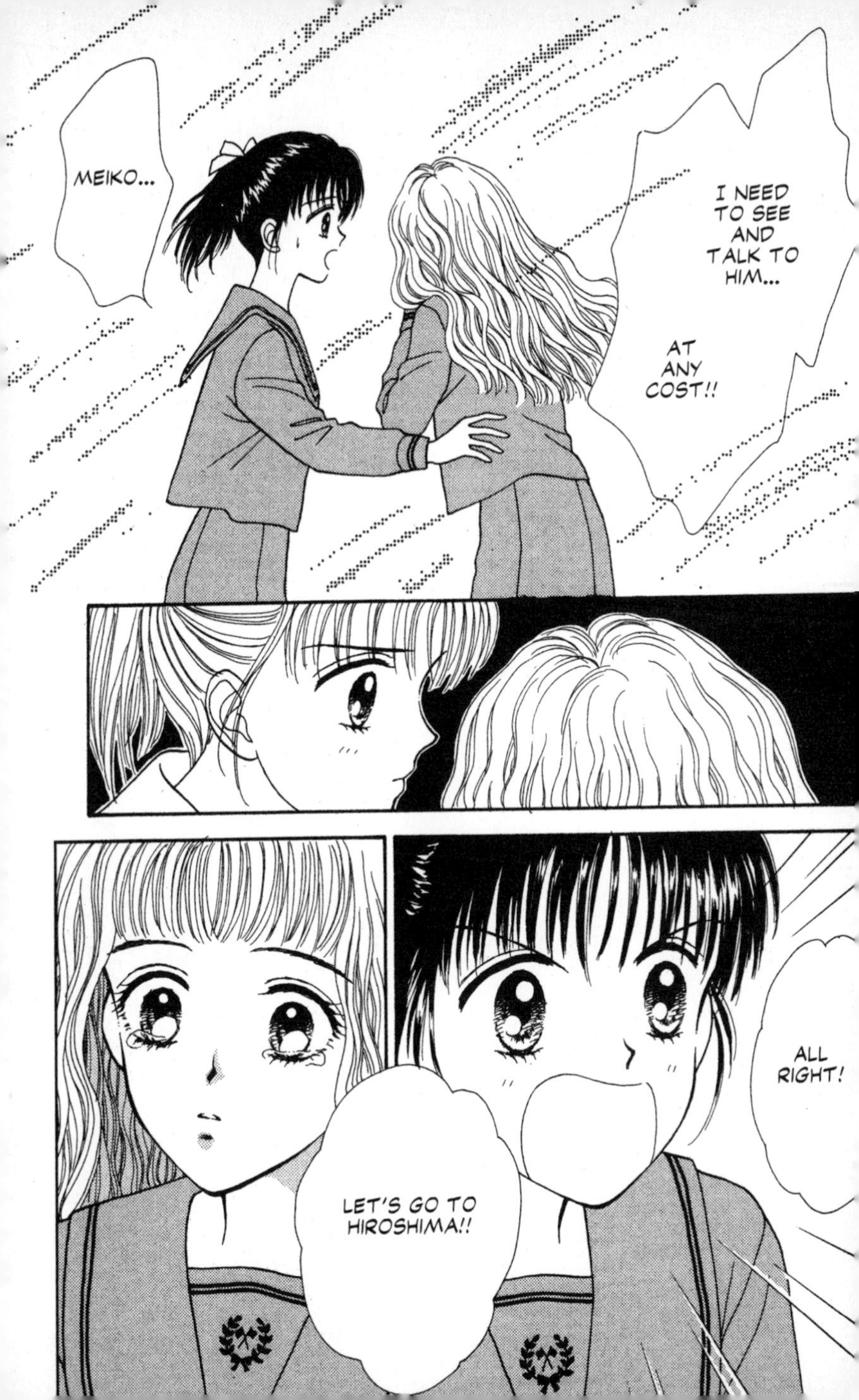
I NEED TO SEE AND TALK TO HIM...
AT ANY COST!!
MEIKO...
ALL RIGHT!
LET'S GO TO HIROSHIMA!!

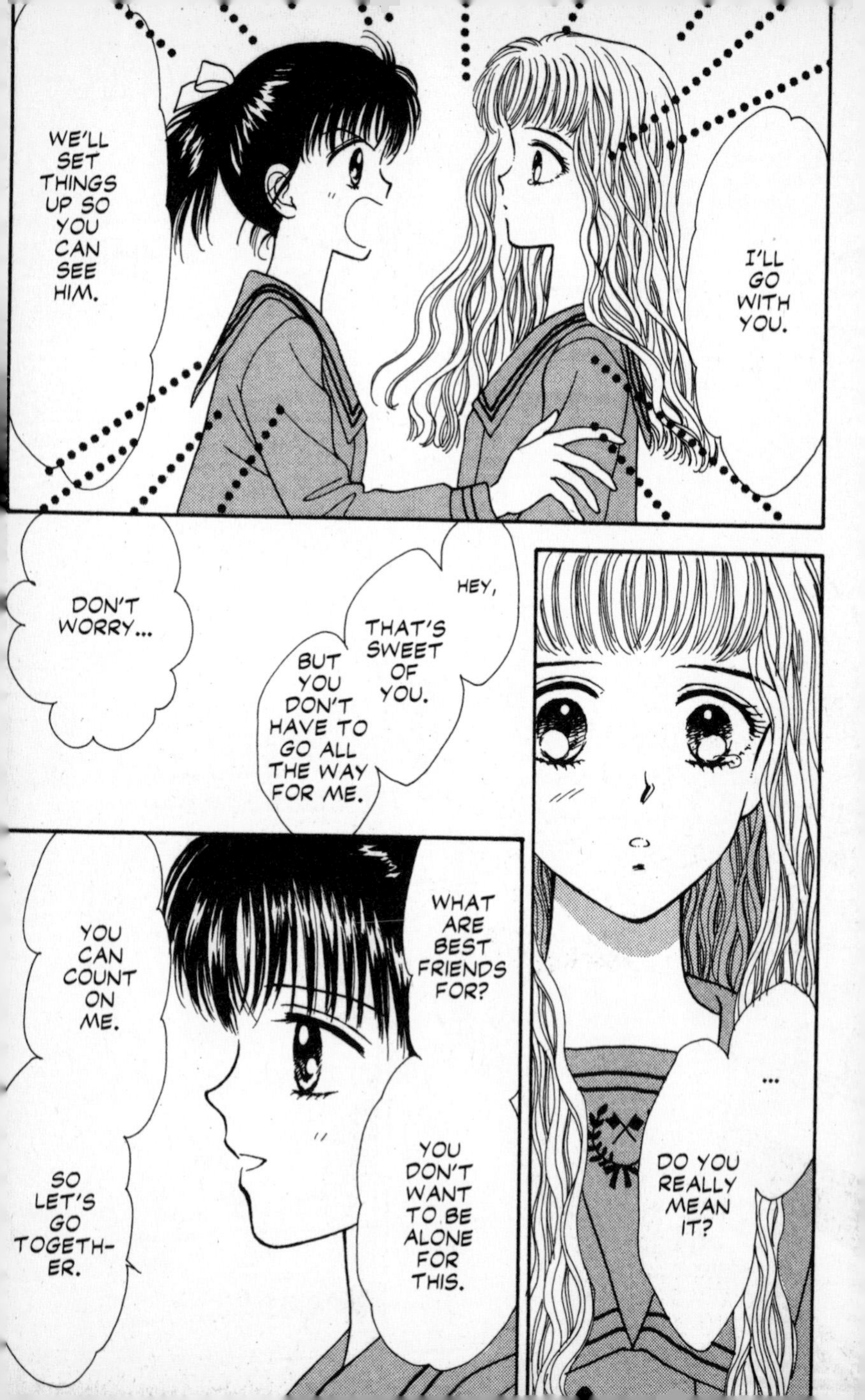
I'LL GO WITH YOU.
WE'LL SET THINGS UP SO YOU CAN SEE HIM.
HEY, THAT'S SWEET OF YOU. BUT YOU DON'T HAVE TO GO ALL THE WAY FOR ME.
DON'T WORRY...
WHAT ARE BEST FRIENDS FOR?
YOU CAN COUNT ON ME.
YOU DON'T WANT TO BE ALONE FOR THIS.
SO LET'S GO TOGETHER.
...
DO YOU REALLY MEAN IT?

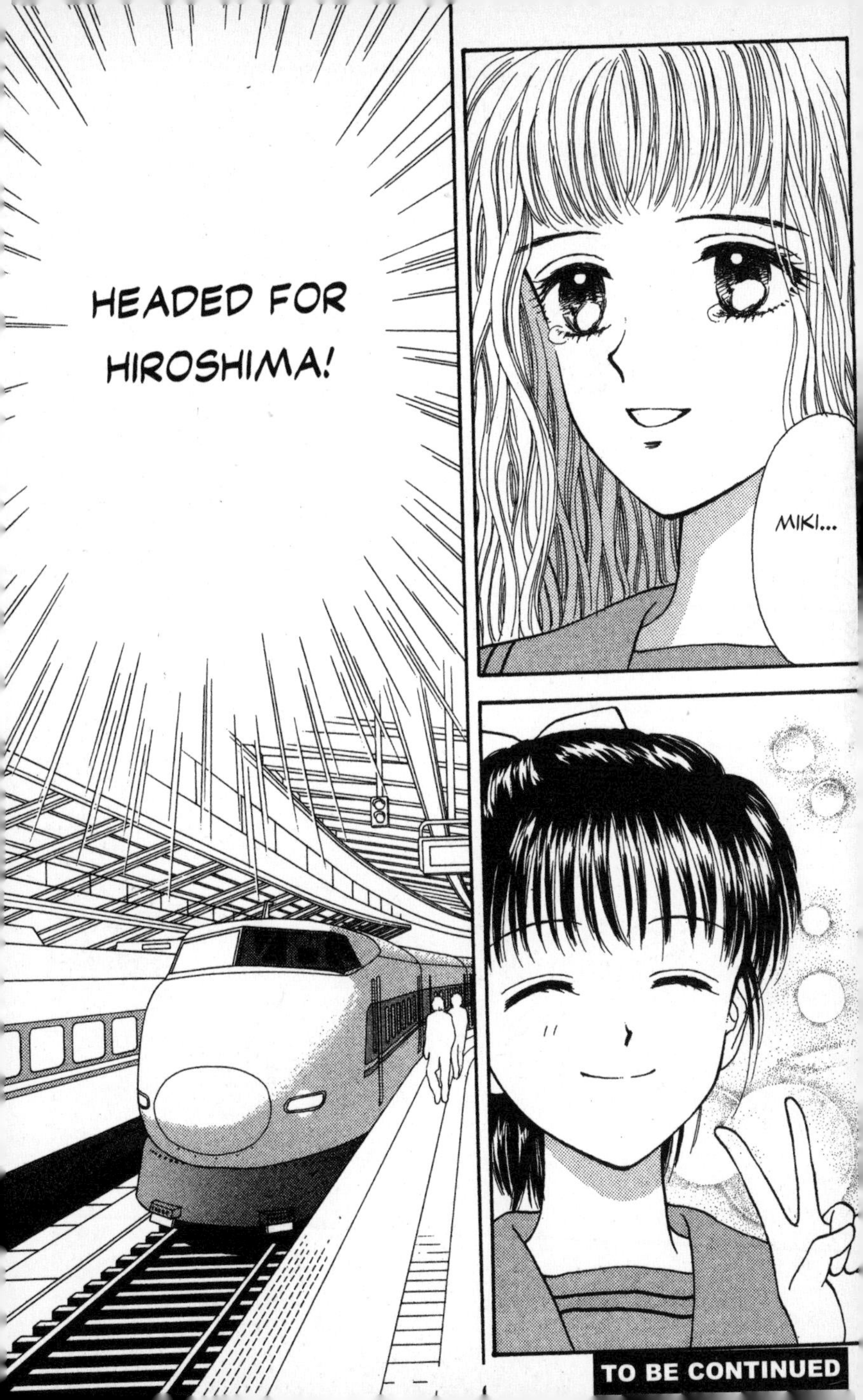
MIKI...
HEADED FOR HIROSHIMA!
TO BE CONTINUED

COMING THIS SUMMER

Marmalade Boy

VOLUME 7

JUST WHEN EVERYTHING SEEMED TO BE GOING FINE BETWEEN MIKI AND YUU, TROUBLE STRIKES. WHEN YUU DOES A LITTLE DIGGING TO FIND OUT WHO HIS REAL FATHER IS, THE TRUTH COULD DESTROY THEIR HAPPY FAMILY. YUU, WHO IS FAIRLY CERTAIN HE'S RELATED TO MIKI BY BLOOD, TELLS HER THEY'RE BREAKING UP. INSTEAD OF COMING CLEAN ABOUT HIS SUSPICIONS, HE SIMPLY SAYS HIS FEELINGS HAVE COOLED. HE ESCAPES THE SITUATION BY GOING OFF TO COLLEGE. MEANWHILE, MIKI DOESN'T HAVE A CLUE WHAT THE HECK IS GOING ON. SHE DECIDES TO CUT HER HAIR AND SAY FAREWELL TO YUU AND TO HER PAST SELF...

WILL THIS STAR-CROSSED COUPLE MAKE UP OR BREAK UP FOR GOOD? YOU'LL FIND OUT THIS AND MORE IN THE NEXT VOLUME OF MARMALADE BOY, COMING THIS SUMMER!

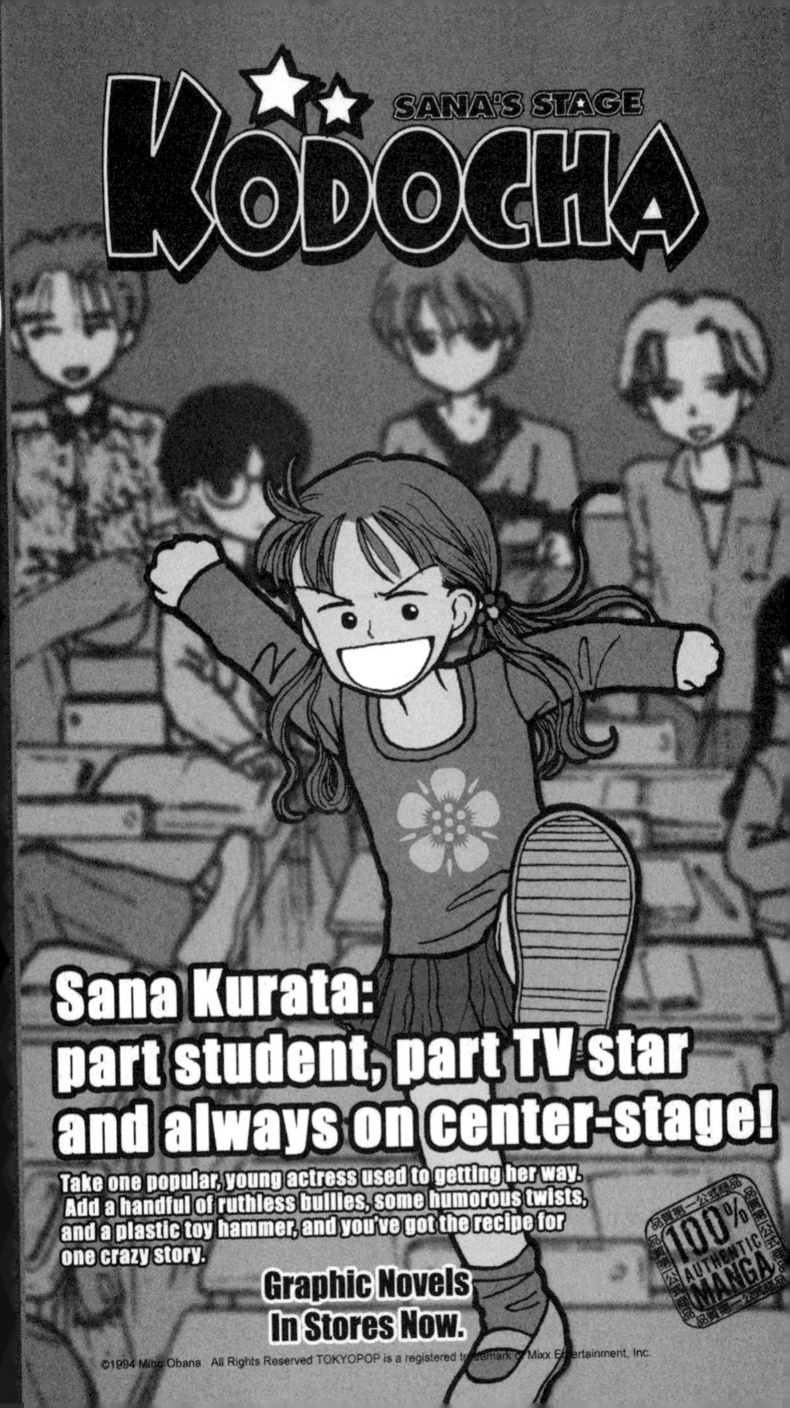
SANA'S STAGE
KODOCHA
Sana Kurata:
part student, part TV star
and always on center-stage!
Take one popular, young actress used to getting her way.
Add a handful of ruthless bullies, some humorous twists,
and a plastic toy hammer, and you've got the recipe for
one crazy story.
Graphic Novels
In Stores Now.
100% AUTHENTIC MANGA
©1994 Miho Obana. All Rights Reserved TOKYOPOP is a registered trademark of Mixx Entertainment, Inc.

Meet Shuichiro, the Man who has Everything.
Handsome bachelor. Wealthy doctor. Just found an angel stuck in his tree.
WISH
A different kind of romance from CLAMP, the creators of Cardcaptor Sakura.
100% AUTHENTIC MANGA
品質第一公式商品
Wish
When you rescue an angel, it will grant any wish your heart desires. So what do you wish for when you're the man who has everything?
Available Now!
WISH © 1995 CLAMP. All Rights Reserved. TOKYOPOP is a registered trademark of Mixx Entertainment, Inc.

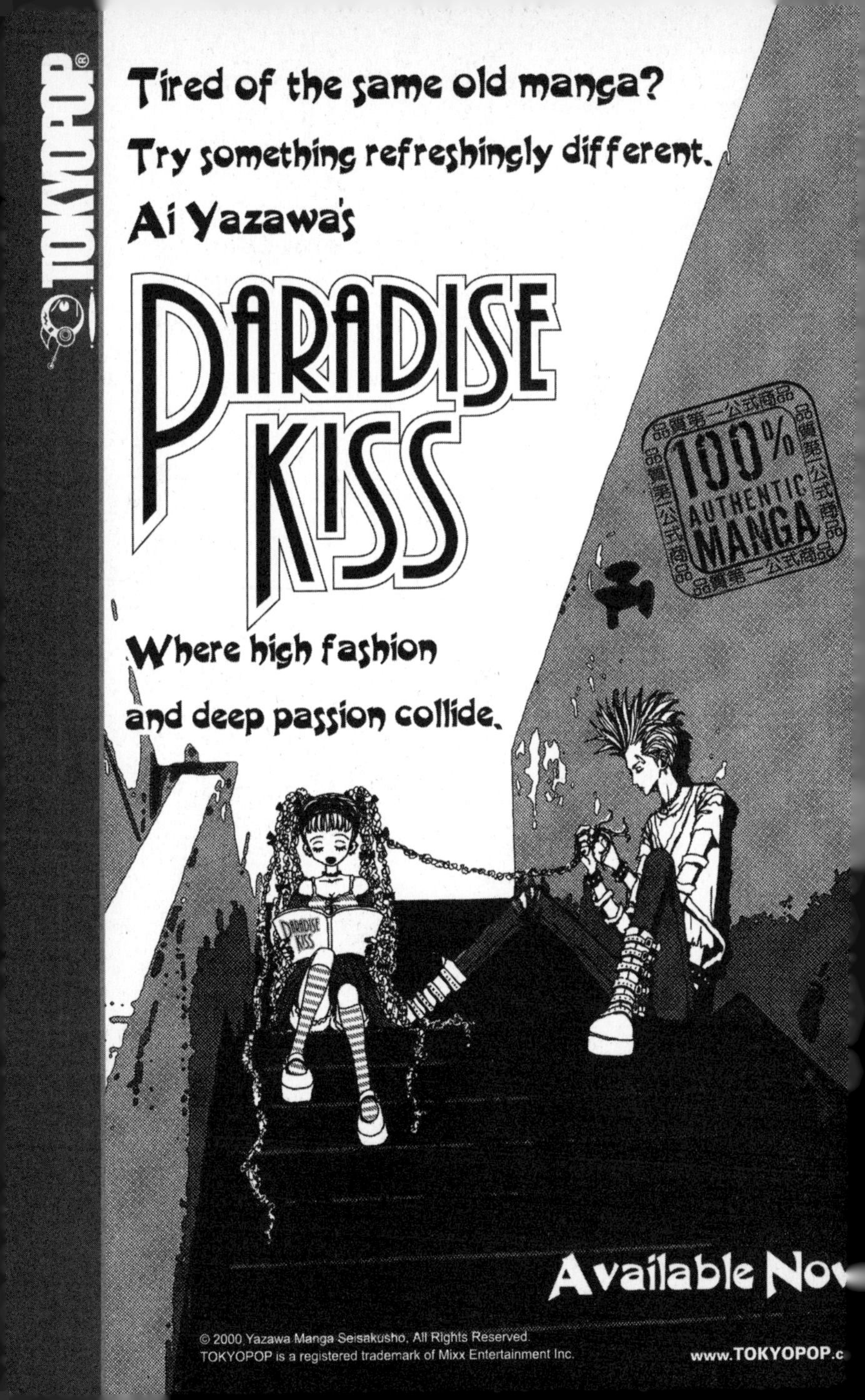
TOKYOPOP
Tired of the same old manga?
Try something refreshingly different.
Ai Yazawa's
PARADISE KISS
100% AUTHENTIC MANGA
Where high fashion
and deep passion collide.
Available Nov
© 2000 Yazawa Manga Seisakusho. All Rights Reserved.
TOKYOPOP is a registered trademark of Mixx Entertainment Inc.
www.TOKYOPOP.c

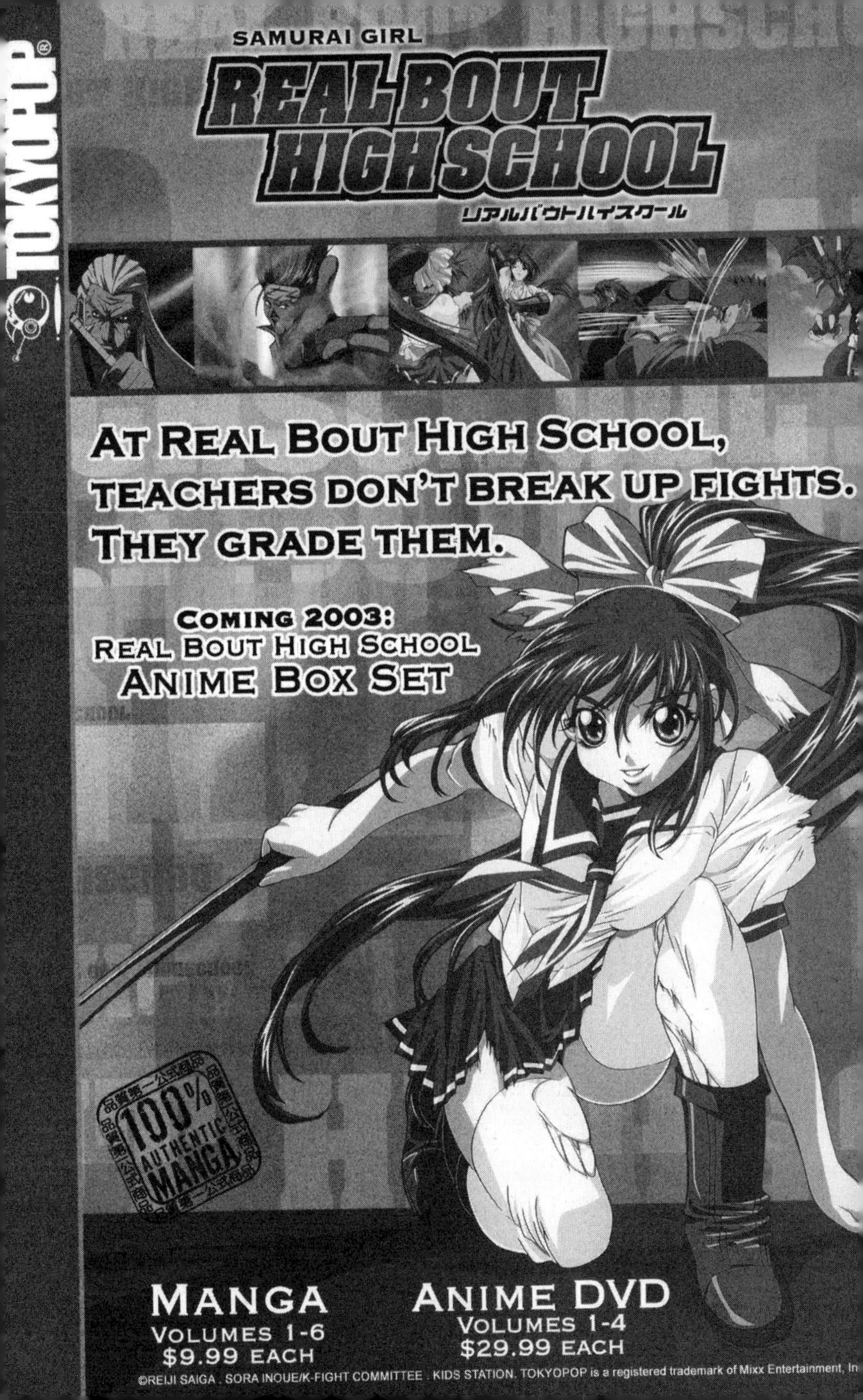
TOKYOPOP
SAMURAI GIRL
REAL BOUT HIGH SCHOOL
リアルバウトハイスクール
AT REAL BOUT HIGH SCHOOL, TEACHERS DON'T BREAK UP FIGHTS. THEY GRADE THEM.
COMING 2003:
REAL BOUT HIGH SCHOOL
ANIME BOX SET
100% AUTHENTIC MANGA
MANGA
VOLUMES 1-6
$9.99 EACH
ANIME DVD
VOLUMES 1-4
$29.99 EACH
©REIJI SAIGA . SORA INOUE/K-FIGHT COMMITTEE . KIDS STATION. TOKYOPOP is a registered trademark of Mixx Entertainment, In

STOP!

This is the back of the book.
You wouldn't want to spoil a great ending!

This book is printed "manga-style," in the authentic Japanese right-to-left format. Since none of the artwork has been flipped or altered, readers get to experience the story just as the creator intended. You've been asking for it, so TOKYOPOP® delivered: authentic, hot-off-the-press, and far more fun!

1
...IT'S A MOCKERY OF LOVE. MOM AND DAD ARE BOTH HAVING AFFAIRS, BUT THEY REFUSE TO GET DIVORCED.
MOM THINKS ABOUT HER FINANCES, AND DAD'S JUST CONCERNED WITH APPEARANCES.
WHAT ABOUT ME?!
DON'T THEY UNDERSTAND HOW DAMAGING IT IS TO WATCH YOUR PARENTS IN SUCH A HOLLOW, SPITEFUL MARRIAGE?
2
I'M...
I'M NEVER GETTING MARRIED.
3
MEIKO...
IS THAT WHY YOU NEVER GO OUT ON DATES?
4
OH, NO! DON'T GET ME WRONG. I JUST HAVEN'T MET ANYONE WHO'S MY TYPE.
I STILL LIKE BOYS. I JUST DON'T WANT TO MARRY THEM.
5
UH-OH. I'VE GOTTA GO.
WHAT'S GOING ON?
6
MY FAMILY'S HAVING DINNER WITH THE MATSUURAS.
I HAVE TO TALK THE FOUR OF THEM OUT OF THIS NONSENSE, NO MATTER WHAT!

DIRECTIONS

If this is your first time reading manga-style, here's a quick guide to help you understand how it works.

It's easy... just start in the top right panel and follow the numbers. Have fun, and look for more 100% authentic manga from TOKYOPOP®!

100% AUTHENTIC MANGA